AF553744

FREEDOM MOVEMENT IN INDIA

1857 AND AFTER

FREEDOM MOVEMENT
IN
INDIA
1857 AND AFTER

Dr. Alladi Vaidehi Krishnamoorthy
M.A., B.T., Ph.D.
Former Professor of History
Osmania University
Hyderabad.

NEELKAMAL PUBLICATIONS PVT. LTD.
EDUCATIONAL PUBLISHERS
(EXPORTERS & IMPORTERS)
NEW DELHI **HYDERABAD**

FREEDOM MOVEMENT IN INDIA
1857 AND AFTER

Dr. Alladi Vaidehi Krishnamoorthy

First Edition : 2010
(Hardback)

ISBN : 978-81-8316-211-1

NEELKAMAL PUBLICATIONS PVT. LTD.
Sultan Bazar, Hyderabad - 500 095.
✆ 24757140, 24757197, 24757944, Fax: 040-24757951

Delhi Office:
BG5/9B, Paschim Vihar, New Delhi-110 063,
✆ 011-25285894
website: www.neelkamalpub.com
e-mail: sales@neelkamalpub.com; sales_neelkamal@rediffmail.com

---

Published by *Suresh Chandra Sharma* for
Neelkamal Publications Pvt. Ltd., New Delhi, Hyderabad
and printed at *Sri Vinayaka Art Printers.*, Hyderabad, India.

Preface

I have written this book with two aims. There are several standard books on the history of the freedom movement in India like, for instance, those by Dr. Tarachand and Dr. R.C. Majumdar but they are voluminous and not within easy reach of many. My purpose therefore is to represent to the readers a book in a manageable form.

In the second place, the history of the freedom movement in India is a subject of study in university courses and in competitive examinations. There is, however, no textbook which serves these twin purposes. As a teacher of the subject for many years, I felt that such a textbook should be made available. In writing this book I have specially taken their needs into consideration.

I have included in the book a special section on the freedom movement in Andhra and Telangana as it is part of the syllabus in all the universities of Andhra Pradesh. This should be of special interest. A detailed chapter on the 1857 revolt forms appropriately the first chapter; and to make the book more purposeful a number of useful appendices and documents have been incorporated.

I am indebted to several scholars whose books have been of great help to me in undertaking this work. But for the invaluable guidance and inspiration provided by my revered father, Padma Buhshan Prof. Mamidipudi Venkatarangaiya, I would hardly have been able to undertake a venture of this magnitude.

– *A. Vaidehi*

FREEDOM MOVEMENT IN INDIA
1857 AND AFTER

1. The Characteristics ... 1
2. Causes of The Great Revolt of 1857-58 ... 5
3. The Meaning And Growth of Nationalism ... 25
4. Religious Reform Movement ... 33
5. Social Reform ... 50
6. Advent of Political Associations ... 55
7. The Indian National Congress 1885 -1905 ... 65
8. Separatist Muslim Politics ... 73
9. The Vandemataram Movement ... 79
10. The Home Rule Movement ... 99
11. Montagu – Chelmsford Reforms ... 105
12. Gandhiji's Entry into Politics ... 113
13. Gandhiji's Earlier Satyagrahas ... 122
14. The Rowlatt Satyagraha ... 132
15. The Birth of the Non-Cooperation Movement 1920-22 ... 148
16. The Course of the Non Cooperation Movement ... 154
17. The Developments From 1921–28 ... 163
18. The Civil Disobedience Movement of 1930 – The Genesis ... 172
19. The Course of the Civil Disobedience Movement ... 178
20. The Resumption of Civil Disobedience ... 188
21. The Revolutionary Movement ... 197

22. The Development From 1929–39 ... 211
23. The Prelude to Quit India Movement ... 222
24. The Course of The Quit India Movement ... 237
25. Other Developments During The Quit India Movement... 242
26. The Period of Negotiations ... 249
27. The Achievement of Freedom ... 263

APPENDIX – I

28. Freedom Movement in Andhra ... 271
29. The Home Rule Movement in Andhra ... 283
30. The Non-Cooperation Movement in Andhra ... 286
31. The Developments in Andhra From 1922–29 ... 293
32. Salt Satyagraha ... 301
33. The Quit India Movement in Andhra and Achievement of Freedom ... 310

APPENDIX – II

34. The Freedom Struggle in Telangana ... 318
SELECT DOCUMENTS ... 327
I. A Himalayan Miscalculations by *M.K. Gandhi* ... 327
II. National Week by *Jawaharlal Nehru* ... 332
III. Speech at the Plenary Session of Second Round Table Conference in London *by M.K. Gandhi* ... 333
IV. Simon Commission; General Survey and Conclusion ... 339
V. Statement Made by His Majesty's Government on June 3, 1947 ... *346*
VI. Objectives of the Resolution ... 352
Index ... 354

❖ ❖ ❖

FREEDOM MOVEMENT IN INDIA

CHAPTER 1

THE CHARACTERISTICS

The dominant characteristics of the History of India after 1858 was the gradual growth of political consciousness and nationalism among the people which led to the movement of the freedom of the country from the alien British Rule. Before we deal with the factors that led to the movement and the history of the movement itself it is necessary to point out in broad outline the nature of the movement and the way in which it differs from the earlier movements for freedom.

Even in preceding ages, both in ancient and medieval India, the country was invaded by foreigners like the Greeks, the Sakas, and the Parthians who brought portions of the country under their rule. In medieval India there were the invasions of the Turks, the Afghans and later the Mughals. All these were aliens and their rule like that of the British was essentially alien in character. Such of those attempts as were made to free the regions conquered by them were by military leaders with a Kshatriya tradition behind them and the instruments they used was a trained army. This was the case, for instance, with Chandragupta Maurya who drove away the Greeks from the Punjab and with Chandragupta II of the Gupta dynasty who put an end to the rule of the Saka Satraps in Malwa, and Western India. In these attempts to put an end to foreign rule the role of the ordinary people was very little. The same was the case in early medieval India when attempts were made to free portions of the country from the rule of the Turks and the Afghans. The lead in such attempts was taken by Rajput rulers. In south India the attempts to liberate the country from the rule of the Sultans of Delhi was undertaken by Bukka and Harihara, who with the help of their armed forces, liberated south India and established the Vijayanagar empire. Here also the role of the ordinary people was conspicuous by its absence.

In later medieval India the Mughals conquered a large part of the country and the attempt to liberate parts of it was undertaken in Maharashtra by military leaders like Sivaji. He defeated the Mughal armies with the help of the guerilla forces and founded an independent Maratha Kingdom. Still later, it was Maharaja Ranjit Singh, the great Sikh leader, who freed Punjab from the rule of the Afghans and founded an independent kingdom. Though in his case, the Sikhs participated in the war of liberation the people of the Punjab as a whole were not actively involved in it. Other examples of this nature may be quoted like the efforts of Rana Pratap to save Rajaputana from falling into the hands of the Mughals.

Unlike all these movements, the one for freeing the country from British Rule was a people's movement. Military leaders or armies had no share in it. It was the people belonging to all categories of life, especially the higher and the lower middle classes, the peasants, and the ordinary workmen who participated in the movement. Consequently, it was entitled to be called a peoples movement. When it succeeded finally in throwing the British out and in freeing the country it was a democratic government that was established.

Not only was the movement that of the people, but it was also a national movement. By the time political consciousness grew among the people the country had already been divided by the British into a number of provinces for administrative purposes. There were also a large number of princely states. There would have been nothing unnatural if the people in the provinces fought separately against the British and founded regional states or all the people in all the provinces joined together during the struggle with the British and then set-up separate states of their own. Regional feelings were strong among the people. The movements for the creation of linguistic provinces which began by about the year 1911 shows how strong the regional feeling could be. Even about the year 1947, there were certain sections of the Sikhs who were anxious to create a state of their own in Punjab which was their home land. In south India there was the Dravidian movement the aim of which was to establish an independent Dravidastan. There were princely States like Travancore and Bhopal which at one stage wanted to remain independent, but by about the beginning of the twentieth century national feeling seems to be getting better of regional sentiment. Such a feeling was present not only among the people in the provinces but also in the princely states. The freedom movement thus helped to prevent the Balkanisation of the country. It was precisely because such a feeling was not shared by a dominant section of the Muslims led by Jinnah that a separate State of Pakistan had to be created.

From this it is but right to infer that the freedom movement was an all-India movement. In this respect also it differs from similar movements in the past. Chandragupta Maurya or Bukka and Harihara or Sivaji for that matter confined their activities to a particular area and so did the Rajput leaders and Ranjit Singh. This was something unique in this history of the country. In the past when empires crumbled the result was the establishment of numerous small states. This however was not the case when the British withdrew from the country as a result of the people's struggle against their rule.

This is also unique if we look at it from the point of view of the struggles carried on in the modern era in other parts of the world to free themselves from alien rule. For example, though the thirteen colonies in America fought unitedly against the British from 1776 to 1783, after they got their independence there was the problem as to whether each colony should be a separate state. Many wanted to maintain the sovereignty of each colony. But a compromise was arrived at as a result of the convention which met at Philadelphia and a federal type of government was set up which permitted a large amount of freedom to the individual states. Even the national feeling did not become deep rooted and an attempt was made by the Southern States to separate from the federation, and set up an independent state of their own. It was only after a devastating civil war which lasted for four years (1860–64) that the secession movement was put down and United States continued to remain one. When Spanish Rule was overthrown in Central and Southern America in the early part of the nineteenth century, twenty independent states came into existence although the people spoke the same Spanish Language and followed only one religion namely Catholicism. This was because national feeling did not exist among them all. The Balkan people in South Eastern Europe fought against the Turks for freedom. But when freedom was won four independent States came into existence because of the absence of a national feeling among them. Contrasted with all this, India remained a single unit, (but for Pakistan) after victory was won in the struggle against the British.

Finally the Freedom struggle against the British Rule was on the whole a non-violent movement. Even extremists like Tilak, Aurobindo, Bipin Chandra Pal, and Lajpat Rai who spoke of Swaraj as the birthright of the people preferred ultimately a non-violent struggle in the shape of passive resistance and non-co-operation with the British Rulers. They considered that an armed rising by a disarmed nation was not exactly a practicable proposition though there was nothing morally wrong to resort to arms to get rid of foreign rule. When in later stages of the freedom movement Mahatma Gandhi, the apostle of non-violence became its leader, the struggle was strictly on non-violent lines. The people knew that he would be their leader and that without his leadership the struggle could not be carried on. Whenever he found his satyagraha movement was taking a violent form, he suspended it. Of course, there was violence during the Quit India Movement of 1942. There was also a revolutionary movement especially in Bengal, Punjab, Maharashtra in the Vandemataram days and during the first world war and for some years after 1930. But these should be regarded as aberrations and exceptions to the general character of the movement which was on the whole non-violent.

It should also be noted that the movement passed through various critical stages. Of them the more important ones are the Vandemataram Movement from 1905–11, the Home Rule Movement from 1916–18 and the Non-co-operation or Satyagraha movements from 1920 onwards. It was after forty years of struggle that the movement attained victory. It was nothing unnatural that it should have taken so long, since it was a struggle against mighty British Empire which had vast military, naval and other vital resources at its immediate command.

❖ ❖ ❖

CHAPTER 2

CAUSES OF THE GREAT REVOLT OF 1857–58

The year 1857 was a crucial year in the history of the country. It witnessed a great uprising in the North initially started by the discontented sepoys but which, in due course, took in certain parts the shape of a national rising aimed at the overthrow of the British power. This great revolt threw at least temporarily the mighty British power into a trough of helplessness and confusion. It appeared as if the edifice of the British Empire in India built over a period of hundred years would crumble to pieces. Actually the year 1857 was most appropriately chosen as it marked the centenary of the Battle of Plassey of 1757 which laid the foundation for British rule in India. There was the fondest hope among the rebels that the great revolt of 1857 would bring to an end the era of British domination over India.

Causes of Revolt

The great revolt was essentially a result of the dissatisfaction among the natives of all walks of life alike- the native rulers, the Mughal Emperor, the merchants, the agriculturists, the industrialists, the religious – minded people, the educationalists etc. As Pandit Sunderlal put it, the British by following various methods brought down the country from a position of one of the most progressive and prosperous nations of one of the most progressive and prosperous nations to that of one of the weakest and poorest countries in the world. They made the loyal Indian soldiers, in obedience to their English Officers, sacrifice their lives fighting against their own countrymen. The Indian rulers, while they adhered to the terms of their treaties with the Britishers faithfully, the Britishers defiantly broke the pledges and the undertakings given to them several times. The European employees of the Indian rulers betrayed their employers at every step. The East India company put an end to the village panchayats and to the indigenous educational system and also destroyed the trade, industries, crafts and other means of livelihood of the people that had flourished for hundred of years. The causes of the great revolt can be discussed under various heads- political, economic, social, religious and military.

Political

The English East India Company was able to acquire a big empire in India mainly due to two reasons. One was the instability and confusion created by the breakdown of the Mughal imperial authority which protected the country from foreign attacks for nearly two centuries. The other was the general apathy of the Indians almost bordering on a lack of patriotism or a love for the country among large sections of the people and the total indifference to matters relating to Government and administration. If sufficient time was given, Marathas or some other power might have succeeded in bringing the country under their control but before such a task could be accomplished the British entered the scene and entrenched themselves in power. Having established an empire in India the British Introduced several measures—revenue, judicial and administrative to consolidate their position and to make the people of India under their aegis. But very soon the Indians realized what they had lost. The authorities were essentially commercial minded. They lacked administrative experience. At the same time, the company's officers were notorious for corruption and incompetence. Ignorance of the local language and customs made matters worse. Many a time they had to depend on their Indian assistants to carry on the administration and most of them were thoroughly dishonest.

Cornwallis as Governor General followed a policy which was completely against Indianisation of the Services. He ordered that all Indians in higher services should be removed. No Indian should get a salary above 80 rupees. As a result the zamindars who enjoyed revenue, judicial and police powers earlier were reduced to mere revenue officers of the company having only the right to collect taxes. Many unemployed Britishers were brought to India and all the expenditure incurred on them had to be borne by the Indians. This policy of Cornwallis was continued by his successor Lord William Bentick who employed Indians in higher services with certain limits but that too with an eye more on curtailing the expenditure of the British wherever possible than providing facilities to the Indians. Their policy in this respect was in marked contrast to that of the Mughals, who after they established their rule, identified themselves fully with the Indians. They employed the Rajputs in administration and posted them to the highest offices. They had great regard for Indian culture. Even though there were some differences among the Hindus and Muslims they respected each other and lived in harmony.

The British had nothing but contempt for the Indians who were eliminated from the political life. It was only after a long time they began to realize the injustice done to the natives by excluding them from higher offices. In the charter Act of 1833 a clause was incorporated that "no native of the said terrorists, nor any natural born subject of his majesty resident therein shall by reason only of his religion, place of birth, descent, colour or any of them be disabled from holding any place, office of employment under the said company". But little effect was given to this in practice. A time therefore came when Indians had to revolt against the British to assert themselves.

The subsidiary Alliance of Marquis of Wellesley and the Doctrine of Lapse of Lord Dalhousie were equally responsible for the great revolt. The two Governors General, pretending to be the friends of the native princes, reduced them to the status of subordinates by implementing the Subsidary Alliance and the Doctrine of Lapse. At times promising to give them benefits of their victories they utilised the services of the native princes and never kept up their promises. Mysore, Maratha, Carnatic, Oudh, Satara, Nagpur, Jhansi were a few of the many states which were deceived by the British. Hence there was lot of discontentment among the native princes too which contributed to the great revolt of 1857–58. Even the people could not tolerate the injustice done to the Indian rulers.

Economic Causes

There was an all round deterioration in the economic condition of almost all classes of people – the zamindars, the mutadars, the rentiers etc., and the agriculturists, the artisans and the handicraftsmen. All had their quota of suffering. The zamindars had to pay heavy taxes to the Government. Many of them could not fulfill the target set for them and their lands were confiscated by the government.

However, it was the agriculturist classes that suffered most. The ryots were overassessed whether it was under the Zamindari, the ryotwari or the village settlement. Even the levies of famine taxes had to be paid and evasion was rendered difficult. They were tortured and the judicial magisterial powers of the revenue officers made their position worse. Adequate attention was not paid either to the extension or the maintenance of sources of irrigation like tanks and wells. Very little was spent on repairs. Loans were not granted to the zamindars and others proprietors to under take these works. Hence the condition of irrigation works was most unsatisfactory. Agriculture being the main occupation of the people neglect of irrigation resulted in immense loss to the cultivators. Further, the collection of land revenue in cash added to the misery of the ryots and their suffering became acute when the prices continued to fall from 1834. The agriculturists had to part with more grain in order to pay the land revenue. In times of famine no attempt was made to formulate a general system of relief.

There was a deterioration in the living conditions of the non-agricultural classes as well as the agricultural classes who engaged themselves in subsidiary occupations like handicrafts. At on time there was a world market for Indian textiles. After the Industrial Revolution in England, the Indian artisans not only lost the foreign market but also the home market. The weavers were subjected to heavy loom tax. Thus the industry which flourished for ages declined rapidly. A majority of handicraftsmen had to give up their traditional occupation. Unemployment increased manifold. The only source of employment – agriculture – was also in a sad plight.

Further as Prof. M. Venkatarangaiya has said, though the East India Company established a regular system of courts for administrative justice in both civil and criminal matters, there was a general complaint that the complicated procedure imported from England, the enormous cost of litigation and the delays involved resulted more often in miscarriage of justice.

The village community which was the backbone of the economic system also suffered. The village community had always been the pride of the people. But changes in the system of land revenue and in the judicial system and the introduction of a highly centralized machinery of administration under which the village officials became the paid servants of the Government instead of being the representatives of the village led to the disintegration of the village community and to dissatisfaction among the villagers.

The Charter Act of 183 aggravated the deteriorating condition of the Indians. By this Act the trade with India was thrown open to all

British subjects except in tea and the trade with china. This resulted in the free flow of English capital and enterprise to India. Several of them purchased agricultural lands and converted them into coffee and tea plantations. They paid high wages initially to the workers to attract their services. Several persons engaged in agriculture believed working in plantations was more profitable. They sold their land to work in the plantation as dependent labourers. Very soon they realized their folly. When there was an influx of labour the land owners reduced the wages, increased the number of hours of work and subjected the labourers to hardship in every possible manner. There was no protection for them from the Government. The British capitalists not only ruined the agriculturists but also the Indian Bankers. The bankers no doubt used to lend money to the agriculturists and collect high rates of interest. The British capitalists established banks in all parts of the country which adversely affected the fortunes of the Indian counterparts. The introduction of railways and telegraphs was certainly beneficial to the people. But all these were intended only to facilitate British trade by providing quick means of transport from ports to inland towns.

Agriculturists and industrialists apart, the educated people were also economically impoverished. It was customary in India to honour learned men by making land endowments. These were known as agraharams and they provided a dependable means of livelihood to the educated middle classes. Even the children of rulers and feudatories were sent to these agraharams for education which were residential centres. The Muslims also encouraged and honoured the educated people in the same manner. The British however had nothing but contempt for the system of education in India nor did they have any regard for those steeped in Indian culture. The learned scholars received no encouragement, and added to this was the fact that the British treated them as uncivilized. The Hindu and Muslim teachers had to give up their ancient profession and the pursuit of traditional learning.

There were Indians who took keen interest in Western education and were conversant with Western literature and ideas. They discovered that in the Western countries the people fought for certain basic and fundamental rights and democracy and achieved them through constitutional methods. The educated Indians wanted to follow the same course in getting their grievances redressed. They hoped that the British would modify their administration to suit the natives. They started political associations like the British Indian Association which would be the media of expressions of the ideas. When the Charter Act of 1853 was under the anvil the members of the British Indian Association made certain suggestions for incorporation in the Act. Some of the recommendations were.

1. Reduction of taxes
2. Construction of canals and anicuts and wells for the development of agriculture.
3. Education through mother tongue and introduction of vocational education and establishment of universities one in each Presidency.
4. Appointment of Indians to higher offices and the enhancement of their pay.

When the charter Act of 1853 was actually passed none of these found a place causing deep disappointment to the educated Indians.

Religious Causes

The public entertained the fear that the Government was bent on suppressing Hindu faith and establishing Christianity. The people were intensely attached to their religion and scrupulously observed the rites and ceremonies enjoined by their religion. They regarded the caste system as a part of the Divine order. They were naturally perturbed when the authorities started making statements in support of Christianity. They believed that the Government was in league with the missionaries in achieving their aim. The charter Act of 1813 increased the strength of the ecclesiastical establishments in India which was paid out of the Indian revenues. Missionaries came to India in very large numbers and carried on systematic propaganda. They established schools which were used effectively as instruments for the spread of their religion. Gradually Bible was used as a classbook in all Government schools. This was resented to by the Hindus as well as the Muslims.

Certain legislation and administrative measures were enforced by the Government which also raised suspicions in the minds of the Indians. The Act of 1850 enabled converts to Christianity to inherit their ancestral property even though they lost their right to render religious service required of them. Again permission was granted to missionaries to construct churches and schools in residential areas of caste Hindus. The governors and high officials collected donations for the missionary school in their official capacity. The Christian missionary could with impunity use highly derogatory language to ridicule the tenets of the

Hindu faith. The interference of the British in the social Practices and customs also was responsible for the growing discontentment among the Hindus. The regulations of 1829 which declared Sati as Culpable homicide was not liked by the upper caste Hindus. There was fear that the government policies would ultimately break up the traditional social structure. The religious and social policies of the British ignited the great revolt of 1857–58.

Military Causes

The immediate cause of the great revolt of 1857–58 was doubtless the discontentment among the Indian soldiers in the British army. Since they took the lead it has come to be called the Sepoy mutiny. The British were able to establish their empire in India primarily with the active assistance of the Indian soldiers. The Indians were recruited in the army in large numbers and given training in fighting. In 1857 out of 3,15,520 soldiers in the Indian army, the number of British soldiers was a low as 15,136. The Indian segment was at least five times the number of British soldiers. The maximum salary an Indian soldier could draw was Rs. 70 and his rank did not rise beyond that a subedar. Added to this discrimination, the religious sentiments of the soldiers were ignored. The company's government progressively ignored and even ran counter to the religious sentiments, beliefs and practices of the Indian soldiers. English officers took to proselytizing the sepoys as part of their work. The immediate cause which instigated the sepoys to revolt was the one connected with the greased cartridge. Prior to 1853 the ends of the cartridges wee broken off by hand by the soldiers immediately before use. But that year new cartridges, whose ends had to be broken off by biting, were issued at a number of places. For a long time the sepoys were not aware of the fact that the cartridges were lubricated with cow and pig fat. It was only in 1857 that they came to know about this. The sepoys were enraged. They thought this to be a surreptitious attempt to defile them religiously. They became infurious because they had been unswervingly loyal to the English even against their own countrymen.

The sum total of the Indian soldier's deep discontent was the persistent indifferences with which their grievances about pay, living conditions and want of ordinary necessary amenities of human life were treated by the English officials and the persistent efforts to propagate Christianity by means fair and foul in the Indian Army.

In the words of Sir William Russell, "we had a war of religion, a war of race and a war of revenge, of hope, of national determination to shake off the yoke of a stranger and to re-establish the full power of native chiefs and the full sway of native religions."

Course of the Mutiny – Delhi

The sepoys played the most prominent part in the great revolt of 1857–58. They had the ability, equipment, and necessary skill to oppose the British. The revolt started at the Dum Dum barracks. One of the Brahmin sepoys refused first to offer his water-filled goblet to a sweeper who belonged to the untouchable caste. The sweeper told the Brahmin with all contempt that while he could bite the end of cow-fat smeared cartridges, how could he claim to be a Hindu of a high caste. He disclosed that the fat smeared cartridges were made at the factory near Barrackpore. The Brahmin sepoy was stunned and this news quickly spread to the battalion. When the new cartridges were given to the Barrackpore Indian sepoys, they refused to use them. One of them named Mangal Pandey became so furious that he ventured to start a religious war against the British Officers. Ultimately he was court martialled and sentenced to death. He was hanged on 8th April 1857. The sepoys held secret meetings to formulate plans for a revolt against the British. They set fire to the bungalows of Englishmen and the Barracks of whitemen at Lucknow, Merrut and Ambala. At Merrut there was a big rebellion. The jails were demolished and Englishmen were killed. Offices were set on fire. Telegraph wires were cut and railway lines were taken over by the revolutionaries. Similar incidents happened in Pherozpur, Muzaffarnagar, Aligarh, Mathura etc. by May 10 the revolt assumed a major dimension so much so that historians regard that date as the actual commencement of the revolt.

The British authorities started a ruthless policy of suppression. They captured the soldiers who rebelled against them tried them and awarded severe punishments. Their clothes were removed and they were then flogged and humiliated.

But all this did not dampen the spirit of revolt of the sepoys. They used every means to free their fellow soldiers from jails. There was the abode of the 72 year old Bahadur Shah II, the last Mughal emperor, who was living on an annual pension from the British. He knew fully well that the might of the British could not be matched by the Indians by any stretch of imagination. He was therefore not anxious to lead a rebellion against the British. But the soldiers were insistent that he should be their leader. They even declared him as the Emperor of India. They forced open the gates of all the prisons in Delhi, and set at liberty all those undergoing imprisonment under the most horrible conditions. Many English men were done to death while a few managed to flee. Not one Britisher was found in Delhi on May 16. Delhi was declared independent and proclaimed as the capital of the Mughal empire once again.

Unfortunately Bahadur shah was undetermined. His vascillating attitude coupled with lack of qualities of leadership did considerable damage to the revolt. The sepoys had no real leader to guide them. Nor was there any unity among them coming as they did from different parts of the country. In fact the entire movement lacked a unified programme of action. In Delhi they started plundering the people and looting the shops. Delhi was in a state of utter chaos.

In the meanwhile the British made arrangements to capture Delhi. They marched with an army towards a hilly area known as the Ridge. But they were pushed back by the Indian soldiers. They then sought the support of Sikhs and the princes of Punjab. The British again entered Delhi with a better equipped army. They attacked Delhi from all sides. The rebels were confined to the fort and were in no position to get help from outside. Their stocks of food, arms and ammunition were depleted. The civilian population was in no mood to come to their rescue considering the suffering through which they had to pass. The British pierced the gates of the fort and made a bold entry into the Capital. Delhi fell into their hands. The captured soldiers were subjected to punishment which was at once heinous and barbarous. The Delhi revolt thus came to an end.

Kanpur

The revolt spread with all its ferocity to several other places. One such centre was Kanpur. It was indeed considered as the real place of origin of the great revolt. The principal leader was Nana Saheb who was the adopted son of the last Peshwa Baji Rao II. The Doctrine of Lapse having come into force he lost his domain and was living on his property. He was friendly with the English who in turn trusted him. The British had a battalion in Kanpur under the leadership of General Wheeler.

The news of the liberation of Delhi reached Kanpur. The Hindus and Muslims celebrated the victory. As a matter of fact Nana Saheb came to know about the news three days before it reached wheeler. The sepoys in the cantonment held secret meetings for similar action in Kanpur. Wheeler mounted efforts against a possible revolt. A contingent of 3,000 sepoys from the headquarters arrived in Kanpur of whom only 100 were Englishmen. He had implicit faith in the loyalty of Nana Saheb to whom he appealed for help. Nana Saheb arrived at Kanpur with a few hundred soldiers. Wheeler put him in charge of the company's treasury as well.

The Indian armymen had secret talks with Nana Saheb in a boat in midstream so as not to rouse the suspicion of the British authorities. On June 4 as Planned the sepoys rose in revolt in Kanpur. Nana Saheb was declared the Raja under the suzerainty of the Delhi Emperor. He thereupon discarded the friendship of the English and declared that he was the leader of the revolutionaries in Kanpur. Money came to Nana in large Quantities from several people. Actually on June 3 an English soldier in a drunken stage shot at and killed an Indian soldier. But no action was taken against him and this ignited the revolt.

Wheeler immediately shifted about 900 Britishers to a safe place of which 400 were soldiers, 376 women and children and the remaining employees. Nana Saheb besieged them from all sides. The food they had was exhausted and as the conditions deteriorated, wheeler was compelled to negotiate with Nana Saheb for shifting his people from Kanpur. Nana agreed to it and 40 boats were kept already for the purpose on the banks of the river at Allahabad. All the Englishmen got into the boats and as they set sail, the boatmen jumped out. This was followed by Nana Saheb's men opening fire on the Englishmen as a result of which many were killed. Though a few managed to escape, the rest of them were captured. Nana Saheb proclaimed himself as the Peshwa.

But as had happened in Delhi the soldiers were most unruly. Nana Saheb could not control them. There was a story current that Nana Saheb never wanted to be friendly with the British and had no intention of being under their control. Even as he appeared to be close to them, he secretly contacted Gulab Singh, the ruler of Jammu, through whom he expected help from Russia.

Revolts broke out in Allahabad, Banaras and other places. In Allahabad there was a British officer by name Nite. He was noted for his cruel behaviour and never spared the Indians even for the smallest offence. He was furious when the army in Kanpur revolted. He marched with a contingent to Kanpur to help wheeler. But he arrived there too late to be able to rescue wheeler. Nite was soon replaced by Havalak as the commander. He attacked Fatepur, an important centre of the rebels and succeeded in occupying it. Having heard about Havalak's success in Fatepur Nana Saheb Immediately marched towards Fatepur. Fatepur and Kanpur were connected by a bridge and if only Nana wrecked towards Kanpur. That was the fatal mistake committed by Nana who failed to realize that it was difficult to fight the English who were equipped militarily with better weapons. Nana sahib was unequal to the task he embarked upon and he had to flee from the battlefield. His lieutenant Tataya Tope continued the fight but he was soon in a helpless position when another battalion under the leadership of Campbell arrived. So he too fled and it was just a matter of time for Kanpur to be reoccupied on December 6.

Central Provinces

The central Provinces played a pivotal role in the great revolt of 1857–58. Jhansi, the chief town in Bundelkhand in the Central provinces, acquired fame in this struggle. It was a Maharashtra dominion under the suzerainty of the peshwas. In 1804, it became a feudatory of the British. In 1853 when the ruler of Jhansi died without a natural heir, this kingdom was annexed to the British empire under the Doctrine of Lapse. The adopted son of the deceased ruler was not recognized as the legal successor. His widow Jhansi Rani Lakshmi Bai who was 19 was sanctioned an annual pension of 60,000 rupees.

The English stationed a battalion in Jhansi. On June 6, the soldiers revolted against the British when they came to know of the greased cartridges. They plundered the treasury and killed several Englishmen before proceeding to Delhi; Lakshmi Bai did not play any part in this revolt in the beginning. But the British who became suspicious were carefully watching her movements. She was infuriated by the attitude of the British who were interrogating her frequently. It roused her ire against the British. Tatya Tope who escaped from Kanpur held secret discussions with her. He had already occupied the fort of Charkāri and collected a big army. He had the support of Nana Saheb and his brother's son Rao Saheb. Rani Jhansi decided to join the revolutionaries and assumed command of the revolutionary army to give a spirited lead. Several hundreds of women also joined her. The British commander Rose confronted the Rani in a battle which went on for eight days. Tatya

Tope as he was proceeding with his army to assist Jhansi was attacked by the British on the way killing 1,500 of his men. The guns too were confiscated. Tatya was thus incapacitated from coming to the rescue of Lakshmi Bai. She fought heroically against the British forces. Her fort was attacked on all sides and in the battle that ensued several of her men were killed.

For a moment she was disheartened and even wanted to commit suicide. She did not want to give up and changed the centre of fighting to Kalpi. She succeeded in meeting the revolutionary leaders namely Tatya Tope, Rao sahet, the Rajas of Shahgarh, Banapur etc. they all decided to make a united effort to humble the British. But they were unable to reach an accord as to who should be the ablest of all but they did not want to accept her leadership for, one thing, she was young and , for another, she was a woman. Time was running out without an accord being reached on this crucial issue. Jhansi Lakshmi Bai took the initiative to march forward. She advanced 42 miles from Kalpi. The others adopted guerilla tactics. There was severe fighting. An English soldier on horse back pierced through her head from behind while another dealt a blow on her chest. Her right eye was wounded. But braving all this, she struck a deadly blow on the horsemen before she finally collapsed. She died a martyr to the cause of the country. She was easily the most courageous person who rebelled against the British. She fought with unsurpassed valour and displayed tremendous qualities of leaderships.

After her death, her soldiers continued the fight. Tatya Tope too was active. It was just then that a person by name Man Singh crossed over to the British side to leak out the location of all the secret centres of the Indians. Thus it was they came to know the hiding place of Tatya Tope. They attacked him while he was asleep and captured him. After the revolt subsided he was hanged to death on 19th April 1859. He was a man for whom nothing seemed to matter where the country was concerned. He was a true hero whose valour and courage have become part of India's glorious history.

Oudh

The toughest revolutionary strong hold was Oudh. Most of the soldiers enlisted in the Company's army hailed from Oudh. Oudh was a strong and rich princely state. During the time Lord Dalhousie it was ruled by Nawab Wazid Ali Shah. He was powerful ruler and a terror to a British. As Oudh occupies very strategic position in the North the British never wanted a strong Oudh. They were therefore eager to annex it. Lord Dalhousie who was known to be one of the most unscrupulous Governors-General India ever had forcibly annexed Oudh on the pretext that the Nawab was despotic and the people were put to suffering. Oudh, unlike in other states, every class and section of the people unjustly ousted from power and deported to Calcutta, there was unprecedented resentment. Within 10 days of the direct establishment of British rule in Oudh, the Hindu and Muslim jagirdars, landlords, farmers, traders, soldiers rose as one man in revolt against the British. The Begum of Oudh by name Begum Hazrae Mahal donned the military uniform of a male and led the army in what she called the Oudh's war of Independence. Except the residency every part of Oudh came under the revolutionaries. For four months the Indians ruled Oudh. No Englishmen was spared and every one of them was killed. The Commissioner of Oudh was among those who lost their lives at the hands of the revolutionaries.

The English had occupied all the other centres of the revolutionaries. The only province left was Oudh. They had in the meanwhile secured a big army and several commanders too were available. They then attacked Oudh fully prepared. With a vengeance the English soldiers massacred the natives, looted the palace and plundered all the wealth which included gold and jewellery besides diamonds and other precious stones. Most of the wealth was sent to England. Cash worth Rupees 60 lakh also was taken away. Thus the last important state was reoccupied by the British. By August 7, 1858, the revolt was in a state of total collapse.

Results of the Great Revolt

The Great Revolt of 1857–58 might no doubt have been suppressed by the British. But they realized that they could no longer rule the country despotically and it was not possible to force obedience by mere might and loyalty could not be extracted by force.

It taught a lesson to them. A revolt was inevitable but if it had no taken place the British would perhaps have continued to believe that all they did was right though it was clear as day light that their motives were utterly selfish and their ambition was total exploitation of the subject people.

In the first instance the British learnt how dangerous it was to interface with the religion of the people. They knew for certain that the main cause of the great revolt was their religious policy. The English were a proud race and they thought the Christianity was the only true religion and the religions of India – Hinduism and Islam were inferior to Christianity. Christian missionaries were indiscriminately encouraged to carry on their activities. Mass conversions of Indians to Christianity did not produce so much as a ripple. The sentiments of the Indian soldiers were brushed aside as noted earlier when the English officers took to proselytising the sepoys as part of their work. And as time went on, the missionary colonels grew louder and more violent in their denunciations of Hinduism and Islam. Front rank politicians in England really believed that the surest way to secure the permanence of English rule in India was to convert en bloc to Christianity all Indians – civil and military. A prominent religious teacher of Christianity, Rev. Kennedy said "whatever misfortunes come on us, as long as an empire in India continues, so long let us not forget that our chief work is the propagation of Christianity in the land until Hindustan from Cape Comorin to the Himalayas embraces the religion of Christ and until it condemns the Hindoo and the Moslem religions. Our efforts must continue persistently. For this work we must make all efforts we can use all power and all authority in our hands."

The revolution was an eye opener to the English that they were mistaken in imagining that the zeal with which they pursued a course of religious fanaticism would yield the desired result. The Queen in 1858 issued a Proclamation immediately after the end of the revolt that the territories in India hitherto in the hands of the East India Company would be taken over by the British government itself and declared that hereafter "none be in any wise favoured, non molested or disquieted by reason of their religious faith or observances, but that all shall enjoy the equal and impartial protection of the law alike and we do strictly charge and enjoin all those who may be in authority under us that they abstain from all interference with the religious belief or worship of any of our subjects on pain of an highest displeasures".

The English further realized that they should not interface with the affairs of the native rulers. Hitherto they held that there should be no independent Indian States, and all of them should be annexed to the British empire. The doctrine of Subsidiary Alliance and Lapse were mainly responsible for alienating the Indian princes and their ultimate resolve to actively participate in the great Revolt. From this the British did not take long to understand that they required steady support especially from the princes in emergent situations and hence they could not afford to antagonise them; in fact they should be treated with the consideration that was their due. Was it not a fact that but for the support of the Indian princes in Punjab and Rajputana, for instance, they would not have been able to stem the rising tide of revolt ? In the Queen's proclamation importance was accorded to the princely states and it was announced "to the natives princes of India that all treaties and engagements made with them by or under the authority of the Honourable East India company are accepted by us, and will be scrupulously maintained and we look for the like observance on their part. We desire no extension of our present territorial possession . . . we shall respect the rights, dignity and honour of our Native Princes as our own". The Indian princes remained loyal to the English as long as they stayed in India.

Yet another lesson that was driven home to the British in no uncertain terms was that they could interfere with the rights of the Zamindars and the landlords only at their peril. An assurance was given to them in the Proclamation that full protection would be given to them in matter of inheritance, and the possession of land. Like the princes, the landlords too stood by the English rulers till the end.

The pillars of the Great Revolt were the educated middle class people. Unless they were pacified the rulers realized that they would continue the agitation in one form or another. Addressing the people of India, the Proclamation declared, "We hold ourselves bound to the Natives of our Indian territories by the same obligation of duty which bind us to all our other subjects. . . . So far as may be, our subjects of whatever race or creed be freely and impartially admitted to offices in our Service, the duties of which they may be qualified by their education, ability and integrity only to discharge. It is an earnest desire to stimulate the peaceful industry of India, to promote works of public utility and improvement and to administer its government for the benefit of our subjects' resident therein". The authorities also realized that in a vast country of the size of India it would be impossible for an alien Government to rule without taking into consideration the opinion of the people. This was revealed especially when they set aside the recommendations of the British Indian Association while passing the charter Act of 1853. This led to the decision to give representation to the natives in the legislatures both at the Centre and in the Provinces. The initiative for this was taken by the Indian Council Act of 1861. This was the beginning of a series of moves which culminated in the final establishment of a popular Government in India. The great revolt it was that laid the seeds for the freedom movement.

The English took extreme care not to ignore the special needs of the army. The Great Revolt was the brain child of the Indian soldiers. They were active participants of the revolt. Actually they were the staunchest supporters of the British for whom they had sacrified everything for their benefit even if it was against the interest of their own country. But the reward they got was precious little. And naturally they revolted against the British when the first opportunity presented itself.

Here it should be noted that a more conservative policy was adopted by the English towards the army after the revolt. They were convinced that it would not be in their interest that the Indian component outnumbered the English five to six times. The number of English soldiers was raised form 45,000 to 65,000. The strength of the India sepoys was correspondingly reduced to 1,40,000. It was decided that henceforward the proportion of the Indians to the Europeans in the army should be two to one. The infantry was to consist of one British and two Indian battalions. The field and other artillery was to be manned entirely by the Europeans. The Bengal Army which was mainly responsible for the revolt was literally liquidated. Nearly 1,20,000 out of 1,28,000 sepoys were either killed in the battle or executed or disappeared. They were replaced not by Bengalees any more but a new force consisting of mainly the Sikhs, the Jats, the Punjabi Muslims, Gurkhas and Baluchis who had proved loyal during the Revolt. The number of sepoys form the upper castes was considerably reduced. In each battalion sepoys belonging to one particular caste or religion were recruited to eliminate the possibility of social cohesion which was thought to be the root cause of the revolt in 1857. A special British battalion was stationed to suppress any rebellion. Changes in the civil and military administration enabled the British to reestablish their sway without being challenged.

The Indians learnt the lesson in the hard way that they could not match the superior armed might of the British even remotely. Many social and religious reformers took it upon themselves to educate the masses and instill in them a sense of nationalism which would make it easy to start an agitation against the British rule on strictly non-violent lines.

Causes for the Failure of the Mutiny

Several reasons are attributed for the failure of the Great Revolt of 1857–58. Mention of them has been made in the appropriate context while discussing the cause of the revolt.

The revolt which first started in Meerut and places near about spread to several places. The sepoys elsewhere were not fully aware of the situation at Meerut. If the revolt had started in all the places simultaneously according to a well conceived plan the British would have found it difficult to suppress the spontaneous movement. The unprepared and premature outbreak of the revolt at Meerut was one of the prime reasons for the failure of the Mutiny.

Secondly, the loyal help and co-operation rendered by certain sections of the Sikhs and the Gurkhas among other Indians to the English against the revolutionaries helped in the quick suppression of the revolt.

As Russell put it, "it must be admitted that, with their courage, the British would have been quite exterminated if the natives had been all and altogether hostile to them. The natives shared the glory of the British. The siege of Delhi would have been quite impossible if the Rajas of Patiala and Jhind had not been our friends and if the Sikhs had not been recruited in our battalions and remained quiet in the Punjab . . . our troops are native troops, natives are cutting grass for our houses, and grooming them, feeding the elephant, managing the transport, supplying the commissionaire which feed us, cooking our soldiers food, cleaning their camp . . . waiting on our offices and even lending up their money". The same was the case with the Goorkhas without whose help the British would not have been able to curb rebel activity in Lucknow. Natives against natives was the slogan of the British and it really paid them rich dividends.

The British had a centralized set-up. All their movements were controlled by the central government at Calcutta. A well organized plan of action to which the commanders strictly adhered was the key to their success. The army commanders had experience in conducting wars elsewhere in Europe. Richdson, Havalook, Rose were names to reckon with. On the Indian side too there were able leaders like Nana Saheb, Tatya Tope, Jhansi Lakshmibai, among others. But they had no military experience that could match effectively with that of the British commanders. To compound the situation for the worse there was no unity among the Indian leaders. Each one of them was highly individualistic and was not prepared to accept the leadership of the other. Hence the kind of unified command which was so essential for a successful pursuit of military operations was singularly lacking. In the absence of an over-all military leader not much could be achieved though they outnumbered the besiegers. Many a time discipline was conspicuous by its absence and disobedience among the soldiers was rampant. The revolutionary soldiers were not exactly and inspired lot. They only wanted money and freedom from the British service. And when they looted they made no distinction between Indian and British. The people therefore were reluctant to encourage the soldiers and the revolutionaries for whom physical destruction became a symbol of action. Even the leaders failed to rise above petty jealousies and considerations.

They lacked national spirit and as one scholar put it, "the cause for which they fought was not unjust but its ethos was hopelessly inadequate."

Finally the revolt was not of any significant dimensions in the country south of the Vindhyas. Event eh few uprisings were local in nature. The troops stationed in the south were available to the authorities to suppress the revolt in the North. The comparative lull in the South enabled the British to retake Banares, Allahabad, Kanpur, Delhi, Oudh etc.

The British were backed by ample resources. They had all the facilities to carry on a war to the bitter end and the Indians soon were outmanouvered by a stronger force. The failure of the Revolt under these circumstances was a foregone conclusion.

The Nature of the Revolt

Historians are not unanimous about the nature of the outbreak of 1857–58. Their views could be classified under three main heads – 1) that it was a sepoy mutiny; 2) a revolution or a war of independence; 3) a great revolt.

Sri H.S. Cunningham considers it as a mutiny which can be traced to a military panic. Sri John W. Kaye calls it a sepoy war or the Indian mutiny. Mutiny according to the New English Dictionary on Historical Principles means "and open revolt against constituted authority, especially the revolt on the part of a disciplined body of soldiers or section of it against its officers. It means a behaviour subversive of discipline and amounting to mutinous conduct". In 1857 sepoys of various military contingents declared open hostility to their English officers. But this was not confined only to the sepoys. If it were therefore only a mutiny of sepoy how was it that there were battles between the British and the native in which people of all classes participated? There was discontentment all round. Thus the merchants were dissatisfied because the government monopolized trade in all valuable merchandise leaving inconsequential business to them. Public servants were badly treated, their pay and status were of a low order compared to the high salaries and other perquisites enjoyed by the Englishmen. The artisans were thrown out of employment and reduced to abject poverty Pandits and Maulvis were disgraced and therefore they considered the English as the enemies of their religion and culture. The litigants thought that the newly introduced stamp paper and the costly legal systems were impediments in the away of securing justice whereas under the village panchayats legal remedies were quicker and far less expensive.

There was a widespread fear among the people that their religion was in danger in the hands of Christians missionaries. All sections of the people in the country thus were thoroughly dissatisfied with the rulers and it was not as though only the sepoys were a discontented lot. The revolt indeed was set in motion by the sepoys, but the very foundations of the British empire in India were shaken since it drew support from people from all walks of life. So it is that the Revolt of 1857 is just not a mutiny as is sought to be made out by some critics. It is on the other hand one of those great events of an epoch making nature.

It is not correct either to describe the outbreak as a war of independence. V.D Savarkar was one of these who said the events of 1857 amounted to an Indian War of Independence which was a planned and organized political and military rising and which aimed at destroying for good the company's power in India. "Its great principles were Swadharma and Swaraj . . . and in these two lies the root principle of the revolutionary war. Asoka Mehta also supports this view. Superficially one can find the ingredients of a revolution. "Revolution means a complete overthrow of established government in any country or state by those who were previously subject to it" (A new English Dictionary definition). For a short while in some places there was indeed a successful overthrow of the paramount power. These who revolted without exception had the desire to free the country from foreign rule and to fight for "Swadharma and Swaraj". All the rebels wherever they were followed the same plan and mode of action. There was to this extent a semblance of unity. There was a common date May 31, 1857 for the general uprising. Above all there was an influential secret organization which secured universal response from people irrespective of caste, creed or occupation. The great leaders of the revolt made common cause against the foreigners to protect their religion and country. And yet it cannot be called a war of independence.

The great revolt did not assume the magnitude of a full fledged war of independence. Nationalism in its real form was not known to the people. They were still medieval in outlook and feudal in temperament. Most Indian rulers and people were interested only in their local regions. They did not rise above petty jealousies. Powerful groups like the Rajputs, the Sikhs and princes continued to render loyal support to the British ignoring national interests. Hence it is wide of the mark to call this revolt a war of Indian Independence.

The rising could most appropriately be called a great revolt, not a mutiny or a war of Indian independence. It was a revolt in which both civilians and the military participated. They fought for a common cause. But it was confined in the main to certain regions. Assam, Orissa, Rajasthan and a large part of Bengal, for instance, did not participate in it. Hence it lacked the character of a national war of Independence. The rivalry between the Marathas and the Rajputs, differences among the Marathas themselves, the treachery of Man Singh, the ruler of Marwar against Tatya Tope, showed that there were still segments which could not think in terms of freeing the country from foreign rule. There was again a fear that if they supported the rebels, they would be subjected once again to the rule of the Muslims. For them Muslims were as alien as the Europeans. The great revolt was not without its communal riots in Shajahanpur, Bareilley etc. The people had not totally forgotten the atrocities perpetrated by the Muslim rulers and not surprisingly some of them preferred the rule of the British to Muslim domination again. At the same time the heroic battles fought during the movement, the magnitude of the operations, the wide and expensive support it received go to prove that the 1857–58 rising had all the features of a great revolt.

THE MEANING AND GROWTH OF NATIONALISM

CHAPTER 3

Meaning of Nationalism

Freedom movement became possible in India as a result of the growth of the feeling of nationalism among the people. The country was conquered by the British when such a feeling was absent. Owing to it growth after 1858 the people began to resist gradually the alien rule, and the time soon came when they began and carried on a struggle for freedom.

Nationalism has several implications. In the first place it creates a feeling of unity among the people of the country. India is a land where there are numerous differences among the people due to variations in the religions they profess, in the languages they speak, in the regions they occupy and in the kind of social system based on caste which took deep root in the country from very early times. With the growth of nationalism the people felt that in spite of these differences they belong politically to one community and in matters political they should ignore these differences and become loyal to the national community.

In the second place, it was argued that they were a single nation because all of them were born and brought up in the same country. The ideas grew that they should look upon the country as their common mother and worship her just as they worshipped goddesses like kali and Durga. Bharata Mata was raised to the status of a Divine Being. The well Known Vandemataram song of Bankim Chandra Chatterjee illustrates this. From this it followed that the people—the children of the mother should work together and take the necessary sacrifices for liberating her from the yoke of the foreigner.

Nationalism in the third place created the feeling that the country belongs to the people and that they alone have the right to be the rulers. The foreigner, even though he might have conquered it, has no moral right to rule. This was what Tilak the great nationalist leader meant when he proclaimed that swaraj was the birth right of every Indian, and he must be prepared to make sacrifices for achieving it. It was this implication of nationalism that made freedom movement inevitable.

Thinkers like Aurobindo widened the scope of the meaning nationalism when they identified it with Indianness (Bharatiyata) – to be an Indian in all matters of life and cease to imitate or follow the British ways of life. Gandhiji also interpreted nationalism in this sense when he gave priority to swadeshi in his scheme reconstruction. According to him, swadeshi meant not only the use of Indian goods in preferences to foreign articles but also adherence to Indian religion, Indian languages, Indian culture and civilization and to Indian modes of political organization like the panchayats. When once nationalism was identified with Indianness and swadeshi in this comprehensive sense, it meant that the people of the country could rule themselves and not be subjected to foreign rule.

Nationalism also implied that the people should make every effort not only to free themselves from foreign rule, but it also created a pride in the country's culture and civilization. During the period of the growth of nationalism there was considerable research into the history of ancient India. It was learnt from the researches that though in the nineteenth century the people were downtrodden there was a time when India had achieved greatness in every field of life, and was also able to carry its culture, religion and civilization to many parts of Asia, like all the countries in South East Asia, Japan and china. It was this pride in the greatness their country that inspired the people to fight for freedom and get another opportunity to spread their culture to many countries in the world. This was specially the message of Swami Vivekananda who told his people that in matters religious and cultural they would once more become the teachers of the Western world. He fulfilled this task when he preached the message of Vedanta the people of the United States at the Parliament of Religions held in Chicago in 1893 and during his tours in the countries of Western Europe in subsequent years. Form this was drawn the inference that it was unworthy of a nation with such significant achievement to its credit in the past to remain subjects of foreign rulers in the modern age.

Finally, nationalism inspired the people to bring about all round development of the country, development in the field of religion, economy, social life and art and literature. This is the reason why the growth of nationalism was also closely associated with numerous religious movements in the country, the social reform movement, a new kind of literature, and the general economic uplift of the people. It was realized by the nationalists that it was only in such an all round development that India could become the equal of the advanced nations in the world. It is only when we understand the meaning of nationalism in the comprehensive sense and with al these implications that it would be possible to estimate its significance in the history of the freedom movement.

Factors Responsible for the Growth of Nationalism – English Education

We have to consider the various factors that were responsible for the growth of nationalism after 1858. Among these factors the first place should be given to the spread of English education and through the knowledge gained from it about the history and movements in the western world in modern times. Through English education the new educated classes had the opportunity of studying English books and also books written in several other European languages like French. These books contained ideas which were not found in Indian literature. Among such ideas were nationalism, democracy, equality, liberty and fraternity which formed the basis of many of the revolutions in the western world like the French revolution. English education was responsible for the idea that the learned classes should cultivate scientific and national outlook on life. These ideas of nationalism first inspired the English educated classes and in course of time they spread through their efforts among the other classes of people. It made them feel that like the people of the western world the British, the French, the Italians and the Americans; they should also become a Nation, and fight for the freedom of the country. Western history acquainted them with the great revolutionary movements which characterized the 18th and 19th centuries, movements like the war of American Independence, the French revolution, the revolts of the Balkan people against the Turks and the national movement in Italy. All this brought a new message to them – the message that they should also become united and fight against the foreign rule and establish a democratic form of government when once freedom was achieved.

It was also the age of science in Western Europe which created a new outlook on the problems with which mankind was confronted. Science exalted the importance of reason and a rational outlook with which alone human problems should be solved. It was this idea that inspired the English educated classes in India and made them critically examine the religious and social institutions which they inherited from the past. They found many defects in the institutions. The movements for religious and social reforms which are characteristics of this age could be ultimately traced to the growth of this rational outlook.

As a result of the spread of education a common language came into existence among the new educated classes. Irrespective of province to which they belonged they began to think on the same lines and established a certain commonality. This would not have been possible if the media of the new education were the regional languages as some people advocated. What Sanskrit served in earlier ages was now served by the English language. It led to leadership of the English educated classes in all walks of public life. This was why the responsibility of leading the freedom movements fell into their hands. In the countries of the western world the educated intelligentia were the main creators of new ideas. Putting these into effect became the work of the affluent middle class, the bourgeoise or the capitalists as they were called. It was the middle class that was responsible for the American and the French revolutions and for the reform movement in Britain. In India, however the British did not encourage the growth of an affluent middle class as the British mercantile community monopolized all avenues for making wealth. Consequently, the burden of putting into effect the new ideas of nationalism and democracy had to be borne by the English educated classes and through the various institutions they created and the movements they led, they undertook this task quite successfully and effectively. English education was thus not a little responsible for the rise of a new leadership inspired by new ideas.

Soon a time came when there was confrontation between the English educated classes inspired by new ideas and the British rulers who felt that if such ideas were allowed to flourish, there would be an end to their rule. This led to the rise of two distinct groups in the country – the party of the educate classes which stood for freedom from alien rule, establishment of democratic and representative institutions and the employment of Indians in the higher ranks of public services and the other led by the members of the European members of the Indian civil service, the non-official European community and the editors of newspapers representing their view. The story of the freedom movement is closely related to the story of this confrontation.

Nature of British Rule

Next only in importance to the spread of English education was the nature of British rule itself which consciously or unconsciously became a factor in the growth of nationalism. British rule created political unity in the country and promoted intercourse between the people of different provinces. It established a centralized form of government under which all power was exercised at Calcutta by the Governor General and his council. Provincial Governors were subordinate to it. The people in the country consequently felt that for the redress of their grievances and for promoting their welfare they should look to the central government for help and bring pressures upon it. It also meant that they must have a central organization to achieve the goal. Thus the British presence became an important factor in the growth of national unity.

Further, to promote their own interests the British paid a great deal of attention to railways and roads, and means of communication like the posts ad telegraphs. But they all helped to bring the people together, an outcome which was not intended by the British. In course of time this led to the economic unity of the country as inter provincial trade developed and businessman all over established close contacts with each other. For several commodities the country became a single market. Such close economic relations created a feeling of unity. People could travel easily from one part of the country to another and to see for themselves the greatness of India in the remains of ancient stupas, temples and other works of art and architecture. These created a pride in the achievements of the country in the past which was at the basis of the growth of self respect.

British rule was also responsible for the growth of national unity in another way. Rulers in ancient and medieval India were content with protecting the existing social and economic order and made no attempt to change it. British however followed an entirely different policy. They introduced new systems of land tenure which ultimately resulted in the majority of cultivators becoming mere tenants of zamindars, talukdars, and other affluent land lords. They levied a heavy land tax on the cultivators which they could not bear. They had to borrow from the rich money lenders at high rates of interest and this created an important class of money leaders in the country along with the affluent landlords. They ryots worked hard, but a good deal of what they produced was to a stage of impoverishment. The system of law and judicial administration introduced by the British was something alien to India. It enabled money lenders to go to the law courts to enforce the contracts entered into by the borrowers who were too poor to carry on litigation with money lenders in the costly courts of justice. The same thing happened to the ryots who mortgaged their lands either to money lenders or to the richer landlords. As a consequence many of the ryots lost their land and they became either rack tenants or agricultural labourers. The traditional system of rural economy underwent a change for the worse from the point of view of the ryots. As very little attention was paid by the government to the construction of new irrigation works, the only exception being the grand anicuts across the Godavari and Krishna built by Sir Arthur Cotton. Famines became more frequent. Little was done to give proper relief to the famine stricken people. In the famines millions of people perished and do also the cattle. Unemployment mounted in the rural areas. Till the days of Lord Curzon no attempt was made to give relief to the debtors. It was during his regime that the first steps were taken for starting co-operative credit societies. But they did not go very far in reducing thc burden of debt.

The lot of the craftsmen who were engaged in producing the fine textiles which were world famous was even worse. As a result of the industrial revolution in Britain imports of cotton cloth into the country increased by leaps and bounds. This led to the decline of handicrafts. The iron industry, the ship building industry, the industry which manufactured military weapons and similar industries suffered a set back with the result that almost all the artisan classes had to turn to land for earning their livelihood. But as there was not enough land for the new classes to take to cultivation the ranks of the unemployed swelled. It was in consequences of this that many of them preferred to go to Natal, Fizzi, and Mauritius, Guayana and other distant lands as indentured labourers. All this led to economic discontent in the country. The British rulers were naturally blamed for the growing poverty and unemployment among the people whose political consciousness was aroused thereby.

The New Literature

The third factor which led to the growth of nationalism was the new literature in the regional languages. Books were written more in prose than in verse and instead of highly flown literary language the spoken language which could be easily understood was used in the new literature. Patriotism was the main theme of writers like Bankim

Chandra Chatarjee. Heroism of the Rajput and Maratha leaders like Sivaji found a prominent place in the new literature. It was a call to show the same kind of courage and heroism which was displayed by the patriots of the past. Ballads were also composed in regional languages and were sung at public meeting by the common people. Even those who could not read and write understood the meaning and spirit of the ballads and became nationalistic minded.

Journalism

A fourth factor which contributed to the growth of nationalism was journalism especially in the regional languages. Regional newspapers found wide circulation and they brought out the growing discontent of the people and made them realise that much of their distress was due to foreign rule. The editorials written in the newspaper of one language were reproduced in the newspaper of other languages, and it created a common stock of political ideas through out the whole country. Similar services were rendered by the nationalist newspapers in English. Among the more important of the newspapers that were responsible for the growth of nationalism may be mentioned the Amrit Bazar Patrika, the Indian Mirror, the Sanjivani, the Bengalee, and Bandemataram in Bengal, the Hindu, the Swedesamitran, the Andhra Prakasika and the Krishna Patrika in Madras province, the Maratha, the Kesari, the Induprakash and the sudharak in Bombay., the Hindustani and the Azad in United Provinces, the Tribune and the Kohinoor in the Punjab.

A sentiment like nationalism would not take a firm root unless is found institutional expression. The political association started in different provinces gave expression to it and later on came the Indian National Congress founded in 1885. It served as a common platform for the political leaders belonging to all the provinces. At every session of the congress the idea was emphasized that the people of India in spite of their differences constituted one nation and they should work together for reforms. It also spread political and economic interest and British Imperialism was their common enemy. It was through the Congress that the people became familiar with the ideas of democracy and civil liberty. It was the congress and other political associations again that promoted democratic thought and it was through this body that a large band of political workers were trained to fight for freedom. Among the factors that contributed to the growth of nationalism, a prominent place should be assigned to the Indian National Congress. The idea of nationalism was indeed borrowed from the west but it was like seed planted in a soil where it could grow and bear fruit.

Geographical, Cultural and Political Unity

Among the factors that led to this culmination a few deserve mention. One was the geographical unity of the country bound as it is by the high mountains and the seas which separate it from the neighbouring countries. The geographical unity furthered the growth of the idea that the people of India belonged to a distinct community with its own individuality. It was this that made the Indians regard the people of the other countries as Mlechas just as ancient Greeks regarded the rest of mankind as barbarians. A second factor was the cultural unity of the people of the country from early times. The large majority of them professed the same religion- Hinduism. They were inspired by the same literature like the Puranas, Ithihasas like Ramayana and Mahabharata and sacred books like the Bhagavad Gita. Centres of pilgrimage were spread all over the country, from Haridwar and Banaras in the North to Rameswaram in the south. Tradition encouraged the people to undertake pilgrimages, and this promoted contacts between people of one part of the country with those in another. In addition to this social system of the country was based on caste which was an institution common to the entire country. All this created cultural awakening among the people and when the English educated classes spread the message of nationalism, people found no difficulty in understanding it. And cultural unity led to national unity for political purposes.

It was not as if the idea of political unity was new to the country The Arthasastra of Kautilya and other treatises on politics and public Administration emphasized the idea that Bharatavarsha was a Chakravartiskshetra, fit to be ruled by one emperor. It was not merely a theory but was given practical effect to by many rulers like the Mauryas, the Satavahanas and the Guptas. Though these empires were short lived they in a way, made the people familiar with the idea of political unity. Even the Turks, the Afghans and the Mughals followed this tradition and founded empires which extended over large parts of the country. What was new in the idea of nationalism as formulated by the English educated classes was that the responsibility for maintaining and preserving the political unity of the country should be ultimately taken over by the people themselves.

❖ ❖ ❖

RELIGIOUS REFORM MOVEMENT

CHAPTER 4

We have already noted that nationalism is a force which leads the people to an all round development and not a mere motivating factors for the fight for political freedom. It was this that inspired many reforms to introduce changes in the religious doctrines and practices so that the country might be in a position to resist the onslaughts against it in the nineteenth century and subsequently by the Christian missionaries and also to make them take pride in the superiority of their own religion. These reform movements affected the Hindu religion to a greater extent than Islam even though there were attempts to reforms the latter also.

Religious reform was not new to the country. It was a continuous process during all the ages. The Vedic religion was transformed to a great extent by the thought embodied in the Upanishads. There were movements like Buddhism and Jainism which brought about significant changes both in doctrines and in religious practices. In medieval India, Hinduism came into contact with Islam. As a result of this emphasis was placed on the ideal of Devotion or Bhakti for achieving salvation. There were also attempts to bring about reconciliation between Hinduism and Islam by placing emphasis on the features which were common to both. Nanak and Kabir played a prominent role in the effort. The Bhakti cult was preached by reformers like Chaitanya, Vallabhacharya, Tukaram and Ramadas. They fought against casteism among the followers of the same religion and even brought the untouchables into the fold of the Bhakti cult. They also contributed to the raising of the status of women in the sphere of religion. We may therefore say that the various religious movements of the nineteenth century followed the earlier tradition, the difference being that they were the outcome to some extent of the confrontation with Christianity and the way in which it was preached by the missionaries.

The Brahmo Samaj – Raja Rammohan Roy

The first among these movements was the establishment of Brahmo Samaj by Raja Rammohan Roy in 1828. Roy was a great student of comparative religions. In his youth he learnt Arabic and Persian and was familiar with the teachings of Koran and its emphasis on belief in one god and the condemnation of idol worship. Later, he learnt Sanskrit and studied the Hindu scriptures with the help of learned scholars in Banaras. After this he wandered in the Himalayas and went to Tibet where he came into contact with the Buddhist teachings. After his return to Calcutta he came into intimate contact with the Christian missionaries and studied the Bible in the form in which it was originally written in Greek and the Old Testament written in Hebrew. He thus became familiar with a number of languages and with all the prominent religions of the day. For a number of years he served the East Indian Company and after his retirement he devoted his time to religious reform.

He found that Hinduism was attacked by Christian missionaries on the ground that in advocated the worship of many gods and of idols, and also because it created barriers between one caste and another. After a study of the Hindu scriptures he came to the conclusion that these doctrines and practices were not found in the early books on Hindu religion like the Vedas and the Upanishads and that they became a part of it in subsequent times. He therefore proclaimed that the purest form of Hindu religion was to be found in the Upanishads, that they all stressed the unity and oneness of god, that they did not advocate the worship of idols and the rigidity in the caste system was only a later innovation. What was needed was for the Hindus to go back to the religion as it was taught by the Upanishads, and that Hindu religion should be reformed on this basis. He argued on these lines in the papers which he started while he translated a number of Upanishads into the Bengali language. He was convinced and he was able to impress on a number of other Hindus who followed him that if this was done all the defects pointed out by Christian missionaries in the Hindu religion could be eliminated. It was to enable the people to follow this reformed Hindu religion that the founded the Brahmo Samaj. The Samaj advocated not the abandonment of Hinduism but the return to its original purer form. The Brahmos according to him should consider themselves as Hindus and not as belonging to a different faith. Like the Christians the Brahmos held weekly prayer meetings at which sermons were delivered. Community worship was encouraged and songs were sung. In this respect they were to some extent influenced by Christian practices.

Ram Mohan Roy interested himself not only in religious reform but also in social reform especially in raising the status of women and in the removal of caste barriers and the uplift of untouchables. He thus became the father of the social reform movements in the country. He advocated the abolition of sati, of female infanticide, the raising of the age of marriage of girls, and convinced Lord William Bentick, the then Governor General, to put an end to them. He started schools for the education of women, advocated inter-caste marriages. He interested himself in politics. That was a time when British rule did not spread over the whole country and there was no question of Indian fighting for freedom. He believed in the blessings conferred by the British rule and expressed the view that in a variety of ways it was far superior to the Muslim rule which preceded it. At the same time he pleaded for freedom of speech and the freedom of the press. In this he was very much influenced by the contemporary revolutionary movements in Europe and he issued an appeal to the Governor General to remove all restrictions on the press. This appeal was considered to be one of the most important documents of the times. He spent the last years of his life in England where he died in 1833. He was buried in the town of Bristol. He was every claim to be regarded as the father of Indian Renaissance.

Devendra Nath Tagore

After his death the leadership of Brahmo Samaj was taken over by Devendra Nath Tagore (1817–1903). The Tagores were a leading family in Calcutta. It was also wealthy one. Devendranath's father Dwarakanath Tagore gave financial help to the Samaj. It was in 1838 that Devendra Nath became a member of the Samaj. He established an association called the Tatvabodhini to hold religious discussions. He laid down a number of rules and regulations for the Samaj and he made their observance a condition of its memberships. He also founded a journal by name Tatvabodhini and made Aswini Kuman Dutt a well known scholar its editor. It carried on propaganda in favour of the Samaj throughout Bengal. He also established numerous branches of the Samaj in different parts of Bengal and thus spread its influence. He emphasized that Brahmos should regard themselves as Hindus–a precondition if the reform movement has to spread among the Hindus. He did not, however, take much interest in social reform. This alienated some of the younger men from him and led to the first split in the Brahmo Samaj. One section came to be known as the Adisamaj and it continued to be led by Devendra Nath Tagore. The other section was the All Indian Brahmo Samaj and Keshab Chandra Sen became its leaders.

Keshab Chandra Sen

Keshab Chandra Sen was as eloquent a speaker as he was a scholar. It was his belief that Brahmoism should become a sort of universal religion and this could be accomplished by introducing into it not only the reformed Hindu doctrines but also the essential doctrines of Christianity. He wanted to ensure that this all comprehensive religion appealed to people belonging to other faiths. He also took great interest in the social reform movement, and especially in the education of women and in encouraging intercaste marriages. He made it a rule that Brahmos should dispense with the Hindu religious practices in the performance of marriages. As a result of his efforts the government passed the civil Marriage Act in 1872 under which men and women who stated that they did not belong to Hinduism, Islam, or Christianity could enter into a civil marriage alliance without resorting to any of the religious practices. The Act could be taken advantage of only by men over 18 years of age, and by girls over 14. Many of the Brahmos in Bengal entered into marriages under this Act. As a consequence the age of marriages was raised and intercaste marriages also became popular.

Keshab Chandra Sen toured the country with a view to making his Brahmoism popular in every province. It was under his influence that the prayer Samaj was started in Poona under the leadership of Mahadev Govinda Ranade. In Madras some of his followers founded the South Indian Brahma Samaj. Keshab Chandra Sen was the first to promote an all- India outlook among many of his countrymen. He was a great patriot. It was his view and he stated it forcibly during his visit to England – that while Indians had to learn a great deal in science and technology from the Europeans, the latter, similarly, could learn a great deal from the religious philosophies of India. He was again the first to put forward this view which was later on taken up with many practical results by religious thinkers like Swamy Vivekananda and Arabindo Ghosh. Though he did much to popularize Brahmoism some of his followers resented his ideas that Brahmos should be considered as Hindus. Moreover, contrary of his teaching, he gave his daughter, who was of the age of thirteen, in marriage to the Maharaja of Kuchbehar who was sixteen, and celebrated the marriage according to Hindu rituals. These factors alienated several of his followers from him, and they formed a separate association called the Sadharana Brahma Samaj of which Pandit Sivanatha Sastry became the leader. As a result of this the original Brahmo Samaj split into three sections. In course of time, this led to the decline of Brahmoism.

Sivanatha Sastry

Sivanatha Sastry, however, did much to popularize his Samaj in different parts of the country and he found many followers in Andhra like Veeresalingam Pantulu and Venkataratnam Naidu. Under their influence, the Raja of Pithapuram became one of the patrons of the Samaj. It was through the activities of these leaders that Brahmoism spread in Andhra.

Influence of Brahmo Samaj

Though the number of Brahmos was small, they exercised a great deal of influence in the public life, especially of Bengal. This movement created a new activity in the field of religion. It was through its efforts that many women in Bengal came out of purdah, took to English education and entered public life actively. Though Brahmoism did not take direct interest in politics, it emphasized the ideas of equality and liberty. Under the leadership of Pandit Sivanatha Sastry it preached that Swaraj must be the ultimate ideal and that it could be achieved by their first taking to social and religious reform and removing all the defects which entered into Hindu religion and the social system. The efforts of Keshab Sen to demonstrate that there was much for the Europeans to learn in the field of religion and philosophy, created a feeling of pride and self-confidence among the people and helped in the strengthening of nationalism.

The Arya Samaj – Dayananda Saraswathi

Dayananda Saraswati was another great religious reformer (1824–1883) who founded the Arya Samaj. His original name was Mula Shankara. He was born in an orthodox saivite Brahman family in

Sourashtra. Owing to some of his experiences when he was a boy he lost faith in idol worship, and he became interested in religion and philosophy. He declined to marry and became a Sanyasi. Like all Indian Sanyasis he wandered in forests and hills in search of a guru who could teach him the essence of Hindu religion. Finally, after fifteen years, he found a guru in Virajananda, a blind Yogi. He accepted Dayananda as his disciple and taught him that the only basis of Hindu religion was the Veda, and that the other sacred books like the Puranas or the epics had no claim to be regarded as of importance. He identified Hindu religion with the religion as was founded in the Vedas. Secondly he also confirmed the faith of Dayananda that idols should not be worshipped. He asked Dayananda to preach the Vedic religion. He told him that this was the only reward which he expected from him as his disciple.

True to the promise made to his guru, Dayananda took upon himself the responsibility of teaching the Vedic religion and carrying on propaganda in its favour in Northern India. On one occasion he came to Banaras, the citadel of Hindu religion and philosophy. In a conference of learned pandits presided over by the Maharaja of Banaras, he challenged the scholars to prove that idol worship had the sanction of the Vedas. They were unable to answer the challenge and yet declined to accept defeat in his hands. A little later he proceeded to Calcutta and came into contact with Brahmo leaders like Keshab Chandra Sen. They agreed with him on two essential matters, that god is one and that idols should not be worshipped. But they refused to agree with his view that the essence of Hindu religion was to be found only in the Vedas. They, therefore, parted company but he accepted their advice that instead of carrying on propaganda in Sanskrit as he was doing all along, he should speak in the language of the people. From then on (1873) he began using Hindi for carrying on his propaganda. Subsequently he visited Bombay and received a warm welcome at the hands of the leaders of Prarthana Samaj. In 1880, he decided that he should embody his teachings in a book and after four years of effort he brought out "Satyartha Prakash" which describes in detail all his teachings. It was in this book that he expounded the view that the Vedas are the only source of Hindu Religion, that they contain not merely spiritual truths but also a large amount of scientific knowledge about railways and many other subject of interest to the scientists in modern times. This was, however, a far fetched conclusion and even though some of these disciples accepted it, it found no acceptance among the scientist or other impartial students of the Vedas. He also pointed out in this connection that the acceptance by the Hindus of the Puranas, the Dharmasastras and other books as authoritative led to the growth of different sects among them and created a split among these sections. The best remedy for this was to accept the Vedas as the sole source of religion just as the Koran for Islam and the Bible for Christianity.

Dayananda Saraswati also expounded the view that the god of which the Vedas spoke was superior to the god as described in Islam, Christianity and several other religions. The Vedic God was Impartial. To him all human being were alike. The Muslims regard the non-Muslims as Kafirs, and the Christians regards non-Christians as Heathens, and the Kafirs and Heathens are not the favourites of God and to receive His favour, they should embrace Islam or Christianity. It is from this point of view that Dayananda stated that the Vedic God was impartial.

Thirdly, Dayananda stated that the only true religion was the Vedic religion and those who believed in his doctrine should try their best to convert the followers of all other religions to Vedic Religion. This was a view which was opposed to Hindu tradition which says that all religions are equally good because they are only different ways of achieving salvation. Dayananda put forward this view because he felt that it was lack of aggressive spirit among the Hindus that helped Islam in medieval India and Christianity in Modern India to convert large number of Hindus into their faith. Hindus should now adopt an aggressive policy and convert the followers of other faiths to the Vedic religion.

Fourthly, he advocated the reconversion into Hinduism of all those who had embraced Islam or Christianity. This again was contrary to traditional Hinduism which was against taking back into its fold those who left it to embrace other religions. Dayananda regarded that this refusal was one of the causes of the weakness of Hinduism and to gain strength it must follow the path which he showed. To this reconversion process he gave the name "Suddhi". More than anything else it was this aspect of this teachings that was most disliked by the Muslims and the Christians. But it logically followed that from the third tenet of this teachings that Hindus should try to convert the followers of other faiths to Hinduism.

For spreading these and other truths contained in "Satyartha Prakash" he founded the Arya Samaj. To the Vedic religion which he expounded he gave the name "Arya" religion because it was the religion taught by the ancient Aryans and to the Samaj he founded he gave the name "Arya Samaj".

It was in Sourashtra that the Arya Samaj was first established in 1875. Within a short time its branches spread into other parts of north India and especially in the Punjab which became the most important centre of the Samaj. Punjab was the province where the Hindus suffered most at the hands of the Muslims. It was, therefore, natural for the educated classes in that province to follow the teaching of Dayananda. They were inspired most by his view that the Arya Samaj should endeavour to convert the followers of other faiths to the Vedic religion. It gave them a great deal of self confidence and his efforts to demonstrate that the Vedas contained a large amount of scientific knowledge also reconciled many of the educated classes to the new faith.

Dayananda was not merely a religious reformer. He advocated social reform as well and called upon all his followers to work for the removal of caste barriers, abolish untouchability and give to women the same status as that of men. It was this last feature that produced many practical results. From this time onwards education spread rapidly among women in Punjab and in all these parts of the country which came under the influence of the Arya Samaj. The general emphasis which he placed on education led to the foundation of a number of schools and colleges by the Arya Samajists. They were of two types. In the first modern English education was imparted, and, in the other, it was the type of ancient Indian education through the Gurukula system that was given prominence. Both types of educational institutions continue to flourish even to the present day.

Dayananda made it clear that Swaraj was the birthright of the people of every country and that India was bound to achieve it. It was he who made the first use of the idea of Swaraj but he also expressed the view that many defects entered the Hindu Society and till all these defects were removed it would be difficult to achieve independence. He, however, called upon his countrymen to make every effort to remove those defects, to cultivate a spirit of patriotism and be prepared to bear the responsibilities of governing themselves. He thus left not only a spiritual message but also a political message.

On the whole his teachings became a source of inspiration not only to the Arya Samajists but also to the Hindus. It instilled in them a pride in their past and served as motivation for the revival of ancient glory. In this way it strengthened the forces of nationalism. It is worthy of note that some of the great nationalists like Lala Lajpat Roy were members of the Arya Samaj.

The Ramakrishna Mission – Ramakrishna Paramahamsa

Yet another great religious reformer was Ramakrishna Paramahamsa (1836–1886). His original name was Gangadhara Chatopadhyaya. He was born in a poor Brahmin family in the village of Ramarpakur in Bengal. He was admitted to the pial school but could make much progress in it. He was, however, interested in the discourses on Puranas given by pandits and also by the wandering ascetics who occasionally visited the village. He would now and then fall into trance and speak of God and his glories.

At the age of twenty he became the priest in a Kali temple newly built at Dakshineswar near Calcutta. While worshipping the idol of Kali he felt that it was not a mere piece of stone as even many educated people believed in those days but the living embodiment of the Goddess Herself. Through a number of traditional religious practices he was able to see the Goddess in all Her glory. He wanted to find the truths in Vaishnavism, Saivism and other forms of Hindu faith and also of Islam and Christianity. For this purpose he came into close contact with the exponents of all these faiths, scrupulously performed all the rituals associated with them. This personal experience gave him a real insight into the fundamental truths of all religions. He came to the conclusion that all religions were similar, that the role of all of them was to reach God and different religions were only different paths to reach him. There was no question of one religion being superior to another and there was no reason why one should give up the ancestral religion in which one was born and brought up and become a convert to other faiths. One of the great lessons which he taught to his disciples and followers was this fundamental similarity among all the religions. It was a lesson so necessary in a country like India with a diversity of religions. Through this lesson he arrested to a great extent the tendency on the part of many Hindus to take to Christianity which was propagated actively by the Christian missionaries.

Secondly, he emphasized the supreme value of religions in man's life at a time when owing to the growth of science and technology there was a decline in spiritual values and greater adherence to materialism. He regarded that the materialistic outlook on life and the pursuit of wealth which it inculcated would promote strife between one nation and another. To give to men and women the peace of mind which they were so much in need of the only instrument was religion and the spiritual values for which it stood. It was also necessary to create harmony in society and between one nation and another.

While he was a priest in the Kali Temple he came into contact with one of the great exponents of Vedanta which occupies a very eminent place among Indian systems of philosophy. What impressed him most in Vedanta was its view that every Individual has the spark of the Divine Being in him. There was a sort of identity between the individual and the Supreme being. From this he drew the conclusion that all men were equal because all were representatives of the Supreme Being. It was therefore unworthy of anyone to treat others as his inferiors. On the other hand, it was the supreme duty of every one to do service to others and uplift them in every way possible. Service to man was the only kind of worship of God which is worthy of human beings. To this interpretation of Vedanta he gave the name "Anshanik Vedanta" – Vedanta as it should be put into practice. It meant that the rich should serve the poor, the educated should serve the uneducated and everyone who some special gift in him should serve others by sharing the gifts with them. This concept of Vedanta as a practical guide to life is a third lesson which he taught to his followers.

He also defended the traditional practices like the worship of a number of Gods and Goddesses on the ground that all these were only forms of the Supreme God and not separate from Him. Out of the same piece of gold the goldsmith makes various kinds of jewellery. One jewel has a name different from that of the others. But that does not mean it has ceased to be gold. Similarly, he defended idol worship as a step which was necessary for people in the earlier stages of their religious development before they could grasp the abstract truths embodied in spiritual philosophy. When such truths were understood there may be no need to continue the worship of idols.

He taught all these lessons to his disciples in simple language that could easily be understood and by means of parables, anecdotes and similies with which they were familiar. That was one of the unique characteristic of Ramakrishna as a teacher of religion.

All this made him great in the eyes of the Bengalees who came into close contact with him. Among them were highly educated people like Keshab Chandra Sen. Ramakrishna became famous as a saint of Dakshineswar who gave a new popularity to traditional Hinduism.

Swami Vivekananda

Among the greatest of his disciples was Narendra Dutta, who late became famous as Swami Vivekananda. Dutta was born in a middle class Kayastha family in Calcutta in 1863. He took the B.A. Degree of Calcutta University and became a keen student of both Eastern and Western Philosophy. At first he had some sympathy for the Brahmo movement. Whenever he met a religious teacher it was usual for him to put to him the question, "Have you seen God? But no teacher was in a position to give him a straight and direct answer. It was in this situation that he heard of Ramakrishna and one day he went to him. Ramakrishna embraced him and told him, "I have been waiting for you for weeks and months and you have atlast come." Datta in his usual way put him the question, "Have you seen God". Immediately came the reply, "I have seen Him more clearly than I am seeing you now". Dutta decided that he was the right teacher for him and from that time on he frequently visited Ramakrishna and learnt from his religious philosophy an also the various yogic practices associated with it. Just before his death Ramakrishna called him to his side and told him, "You are not an ordinary man. You are God Narayana Himself and it is now your duty to devote all your life to teach not only the people of India but also the people of the whole world the Supreme value of Vedanta". Datta promised to do so, became a Sanyasin along with many of this friends. For some years he devoted himself to the study of Vedanta and other systems of philosophy along with his friends who also became sanyasins and founded the Ramakrishna Mutt to carry on propaganda on the lines laid down by his master, Ramakrishna.

We have already noted Ramakrishna's emphasis on putting Vedanta to practice by each one serving the others. This impressed Vivekananda and for this purpose he founded in due course the Ramakrishna Mission whose main purpose was to render service to those who were in need of it.

Vivekananda (the name which he assumed after he became a sanyasin) was not content with carrying on propaganda only in India. He heard of a meeting of the Parliament of Religions in 1893 at Chicago in U.S.A. He decided to participate in the deliberations of that parliament and to convey to the delegates assembled there the message of Vedanta. With the help of his admirers and friends he got the necessary financial help which enabled him to go to Chicago and participate in its deliberations. Besides hundreds of delegates representing all the religions of the world, there were more than ten thousand people who eagerly listened to all their speeches. Vivekananda was then only thirty years of age. He was dressed in yellow robes with a yellow turban. Unlike the other delegates who spoke only in praise of their religion and of the need for all others to follow it, Vivekananda spoke of the Vedanta which stood for equality of all religions. It was this impassioned plea that deeply impressed the large audience. He was greatly praised for putting this Truth before them. Many American papers wrote editorials in his praise and the eloquence which he displayed while speaking in the parliament. They even said that it was foolish on the part of the Americans to send missionaries to India, the house of spiritual philosophy like the Vedanta, which stood for equality of all religions. At all subsequent meetings of the parliament which he addressed more and more people came to listen to him and he became a celebrity in U.S.A.

He spent four years in that country, visiting city after city, and addressing large audiences on the spiritual teaching of India. In order to give permanence to his work, he established a number of Vedanta centres in many of the cities of United States and entrusted their work to sanyasins trained in the Ramakrishna Mutt. Through these centres many Americans became familiar with the teaching of the Vedanta and admirers of the spiritual learning of India. This was the greatest service which Swami Vivekananda rendered to the country of his birth. For more than a country the westerners were under the impression that the people of India were uncivilized and their culture was of an inferior order. The work done by Vivekananda and by the Vedanta centres dispelled this view and gave to India a high place among the cultured nations of the world.

From America Vivekananda went to England and several countries on the continent of Europe carrying the message of the Vedanta to a large number of people. They also came to revise their views on the nature of Indian civilization and culture and gave to them a very high place among the cultures of the world. In 1897 he returned to India. After this triumphant tour he was warmly and enthusiastically welcomed by his countrymen who found in him the greatest Indian spiritual ambassador to the countries of the west. From Colombo in Ceylon to Almora in the far North, meetings were arranged to listen to his inspiring message. The essence of the message was that India had a rich spiritual wealth and it was this wealth that kept the nation alive in contrast to ancient Greece, Rome, Egypt and other countries whose cultures though great and glorious in ancient times, perished in course of time. India's cultural heritage according to him was as much alive then as it was four thousand years ago.

He also told his countrymen that in ancient times India carried her spiritual wealth to various countries in Asia as far as China and Japan, and was recognized as a great teacher. There was need even now for India to carry on this work. And Indians should train themselves to discharge this responsibility effectively and successfully. Under no circumstances should Indians forget that India's greatness was mostly due to the spiritual wealth which she possessed and they should make every effort to enrich this wealth and be of service to the rest of mankind. It was this message that created a sense of pride among the educated classes in the country. It made it clear to them that there was nothing to be ashamed of in their religion, in the kind of life for which it stood. Nationalism always stands for legitimate pride in all its achievements and it was given to Vivekananda to create this kind of pride among his countrymen it was how he contributed to the strengthening of nationalism in the country.

He spent most of his time after his return from America touring the country in the course of which he found that people were generally down trodden. The large majority of them were poor. Many were treated as untouchables. He regarded this as a great blot on Hinduism as it was practiced. He called on his country men to remove poverty and untouchability. He preached in a way socialism though the term as such was not used by him.

Vivekananda was a great patriot and a staunch nationalist. Though he did not plead the cause of Swaraj directly his teachings contributed to the strengthening of national feeling among the people and leading the way to the demand of Swaraj in due course. To carry on his work, he established a training centre at Mayavati, He started a magazine "Prabuddha Bharata." He studied the various system of Yoga, practiced them and wrote on them and they have been subsequently published in a number of volumes. He was a great intellectual and he spent most of his time carrying his message to every part of the country. This incessant and untiring work led to a breakdown of his health and he passed away prematurely at the young age of thirtynine. But his work as a religious reformer has obtained a place of permanence in the country.

The Theosophical Society – Madam Blavatsky and Colonel Olcott

Another important movement which contributed to the strengthening of nationalism was the Theosophical Movement. The Theosophical Society was founded in New York in 1875 by Madam Blavatsky, a Russian who belonged to an aristocratic family, and by Colonel Olcott, an American. Its object was to promote Theosophy which means Divine Wisdom. They drew a distinction between knowledge and wisdom. Wisdom consists in the capacity to use knowledge for the right purposes. The founders of the society felt that though scientific knowledge increased in the western world it was used only for the pursuit of wealth and for the manufacture of weapons for warfare. This harmful use of knowledge could only be corrected by the spread of Divine wisdom which was propagated from the earliest times by the founders of great religions.

Blavatsky and Olcott came to India in 1879 and established branches of the Society in different towns and made Adyar in Madras the centre for all the activities of the Society both in India and abroad. The selection of India as the head-quarters of an international organization like the society exercised a special influence on the educated classes in India.

Besides this the founders and members of the Society believed that the countries of Asia, and among them India in particular, were places where Divine wisdom originated. It was from them that the westerners borrowed from very early times their knowledge of religious and spiritual life. They also emphasized that even in the contemporary age it was mainly from India that they had to learn the highest truths of religion and philosophy. In particular they emphasized the truth contained in the two doctrines of Karma and Rebirth which formed the special features of Hinduism and Buddhism. They popularized these doctrines in the western world along with the Yogic practices which were also a special feature of the Indian system of religion and philosophy. Through their efforts, the rest of the world and especially the west came to realize that they had much to learn from India.

All this created among the educated classes in the country a natural pride in their ancestral religion. For about a hundred years Hinduism was subject to attack by the Christian missionaries and several among the English educated classes became converts to Christianity while many more were not able to decide as to a whether they should follow Hinduism or give up all faith in religion. Quite a few of them became atheists or agnostics and it was in this situation that the Theosophical Society carried to them the message that India was the home of spiritual knowledge and it was best for all mankind to learn it and put it into practice. Reformers like Dayananda and Vivekananda emphasised this standpoint but there was nothing unnatural in it as they were all Indians. The expression, however, of a similar view by Westerners who founded the Theosophical Society dispelled from the minds of the educated classes and doubts that might still have lingered among them as to the spiritual superiority of that they inherited from the past. This strengthened the sentiment of nationalism among them.

Annie Besant

In 1893 Annie Besant who by that time had become a convert to Theosophy came to India to carry on propaganda on its behalf. For years she was a rationalist and an atheist. She took a prominent part in England in socialist and other radical movements. In 1889 when she was forty three she came across the book entitled "The Secret Doctrine" Written by Madam Blavatsky. She had to review the book in a magazine entitled "review of reviews" edited by William Stead. She immediately became convinced of the truths contained in the book, gave up her atheism and became one of the most active members of the Society. It was with this background she came to India in 1893 she was a great orator and could sway large audiences by her eloquence. She addressed meetings all over the country and popularised the ideas of Theosophy to a greater extent than was done by Blavatsky and Olcott. She believed that in her former birth she was an Indian and that in this birth it was her duty to redeem her past debt to the country. This served as a motive force which made her work incessantly for the uplift of India in all walks of life. It was education that first attracted her attention. She criticized the existing system of English education, as religion and morals had no place in it. She started the central Hindu college at Banaras to impart English education along with religion and morals. She gave as much importance to the education of women as to that of men. She insisted that admission should be given in the Theosophical institutions only to unmarried girls and boys which were in the true spirit of ancient Indian Brahmacharya. It was this college that was the nucleus for the Banaras Hindu University.

Annie Basant got interested in social reform especially in raising the age of marriage, improving the status of women and removing untouchability. She however emphasized that in these matters Indians should not imitate the west but proceed on truly national lines. It was in 1914 that she started taking keen interest in Indian politics. She founded the Indian Home Rule League on 1916 and carried on vigorous propaganda in its favour through speeches and by issuing books and pamphlets.

She suffered internment at the hands of the Madras Government for her Home Rule activities. This added to her popularity in the country. In recognition of her services she was elected president of the Indian National Congress in 1917 and she continued her political activities till 1920 when Gandhiji became the recognized political leader in the country. She differed from him on matters relating to civil disobedience and her popularity slowly diminished. But all the same she continued her activities till the last days of her life especially educational, as enthusiastically as ever. She left a rich legacy of national work.

As we have noted above the Theosophical movement created among the English educated classes a real understanding of Indian religion and made them take pride in all that India achieved in the past. It served as a big factor in inducing them to work hard for creating an equally bright future for the country.

The Impact of Religious Movements

When we review the history of religious movements in the nineteenth century we find that all of them brought about a reawakening among the people of India in almost all fields of public life. They were responsible for creating an all India outlook among the educated classes. They created a sense of pride in the achievements of India in the past and made them realize that their effort should be directed to an all round development of the country. That was the message of Dayananda, Vivekananda and the Theosophical society. They placed the ideal of service before them and this was responsible for the great sacrifices which the people made later when the freedom struggle assumed a new form under the leadership of Gandhiji. The religious movements were directed against attempts made by the Christian missionaries for the cultural conquest of the country. They achieved complete victory in this respect. Naturally this infused confidence in the people that they could equally achieve victory in freeing the country politically too.

SOCIAL REFORM

CHAPTER 5

Factors Responsible for Social Reform Movement

The social reform movements in the country originated in the idea that there should be an all round development of the people and that unless the social evils were removed it would not be possible for the people to achieve real victory in the political field either. Apart from this the spread of English education was greatly responsible for the social reform movement. It did this in two ways. In the first place it created a rational outlook on various problems confronting the country. So far as the social system was concerned it encouraged the English educated classes to test every one of their institutions from a rational stand point. When so tested, they found that the inequality between men and women, the caste barriers and the institutions of untouchability were all opposed to reason. Secondly, the English educated classes were influenced by the institutions of the West and they found that in these institutions greater emphasis was placed on the equality of men and women, on the removal of class barriers. That was the message of the 18th century philosopher like Voltaire and Rousseau in France and Thomas Paine and John Stuart Mill in England. This led the English educated classes to work for social reform and to see that Indian society became as free as the Western society.

Besides this, the Christian missionaries exercised a great influence on the growth of the social reform movement in the country. They were not only critical of the Hindu social system but also did constructive work especially in the field of education of women and in the elevation of the untouchables. They were the first to start schools for girls and also to spread education among the untouchables whom they converted to Christianity. All this induced the English educated classes to attach considerable importance to social reform.

The Aims of Social Reforms

The three fields in which the educated classes wanted to bring about reform were – improving the status of women, the removal of caste barriers and untouchability. In actual practice however it was the first that received the largest attention at their hands. This was only natural because the evils that affected women were brought home more directly to the English educated classes than the evils of caste barriers or of untouchability. Most of the evils that affected women's lives were found only among those who belonged to the higher castes. Practices like sati, infanticide, child marriage and compulsory widowhood were more prevalent among them and it was the members of the higher castes that first took to English education and came into contact with Western culture. They therefore turned their efforts to remove them.

Raja Ram Mohan Roy

Raja Ram Mohan Roy was doubtless the first great social reformer. It was mainly through his efforts that Lord William Bentick, the Governor General, abolished by legislation the practice of sati. Later, several governmental efforts were made to abolish infanticide, prevalent to a great extent among the kshatriyas and the Rajputs. They succeeded in their efforts by about 1850. The work of social reform which began with the abolition of sati was continued through voluntary effort on the part of the English educated classes. The Brahmo Samaj gave a prominent place to social reform in its programme of work. We have already seen that it was through its efforts that the Civil Marriage Act which raised the age of marriage was passed by the government. Much earlier than this through the efforts of Iswar Chandra Viday Sagar, principal of the Sanskrit College in Calcutta and an eminent scholar, the Government of Dalhousie enacted a low permitting marriage of widows. These constituted the earliest efforts in the direction of social reforms.

Controversies Regarding Social Reform

Several controversies arose not only among the social reformers but also between the social reformers and orthodox sections in connection with the content and nature of the movement. One was whether social reform should be regarded as a part of religious reform or separated from it. The followers of the Brahmo Samaj regarded it as a part of religious reform. But Dayananda Saraswati, among others, made it clear that social reforms was not inconsistent with Hindu religion, that religion and social reform dealt with different aspects of man's life and that it was wrong to bring the two together. It was this view that ultimately gained strength in the country and prompted social reform.

The second source of controversy was the relationship between political and social reform. Many among those who founded the Indian National Congress were equally interested in social reform. But a keen debate arose as to whether the platform of the Congress should be used for carrying on the propaganda in favour of social reform. As early as in 1886 Dadabhai Naoroji said that it was not desirable to discuss the problems of social reform at the annual sessions of the Congress. He pointed out that while there was a large amount of agreement in regard to political issues, the same was not the case with respect of social problems. These problems varied between one province and another, and between one caste and another and among different religious communities. The discussion of such problems by the National Congress could disrupt unity and it was, therefore, best to leave the work of social reform to other organizations. It was because of this view that another organization called the National social organization was started by Ranade and others. This conference usually met in the same pandal in which the National Congress was held soon after the session was over. Even this was objected to by Tilak when the Congress held its session at Poona. Though his opposition prevented the National Social Conference from meeting in the Congress pandal that year, the objection to it weekend in course of time. The conference continued to hold its session immediately after the session of the congress and passed resolutions of a recommendatory nature on matters relating to social reform leaving to provincial organizations the responsibility of putting them into effect.

A third source of controversy was on the priority to be accorded to social reform and to political reform respectively. The Moderates urged that social reforms should have a place of priority. Their plea was that unless social evils were removed national unity could not be achieved and without the achievement of national unity. There could be no progress in the direction of self Government. Extremists like Bal Gangadhar Tilak took a different line. It was the political dependence of the country on the British that Stood really in the way of progress in all fields of national life, and unless self government was rapidly achieved reform in society would not be possible. It was also pointed out that the government officials especially the members of the Indian civil service emphasized the view that social evils should be removed first before Indians could claim the right to the self government. They did this mainly to divert the attention of the people from political agitation which was detrimental to the interests of the British. It was, therefore, a mistake to insist on precedence to social reform. It would really amount to promoting the vested interests of the British rulers. The controversy however continued, and it was one of the reasons why as time passed the enthusiasm for social reform weakened. This weakening was also due some extent to another controversy as to whether people should call upon the government to legislate on matters of social reform or whether they should carry it out through the efforts of their own, independently of governmental legislation. Here again the politicians who belonged to the extremist or nationalist school preferred voluntary efforts arguing that the Government especially when it was alien should not be permitted to enter into the social field and that it was quite possible to bring about social reforms by educating the public opinion. This view ultimately prevailed because the Government also came to feel that they would be taking an unnecessary burden upon themselves by intruding into the social field. The result was that for more than thirty or forty years until the Sarada Marriage Act was passed Government refrained from any kind of social legislation.

What deserves to be noticed is that the gradual spread of education among women gave them the needed impetus to solve the problems affecting their status by their own efforts. The developments or railways and the factory system in industry led to a weakening of the caste barriers. It was not possible during railway travel for people to strictly observe restrictions in regard to food or practice untouchability. Similarly, in factories people belonging to all castes worked side by side and caste barriers lost this rigidity to some extent. The same was the case when women and men worked alongside of each other in factories and industrial concerns. All this made social reforms practicable without the need for aggressive propaganda as in earlier days.

Later on the enfranchisement of large number of untouchables along with the members of the higher castes led to a great extent to raising the status of untouchables. Politicians who stood as candidates for legislatures had to seek the vote of the untouchables. Naturally, this compelled them to show to them a certain amount of respect. Dr. Ambedkar and others also organized the untouchables to fight for better status. The point to be noted is that without the need for any special social reform agencies, the changes in the economy of the country and in the political system brought about a transformation in the social system. In some parts of the country each caste made its own efforts to solve its problems and this also resulted in bringing about greater between caste and caste.

ADVENT OF POLITICAL ASSOCIATIONS

CHAPTER 6

We have now to study the influence of nationalism on the growth of political associations. In tracing the history of these associations two clear stages could be discerned. In the first stage, associations were confined to particular provinces. These could appropriately be described as provincial in character. There was not much of contact between those in one province and in another, due mainly to lack of means of communications. In the second stage, we find a movement for starting an all India political association and it was in the attempts made for this purpose that the influence of nationalism on political organization was felt. It fructified in the establishment of the Indian National Congress in 1885.

In the first stage it was only in those provinces where English education was spread that associations were started. This was only to be expected because it was the English educated classes that started them. So we find such associations in the coastal provinces of Bengal, Bombay and Madras. The inland provinces were slow to follow because English education started there much later than in the three coastal provinces. In starting these associations the English educated classes were influenced by two factors. One of them was the existence of such associations in Britain which through peaceful agitation were able to get from the government of the day the concessions and reforms they wanted. The English educated classes in India very much influenced by these ideas and institutions which were prominent factor in inducing them to start century and this was a prominent factor in inducing them to start similar association in the provinces. In addition to this, it was the British mercantile community that first set the example of starting political associations what with its influential position especially in the coastal provinces. Its examples was followed by the Indian educated classes. This is why associations were in the earlier stage started in Bengal, Bombay and Madras.

The British Indian Association

By 1858, the British Indian Association in Calcutta, the Bombay Association in Bombay and the Madras Native Association in Madras had come into existence. All of them were found before 1858. But gradually they lost their influence owing to a variety of circumstances. The British Indian Association consisted mainly of Zamindars. But, in the meanwhile, a middle class of English educated people consisting of lawyers, government employees, journalists and teachers came into existence, and they did not find much scope for their activities and their point of view in these associations. They therefore found it necessary to start their own association which would represent their point of view. In addition to this, the British Indian Association confined its activities mostly to Calcutta and din not find a place for the educated classes in the districts. Sisir Kumar Ghosh, editor of The Amrit Bazar Patrika started the India league in 1875, and Surendranath Banerjee and Ananda Mohan Bose and their friends set up the Indian association. They wanted to make this the central association for the entire country. Surendranath Banerjee started branches of this association in different parts of North India. In the course of his tours between 1877 and 1879 to carry on propaganda against lowering the age of candidates appearing for the Indian Civil Service competitive examination held in England from 21 years to 19, he tried to convince the people of the need for making the Indian Association and all India one. His efforts did not succeed immediately because the then existing provincial association did not want to lose their identity by merging in an association dominated by the Bengalis.

The Bombay Association

The Bombay Association started in 1853 ceased to be active after 1862. Bombay was a city dominated by merchants. They were the most influential class. They were more interested in commerce and trade than in politics which did not bring any immediate gain. The English educated class could do little without the cooperation of the mercantile community. Moreover Bombay was a cosmopolitan city consisting of Parsis, Gujaratis, Maharshtrians and Muslims. It did not belong to any one community as for instance Calcutta, where the Bengalis were dominant. It was only when there was co-operation among all the communities that political activity was possible and this was why Poona became the centre of political activity in the Bombay presidency for a long time. Poona was a city of the Maharashrians. Memories of the independent and imperial glory they enjoyed under the peshwas were still fresh. They were also led by the influential community of Chitpawan Brahmins to which eminent persons like Tilak, Gokhale and Ranade belonged. There was a great deal of cooperation among them and the Sarvajanik Sabah that was started in 1870 became the most important political body in western India. Under the leadership of Ranade it educated the ordinary classes of people in politics, brought their grievances to the notice of the government through its representatives and reports and also worked in the rural areas among the peasants. All this led to its commanding influence. But later on differences arose in the association between the moderates led by Ranade and Gokhale and the extremist led by Tilak, and there also came into being a non-Brahmin organization which opposed the Sarvajanik Sabha on the ground that it was dominated by the Brahmins. In 1855 through the efforts of Telang, Tyabji and Pherozshah Mehta, the Bombay Presidency Association was set up and it grew in influence in due course.

The Madras Native Association

The Madras Native Association was started in 1853. Though it was active till 1862, and many of the representations which it made to the British parliament in connection with the revision of the Charter in 1853 received great attention, it became almost defunct after 1862. There was then no leisurely class and Zamindars in Madras as in Calcutta. Education also did not spread so rapidly as in Bengal and the number of lawyers and doctors who could take part in politics was limited. For a long time there was no leading newspaper in the Presidency until the Hindu was started in the year 1878. In 1884 however many who belonged to the younger generation of the educated classes started the Madras Mahajana Sabha which became the most important political association in the Southern Presidency for a fairly long time under the leadership of Anandcharyulu.

During this period the leading politicians in the province felt that in addition to the provincial associations there should be an association of all India character which would prove effective in bringing before the authorities the needs of the people as a whole and the reforms required to satisfy such needs. But there was no agreement among them as to what its shape should be. As early as in 1853 the British India

Association of Calcutta suggested that body should be recognized an all India organization. But as pointed out above its suggestion could not be carried out.

The East India Association

In 1865 the Indian residents in Britain, including the students and the members of the mercantile community, formed an association representative of the Indians in all the provinces. It was called the London Indian Association. But it worked only for a very short time. In 1866, with the same object, the Indians in Britain established the East India Association. Dadabhai Naoroji took active interest in its work and tried to establish branches in Bombay, Madras and Calcutta. It was only the Bombay branch that worked successfully for some time. It sent reports on India to the association in Britain and also contributed funds for its work. But as membership in the East India Association was open to non-Indians interested in Indian affairs, advantage was taken of this by the retired members of the Indian civil service and their numbers grew with time. They did not correctly represent the Indian point of view and hence it lost all popularity among the educated classes in India and not surprisingly the Bombay branch became defunct. Similar attempts were made from time to time to start all India bodies in England, but without success. They however drove home the lessons to the political leaders in India that any all India political body if it should serve the real purpose should be established in India itself and not in Britain. This was a significant lesson indeed.

Need for all India Political Body

This idea was taken up in another form when the representatives of Bengal and Sarvajanik Sabha attended the Deshi Durbar held by Viceroy Lytton in 1877 to proclaim Queen Victoria as the Empress of India. They decided as a first step there should be a national press union and that it should hold annual conference not only to explain the grievances of the press but also to discuss question of an all India character and make representation to government. Two such conferences were held in Calcutta in 1878 and in Bombay in 1879. Though similar conferences were not subsequently held these gave fillip to the idea that there should be an all India political body.

Surendranath Banerjee and Indian National Conference

In 1883 Lord Rippon, the liberal Viceroy referred in the address delivered at the convocation at Calcutta to the fact that different kinds of public opinion were being expressed by different bodies in the country and said that government was not able to find out what the true public opinion in general was and it would be better if steps were taken to create a common public opinion. The suggestion was taken up by Surendranath Banerjee who was already moving in that direction. In the later part of 1883, he organized under the auspices of the Indian association a National Conference to which he invited delegates from the political bodies in all the provinces. Though delegates did not come from all the provinces several of them were represented in it and it passed resolutions on subject like the representation of elected representatives on Indian legislatures, the raising of the age of candidates for the Indian Civil Service examination and the separation of the judiciary from the executive – the subject on which resolutions were passed by the Indian National Congress when it met in 1885.

Ilbert Bill and European Defence Association

This attempt to hold a national Congress was also influenced by the agitation organized by the Europeans in India over the Ilbert Bill introduced in the Legislative council by Ilbert, the Law Member, in 1883. Its aim was to confer on the Indian magistrates who belonged to the I.C.S. the same right to try European criminals as the European members of the service Possessed. The Government of Lord Rippon, the provincial governments in India and the Home authorities felt that there should be no invidious distinction between the European and the Indian members of the Civil Service in the matter of crime – a distinction which existed till then. But the European communities in their racial arrogance resented the extension of the right to Indians whom they regarded as an inferior race and therefore unfit for trying men of a superior race. They set up a European Defence Association of an all India character, collected a defence fund of one and a half lakhs rupees and carried on a provocative agitation in all parts of the country. So fierce was the agitation that Rippon had to yield in certain essential respect in regard to the Bill, and finally introduced a clause in the Bill that while trying Europeans accused of crime half the jurors should be Europeans. This additional clause was incorporated in the Ilbert Bill and passed into law, and thought it gave the Indian magistrates and same right as was possessed by the European magistrates it safeguarded the interests of the Europeans accused of crime. It amounted to the perpetration of the invidious distinction in another form and a negation of the principle of equality before law.

The establishment of the European Defence Association and the pressure which it brought upon the authorities taught a lesson to the Indian political leaders. They soon realised that unless they too had, like the European Defence Association, an all India Association of their own they would not be able to counter the activities of the European community and bring sufficient pressure the authorities to concede their demands.

It was under circumstances like these that the National conference was held 1883 and second conference of a similar type was held in December 1885. The second conference was organized by the Indian Association in co-operation with the British Indian Association and the Muslim Association in Calcutta. This was an improvement on the conference held in 1883. The second conference were participated by delegates from a larger number of places in the country than the first. It passed resolutions similar to those passed in 1883.

Naturally Surendranath Banerjee expected that the National conference which he organized in 1883 and 1885 should become permanently the All India Political Association on which there was considerable agreement among the Indian political leaders. But his expectations were not fulfilled and it was the Indian National Congress which was organized towards the end of 1885 through the efforts of A.O. Hume that became the All India Political Association.

Hume and the Indian National Congress

It is necessary to find out what induced Hume to start the Indian National Congress when there was already an Indian National Conference organized by Surendranath Banerjee and why the Congress secured a permanent place as the All India political association.

Hume came to India in 1849 as a member of the Indian Civil Service. He had a liberal outlook from the beginning and sympathized with the aspirations of the Indian people especially of the English educated classes. He took great interest in educational and social reform and in temperance and even tried when he became a Secretary in the Central Government to influence adoption of liberal policies in view of the growing discontent in the country. But the other members of the Civil Service did not like the radical outlook and so also Lord Lytton. His claims to become a member of the Viceroy's Executive Council were overlooked because of his liberal outlook. He consequently resigned in 1892 from the I.C.S., and instead of going back to England he settled down in Simla and decided to work for the welfare of the people of the country. He came into intimate contact with the Theosophical Society and this further strengthened his pro-Indian outlook.

Simla being the summer capital of the Viceroys, Lord Rippon, the new Viceroy, was there in 1882 and Hume discussed Indian problems with him. He became a close friend of the Viceroy. Indian political leaders knew of this and they placed great confidence in Hume who served as a link between them and the Viceroy.

At the time of the Ilbert Bill controversey, Indian Political leaders thought that Rippon's compromise on the Bill was unjust. They tried to hold protest meetings against him. But Hume persuaded the Indian leaders not to do so and convinced them that Rippon was a man of good intentions and that he would carry out liberal reforms like local self government. Due to the influence of Hume, the Indian Leaders place implicit confidence in Rippon and abstained from all agitation against him and welcomed the reforms he carried out.

During the year 1883–1885, Hume bestowed thought on the need for creating an All India Political Association which would be of a different type from that of the National Conference organized by Surendranath Banerjee. He believed that India's connection with Britain was a providential act and that it should be maintained without any break. He also believed that the English educated classes were the real leaders of the people, that the Indian princes the zamindars and bigger landlords had not much influences and the English educated classes should rally round the British government if the connection between India and Britain should be maintained and that this would be possible only if the government on its part was prepared to concede the demands of the English educated classes.

In the third place Hume drew a distinction between the moderates and the extremists. Among them he regarded Surendranath Banerjee as an extremist and a follower of Mazzini, the great Italian leader, anxious to bring about a revolution in the country. Hume therefore wanted to create an all India association in which the moderate Indian leaders would be the dominant members and this also influenced him in the steps which he took in those years 1883–1885 to organize the Indian National Congress.

Fourthly, there was in those days a fear among the British authorities that the Russians would invade the country with the hope that the educated classes prefer their rule to British rule Hume wanted to show to the Russians that there was no basis for such a hope, and this was why he wanted to start a Congress consisting entirely of the moderates. Hume worked in the direction of creating an all India organization consisting of the moderates and loyal elements among the English educated classes.

He set up in 1884 the group of Indian politicians who formed the inner circle and thought its efforts politicians from the different parts of the country came to Bombay in 1884 to participate in function organized for bidding farewell to the popular Viceroy. Hume was also present in Bombay on that occasion and in consultation with the leaders who were present there he expanded the inner circle into what was called the India National Union. All the leaders agreed that the union should meet in a conference in the later part of 1885. From then on he took more decisive steps the same direction and persuaded the Sarvajanik Sabha to organize a conference under its auspices in Poona in December 1885. He did not however give much publicity to all this, it was more or less done in secrecy. From Poona he went Madras and held discussion with Madras politicians who had joined the Madras Mahajana Sabha by that time. He also visited Calcutta, held discussion with several politicians there though not with Surendranath Banerjee. These discussion convinced him. He had full support of almost all the Indian political leaders in his attempt to establish an all India political body of which the conference to be held in 1885 would be the nucleus.

Finally, he put his views before Lord Dufferin, the new Viceroy, who also agreed with him in what he proposed, but suggested that this all India body should serve the same function in India as the opposition party served in British politics. After this Hume went to Britain to put up the proposal before liberal politicians, members of parliaments and editors of newspapers and obtained from them an opinion favourable to the idea.

As all this was done without much publicity Surendranath Banerjee was not aware of it. This was why he convened the session of the Indian National conference from 27th December 1885 little knowing that the conference proposed by Hume and his co-workers was to be held between 25th and 31st December 1885. When Banerjee sent circulars asking the political bodies in different provinces to send delegates to his conference, Sarvajanik Sabha got confused and did not know exactly what to do. It waited till Hume's return from Britain and on December 2, the leaders of Poona held discussions with him and ultimately it was decided that the name Congress should be given to the body that would be meeting in Poona at the end of December and that the dates should be changed to 28th December to 30th December so that there might be no conflict between it and the National conference at Calcutta. But due to the outbreak of cholera in Poona in December the venue of the congress was changed to Bombay. This was how the Indian National Congress took birth as all Indian political organization and Hume came to be called the father of the Indian National Congress.

As planned the Congress met in Bombay on 28th December 1885. Seventy two delegates came from different provinces, and among them were lawyers, journalists, teachers, members of legislatures and municipal bodies and persons belonging to different religious communities. It is therefore entitled to be regarded as a National body and deserved the title Indian National Congress. It was presided over by W.C. Bonerjee, an eminent lawyer from Calcutta. He carried on the deliberations for three days and a number of resolutions were passed – that a Royal commission should be appointed to make an exhaustive enquiry into Indian affairs, that the Secretary of State to India Council should be abolished, that representation should be given to persons elected by the people in legislatures – provincial and central – that competitive examinations should be held simultaneously in England and India and that military expenditure should be reduced and a part of it should be borne by the British Government. These were similar to the resolutions passed by the various political associations in the country and by the Indian National Conference in 1883 and 1885. But it secured special importance because the Congress turned out to be a much more representative body than all of them.

Why the Indian National Congress Achieved Permanence

The Indian National Congress thus started secured permanence in the political history of the country, and it was under its auspicious that the struggle for freedom was carried on to a successful competition.

The history of the freedom movement is indeed the history of the Indian National congress especially from 1920 when Mahatma Gandhi became its undisputed leader as well as the leader of the freedom movement.

Yet another reason for the Congress securing permanence and not the National Conferences of Surendranath Banerjee is the fact that Hume who commanded the confidence of Viceroys like Rippon and Dufferin and a large amount of support from the Majority of the politicians of those days was intimately connected with it. There was of course the suspicion that Surendranath Banerjee was and extremist and an advocate of revolution and that his conference would become a revolutionary body. There was a feeling that the British authorities would ban ultimately and organization started by Surendranath Banerjee. This also attracted the political leaders to the congress instead of to Banerjee's Conference. Banerjee also realized this and instead of forcing a conflict between Conference and the Congress he himself became an active supporter of the Congress which was a measure of his patriotism. All this enabled the Indian National Congress to obtain a permanent place in the political history of the country.

In this connection an observation made by Gokhale in 1913 is extremely relevant... "No Indian could have started the Indian National Congress. If an Indian had come forward to start such a movement embracing all India, the officials would not have allowed it to come into existence. If the founder of the congress had not been a great English man and a distinguished ex-official such was the distrust of political agitation in those days that the authorities would have at once found some way or the other of suppressing the movement."

It has to be noted that though Hume was entitled to be called the Father of the Indian National Congress the idea that there should be an All Indian political association did not originate from him. It became a part of Indian political thinking from 1853 itself and as referred to above, it gained strength from time to time through the efforts of the Indian Association, the Sarvajanik Sabha and several other political bodies. What Hume did was to concretise the widespread opinion in favour of the establishment of an all India body and through intensive activity and give it a real shape and form. It was the organisation set up by him that secured permanence owing to a number of favourable circumstances referred to above.

THE INDIAN NATIONAL CONGRESS – 1885–1905

CHAPTER 7

Nature of its Organisation

The years 1885–1905 may be regarded as the period of infancy in the history of the Congress. When it was started it had no definite organization like the other political associations of the time. There was no general membership paying regular subscription. It had no president, no managing or executive committee nor a place for locating its office. It had only a secretary and Hume held this office till a system of election was introduced in 1888. Even then for some years Hume was elected secretary. The only business transacted by the Congress was to hold annual session at some place decided upon by the previous session, discuss Indian questions and pass resolution. As no other business was transacted till the next session was held, and as the work of propaganda on behalf of the Congress was carried on by the existing provincial association and by the district associations which were started about this time no need was felt by the congress itself to create its own instituting for the purpose.

The arrangement for every session was made by a reception committee consisting of local leaders. They and other leaders of the concerned province raised subscription and donation to meet the expenses of the session, arranged for lodging and boarding of the delegates and when the session was over prepared the report of the proceedings for publication. The committee was then dissolved and thus it was a temporary body though a highly importance one. But at the third session of the Congress many delegates proposed that the subjects for discussion should not be settled as was done hither to by Hume in association with two or three of his intimate colleagues, and there should be a subjects committee elected by the delegates attending the Congress session. The idea was accepted and from 1887 a subjects committee representing each of the provinces together with some ex-officio members came to be elected and decided the subjects for discussion and the wording of the resolution. But this too was a temporary body ceasing to function after the session was over. It was at this time the idea took shape that the congress should not merely be a three day affair, and that it should do work among the people all through the year. This did not however materialize though in pursuance of it standing committees in each province were created, but they were not very active.

It was fifteen years after the establishment of the Congress that an All India Congress Committee was established consisting of delegates who met at the annual session. It became the most important body of the Congress and guided it in every respect. It had an honorary secretary and a paid joint secretary and its office was located at an important place in the country. By 1900 the Congress had a well - conceived organization set-up with bodies attached to it, some temporary, others permanent and an office for carrying on its work. Even then it had no regular members who paid subscription.

Sessions of the Congress were however regarded as of great importance by the political leaders in the country. They were the only occasions when persons from different provinces could meet, hold discussion on all India problems, pass resolutions and make representations to the Governments both in India and Britain. Most of the leading persons interest in political attended the sessions. Almost all of them belonged to the English educated community. One reason for this was it was only among them that the idea of nationalism and political consciousness took a deep root. Secondly, proceedings of the Congress were all in English. Among them were all the professional classes – lawyers, journalists, teachers, doctors and eve Government employees in the early stages. But lawyers were the most active of all of them. They attended the sessions in large numbers, so much so that the Government came to regard the congress as an association of lawyers in the main. But there was nothing unnatural about this. The lawyers belonged to a profession which was independent of Government patronage. Through their clients they came into contact with different classes of people and understood the trends of public opinion. They could therefore speak better on behalf of the people than others. Even in the Western countries it was the lawyers who took great interest in public life.

In the first session of the congress there were only seventy two delegates. But the numbers went on increasing as years progressed. The increase was so large that reception committees found it difficult to make arrangements for their boarding and lodging. A rule was introduced that the number of delegates should be limited to five for a million of population. But even then partly owing to the growth of population and the rising popularity of the Congress the number of delegates attending the session increased. For example while in 1886 the number of delegates attending the session was 434, in 1887 it was 607, in 1887 it was 1248 and in 1888 it was 1859.

Reasons for the Popularity of the Congress

One reason for the popularity of the Congress was that it attracted persons of all communities and from all provinces. Those who attended its sessions and especially those who participated in their proceedings became leaders in the districts after their return from the Congress session. Their names appeared in the newspapers and they were looked upon as guides in all political matters by the local people. It was they who took an active part in organizing provincial and district conferences. Though the delegates belonged to all communities, a controversy arose immediately after the formation of the Congress on the desirability of the Muslim participating in it. The Government did not like the growing popularity of the congress and it dissuaded in a variety of ways. Muslims from attending its sessions. Sir Syed Ahmed Khan, an eminent Muslim leader of the time, agreed with the views of the government and he dissuaded the Muslims from attending its sessions. But there were other Muslim leaders like Badruddin Tyabji who argued that though the Hindus and the Muslims belonged to two different religions there was much in common between them in all secular matters and it would be in their interest to participate in the deliberation of the Congress which tried to promote the welfare of the people as a whole and not of any particular community. To dislodge their fear that the majority of the Hindu delegates would adopt by sheer force of their numbers resolutions detrimental to the interest of the Muslims, a rule was introduced at the third session of the Congress that any resolution which the delegates belonging to any minority community like the Muslims were opposed to should not be taken up for discussion at the session of the Congress.

Consequently the number of Muslim delegates attending the congress also started increasing. If in the first session their number was two, in the second session it was thirty three and in the sixth session it went up to one hundred and fifty six. Whatever the Government and persons like Sir Syed Ahmed Khan might say the Congress remained a national body in its composition even though in a country like India where Hindus were in a majority there was nothing surprising in the Hindu delegates outnumbering the Muslim delegates or those belonging to other minority groups. This was also the case in Britain when the Civil War in the days of Charles I, the Glorious Revolution in 1688 and the agitation for parliamentary reform in the nineteenth century were all led by small minority groups like the puritans, the landlords and the rising middle class. The general trends in the history of the world were ignored by the British Government when they complained that the Congress was representative of only a small group of people and not the entire nation.

The Work of the Congress – Its Moderatism

In the period 1885–1905, the work of the Congress was characterized by what may be called Moderatism. It was moderate both in its aims and in the method of action followed to realise the aims. Its aim was not the achievement of Swaraj or even internal self-government like that which prevailed in some of the British colonies like Canada and Australia. It only demanded certain reforms and changes in the system of Government and administration like the representation of the Indians in larger numbers in the legislatures through a system of election, admission of Indians into the higher ranks of public services as was provided for in the charter Act of 1833 and in Queen Victoria's Proclamation, lowering of taxes, reduction in public expenditure, removal of excise duties on Indian textiles, etc.

For achieving these objectives it was determined to follow only constitutional methods. It never wanted to resort to violence or revolutionary activity. It was merely content with making representations to the government in India and Britain in carrying on peaceful agitation in favour of the reforms it advocated. It believed like Hume that the connection between England and India should be permanently maintained that on the whole British rule in India was advantageous to the people even though it produced a few evils. It believed in peaceful agitation for their removal because such a method was a great success in Britain and also because the British were a democratic people and they would respect the wishes of the people of India. They also believed that since it was the members of the civil service in India and the Anglo Indian community that stood in the way of reforms, they could make a representation to the people in Britain who were the ultimate rulers of India, and were in a position to over rule the members of the Indian Civil Service and do justice to the Indian people. In all the resolutions of the sessions of the Indian National Congress the first place was therefore given to the expression of loyalty to the rulers in England and to a faith in their sense of justice.

In spite of the moderatism, the Congress was not able to get the reforms which it demands from the British. The Indian Councils Act of 1892, the raising of the age of candidates appearing for the I.C.S. examination in Britain, and the appointment of the Welby Commission to enquire into the finances of India were the only steps taken by the British authorities in response to the Congress demands Moderatism failed to achieve its objectives limited as they were and this was responsible for the growth of extremism among a section of the political leaders in the country.

British Hostility Towards the Congress

Not only did the British authorities fail to respond even to the reasonable demands of the Congress but they also became hostile to it in course of time. They argued that even though the Congress adopted a policy of moderatism for the time being, it would sooner or later become an extremist body making all kinds of demands which could not be fulfilled by the Government. They also thought that the activities of the Congress would lead to a revolution which would bring to an end the British rule. The British were able to conquer India at a time when there was no national feeling and naturally they would not be friendly to a body which called itself national and which tried to spread the spirit of nationalism in the masses also. Leaders like Dadabhai Naoroji made it clear that they were not agitating for Home Rule like the Irish and there was no danger of such and agitation in India. But the British continued to be hostile to the Congress and Lord Curzon the Viceroy, said that he would see during his administration the disappearance of the congress as a political body. This attitude of the British led to the growth of extremism which was an important phase in the history of the freedom movement.

It should be noted that there was disagreement between the aims of the English educated classes and of the British not only during this period but also during all the 90 years of the rule after the revolt of 1857–58. The English educated classes were influenced not only by the idea of nationalism which was characteristics of Western history in the nineteenth century, but also by the ideas of democracy. It was their ambition though not immediately but ultimately that a representative form of Government should be introduced by the British in India. For one thing it was considered to be the ideal from of Government by the British as well as other European thinkers of the age, and for another it was this form of Government which found a place in many of the western countries and in the United States of America. The English educated classes also wanted to be treated as the equals of the British in all matters because they were the citizens of the same empire and that there should be no difference between the British citizens in one region and those in another. They argued that the introduction of representative institutions and the according of equality of treatment to Indians would not weaken the British hold over India and instead strengthen the bond of connection between the two countries. It was on these grounds that they wanted the British to fulfill the promise made in the Charter Act of 1833 and in Queen Victoria's Proclamation and admit Indians into all ranks of civil and even military services.

The British however were not prepared to accept any of these claims made by the English educated classes. In their view democracy was a form of Government which suited only the British and other Westerner and that the people of India had for centuries been accustomed to a despotic form of government and it would therefore be in the best interests of the country that the enlightened despotism of the British continued. They pointed out that for the maintenance of the British rule, civil and military service, especially of higher ranks should be manned only by the British. The British had inborn talent for administration which the Indians did not possess however educated they might be. Administrative talent was something inborn among people and could not be acquired by superficial education. Moreover India being a land of different communities, speaking different languages with different economic interest it could never become a nation as is understood in Western countries, English education was confined only to certain sections of the people, the higher castes in all the provinces. Admission to higher ranks of Public Services would be a monopoly of those belonging to the higher castes. Other communities in the country, the Muslims, the Jats, the non – Bramins who did not take to English education in large numbers would resent the authority of the higher Hindu castes and it would create discontent among them. Several of them like the Jats and the Rajputs liked military tradition and discontent among them would weaken the British rule in the country. The British required more the loyalty and the devotion of such military communities and not of the Bengalis or higher middle class who could only wield the pen and not the sword. These were some of the arguments used by the British to oppose the demands made by the English educated classes through the Indian National Congress.

The truth was that conceding the demands of the English educated classes and the Congress would adversely affect the material interests of the British people. India was a market for all the goods they produced. It supplied to Britain raw materials like cotton, jute and consumers goods like tea. The growth of trade with India was a source of profit to the British mercantile community and to the shipping interests and also to the banking concerns in Britain and to similar British Interest in India. The middle class youth of Britain found lucrative service in India in both the civil and military fields. The introduction of democratic institutions, the admission of Indians to the rank of public services and other demands made by the English educated classes and the congress would harm the British interest. That was the main reason why they opposed the demands of the Indian political leaders and even went to the extreme in proclaiming that the whites were destined by the virtue of their superior racial quality to rule over the coloured races, that it was the intention of providence that it should be so and that the Indian demands were against such an intention.

The British even deliberately adopted a policy of divide and rule to weaken the forces of nationalism and the hold of the Congress over the people. They succeeded to a considerable extent in separating an influential section among the Muslims from the national movement and the Congress. They also saw to it that the zamindars the rich landlords and the Indian princes kept themselves away from the congress and did not contribute to the finances of the congress, they did not however succeed in permanently weakening forces of nationalism though it had to suffer a little setback as a result of the policy of the British.

In addition to the policy of divide and rule, the British tried to satisfy the moderates in the Congress, the zamindars and some other interests through the reforms which they introduced as, for instance, the Indian councils Acts of 1892 and 1909. But in all these reforms especially of 1909, they took steps to favour the interests of particular groups and the reforms were never really meant to transfer power into the hands of the Indians even to limited extent. This brief account gives an idea of the responses of the British to the growth of nationalism in the country and to the activities of the Congress. This attitude continued to be, with certain modifications, the guiding principle of the British rule till the end.

SEPARATIST MUSLIM POLITICS

CHAPTER 8

Separatist Muslim Politics

Even as the English educated classes in the country developed a sense of national feeling and gave concrete form to it by establishing the Indian National Congress, a group among the Muslims especially those who belonged to the aristocracy and the landed gentry felt that their political interests were different from those of the Hindus and it was desirable that they should not identify themselves with the national movement or with the Indian National Congress. It should however be noted that all the Muslims did not share this feeling. And yet those who started the separatist idea gained influence in course of time and this ultimately resulted in the partition of the country into two independent states- India and Pakistan – when in August 1947, the British withdraw and freedom was achieved. It is this that gives importance to the cause of the separatist Muslim politics.

Causes for the Separatist Movement

Several factors contributed to the growth of this movement. The Muslims came to India in the eleventh century as invaders and conquerors. It was not the first time that foreigners invaded and brought large areas of the country under their control. There was however an essential difference between the earlier conquerors like the Indo-Greeks, the Kushans, the Sakas and Huns ad the Turks, the Afghans, the Mughals and the other Muslim invaders. The earlier conquerors were attracted by Hindu culture and civilization and merged themselves in the Hindu social system and several of them were recognized as Kshatriyas. It was due perhaps to the fact that the Hindu culture of those days was in many respects superior to their own cultures. This was not the case with Muslim conquerors. They had a distinct religion and culture which they thought was not in any way inferior to that of the Hindus. They were also repelled by some of the features of Hinduism like polytheism and idol worship and by the system of caste which formed an integral part of Hindu society. They resented any idea of embracing the Hindu religion and culture, kept themselves aloof and did not merge into the Hindu social system. On the other hand they spread their own religion in the country and strengthened themselves in everyway. The result was that though the Hindus and the Muslims existed side by side as inhabitants of the same country for nearly eight centuries, they lived as two distinct entities each trying to maintain its own individuality. This was the main historical factor that was behind the Muslim separatist movement in the latter part of the 19th century.

Powerful sections of the Muslims did not forget the fact that they ruled over a large area of the country and all sections of the Hindu population for several centuries and this created in them a feeling of superiority which they were not prepared to give up even after they lost their power and became subject to the British rule along with the Hindus in the 18th century. The memories of their imperial rule were also a factor which prevented the two communities from becoming a single nation.

It should also be observed that Muslims in whatever country they lived considered themselves to be a part of a wider world community, as Islamic people, spread as they were in the continents of Africa, Asia and Europe. They developed close cultural ties with their religious brethren abroad and such ties were strengthened by the fact that all the important religious centres of the Muslims were in Arabia and countries in West Asia. This was also the case with Muslims in India. They had close spiritual and cultural affinity with their religious brethren in countries outside India. This is not the case with the Hindus. Right from the middle ages, their religion and culture and civilization were confined to India itself. The attachment of the Muslims to people in the Islamic lands – natural as it was – made them a community separate from the Hindus and created and urge that they should not become merged in the Indian nation which was slowly being built up from the second half of the 19th century.

The renaissance movement which led to the awakening of the people of India in the 19th century affected the Hindus much earlier than the Muslims. The Hindus took up English education from 1820 but the Muslims lagged behind and took to English education only from about 1870. There was thus a gap of nearly half a century in the movement of modernization as between the Hindus and the Muslims. As English education spread among the Hindus and as it opened the door to Public services and to professions, the Hindus gained entry in fairly large numbers into these services and profession by the time the Muslims realized the value of English education. The Hindus were certainly not responsible for the failure of the Muslims to opt for the new education. It was more the outcome of the view held by the influential Muslim religious teachers who insisted that there was nothing new to be learnt through English education, that all the Muslims had to learn was to be found in Arabic and Persian and that English education might weaken the faith of the Muslims in their own religion and induce them to become Christians. This historical factor was not appreciated by the Muslims and they attributed their backwardness in English education to the Hindus'. Government also did not do anything special to encourage Muslim education before 1870. This near monopoly of public services and professions by the Hindus was resented to by the leaders of the Muslims community and this also was instrumental in keeping them aloof from the English educated classes among the Hindus.

The British also contributed to this separatist feeling between the two communities. In the early days of their conquest they received much sympathy and support from the Hindu community and it was mostly the Muslim including the Mughal emperor that lost power at the hands of the British. Since the British though that the threat to their rule would come only from the Muslims they showed a great deal of favour to the Hindu community. The hostility towards the Muslims was behind the great revolt of 1857 more than the Hindus. In consequences of the revolt, the Muslims lost their lands and jobs under the British government and large sections of them become impoverished. But soon enough the British began to change their attitude towards these two communities. That was due to growth of nationalism among the English educated, and the starting of numerous political associations by them.

But as English education was mostly taken advantage of by the Hindus till then, it was that they were first influenced by the national feeling and were active in politics. Consequently the British wanted to weaken the growth of national feeling in the country and this was accomplished by their policy of divide and rule by showing special favours to the Muslims. This was a potent factor in promoting the separatist movements.

Sir Syed Ahmed Khan

It was about this time that Sir Syed Ahmed Khan made his appearance on the Indian political scene. He was born in Delhi in an influential Muslim family, held a number of judicial jobs under an influential Muslim family, held a number of judicial jobs under the British, helped them a great deal in the days of the great revolt of 1857–58 and saw how the revolt brought about a change in the fortunes of the Muslim community owing to the suspicions entertained by the British that the Muslim community owing to the suspicions entertained by the British that the Muslims were responsible for the revolt. After he retired from service, he devoted himself to the cause of the uplift of the Muslim community and to see that they got their due place in the political and economic life of the people commensurate with their past greatness. He was quick to realise that Muslims could not be uplifted unless it is or be with the active help and support of the British rulers. Their educational backwardness and many other evil consequences which it brought could be removed with the special help of the Government. By themselves they would not be able to compete with the educated sections among the Hindus who occupied important places in the professions and in the public services. With a view to getting the sympathy of the Government, he wrote books to dispel from the minds of the rulers that the Muslims were behind the revolt of 1857 and he wanted to convince them that the Muslims were a loyal people ready to stand by the British authorities. His views were quite welcome to the British government. If the Muslim community came to their support it would weaken to that extent the growing strength of Hindu nationalism.

At one time Sir Syed Ahmed thought of Hindus and Muslims as forming a single nation, that they were like the two eyes of the Indian people and through they belonged to different religious communities they should work together in matters which were secular in character. But gradually he changed his view since he did not want to estrange the Muslim community from the British Government whose support he wanted for Muslim uplift. So he gradually came under the spell of the British policy of divide and rule, especially as they came to show special favours, and grant special concessions in education and other fields of public life to the Muslims. This was why he advised the Muslims not to participate in the deliberations on the Indian National Congress. He argued that it was a body dominated by the Hindus and that Muslim interests would suffer if they had elected representative on the legislatures as the Hindus were everywhere in a majority and admission of the Hindus in a large numbers into the public Services would only benefit the Bengalis and the Hindus who were highly educated. He also argued that in a country where there were different religious communities each with its own cultural traditions, democracy would not work, and democracy in India would mean the rule of the Hindus over the Muslims, a rule which should never to be tolerated by the Muslim communities which for centuries ruled over the Hindus.

In all this he was also influenced by the two British principals of the Aligarh College – Beck and Morrison who furnished him with additional arguments as to why the Muslims should not join the nationalist movement of the Congress. Sir Syed Ahmed Khan thus played a vital role in the separatist politics of an influential section of the Muslim community.

Though this kept away a large number of Muslims from the freedom movements carried under the auspices of the Congress under the leadership of Mahatama Gandhi, (except during the time of the Khilafat movement) it was recognized that Sir Syed Ahmed Khan's policy contributed much to the promotion of the special interests of the Muslim Community.

This was but one aspect of the role of Sir Syed Ahmed Khan - the political aspect. But there was also another aspect to his work. It was he who was responsible for the awakening of the Muslim community in the various fields like religion, education, and social affairs. It is the option of many historians that in relation to the Muslims he played a role similar to that of Raja Ram Mohan Roy in respect of the Hindus.

He pointed out that the Muslims should take to English education and Western learning if they were to become an enlightened community. Without knowledge of modern science such as enlightenment was not possible and English education was a window of the world. He thus refuted the argument of the Muslim religious leaders who discouraged the community from taking to English education. His attempts to improve Muslim education culminated in the founding of the Aligarh College which later on developed into the

Aligarh University. To satisfy those who opposed English education he gave in this college and other institutions he started, and important place to the teaching of Islamic classical languages like Arabic and Persian. He got many books translated from English to Urdu and made it a fitting medium for imparting modern education. He also attempted to bring about certain changes in the religious beliefs and practices of the Muslims community which had no support in the Koran, the only authoritative guide in religious matters for the Muslims. In this, however he did not meet with complete success because of the opposition of the theologians who had a big following among the masses. All the same, we have to recognize that Sir Syed Ahmed Khan was as much a leader in the educational and religious life of the Muslim community as in their political life. He is truly the maker of the modern Muslim community in India.

THE VANDEMATARAM MOVEMENT

CHAPTER 9

The freedom movement in India in the real sense of the term began only after 1905 with the rise of what is known as the Vandemataram movement. It was a movement which was started by the people of Bengal to annul the partition of the province carried out by the autocratic Viceroy, Lord Curzon despite the united opposition of all the Bengalis. In leading the movement, the Bengalis put into effect the philosophy and the programme of the Nationalists who in books on history are generally called the Extremists to distinguish them from the Moderates who dominated the Congress all these years. It is therefore necessary to know at the outset what the deals and the programme of action of the National were.

Nationalists Versus the Moderates

The nationalists came into prominence as a result of the failure of the Moderates during the first twenty years of the existence of the Congress. We have already seen that very few of the demands made by the Moderates were conceded by the British. In addition to this the authorities dubbed the English educated class as a microscopic minority in the country and said they had no right to speak in the name of millions of people. They also argued that not only then but also in the forceable future it was not desirable or possible to introduce democratic or representative institutions in the country and that for the peace and prosperity of the people, British despotism should continue. To weaken the national movement and the Congress they also adopted the policy of divide and rule and succeeded in separating an influential section of the Muslims from the national movement. All this roused the emotions of many eminent persons belonging to the congress and in course of time led by persons like Balagangadhar Tilak in Maharashtra, Auro Bindo Ghosh and Bipin Chandra Pal in Bengal, Lala Lajpat Rain in

Punjab they formed themselves into a party of Nationalists. What has to be noticed is that it was the failure of the Moderates and the methods of constitutional agitation and petitions which they adopted that led to the rise of the Nationalists party.

The Nationalists put forward the ideal of Swaraj-complete freedom from British rule as the objective which the Congress should achieve. They believed that every nation had a right to govern itself and that under no circumstances there was justification for foreign rule. They considered that the question whether the Indians were fit for self-government or not was irrelevant and advocated that Swaraj should be achieved not in the remote future through a process of gradualism but immediately. Thus the ideas of the Nationalists were different from those of the Moderates who were contended with a few reforms.

In their method of action too the Nationalists differed from the Moderates. They were convinced that constitutional agitation would never make the British give up their authority which gave them numerous advantages. At no time and in no country in the world imperial rule came to an end as a result of peaceful agitation on the part of the subject people, it was only through resort to arms that, for example, the Dutch in the 16th century, and the Americans in the 18th century gained independence. There was also nothing morally wrong in a subject people resorting to arms for achieving a right end like the country's freedom. Sacred books in India like the Gita supported the ideas of righteous war. But at the same time the Nationalists believed that resort to arms was not a practicable proposition in the conditions which prevailed in India under the British rule. The people were disarmed by the British and to collect arms on a large scale and train people to use them effectively were not practicable. Moreover, in such a war, the British with their military superiority were bound to come out victorious. This was proved by the way they suppressed the great revolt of 1857 – 58. It was therefore necessary a new kind of pressure was brought to bear on the British to compel them to surrender their authority.

Passive Resistance or Non-cooperation

Non-co-operation or passive resistance was what the Nationalists conceived in this context. They pointed out that it was because the people of the country co-operated with the British that their rule became possible and therefore withdrawal of such co-operation could make their rule impossible. This withdrawal of co-operation should extend to every field of public life. For example they argued that because the people co-operated with the British in using cotton cloth imported from Britain that the Indian textile industry declined and millions of artisans were impoverished. Non-co-operation in economic sphere would mean the boycott of British cloth. Such a boycott on a large scale would bring down the profits of the British mill owners and create unemployment among the British labourers and they would consequently bring pressure on their Government to yield to atleast to some of the demands of the Nationalists. So went the arguments which the Nationalists used in their advocacy of the boycott of the British goods.

Similarly the people should boycott schools and colleges established by the Government or aided by it. They pointed out that the education imparted in these institutions only trained the youth to become loyal supporters of the British Government. It denationalized them. The idea of nationalism became alien to the large majority of youth. It did not provide all of them with employment. It was therefore desirable to boycott such educational institutions.

In the third place there should be boycott of the courts of justice established by the British. These courts made litigation very costly. Justice was considerably delayed. These courts did not serve any useful national purpose and their help should not be sought by the people.

The entire administration was run by the Indians who were willing to be employed in the clerical posts and in the lower ranks of public services, in police and other departments and in courts. It was because of this that the British were able to rule the country and by the same token if the Indians refused to serve in any capacity under the British, it would be next to impossible for the latter to import thousand of British personnel to run the administrative machine. So this would result in the automatic collapse of the administrative machinery. Finally at the opportune time Indians should refuses even to pay taxes.

These were the various forms of non-co-operation the Nationalists envisaged. Their approach was however not merely negative. In the place of British goods they advocated the use of Swadeshi or Indian made goods even though they were a little more expensive than the British goods. Swadeshi was the positive aspect of the boycott of British goods. Similarly in the place of educational institutions managed or aided by the British they wanted the establishment of national school and colleges. The spread of national education was the positive side of the boycott of educational institutions. Similarly they advocated the establishment of panchayat courts in the place of British courts. We have thus to note that non co-operation had a negative as well as a positive aspect.

The method of programme of action was also called passive resistance because it meant resisting or opposing the British rule not through resort to arms but passively through the various methods of non-co-operation. Whether a war was violent as was the case with all wars of independence or took the form of non-co-operation, resistance was a common feature. Without resistance the ruling power would not yield. But since the resistance did not take the form of active fighting, the Nationalists called their method of action passive resistance.

It may be incidentally noted that it was this method of non-co-operation that Mahatma Gandhi made use of when he became the leaders of the freedom movement in the country after 1920.

The Nationalists also believed that unless the masses of people were brought in large numbers into the congress fold and thus into the national movements it was not possible to achieve success. They pointed out that the failure of the Congress under the leadership to the Moderates was to great extent due to the congress being unrepresentative of the masses. They also pointed out that the British authorities refused to pay much heed to the resolutions of the congress because of this unrepresentative character. According to them it was only a mass organization that could effectively bring pressure on the British rulers.

Nationalism as a Religious Creed

How to enlist the support of the masses was the problem to which the Nationalists had to find a solution. They felt that what appealed most to the people of the country especially to the Hindus who constituted the majority was religion. It was therefore by appealing to the religious instincts of the people that they could be brought into the political movements. This appeal assumed two forms. In the first place Aurobindo and Pal argued that nationalism was not a mere political creed, that it should become the religion of the people in the 20th century. It meant that they should be as much devoted to nationalism as they were to their traditional religion for thousand of years. If a religions has a god or goodess to be worshipped, nationalism as a religion centred itself round the worship of the country as the mother of the people. They should worship "Bharat Mata" just as they worshipped Kali, Durga and other goddesses. They should be prepared to sacrifice everything for the Mother and liberate Her from the thralldom to which she was subjected at the hands of the British. The worship of the country as the Mother became a central feature of the doctrine of nationalism preached by the Nationalists. It was the sort of language which could be easily understood by the people. It was this that gave popularity to Bankim Chandra's song of "Vandemataram". The song was sung from 1905 at all public meetings. Badges with Vandemataram inscribed on them were worn by a large number or people especially the students and the youth. The cry of Vandemataram rented the air when people went in procession on the streets. All this originated in Bengal in connection with the movement for the annulment of the partition of Bengal. That was why the movement was known as the Vandemataram movement and it gradually spread to every part of the country.

In the second place, the Nationalists made use of the traditional religious festivals to spread their political ideas. In Maharashtra, the Ganapati festival was one of the most popular festivals and almost all classes of people participated in it for days together Tilak and his followers took an active part in its celebration and utilized the occasion for the spread of their political teachings. This easily caught the imagination of the people and brought many of them in due course into the political field. Coupled with this was the Sivaji festival which was started by Tilak to eulogise Sivaji who freed Maharashtra from the Yoke of Bijapur and the Mughals. In a way the festival made the people of Maharashtra feel that what Sivaji did in his day should be done now by his countrymen. They should sacrifice everything to free the country from the alien British.

In their inimitable style Aurobindo, pal and Lajpat Rai appealed to the religious instincts of the people. They succeeded in bringing large numbers of then into the national movements. The opportunity came for making use of the ideals of the Nationalists and their method of action when the Bengalis started the agitation for annulling the partition of their province. To understand the significance of the movements we have to know why they opposed the partition.

Partition of Bengal and Lord Curzon

Bengal at one time consisted of not only Bengal proper but also Bihar, Orissa, Chota Nagpur and Assam. It was the biggest Indian province. It was however administered by a single lieutenant Governor without the aid of an executive council though small provinces like Madras and Bombay were administered by a Governor with an executive council. From 1870 a move was set afoot to reduce the size of the province to make the administration more efficient and effective. For this purpose Assam was separated from Bengal in 1874 but it did not reduce significantly the size of Bengal. So the problem of reducing its size continued to trouble the authorities. Various solutions were put forward but none was found satisfactory until Lord Curzon, the Viceroy between 1898 and 1905, took up the question seriously, worked out a scheme of partition and put it into effect with the consent of the Home government in 1905.

And in this Curzon was motivated by ill-will towards the Bengalis in general and the Hindu section of the Bengalis in particular. Bengal was in the forefront of the national movement right from the very beginning and the Bengalis also dominated the Congress from 1886. Curzon wanted to cut the Bengalis to size as it were and it was for this purpose that he divided the province into two – one consisting of East Bengal and Assam and the other of West Bengal Bihar, Orissa and Chota Nagpur. Ever since the Battle of Plassey all the Bengalis lived together in one province. But the partition implemented by Curzon divided the Bengalis into two sections. This was resented to by the people as they were aware of the evil motives that influenced Lord Curzon. They suggested that the size of Bengal could have been reasonably reduced without affecting them by separating Bihar, Orissa and Chota Nagpur from the province. But it did not meet with the approval of Lord Curzon as he was bent upon weakening the political influence of the Bengalis in the country.

The other motive which influenced him was equally sinister. In east Bengal the majority of the people were Muslims. They never wanted a separate province of their own. They were also against partition when they first came to know of it and joined the Hindu Bengalis at all the protest meetings. But Curzon brought them round by telling them that in a province of their own they could pursue their policies as they liked without being influenced by the Hindu nationalists.

This satisfied then and they became staunch supporters of partition. It was clear that Lord Curzon and the British authorities were determined to give effect to the policy of divide and rule, and the partition of Bengal admirably served this purpose. As a result of the partition the Hindu Bengalis became a minority in both the provinces. In East Bengal they were outnumbered by the Muslims and in West Bengal by the people of Bihar, Orissa and Chota Nagpur. As a minority they lost all the political influence which they exercised in the past and this was when they started an agitation for annuling the partition.

Between 1903 when they first came to know of the scheme of Lord Curzon and 1905 when it was put into effect, the Bengalis held thousand of meetings not only in the city of Calcutta and bigger towns but also in the rural areas to pass resolutions protesting against the partition. They sent representations to the authorities but all this had no effect. It was then the constitutional method or agitation failed that they decided first in boycott of British goods and gradually adopted the other forms of non co-operation as suggested by the Nationalists.

Although it was started to annul the partition in the initial stages, it later became a demand for the achievement of Swaraj. In the beginning the movement was confined to Bengal. But within a year it was taken up in some form or other by the people in other provinces also, and to a limited extent it became an All India movement. These developments gave a special significance to the movements which was regarded by the historians as the first phase of the Freedom movement.

Genesis of the Vandemataram Movement

The movement went on from 1905 to 1911. It was only in 1911 that partition was annulled and a united Bengal was restored. With this the movement also came to an end though it left a number of other important effects. It was the first impressive victory of the people against the British Government.

On July 6, 1905 a weekly newspaper in Calcutta suggested for the first time that they should boycott British goods to bring pressure upon the commercial manufacturing interests in England, and through them on the Government. The suggestion was eagerly taken up by all the newspaper in Bengal and huge public meeting was held on August 7 to consider the suggestion. Complete hartal was observed on that day and the meeting unanimously passed a resolution that British goods should be boycotted until the partition was annulled.

September 5 was the Durga Puja day, a day sacred to the people of Bengal. On that day thousands of people proceeded to the Kali temple and took a vow that they would boycott British goods and adopt Swadeshi. They also took a vow that as all the ills which the country suffered from were due to foreign rule, they should make every effort to overthrow it and liberate the mother country from such a yoke. This was how the Vandemataram movement became a movement for freedom as this date is generally regarded by historians as the date of the real beginning of the freedom movement.

On October 16, partition came into effect. The day was observed as a day of hartal and fasting. Rabindranath Tagore set the tone for a general revolt against the partition by composing a special poem to give expression to the feelings of the Bengalis and the tragedy of partition and called upon them to bathe in the holy Ganges early in the morning to observe the ceremony of Rakhi Bandhan which for the Bengalis was an external symbol of their unity. Though the Government banned the singing of Tagore's poem in public, the people ignored the ban and repeated the poem with great fervour.

In course of time the message of boycott spread among all classes of people in Bengal. The students were inspired by it, and they refused to attend examinations as it meant writing on foreign paper. They also declined to wear foreign shoes. They went to school and colleges bare foot and continued to do so in spite of the punishments awarded to them. Washermen refused to wash foreign cloth, shoe repairers to repair foreign shoes, cooks to serve in houses in which foreign goods were used and priests also declined to officiate at religious ceremonies in the houses of such people. The popular commentators on the puranas gave a new meaning to the stories recorded in them. Even the sanyasis entered the scene by preaching boycott in the course of their religious sermons. Women belonging to aristocratic families who observed strict purdah came out of their houses preaching in the open the message of boycott and swadeshi. In this the Zamindars also co-operated with the other political leaders and the boycott thus became the first national movement.

The advocates of the movement were not content with merely preaching the message. They undertook picketing on a large scale of the shops where foreign cloth was sold and pleaded with the shopkeepers not to sell them and their customers not to buy them. Sometimes when the shop keepers refused to take back the cloth and refund the money to the purchasers the picketers paid the money to the shop keepers and made a bonfire of all the cloth thus purchased. This led to quarrels with the shop keepers and the volunteers who were picketing. As the students took a prominent part in the whole process the police entered the scene, lathi charged the students volunteers and inflicted serve injuries on them. But this did not affect in any way the enthusiasm and determination of the students in picketing.

Boycott of foreign cloth was invariably accompanied by the advocacy of Swadeshi – the use of indigenous cloth in its place, even though the Moderates while welcoming Swadeshi expressed opposition to boycott. They failed to recognize that boycott would not be a success unless foreign goods were replaced by Swadeshi.

As a result of the two movements going alongside of each other there was in the course of the year 1905 an appreciable fall in the quantity of foreign cloth imported into Calcutta and other parts of Bengal. Originally the boycott was restricted to foreign cloth but gradually it was extended to other commodities like salt, sugar, cigarettes etc. Along with the decrease of the imported commodities there was increase not only in the cloth produce by mills in Bombay, Ahmedabad and other manufacturing centers, but also in the handloom products in Bengal itself. It was not merely the economic effect of boycott of Swadeshi that impressed the people but also its larger political effect as a means of bringing pressure on the British authorities to concede Swaraj.

It was again in 1905 that the first steps were taken by political leaders in Bengal irrespective of the parties to which they belonged to establish a Council of National Education, and to start schools and colleges under its auspices. A meeting for this purpose was organized in the latter part of that year. Large donation were made for starting national schools as in those days there was a widespread opinion that the education imparted by the Calcutta University and other institutions managed or aided by Government denationalized the students and made them slavish admirers of everything British. The movement received special impetus as government severely punished those students who took part in the boycott and Swadeshi movements. They fined them, issued instruction that they should not be permitted to appear for the public examinations and the institutions in which they studied should not get Government grants. Various other penalties were inflicted on the teacher and managements of such institutions.

The leaders of all political bodies in Bengal and even independents who never took part in political life condemned this policy of repression. To impart education to students who suffered at the hands of the Government and to provide employment to the teachers who were penalized they started national institutions and taught a new type of national education.

We have already noted that Nationalists included these items-boycott, swadeshi and national education in their scheme of non-cooperation and all of them were put into effect by those who led the Vandemataram movement.

Bengal was fortunate in having a large number of leaders like Surendranath Banerjee, Bipin Chandra Pal, Aurobindo Ghosh and Aswin Kumar Dutt. They had long experience of public life and were fearless critics of the policies of the Government able to sway lakhs of people assembled at public meetings. The province also had a number of newspapers which roused the sentiments of nationalism and patriotism among the people and preached effectively the message of Swaraj. In addition to newspaper like the Bengalee and the Amrita Bazar Patrika new ones like the Yugantar, the Sandhya and the Vandemataram were started. Many of the literary figures including Rabindranath Tagore wrote special poems and books in support of the movement. Association were also started to carry on propaganda in favour of the movement. There was thus a convergence of many fortuitous circumstances which enabled the people to carry on the movement with zeal and enthusiasm in the face of the repressive methods adopted by the government.

Repression by the Government

Restrictions were placed on public meetings, newspaper and the activities of various political associations. The police resorted to all sorts of cruel methods to punish those who participated in the movement. As if the old penal code was not adequate for this purpose, numerous new laws were passed with a view to giving additional powers to district magistrates to arrest and keep in jails persons they suspected. Very few of them were brought to trial in the law courts.

Among the repressive laws enacted during the Viceroyalty of Lord Minto who succeeded Lord Curzon was the Seditious Meeting Act which empowered magistrates to forbid holding of meetings and to regulate and control the meeting permitted by them. Another Act was the Explosive Substances Act of 1908 to restrict and penalize the activities of those suspected of manufacturing bombs and explosives. The third Act was the Newspapers (Incitement to offences) Act under which magistrates could prohibit the printing of newspapers, demand large deposits from them, confiscate such deposits when they were suspected of writing seditious articles and even to confiscate the press in which such papers were published. The Indian press Act was passed in 1910 and more restrictions were placed on newspaper and printing presses.

The result was that a severe blow was dealt to the freedom of speech, freedom of the Press, freedom of association and all other fundamental freedoms which at least to a limited extent Indian citizens enjoyed with the British citizens.

After the congress split in 1907 several nationalists leaders were tried under charge of sedition and severe punishment was inflicted on them. Among them was Bal Ganghadhar Tilak, the great Maharashtrian leader, who was imprisoned for six years in a jail in Mandalay from 1908. Aurobindo was arrested during the Alipore bomb case. The Government however could not get sufficient evidence to prove the charges against him after keeping him for one year as an undertrial prisoner freed him in 1909. He grew disgusted with politics and in 1910 retired to Pondicherry where he spent the rest of his life in investigation into Yoga and in literary writing. Lala Lajpat Rai went into voluntary exile and spent sometime in Britain and America. The policy of suppressing the leaders in one form or another was extended to all the provinces and in 1908 the Andhra Patriot, Gadicherla Harisarvothama Rao, was made to suffer three years rigorous imprisonment. With shackles placed on great leaders like these nationalist movement lost its original momentum and the Moderates took command of the Congress.

Repression by the Government was also the offshoot of a deliberate creation of a split between the Hindus and the Muslims. This reached its climax when Fuller became the Lieutenant Governor of the newly created province of Eastern Bengal and Assam. Immediately after he assumed office he openly stated at a public meeting that he had two wives – the Hindus constituted one and the Muslim the other. But the Muslim wife was his favorite. This gave encouragement to the Muslims to oppress the Hindus with the confidence that the Government will not take any stringent action against them. It led to the outbreak of communal riots in many parts of East Bengal especially in places like Comilla and Khulna in 1907 where the Hindus formed a small minority following which many of them lost their lives. Their shops were looted, houses burnt temples and idols broken, and their women ill-treated and kidnapped. No action was taken by the police to prevent or suppress the riots and when some were actually tried in the law courts. It was only the Hindus that were punished.

Among the repressive measures of Fuller was the dispersal of the conference held by the leaders of both West and East Bengal at Barisal in 1906. He made raising of the slogan of Vandemataram a crime. He did not like the idea that Bengalis whom the government separated should display the courage to come together in a conference at Barisal. Surendranath Banerjee attended the conference and protested against the slogan of Vandemataram being declared illegal. He was arrested and fined. On the second day of the conference and order was issued that unless the delegates gave an undertaking that they would not raise the cry of Vandemataram the conference would be dispersed. The leaders having refused to give such a guarantee the conference was forcibly dispersed. This did not however result in the weakening of the Vandematarm movement. It only received further impetus and protest meetings were held throughout the country condemning the repressive policy of Fuller. This step taken by him was one of the causes for widespread sympathy which the people of all other provinces showed towards the Vandemataram movement in Bengal.

Fuller adopted many other repressive measures before he resigned his office and his resignation was accepted by lord Minto, the Viceroy, with the approval of Morley, the then Secretary of State for India. They also did not like the extremes to which Fuller went in the execution of the repressive policy.

In spreading the message of boycott, Swadeshi and national education, Bipin Chandra Pal's tour in Andhra in April and May 1907 was a great significance. He delivered lectures in Vishakhapatnam, Kakinada, Rajamundry, Vijayawada, Musulipatnam and several other places. This electrified the entire region and convinced the people that in winning their object of Swaraj boycott and other weapons tried in Bengal should be used by them. Swadeshi shops were opened in almost all the towns and national education received encouragement culminating in the establishment of the Andhra Jateeya Kalasala in Musulipatnam under the direction of Kopalli Hanumanth Rao, a leading advocate.

The Terrorist Movement

The repressive policy adopted by Fuller and Minto only drove the Vandemataram movement underground. It led to the growth of a revolutionary or the terrorist movement as the British called it, a movement which continued with varying fortunes till 1919. The revolutionaries like the nationalists believed that their goal was immediate Swaraj. But they did not share the view that through passive resistance it could be achieved. In no country of the world and at any time was imperialism put an end to without the use of armed force against the imperial rulers. They decided upon using violence against individual officials, both British and Indian. This led to several assassinations. For this purpose the revolutionaries manufactured bombs of explosives, collected arms in a variety of ways, and even tried to bring about a large scale armed rising with the help of the German arms during the first World war. The attempt made by the German embassy to send arms to India to help the revolutionaries free of cost came to be known to the British and they captured the ships that were bringing those arms.

Another aspect of the attempt of large scale armed resistance during the first World War was the return to India of a large number of Indians settled in U.S.A. They were mostly Sikhs. They organised a party called the Ghadar Party in U.S.A., ran several news paper in English, Hindi and other Indian settlers not only in U.S.A. message of revolution among the Indian settler not only in U.S.A but also in other countries of the Far East and South East Asia. The Sikh immigrants carried on negotiations with some of the sepoy regiments in India and encouraged them to rebel against the authorities. But their plans were miscarried as a result of the infiltration to the ranks of the revolutionaries a number of police informers.

The outcome of all that in a number of conspiracy cases hundreds of revolutionaries, some real and others only suspected, were tried and sentenced to death or transported to the Andaman's to undergo long spells of jail after rigorous imprisonment in India. Historians affirm that the punishment given to those suspected of sympathizing with revolutionary movement was far worse than the atrocities committed by Hitler against the Jews and others in Germany. This reference to the revolutionary movement in Bengal during the Vandemataram movement and the years that followed is appropriate for the reason that it was the outcome of the policy of repression adopted by Viceroy Minto with the approval of Morley and later by Hardinge.

Lord Hardinge and Annulment of the Partition

Minto left India in 1910 and was succeeded by Lord Hardinge. As soon as he arrived in Calcutta, Hardinge could see that inspite of the repressive policy the revolutionary activity continued and there was no peace or order in any province or in the country as a whole. He realized that really something should be done immediately to bring peace to the Province of Bengal and this was all the more necessary in view of the proposed visit of King George and his consort to India in December 1911. He felt that the partition of Bengal was the root cause of the disorder and lawlessness that prevailed in the provinces and unless steps were taken to annul the partition, peace could not be restored. Lord Grewe who succeeded Morley as the Secretary of State for India shared the view and he approved of the proposals made by Hardinge for the restoration of peace. These proposals had the consent of the British Cabinet also.

Among the proposals made by Hardinge were 1) The partition should be annulled and East Bengal and West Bengal should be united into one province 2) Assam should be separated from Bengal and made province as it was prior to the partitions. 3) Bihar, Chota Nagpur and Orissa also should be separated from Bengal and constituted into another province and 4)the capital of India should be shifted from Calcutta to Delhi.

These proposals gave satisfaction to all the concerned people not only to the Bengalis but also to the people of Assam who never liked the idea of being tagged on to East Bengal as well as to the people of Bihar who were Hindi speaking and who disliked Bengali domination over the province right from the days of the Battle of Plassey. Patna became the capital of the province of Bihar, Orissa and Chota Nagpur and this was the precursor of the organization of the Indian provinces of a linguistic basis though it took several years before the principle was applied to Orissa. The transfer of the Capital from Calcutta to Delhi found favour with many classes of people and to the Hindus and the Muslim alike.

Delhi was more central than Calcutta and it had early association with empires in ancient India and also with the Sultanate and the Mughal Empire.

Hardinge suggested that all the proposals should be announced by King George at the Durbar to be held in Delhi. Accordingly it was in the Imperial Durbar held on 12 December, 1911 that the proposals were announced by the king Emperor and this gave additional significance to his proposals.

The Vandemataram movement yielded successful results. The difficulties and troubles of the people of Bengal ended in final victory-the first of its kind which the people won against the alien rulers.

The Outcome of the Movement

The main outcome of the Vandemataram movement was clearly the annulment of the partition of Bengal the purpose for which it was started. But it produced other effects too. One was the growth of the revolutionary movement. The second was the split in the Congress and the third was the enactment by the government of the Indian councils Act of 1909.

From 1903 the Bengali delegates who attended the annual sessions of the Congress pleaded for the passing of a resolution condemning the proposed partition of Bengal. But there were delegates who were opposed to passing such a resolution on the ground that the issue was purely a local one and should not be considered at a meeting of the Congress which was an all India body. They said that the subject could well be discussed in a provincial conference confined to Bengal. The Pressure of the Bengali delegates was so intense that in the sessions of 1903 and 1904 resolutions were passed protesting against partitions. When the congress met in December 1905 at Varanasi (Banaras) under the presidentship of Gokhale, partition was already an accomplished fact and to get it annulled Bengalis had already started the boycott and Swadeshi movements. So Bengali delegates now wanted that the Congress should give its approval to Boycott and Swadeshi movements. The moderates who dominated the Congress were against passing a resolution. Ultimately a compromise was arrived at between the Moderates and the Nationalists. A resolution welcoming the Prince and Princess of Wales who proposed to visit India was coming up for discussion. The Nationalists were against extending such a welcome. They threatened to oppose the resolution on the subject. The moderates felt that the resolution must be passed unanimously. So they affected a compromise with the Nationalists according to which they gave indirect support to boycott while the Nationalists absented themselves from the meeting when the resolution welcoming the Prince and Princess of Wales came up for discussion and the Moderates were enabled to carry it unanimously.

By December 1906 the Vandemataram movement gained momentum and the delegates from Bengal wanted that the session of the congress to be held in Calcutta in December 1906 should be presided over by Tilak, the foremost Nationalist, and that resolutions favouring boycott, Swadeshi, national education and Swaraj should be passed. But the Moderates maneuvered to prevent Tilak from presiding over the session and invited instead Dadabhai Naoroji, the grand old man, residing in Britain. Tilak did not want to contest and the Congress met at its annual session in Calcutta under the presidentship of Dadabhai Naoroji.

The atmosphere in Calcutta was all in favour of the Nationalists objectives. The moderates tried their best to prevent resolutions on the four subjects noted above from being passed. In the course of his presidential address, Dadabhai Naoroji stated that the objective of the Congress should be Swaraj, though he did not define the term but meant by it only colonial self-government. Heated discussions took place in the subjects committee on the resolution with regard to these four subjects. It appeared at one stage that the Congress session would break up. But wiser counsel prevailed and ultimately resolutions in favour of boycott, Swadeshi, and national education were passed through the objective of the Congress was defined to be self-government on colonial lines. This was a great victory for the Nationalists.

The Government reacted to this by accusing the moderates of aligning themselves with the Nationalists. And they even threatened that might lead to an indefinite postponement of the reforms which they wanted to grant. Moderates therefore were eager to cancel at the next session the resolution passed at Calcutta and if that was not possible at least not to repeat them at the session to be held in 1907.

The session of 1907 met in Surat even though at the Calcutta session Nagpur was selected as the Venue. Surat was the center of the Moderates. It was completely under the control of Sir Pheroze Shah Mehta. The nationalists wanted Lajpat Rai to preside while the

Moderates preferred Rash Behari Ghosh. When the venue was shifted to Surat, Lajpat Rai declined the presidentship and Rashbehari Ghosh was elected president.

The Congress met at Surat but the Nationalists found that the subjects to be discussed and voted upon were prepared by the reception committees, that there was no reference at all to the resolutions passed at the Calcutta session-boycott and other subjects. Arabindo and other Nationalists insisted on the resolutions on these subjects being repeated at the Surat session. Tilak made it clear that he would oppose the election of Rashbehari Ghosh and the proposed resolutions on these subjects being repeated at the Surat session. He was not given any opportunity to speak even though he got up on the platform determined to oppose the election of Rashbehari as President. Commotion arose in the hall when the Congress, met Shoes were hurled and Surendranath Banerjee and Sir Pheroze Shah Mehta were hit. Immediately the chairman of the reception committee announced that the session would not be held and dissolved the meeting. Thus ended the Surat session without transacting any business. Efforts were made to effect some compromise but the Moderates were not prepared for it as they had in their mind the threat by the authorities that the reforms would be postponed if they came to an understanding with the Nationalists.

After the dissolution of the Surat meeting the Moderates who were in a majority in the Congress appointed a committee to draw up a constitution for the congress, and in the constitution thus framed clauses were introduced to the effect that only those who believed in colonial self government and in constitutional methods of agitation should be elected as delegates to the Congress. This automatically excluded the Nationalists and from 1908 the congress became a completely moderates –dominated body, thoroughly loyal to the Government and upholding its policies. It ceased to represent the people as a whole. It soon lost all the popular support which it commanded before the Surat split and even attendance at the annual session showed a gradual fall till it numbered only about 300 during one of its sessions.

Minto Morley Reforms

The Vandemataram movement led to the enactment of the Minto Morley reforms or the Indian Councils Act of 1909. From the very beginning Morely was in favour of introducing reforms to satisfying the

Moderates. Minto however felt that there was no need at all for reforms. But he was not able to bring round Morely to his point of view. He saw to it that the reforms should be utilized to create further split between the Hindus and the Muslims which would weaken the nationalist movement in the country. The Moderate leader Gokhale went to Britain and had a series of meetings with Morely and tried to convince him that some kind of colonial self government should be introduced in the country. Morely however was adamant. In his view self government under which the executive would become responsible to an elected legislature could never be introduced in India and that the utmost he could go was to enlarge the Indian element in the legislatures-central and provincial –and to give it powers to discuss the budget and for putting supplementary questions and moving resolutions on matters of public interest. Gokhale was disappointed, but he and the moderates were satisfied with the few concessions that Morely proposed to grant.

What is worthy of note is that for the sake of such minor concessions they were prepared not to come to any type of compromise with the Nationalists and even drive them away from the Congress.

When the Muslims came to know that Morely was going introduce reforms they wanted to make sure that they got separate electorates and weightage in representation. They went on a deputation to Minto in the later part of 1906 and got assurances from him covering both these points. Morely was against both these measures. He wanted joint electorates and not communal electorates. But Minto brought pressure on him and convinced him that to ensure the loyalty of the Muslim community they should be given weightage and special electorates. Morley ultimately yielded to him. Though provision was not made for them in the Act itself, they were introduced into the rules and regulations which were passed by the Government of India and approved by the Secretary of State.

The Moderates welcomed the Act initially but later when they came to know of the communal and special electorates, they were disappointed. But they were helpless in the matters. The Act was passed in 1909 and it came into effect along with the rules and regulations. Under the Act the strength of the Imperial legislative council and the Provincial Legislative councils was increased. The total number of members in the Imperial Legislative Council was 68 excluding the head of the Government and the experts. There were three classes of electorates and members were elected separately from among these constituencies – General, Muslim and special. The following table indicates the strength of the Legislative council at the Center and the Provinces as well as the allotment of the membership to the various categories.

Legislative Council	*Elected*	*Nominated Non-official*	*Nominated official*	*Tatl*
India	25 (27)	7 (5)	36	68
Madras	19(21)	7(5)	20	46
Bombay	21	7	18	46
United Provinces	20(21)	6	20	46(47)
Bengal	26(28)	5(4)	20	57(52)
E.Bengal and Assam	18	5	17	40
Punjab	5(8)	9(6)	10	24
Burma	1	8	6	15
Bihar and Orissa	21	4	18	43
Assam	11	4	2	24

From the table given above, it can be seen that there was no non-official majority in the legislative council. In the provinces, though provision was made for a non official majority the non officials were elected through a variety of constituencies–general Muslim and Special. There was no prospect of all these working together as a single group and though there was a non official majority the government was able to have its way.

The act of 1909 empowered the councils to discuss the budget at length before it was finally adopted, to propose resolutions on it and to vote upon them not only on the Budget, but on all matters of general public importance resolutions might henceforth be moved and voted upon. The resolutions were to operate as recommendations to the executive government. The right to put questions to the government was enlarged by allowing the members asking the original question to put supplementaries.

Though there was apparently an enlargement of the legislatures and an increase in the powers, there was nothing to constitute a real transfer of authority from the British into the Indian hands. The reforms afforded no answer to the Indian political problem. Narrow franchises and indirect elections failed to encourage among its members a sense of responsibility to the people generally, and made impossible for the members who had votes to use them with perception and effect. The concept of a responsible executive wholly or partially amenable to the elected councils was not recognized. Power remained with the Government and the Councils were left with no functions except that of criticism. The non-responsible form of Government continued till under the Act of 1919 Dyarchy and along with it, partial responsible Government were introduced in the provinces. This accounts for disappointment caused to the Moderates.

The Long Period Effects of the Movement

Among the long term effects of the Vandemataram movement was the spread of political consciousness and national sentiment among a large section of the people. Before 1905 this was confined only to the English educated classes. During the Vandemataram movement, the boycott, Swadeshi and the work of the revolutionaries led to an awakening of large sections especially the lower middle classes and to some extent even among classes much lower. All this enabled Gandhiji to get response to his Non-co-operation movement when he started it in 1920. People gave up all fear of the police and the authorities and they were prepared to face the challenge and undergo any amount of suffering for the sake of the freedom of the country. It could be said that this movement prepared the ground for the freedom movement under the leadership of Gandhiji. That is why the Vandemataram movement is regarded as the First phase of the freedom movement.

❖ ❖ ❖

THE HOME RULE MOVEMENT

CHAPTER 10

Character of the Movement

The Home Rule movement which was carried on vigorously by Tilak and Annie Besant for two years from 1916 jointly was the second phase of freedom movement in India. It differed from the Vandemataram movement in certain essential respects. It was in the first place an all India movement not restricted to any single province. Secondly it aim was not complete Swaraj but Home Rule or internal self-government. Even Tilak became a convert to this idea by the time he was released from jail in 1914. He said that it was not necessary that India should cut off its connection with Britain for political progress, that home rule of the type enjoyed by the colonies in Australia and Canada was as good as Swaraj and the people of India should strive for it. Besant was also of that view from the very beginning of her political activity. Throughout her career she emphasized that the British Empire should be converted into a Commonwealth in which India along with the other colonies should be equals of Britain and this was the basis of her advocacy of Home rule in the year 1916 and 1917. Finally the movement was not carried on under the auspices of the Congress. Separate Home Rule Leagues were started by Tilak in Western India and by Annie Besant in Madras 1916. Besant wanted to start it in 1915 but the Congress leaders promised that they themselves would take up the matter and that there was no need for a separate League. She found that the Congress was not serious about the matter and after waiting for a few months she started the League in 1916 a few months after Tilak started that of his.

Activities of Tilak and Annie Besant

To carry propaganda in favour of the movement, Besant started a weekly called the Commonwealth and a daily by name the New India. She wrote powerful articles on the need to introduce Home Rule immediately. In addition to these she published books and pamphlets, opened reading rooms and formed discussion groups. In this respect she made use of the numerous branches of the Theosophical Society which were active in those days in almost every part of the country. Tilak also made use of his two papers Marathi and Kesari for purposes of propaganda. In addition to this he toured Maharashtra, Karnataka, Central province and Gujarat, and addressed huge public meetings. In Maharashtra and Central Province he spoke in Marathi, the language of the people and in other provinces also he advised his followers to speak in the regional languages. This enabled him to carry on the message of Home Rule effectively to the ordinary people. He and his followers addressed meetings even in villages. There was an understanding between Besant and Tilak, the former Working mostly in the areas in the South and North while Tilak confined himself to the West.

Reference has to be made to several other developments in the period after 1914, the year in which Tilak was released from prison. By that time Besant who all along concentrated on religious, educational and social work decided to enter the political field as she felt that political advancement was the key to progress in every other field of public life. She was an Irish woman and she was familiar with the Home Rule Movement in her country. She imported into India the propaganda model with which she was familiar at home.

Unity Between the Moderates and the Nationalists

Before she took up the cause of Home Rule she wanted to bring about unity between the Moderates and the Nationalists and make the Congress once again a body representative of all groups and points if view. For this purpose she carried on negotiations with leaders like Gokhale and Pherozesha Mehta. She also talked to Tilak who was equally in favour of a united Congress. He however insisted that there should be some changes in the constitution of the Congress so as to facilitate re-entry of the Nationalists. Though the majority of the Moderates were disposed favourably towards a united Congress, Pherozeshah Mehta and Gokhale were against Tilak's entry because of the fear it might lead to domination by the nationalists. With the death in 1915 of Gokhale and Pherozeshah Meta negotiations for a united Congress commenced. Certain changes were made in the constitution of the Congress and the Nationalists joined it at the Lucknow session in 1916. As a result of this the Congress once again became a leading all India political body, a position occupied before the Surat split.

The Congress and the Muslim League come Together

A significant development in this period was the willingness of the Muslim League to work in unison with the congress. Since 1911 the Muslims became alienated from the Government for a variety of reasons. One was the annulment of the partition of Bengal without consulting them. The more influential factor was the policy which the British followed towards the Muslim States in Africa and Turkey. That was a time when the aggressive European people, the French, the Italians, and Russia were encroaching upon the Islamic States one after another and Britain also followed a similar policy more or less in alliance with them. Many Muslim states lost their independence and in the Balkan war of 1912–13 Turks were defeated losing much of their territory in Europe. The Muslim felt that the British were responsible for the gradual collapse of the Islamic States. This made them come closer to the congress. In 1916 they agreed to work almost as a single body. The league also accepted self government as was obtained in the colonies as its goal. There was thus no difference between the ultimate goal of the Congress and the league. All in all the year 1916 was eventful as it witnessed the coming into existence of a reunited Congress, the coming together of the Congress and the Muslim league and also the establishment of the Home Rule League.

At the sessions of the Congress and the League which were held in Lucknow in 1916, the reforms scheme called the Congress League scheme was jointly prepared and resolutions were passed by both the bodies urging the British Government to declare colonial self-government as the objective of its rule in India and that immediate steps should be taken to introduce reforms to further this objectives.

The Memorandum of the Nineteen

In the same year 19 non-official members of the Imperial Legislative Council also prepared a memorandum in favour of colonial self-government and submitted it to the Viceroy. Thus there was a general movement in the country in favour of Home Rule or internal self-government.

The First World War and its Effects

Another factor which took the country in the same direction was the First World War which broke out in 1914. During the War, Indians contributed large military contingents and Indian Sepoys fought on all fronts including Europe, North Africa and East Asia, The expenditure for raising the contingent and for maintaining them was borne by the Government of India. In addition to this a gift of rupees hundred crores was made by the Government of India to Britain while large donations were made by the Indian princes and the people for the war fund. All this made the Indian politicians feel that in return for the sacrifices which India made for the victory of the British, the latter should be grateful and grant numerous political concessions to the country. The consequences of the World War and the part played by the Indians in it thus raised new hopes among Indians.

The British and their allies the Americans proclaimed that the principal aim of the War was to spread the ideal of democracy in the world and to liberate subject people from the yoke of imperial rule. India political leaders thought that this would apply to their country also. They expected that by the end of the War India would make progress in the direction of self-government. This was why Tilak argued when he came out of prison in 1914 that India should support the British with men and money for the war. Gandhiji who returned from South Africa in 1915 also argued on similar lines.

The First World War thus changed radically the political atmosphere in the country. But there was not much of a change in British attitude at least in the beginning. They disliked the agitation carried on by Tilak and Annie Besant in favour of Home Rule. They placed various restrictions on Tilak in Delhi and Punjab.

Montagu's Announcement on August 20, 1917

More harsh steps were taken against Besant. The Governor of Madras recommended her deportation to England. But the Governor General of India was not in favour of it. Ultimately large deposits were demanded from her under the Press Act while a sum of 20,000 rupees which she paid in the shape of deposits were forfeited. She had to stop the publication of her news papers for some time. Finally the Government of Madras interned her along with two of her colleagues at Coimbatore in order to put a stop to her activities. But this resulted in an agitation throughout the country for her release and some members of the Congress and the League even went to the extent of proposing a passive resistance movement to get her released and to support the causes of the Home Rule movement. The Madras Provincial Congress Committee passed a resolution in favour of the adoption of passive resistance. But before events took a serious turn, there came and announcement by Montagu, the secretary of State for India, in the house of Commons on August 20, 1917 stating that the ultimate goal of the British in ruling the country was the establishment of responsible government. Montague also ordered the cancellation of Besant's interment.

With this announcement Besant felt that there was no need for further propaganda in favour of Home rule. Though Tilak continued the agitation a little longer every one felt that steps should be taken to introduce responsible government in accordance with Montagu's announcement. We may therefore say that the Home Rule movement ended as victoriously as the Vandemataram movement.

A brief reference may be made to the circumstances which led to the announcement of Montagu in the House of Commons. From the very beginning of her War certain political leaders in Britain Strongly felt that with a view of getting the full support of India for the War some concessions per force have to be offered. Chamberlain, the Secretary of State, took the initiative in the matter but before he could formulate any scheme he resigned to make way for Montagu who was a man of liberal views. Montagu showed sympathy for Indian's aspirations even when he was the under secretary of State for India. Now that he became the Secretary of State he worked upon the ideas of Chamberlain. The announcement that he made on August 1917 in the House of Commons was the outcome of all these efforts.

The announcement declared that responsible government was the ultimate goal of the British Rule in India. Responsible government means a government where the executive is responsible to the legislature elected by the people and it amounted to self government in the accepted sense of the term. It also stated that responsible government would be introduced through stages. Further the British government alone would decide the nature of the responsible government that was to be introduced at each stage which in turn depended on the way Indian representatives conducted themselves in the exercise of the power granted to them.

In accordance with this announcement Montagu came to India and along with Viceroy Lord Chelmsford he undertook a tour of the country, interviewed political leaders and received representations from political associations and ultimately prepared the well known report on Indian Constitutional reforms (Montagu–Chelmsford Reforms) which became the basis of the Government of India Act 1919.

MONTAGU CHELMSFORD REFORMS

CHAPTER 11

Evolution of Responsible Government

In tracing the course of events leading to the passing of the Montagu- Chelmsford Reforms or the Government of India Act 1919, note has to be taken of the famous Despatch by the Viceroy, Lord Hardinge, to the Secretary of State proposing the annulment of the partition of Bengal, the Creation of new provinces, and the transfer of the capital from Calcutta to Delhi. It was in this Despatch that the right of the Indians to have a share in the administration of the country was first officially recognized. The Despatch also pointed out that these could be best accomplished in a federal framework in which provinces would enjoy some degree of autonomy.

In 1914 the First World War broke out. Reference has already been made to the change it brought in the outlook of the Indian leaders culminating in the union of the Moderates and the Nationalists in the Congress and the coming closer of the Congress and the Muslim League, the preparation jointly by them of a scheme of reforms and also of a memorandum on the same subject by nineteen non-official members of the Imperial Legislative Council. These were followed by the Home Rule movement. All these had an impact on the British politicians.

The next phase in the scheme of reforms relates to Chamberlain, Secretary of State for India, who was keen introducing a measure of reform which would give concrete form to the desire of the Indians to have a share in the Government. He realized that the policy of divide and rule would not always succeed as was indicated by the coming together of the Congress and the league. Britain was also in need of loyal support of the Indians in the World War. Influenced by these factors he asked Chelmsford to make proposals for a new scheme of reforms. But Chelmsford purely on the advice of the members of his executive who were drawn from the Indian Civil Service and who were opposed to any kind of political advancement. He only suggested to further enlargement of the legislative councils and a few changes in the system of local government Chamberlain was not satisfied with this. But before he could work out a more liberal scheme of reform he had to resign his office. This was taken over by Montagu who was till then the Under Secretary of State for India.

Montagu was a man of liberal views. In the controversy on Hardinge's Despatch he expressed in favour of conceding to the Indians a large share in the Government of the Country. As Secretary of State he adhered to that view. By that time there came into existence in Britain the Round Table Group under the leadership of Lionel Curtis. This group worked on a scheme of responsible government for Indian in various stages it should be introduced firstly into the provinces. The subjects under provincial control should be divided into a reserved half and a transferred half. The latter should be made over to ministers commanding a majority in the legislature.

Montagu came to know of the Scheme prepared by the Round Table Group. He accepted it for all practical purposes as a sound scheme for introducing responsible government in India in stages. He had discussions with the leading members of the Congress and with their approval he made the famous announcement in the House of Commons on August 20, 1917 to which reference has already been made.

Montagu Chelmsford Report

In 1917 Montagu visited India and toured the country for five months along the Viceroy Chelmsford. He listened to suggestions from various British leaders and associations but he had already made up his mind that the scheme prepared by the Round Table Group was the best to be put into effect. It was on these lines that he and the Viceroy drafted their report on Indian constitutional reforms which received the approval of the Cabinet in July. 1918and it was published for public discussions. He took in to confidence the Moderate leaders to whom he explained the broad features of the scheme of reforms, obtained their approval and consent to work the new scheme. Bringing them round was the main purpose of his visit to India and he succeeded.

Reaction of the Indian Political Parties to the Report

In August, 1918 a special session of the Congress was held at Bombay under the presidentship of Hassan Imam. The Moderates boycotted the session and met separately in another conference, and formed the All India liberal Federation. At the session of the Congress, several suggestion were made for liberalizing the scheme prepared by Chelmsford and Montagu, especially, that all subjects at provincial levels should be transferred to the ministers responsible to the provincial legislatures and that at the center also some subjects should be made over to responsible ministers. The Moderates at their conference made suggestions which were more or less similar to those made by the Congress. There was, therefore, no fundamental difference between the two sections. But as a result of the pressure brought on them by Montagu they seceded from the Congress, just as they did in 1907 due to the pressure of Moreley and brought about a split in the Congress with a difference. In 1907 though the Nationalists were driven out of the Congress, they continued to enjoy the confidence of the people of the country. As a result of the split in 1918 the Moderates voluntarily went out of the Congress, and owing to the boycott of legislatures during the first non-co-operation movement, they were able to get elected into the legislatures and form ministers in the provinces. Ever since 1914 when the Congress decided on entry into the legislature the Moderates were defeated in the elections and therefore ceased to play any role in Indian politics. The movement under the leadership of Mahatma Gandhi was the greatest event in the history of the country after 1920, and the Moderates had little to contribute to the movement.

Changes Introduced by the Reforms – Home Government

Significant changes were introduced by the Montagu Chelmsford reforms which were embodied in the Government of India Act passed by the Parliament in 1919 and put into effect in January, 1921. These could be studied under four broad heads. India was governed bodies at four levels from 1858. At the top were the parliament, the secretary of State for India, and his Council. The parliament was accepted as the highest sovereign body for all-purpose of government, and the Government of India Act, 1919 did not bring about any change in its sovereignty. In practice, however, parliament relaxed its control over the transferred subjects in the provincial government. So far as the Secretary of State of India and his Council were concerned, there were two important changes. All the expenditure incurred on the Secretary of State and the Council was hence forward placed on the estimates of the British budget, and the Government of India had no responsibility in sharing the expenditure Secondly, the control of the Secretary of State was also relaxed to some extent on provincial governments. Further a new office called the High Commissioner of India was created by the Act. He was to be appointed by the Government of India and his salary was to be borne by it. Some of the functions of the Secretary of State were transferred to him. As a matter of fact he acted as an agent between the Government of India and the Home Government.

Central Government

The next level of Government was the Central Government of India. Important changes were introduced into it by the Act of 1919. Henceforth the Imperial Legislature came to consist of two Houses the Legislative Assembly and the Council of State. The Council of State was to consist of 60 members out of whom 33 were to be elected and 27 nominated by the Governor General. Of the nominated members not more than 20 should be officials. The life of the Council of State was five years. The Legislative Assembly consisted of 145 members of whom 103 were to be elected and the remaining nominated. Of the elected members 51 were elected from the constituencies, 30 from Mohemmadan constituencies, 2 from the Sikhs, 9 from Europeans, 7 from the Land holders and 4 from the members of Indian mercantile community. The life of the Assembly was three years. The franchise was slightly widened. The number of voters for the Legislative Assembly came to about a million. But this was to small a number for a country with a huge population. Further the right to elect to the council of State was restricted to men with property and large income. Their numbers came into to about 17,500. Even for the Legislative Assembly the qualification of the voters was either the payment of municipal taxes of not less than Rs. 20-/ per annum or ownership of houses of an annual rental value of Rs. 180/- or the payment of Income Tax on an annual income of about Rs. 5,000/-. Thus there was a restricted franchise for both the Houses.

The powers of the Central Legislature extended to making laws, subject to a few exceptions, on all matters within the jurisdiction of India. They could also discuss the budget, propose motions and vote upon them. Neither the budget nor bills would have legal validity unless they were passed by both the Houses of the Legislature. They had ofcourse to receive the approval of the Governor General before they were placed in the statute book. But the Act conferred what is known as the power of certification on the Governor General. In the exercise of this power, it was open to him to certify a Bill into law even if it was not passed by the Houses of Legislature if he felt that such a law was necessary for the safety of the country and for the maintenance of law and order. This enabled him to administer the country as despotically as he did before. There was therefore no real transfer of power in so far as the Central Government was concerned even though the elected members were in a majority. What the Act did was to give more opportunities to the representatives of the people to give expression to public opinion and to expose the autocratic nature of the Government.

Provincial Government

At the third level were the provincial governments. Madras, Bombay, Bengal, United Provinces, Punjab, Bihar and Orissa, Central Provinces, and Assam were constituted into "Governors Provinces". In these provinces the subjects to be administered were divided into two categories – reserved subjects and transferred ones. The reserved subjects were administered by the Executive council, the members of which were responsible not to the legislature but to the Governor. The transferred subjects were in the hands of the ministers who commanded the confidence of the majority of members in the Provincial Legislative Council. The transferred subjects included Local Self Government, Medical administration, Public Health and Sanitation, Education other than European and Anglo-Indian Education and Central Universities, Agriculture, Veterinary Department, Co-operative Societies, Excise, Registration, Religious and Charitable Endowments, Development of Industries etc. In regard to all these the ministers could have their ways as long as they commanded a majority in the legislative Council. Thus came into being what was known as Dyarchy. It means the existence of dual form of Government within the provinces - Government over reserved subjects and Government over transferred subjects.

Responsible Government also implies a legislature which contains majority of elected members; provision was made for 70 per cent of the members in each legislature to be elected, some by the general constituencies and a few in communal and special constituencies. The remaining 30 percent were nominated by the Governor even though among those nominated the non-official preponderated. The official element was considerably reduced in the Legislative Council. Members elected were chosen by general, communal and special constituencies as for example (besides separate electorates for Muslims) Sikhs in the Punjab, Anglo-Indians in Madras and Bengal, and Europeans in all provinces except the Punjab, Central Provinces and Assam and so on. In madras 13 of the elected seats fell to special, 20 to communal and 65 to general constituencies while 28 seats were reserved for non-brahmins.

The legislative council had power to make laws on all matters reserved as well as transferred within the jurisdiction of the provincial Government. The Budget also should be voted by the Council before it could be put into effect. Bills passed by the Council how ever had to be approved not only by the Governor but also by the Governor General before they became laws. Generally however such Bills were automatically approved. But as in the case of the Central Government the provincial Government had power of certification on reserved subjects generally and under special circumstances on transferred subjects. Any bill relating to the reserved subjects or any item of the budget relating to it may be given legal validity by the Governor if he considered that it was necessary for safeguarding the public interest, law, and order. So the Governor continued to exercise the same unbridled authority over the reserved subjects as he did before 1921.

At the bottom were the local bodies – municipalities in urban areas and local boards in rural areas. The Government of India Act of 1919 made no changes in their composition and powers as it was thought that should be left to the ministers who were in charge of local self government.

Beginnings of Federalism

Further the 1919 Act introduced and element of federalism into the Indian Government. Under the rules and regulations framed to settle the details of Act, a division was made between the subjects to be administered by the Central Government and the provincial Governments. Thus there were the Central subjects and provincial subjects. "Where extra provincial interests predominate the subject is treated as Central, while, on the other hand, all subjects in which the interests of a particular province essentially predominate are provincial". Among the Central subjects were military matters, foreign affairs, tariffs and customs, railways, post and telegraphs, income tax, currency, coinage and public debt, commerce and shipping and civil and criminal law. The important provincial subjects were local self-government, medical administration and public health, education (with certain exceptions) public works and irrigation, land revenue administration, famine relief, agriculture, forests, law and order. Separate finances were also allotted for the administration of subjects within the Central and provincial Government. For example, land revenue and excise on alcoholic liquor were allocated to the provinces whereas customs and income tax were treated as Central revenue. Ordinarily, it became a convention for the Governor General not to interfere with the administration of subjects allotted to the provinces. As provinces had independent financial resources they were free to administer these subjects in any way they liked. The division of subjects and the division of financial resources are the essential characteristics of federalism. Though these were not embodied in the Act itself and were only put into effect through rules and regulations, they had in practice the same effect as provisions in a parliamentary Act. This is why the beginnings of federalism in India could be traced to the Act of 1919.

Defects of the Reforms

The Act of 1919 did not give full satisfaction to the Indian political leaders or the people. In the first place, it did not bring about any transfer of power at the centre. This was its most serious defect. Even in the provinces where power was transferred and the scheme of diarchy was introduced, the transferred subjects were considered less important than the reserved ones. Moreover, finance was a reserved subject, and the ministers who had to administer transferred subjects had to depend upon the Executive Council for the money they needed. This stood in the way of any big changes to be introduced in education, agriculture and other subjects, as well as social and economic development of the country. Diarchy would have been more effective if along with the division of subjects financial powers were granted.

In the next place, the Legislative Council was so constituted that it was not always possible for the ministers to get the majority of the elected members on their side. The members were elected by various types of constituencies general, communal and special. They had no common interest and they did not work together. The result was to get a majority in the legislature the ministers had to depend on the support of the members nominated by the Governor and on official members. This brought them under the virtual control of the Governors and the purpose of dyarchy was defeated.

Defects like these became apparent during the course of the working of diarchy after 1921. Even the Moderates who joined the ministries complained that they were unable to exercise real power. This was why there was an agitation in the country after 1921 not only by the Congress but also by the Liberals that diarchy should be abolished and that control over all subjects in the provinces should be placed in the hands of responsible ministers – a change that was introduced by the Government of India Act of 1935. This dissatisfaction with the Act of 1919 was a very important factor in further strengthening the freedom movement under the leadership of Mahatma Gandhi.

CHAPTER 12

GANDHIJI'S ENTRY INTO POLITICS

Gandhiji's Leadership of the Freedom Movement

With the entry of Mahatma Gandhi into the political arena in 1919 the freedom movement entered a new phase. It provided the country with a leadership which was accepted by the masses from one end of the country to the other. To wage a country –wide struggle for achieving freedom, central leadership was absolutely necessary. This was all the more so in a country with numerous divisions among the people religious, linguistic, regional, economic and social. To bring all of them together on a common platform, a single leader was essential and such a leadership was provided by Mahatma Gandhi. It is true that even before 1919 there were persons like Gokhale, Pherozeshah Mehta, Surendranath Benarjee, Bal Gangadhar Tilak and Lala Lajpat Rai who had wide reputation. But they did not command the confidence of all sections of the people, Gandhiji was able to lead the people in the real sense of the term and make them do what he wanted them to do. He was able to command this position right through till the freedom struggle came to a successful fruition.

Mahatma Gandhi became an all India Leader because of his saintly character and simple living. In India people were always attracted by saints who conveyed a spiritual message and who led a simple and austere life. Gandhiji was primarily a man of religion. Even his policies were influenced by religious principles. He always said that life is one and it cannot be divided into compartments. Consequently religion and politics should go together. It was his spiritual message, especially the stress on truth and non-violence that appealed to the masses. He not only placed before them the highest spiritual values but also led the life of a simple man.

In a poor country he said no one had right to lead a life of comfort and luxury and that too at the expense of the common man.

He practiced what he preached and took to his loincloth and to simplicity in food and in every aspect of living. This was the secret of his hold over the Indian masses.

Ever since he returned to India in 1915 from South Africa he took up for solution the problems which affected the peasant and of the ordinary workers. The earlier satyagrahas in Champaran, Kaira and Ahmedabad were intended for that purpose. In this he differed from the other Indian political leaders who took little interest in the problem of the ordinary people though they did not ignore them. But Gandhiji's emphasis was entirely on their problems and especially of those which affected the people in the rural areas. The masses discovered in him a real friend and this was another factor which enabled him to become their undisputed leader.

It was not merely the masses that were attracted towards him. Even intellectuals whose outlook on life was entirely different from that of his and who did not even sympathise with his philosophy or with his importation of religious ideas into politics were attracted by his personality. He had something charismatic about him and this enabled him to command the confidence of persons like Motilal Nehru, Jawaharlal Nehru, C.Rajagopalachari, C.R. Das and others. There was some thing inexplicable in this phenomenon. But Jawaharlal Nehru gave an explanation: "Inspite of the closest association with him (Gandhi) for many years. I am not clear in my own mind about his objective. I doubt if he is clear of himself. One step is enough for me he says, and he does not try to peep into future or to have a clearly conceived end before him.... How (then) came we to associate ourselves with Gandhiji politically and to become, in many instances his devoted followers. The question is hard to answer ....Personality is an indefinable thing, a strange force that has powers over the souls of man, and he possesses this in an ample measure. He attracted people. They did not agree with his philosophy of life, or even with many of his ideals. Often they did not understand him. But the action that he proposed was something tangible. Any action would have been welcome after the long tradition in action which our spineless politics had nurtured brave and effective action with him although we did not accept his philosophy". Gandhiji supplied the central leadership for the freedom movement. He commanded the confidence of both the ordinary people and the English educated classes in the country. This is a significant contribution to the freedom movement.

His important contribution was the weapon of satyagraha which he effectively used for carrying on the struggle for freedom. Satyagraha was his new discovery. Before him the Moderates who dominated the Indian political scene believed in constitutional agitation. But when it failed as it did they had no substitute to offer. The Nationalists thought of passive resistance but they were not able to practice it in a big way. In all other countries where the people fought for national freedom war was the usual form resorted to, but Gandhiji's Satyagraha become as effective as war itself.

The third contribution made by Gandhiji to freedom movement was the use he made of the Indian National Congress for organizational and Propaganda purposes. We have already seen that when Besant and Tilak carried on the Home Rule Movement they did not make use of the Congress but started separate Home Rule Leagues for this purpose. Even Gandhiji did not make use of the Congress when he carried on his first three satyagraha campaigns or even when in 1919 he undertook the Rowlatt satyagraha. By the end of 1919, he was convinced that an all India organization like the congress with a country wide reputation, a long period of service to its credit, with branches in the shape of better Congress committees in all the provinces would serve the purpose better than adhoc sabhas which he established in 1919. So, by the end of 1919, he wanted to capture the Congress and make it the organizational instrument for carrying on the freedom struggle. But the Congress which he utilized for the purpose was entirely different from the Congress as it then existed. He transformed it into a mass body with branches spread all over the country at all levels-provincial, district, taluka and village. This transformation was necessary if the struggle was to be a real people's struggle and if it was to produce an irresistible pressure upon an alien Government. It is true that Tilak tried to bring the masses into the political struggle, but his efforts were confined in the main to Maharashtra. It was Gandhiji that gave a mass character to the freedom struggle and the congress a people's organization to the core.

Gandhiji's Experience in South Africa

It is necessary to know a few details about his early life and the influence which they exercised on him – the influence which was really responsible for all the work he died in India from 1915. Gandhiji was born in a Vaisya vaishnavite family in the small Indian state of Porbandar in Kathaiwar in 1869. His mother was a woman of great piety making frequent visits of temples and observing long periods of fasts. His father was the Diwan of Porbandar first, and of Rajkot later and was fond of listening to the Ramayana of Tulsidas and to various Puranas expounded to him by the Pandits who visited his house. This created in Gandhiji a religious and spiritual outlook on life. In 1888 he went to England to qualify himself for the Bar and returned to India in 1891. He was not however a great success as a lawyer. In 1893 he was invited by Guajarati Muslim merchants residing at Natal in connection with a law suit. He accepted the invitation, went to South Africa and spent twenty years in that country. It was there that almost of his political ideas were developed and with these ideas he returned to India in 1915.

Gandhiji did not take long to realize that the Indian settlers in South Africa were subjected to humiliating disabilities. Most of them were labourers working in plantations and mines. There were besides hawkers and petty shop keepers. A few were businessmen carrying on trade on a fairly large scale. But whatever be the category to which they belonged their presence was not liked by the White rulers of the country. Indians first went there as indentured labour and what the Whites wanted was only such labourers and not free Indians with whom they were not in a position to compete since the Indians were accustomed to simple living. They worked for lower wages than the whites and also for a lower rate of profits than the white shopkeepers. To get rid of the Indians they imposed all sorts of disabilities on them and discriminated against them in a variety of ways. They treated them as untouchables, made them live in separate localities, face various obstacles in their trade and curtailed their freedom of movement, Gandhiji was not the man to tolerate any kind of injustice which men and women suffered and he was therefore determined to remove the disabilities. In the beginning he adopted only constitutional methods of agitation. He started the Natal Indian Congress and a newspaper called the Indian Opinion to educate the Indians to create public opinion in regard to their rights. He made representation to the Governments in South Africa, in Britain and also in India that steps should be taken to remove the disabilities imposed on the Indians. But these representations were of no avail.

During this period, he like the Moderates in India was a firm believer in the British system of Government. He was confident that through constitutional agitation, the British who were the rulers of South Africa would do justice to Indians even though the local government of the four provinces there discriminated against them. He also believed that every citizen of the British empire should be loyal to the authorities. He gave practical effect to this by organising an ambulance corps consisting of Indians during the Boer war between the British and the Boers in Transvaal. Later on when the Zulus rose in rebellion he raised a similar ambulance corps and worked whole heartedly. But neither representation nor this loyal and devoted service produced any change in the racial politics pursued by the provincial Governments in South Africa or on the authorities in Britain. In 1906, the provinces in South Africa obtained self government and this meant they were free to pursue their policies of racial discrimination with less difficulty.

Gandhiji was in a dilemma. He began to seriously think as to what he should do when protests, representations, and other method of constitutional agitation failed in removing the injustices. It was then that the idea of Satyagraha dawned in his mind. He made use of it in successive stages for seven years from 1907 to 1914 until under its influence the Government of South Africa partially yielded and removed some of the more serious disabilities imposed upon the Indians. Gandhiji concluded that Satyagraha was a weapon which would bring success in a peaceful war of resistance however mighty the rulers might be.

The Weapon of Satyagraha

Satyagraha rests on a number of principles. The first of them is that men and women should not keep quiet when they are subjected to social injustices. To do so is cowardice and derogatory to self respect. Injustice must be resisted at all costs and if constitutional methods fail resistances should take the form of opposing the authorities' not through war but through self suffering based on truth and non violence. To him non violence was the highest of all the virtues to be practiced and under no circumstances should there is a departure from it when the end to be achieved was a right one. According to Gandhiji war involving as it did violence was tantamount to collective murder. In every country law recognizes that murder is a crime and collective murder should also be regarded as a crime according to him. The problem therefore was how to bring pressure on those perpetrating injustice to remove them with out recourse to violence. He was convinced of the need for peacefully disobeying the law on which injustice was based and wanted the persons to suffer the penalties consequently imposed upon them without hating those who rendered injustice. This kind of self-suffering would ultimately bring about a change in the attitude of the authorities. His basic assumption was that there was a divine element in every one, that human nature was consequently good and that in the final analysis if not immediately no one would want anybody else including enemies to undergo suffering for long periods of time. His heart would melt as it were and he would then see the wrong in rendering injustice and then enter into a compromise with the opponent and remove justice. In this non-violent resistance it is only those who resist that suffer unlike in a war in which both sides suffer. Non-violent resistance is thus less expensive than a violent one. It is considerations like these that made Gandhiji take to the weapon of Satyagraha which literally means grasping truth firmly and to him truth and non-violence went together. From his experience in South Africa he came to the conclusion that Satyagraha was a weapon, which could effectively be used in removing injustice – political, economic and social in India too.

Influence of his Experiences in South Africa on his Ideas and Plan of Action

In India tradition Rishis undertook penance, which meant severe itself suffering for the sake of getting boons from God or for attaining salvation. The principle underlying Satyagraha consisted in the view that self suffering should be used not only for individual salvation but also for the collective good of the people. No one thought of it in this way and Gandhiji was the first man to do it. When he returned to India he was determined to make use of it for the achievement of the freedom of the country. He brought therefore a new weapon for carrying on the struggle against the alien rulers.

Faith in Masses

There were several other beliefs which became part of his public life as a result of his experiences in South Africa. Indians there were illiterate, ignorant and poor. They all belonged to the lower strata of society. But Gandhiji was able to transform them into Satyagraha fighters willing to undergo imprisonment and other penalties. This created in him an abundant faith in the common man and his willingness to suffer for a righteous cause. He identified himself fully with the masses on his return to India and takes up their problems, win their co-operation for fighting for Swaraj. And in the process he transformed the Congress into a mass organization.

Faith in Women

Among those who took part in Satyagraha in South Africa were a large number of women. They resisted the Government as heroically as men did. This made him realise that in any struggle to remove collective injustices; women should also play as prominent a role as men. That was why when he started his non cooperation movement in India; he enrolled a large number of women. This was an important factor in the emancipation of women in India. What the social reformers were not able to achieve even after nearly a century of propaganda, he was able to do within a short period. If in the freedom movement women played an important role and if in free Indian women are occupying high positions in public life and taking a prominent part in all fields of constructive work, the credit must go to Gandhiji.

Removal of Untouchability

Untouchables were among those who participated in satyagraha in South Africa but the other Indians did not look down on them as untouchables because of the influences of Gandhiji's teaching and they welcomed them into their ranks fighting for a common cause. Untouchables fought as enthusiastically as the members of the other castes and this was responsible for Gandhiji devoting himself after his return to India to the cause of the removal of untouchability and Harijan uplift.

Promotion of Hindu Muslim Unity

In South Africa Muslims residents showed willingness to fight along side of the Hindus in the Satyagraha movement. We have already seen that he went to South Africa at the instance of a Muslim merchant. He came into close contact with the Muslims, and helped them in getting trade licenses and obtaining permission to build mosques. The Muslims too accepted him as their leader. This made him a firm believer in Hindu-Muslim unity and its practicability. After he returned to India he became a great champion of Hindu-Muslim unity and devoted his public life to achieve it. This is also the reason for his taking up the Khilafat cause and working with the Ali brothers.

The Need to Achieve Swaraj for India

When Gandhiji first went to South Africa he was loyal and devoted to the British Empire. He believed in the British sense of justice. But while the British did nothing to remove the injustices perpetrated on the Indian in South Africa which was then under the British rule, his faith in British empire and in British sense of justice began to wane. He became a staunch nationalist and from 1905 the idea got embedded in his mind that India cannot make any progress until it achieved Swaraj. When he returned to India he therefore decided to work to free India from British control. This belief in the country's freedom was the outcome of his experience with the British Government in South Africa.

Opposition to Western Materialism

When he was in South Africa he realized that western civilization was materialistic in character, that under the influence of industrialism and science and technology western people cared only for the material comforts and were becoming totally irreligious. It was industrialism that was responsible for the imperialistic policy which the British adopted and the use they made of their dependencies in Asia and Africa for their own material advantage impoverished their subject people. He also attributed the World Wars to the competition and rivalry among the Western nations for imperial glory and possession. He therefore condemned the Western civilization and asserted like Swami Vivekananda the superiority of Indian culture to Western culture. This was at the heart of his advocacy of Swadeshi in all fields of life. His emphasis was on cottage and small scale industries and spinning and weaving and other items of constructive work to which he gave as much prominence as for freedom.

It was while he was in South Africa that he made experiments in the Ashram type of life. He started the Pheonix farm and later on the

Tolstoy farm in which Indians lived together as a community participating in manual work and leading a simple life under strict discipline. Many Satyagrahis underwent this kind of discipline. When he came to India in 1915 almost the first thing he did was to start an Ashram – Satyagraha Ashram as he called it on the banks of the Sabarmati in Ahmedabad. It was his belief that though the masses should fight for the country the leadership should be assumed by trained Satyagrahis. The purpose of his Ashram was to supply trained men and women. Later when he started the non-co-operation movement, these were among the front rankers of the movement.

The above survey demonstrates that all the ideas and methods of action which motivated Gandhiji after his return to India in 1915 were based upon his experiences in South Africa and that he was a product of such experiences. It is this that gives significance to his twenty years of life in South Africa an understanding of which is necessary to appreciate the part he played in the freedom movement in India.

GANDHIJI'S EARLIER SATYAGRAHAS

CHAPTER 13

Contrast Between Gandhiji and other Political Leaders

On his return to India in 1915 Gandhiji instead of entering politics immediately accepted the advice of Gokhale whom he regarded as his political guru that he should first tour the whole country, study the general situation and understand its problems Though he had high personal regard for Gandhiji and appreciated all the work he did for the Indians in South Africa there were fundamental differences between the two. It was not only Gokhale but almost all the English educated political leaders of those days differed from him. In the first place they did not like his idea of involving the masses in political life. They thought that the masses would easily get excited and they might resort to violence. In the second place they had high regard for western civilization and culture unlike Gandhiji. Even from the days of Raja Rammohan Roy they believed that India would gain by contacts with the western culture. That was why they undertook various measures to spread English education and make use of the western methods of political work. Gandhiji however had nothing complimentary to say about the western culture. He believed in a system of education through the mother tongue with emphasis on religious and moral values, and which was relevant to the Indian way of life, especially in the rural areas. Thirdly they did not like Satyagraha. What ever it might have achieved in South Africa they believed that in a vast country like India with numerous differences among the people, open resistance to government through the use of this weapon would ultimately lead to lawlessness and disorder. This was why Gokhale advised him not to enter politics immediately.

Gandhiji accepted his advice and during the year 1915–1916 he went round the country and though he addressed public meetings he did not touch on politics. The subjects on which he spoke were related to Swadeshi and problems akin to it. Though he attended the Lucknow Congress in 1916, the only resolution on which he spoke was on the need for putting an end to indentured labour in South Africa. He also attended a session of the Muslim League in the same year and spoke on Hindu Muslim unity. On the political issues which came up for discussion in the congress as well as the session of the League he kept silent as he thought that participating in discussion on those subjects might compel him to identify himself with one party or other. The only exception he made to this general rule was the threat to resort to Satyagraha in case the system of indenture labour in South Africa was not abolished. He also took up the cause of the Ali brothers- Muhammad Ali and Shoukat Ali who were sentenced to imprisonment for their Pro – Turkish activities during the First World War. He made several representations to the Viceroy urging that they should be released from prison.

He accepted the leadership of the Gujarati Sabha, a political body. But there also he did not enter into controversial politics although he introduced some important changes in its methods of working. He insisted on all the deliberations of the Sabha being carried on in Gujarati language instead of English. He called upon political workers associated with the Sabha to carry on their propaganda for educating the people by going to the rural areas and working in their midst throughout the year instead of merely being satisfied with holding annual conferences and passing resolutions and sending representation to the government. There were very important changes which were introduced into public life first in Gujarat. Gradually under his influence they spread to other parts of the country. He gained sufficient knowledge of the political situation in India by the end of 1916. He had however a regrettable experience during this period bringing out clearly the difference between his outlook and that of the other political leaders. He applied for membership of the Servants of India Society started by Gokhale. Gokhale hesitated to admit him. He asked him to wait for a year. Meanwhile Gokhale died and in 1916 the new president of the Society, Mr. V.S. Srinivasa Sastry and the other members declined to admit him. He wanted to serve the country through this society. He therefore felt a little disappointed when membership was denied to him.

His Satyagraha in Champaran

It was at the Lucknow session of the Congress in 1916 that one of the leaders from Bihar brought to his notice the sad plight of the cultivators in the Indian plantations in the district of the Champaran and requested him to take up their cause and remove the injustice they were subjected to by the planters. Gandhiji initially hesitated but the Bihar leader, Shukla, persisted and ultimately Gandhiji decided to visit Champaran and see what could be done to improve the lot of the indigo cultivators.

Champaran was a zamindari area. The zamindars however leased out their lands to the indigo planters who were Europeans. Those planters compelled the cultivators to raise indigo on 1/3 of the area cultivated, fixed arbitrarily the price at which they should sell it to the planters, imposed various cesses on them and tyrannized over them in many other ways. Politically Bihar was a backward province. The Congress leaders did not show any interest in tackling a problem of this nature.

Gandhiji was not known to come to any decision unless and until he made a through study of the problem and examined it not only from the point of view of those who suffered injustice but also those who inflicted it. He decided on pursuing this course in Champaran. He first met the European planters for the purpose as well as some officials. But they did not like his intrusion and decided on preventing him from carrying on his work. The district magistrate issued a notice that he should quit the area Gandhiji refused and resolved to disobey it and suffer the penalties. This is the Satyagraha which he tried there in the first instance. The magistrate issued a notice that he should appear before the court. At the same time the district authorities acquainted the provisional Government of the action they were taking against Gandhiji. The Provincial Government however did not like the action of the district authorities and asked them to withdraw the notice and allow Gandhiji to go ahead with the work of investigation his Satyagraha thus ended in a victory.

Gandhiji next recruited a number of volunteers and among them were persons like Rajendra Prasad who was then a young advocate in Patna, and Kripalani who was a teacher. With their help he collected evidence from the peasants and those who had first had experience of the wrongs suffered by the cultivators, but before he could proceed further, the provincial Government got jittery especially as he toured in the rural areas while collecting the evidence. They then ordered that he should leave the district but he disobeyed it just as he disobeyed the notice of the district authorities. This was a new experience for the authorities unprecedented in the history of British administration. They did now know exactly what to do. They wrote to Delhi. Meanwhile, Gandhiji was also carrying on correspondence with the Government in Delhi and he suggested that a committee should be appointed to go into the entire subject of the condition of the cultivators in Champaran. The First World War was on and the Government had to depend more and more on the support of the people both for getting recruits and for finance. They therefore did not like the idea that a man of the stature of Gandhiji should be proceeded against at such a crucial time. They advised the provincial Government to drop the case against him, appoint a committee of enquiry with Gandhiji also as one of these members. This was a great triumph for him and for his Satyagraha. The committee carried on an enquiry and unanimously came to the conclusion that the grievances of the cultivators were genuine and recommended that action should be taken to remove them. Among the recommendations were that the planters should abstain from doing anything which compel the cultivators to rise in revolt. They should not collect any cesses from them and at the same time they recommended what other concessions needed to be granted to them. Thought all their grievances were not removed, these recommendations did improve the economic position of the cultivators considerably. The provincial Government accepted the recommendations and gave effect to them.

Thanks to the successful Satyagraha at Champaran Gandhiji became the undisputed leader of the people in the rural areas not only of Champaran but also in the other districts of Bihar. The people reposed complete confidence in him and became his trusted followers in every movement he launched. They lost all sense of fear of the European and other officials and became assertive. The province of Bihar as a whole became politically conscious. Gandhiji was able to get a large number of persons belonging to younger groups as his followers.

In this connection it is worthy of notice that in his Satyagraha Gandhiji did not seek the help either of the Congress or of the senor political leaders. He relied entirely on himself and on those who voluntarily became his devoted followers. This attracted the attention of the people in other provinces also and soon recognition came to him as the only man who had the mettle to become an all India leader. The efficacy of the weapon of Satyagraha in removing injustice from which the people suffered and even in getting Swaraj was clearly established.

It was not as if at Champaran, Gandhiji concerned himself merely with the problem of indigo cultivation. He sent volunteers into villages to spread literacy among the peasants, teach them modern rules of health both in theory and practice, to bring about the uplift of the harijans and to start cottage industries. He inculcated in this way the idea of service to the ordinary people among his educated followers. This also enhanced his popularity in Bihar and they came to believe just as he did that political freedom though of great values was not the only desirable end to be sought after and that what was really needed was the improvement of the masses in all directions. Gandhiji's Satyagraha in Champaran made him an all India leaders and the guide, friend and philosopher of the masses.

Satyagraha of the Peasants at Kaira

The next Satyagraha was in the district of Kaira. The situation in Kaira was very much different from that at Champaran. The peasant there were not so illiterate and ignorant or so impoverished as those in Champaran. There was an affluent class known as the patigars. They not only carried on agriculture in an efficient manner but also had trade connections with east Africa where a number of Gujaratis were settled as traders in those days. In spite of their affluence, they did not find it necessary to take the politics. It was only under the influence of Besant's Home Rule Movement a few branches of which were set up in the area that there was a beginning of a political awakening among them. They were also influenced by what Gandhiji did as the president of the Gujarati Sabha to which reference is already made. In 1918, they had a special problem to solve for which they sought the help of Gandhiji. There was a total failure of rains. The agricultural income touched a new low and the war led to a big rise in prices. The Agriculturists barring the rich were not in a position to pay the land revenue. They were at the same time unwilling to sell their movables and cattle to pay their dues. They made representations to the Government but the districts officials were of the view that the failure of the crops was not such as to warrant either to remit the land revenue in full or do reduce it. The peasant did not know what to do in the circumstances. They approached Gandhiji for advice. He told them that he would examine their case and if he as really convinced that there was failure of crops, he would help them. He toured the villages, collected evidence and came to the conclusion that there was really a case for remission of land revenue. He made representation to the district authorities and to the provincial Government and when these failed, he approached the Central Government in the hope that they would be fair, just as they were in Champaran. But they refused to interfere in the matter. It was that Gandhiji advised the cultivators to resort to Satyagraha. It meant that they should not pay the land revenue and they should suffer all the penalties that followed non-payment. He asked them to sign a pledge to the effect. And he also made it clear that under no circumstances should a pledge once taken be broken. It was thus the Satyagraha movement was started by the whole body of peasants in Kaira District. The movement continued for about two months with great vigour. It had the desired effect on the provincial Government and the district authorities in that a number of concessions were granted. Though they did not remit the entire land revenue the concessions granted gave substantial relief to the peasant Gandhiji advised them that they should be satisfied with the relief which they accepted. The Satyagraha thus ended in victory for the peasants.

If in Champaran it was Gandhiji who offered Satyagraha in Kaira the entire peasant population took part in it. They were willing to undergo the penalties imposed upon them and they learnt that self-suffering proved to be a rewarding exercise. This created a new confidence in non-violent struggle. Gandhiji had truly become the leader of the masses in the rural areas of Gujarat too. He first brought Bihar under his control and then Gujarat. Both these provinces became his staunch followers in all other movements.

Gandhiji chose his own sub-leaders to run the movement and among them was Vallabhbhai Patel who was at that time an advocate in Ahmedabad. Patel himself was a Patigar. He had English education, proceeded to England for higher studies became a barrister and enjoyed lucrative practice in Ahmedabad. Following Gandhiji's appeal he became his lieutenant and, in fact he was the real leader of the Satyagraha Movement in Kaira. He commanded the confidence of the peasants in the district and he displayed consummate ability as an organizer. Hence forward he became one of the most important persons in Gandhiji's Camp. The movement in Bihar brought Rajendra Prasad and Kripalani close to Gandhiji, while Gujarat gave him Vallabhbhai Patel. In the course of the campaign Gandhiji obtained the help of some members of the Home Rule League in Bombay who were mostly Gujaratis and this brought him into close touch with Bombay leaders. They were of great help to him not only during this Satyagraha but also the Rowlatt Satyagraha of 1919. The Kaira Satyagraha attracted nationwide attention and it marked yet another step in raising the stature of Gandhiji as an all-India leader.

Gandhiji's Satyagraha at Ahmedabad

The third Satyagraha which Gandhiji undertook was in Ahmedabad. Ahmedabad had for long been a commercial center. Numerous textile factories were established in the city and the mill owners made huge fortunes. The factories provided employment for nearly two lakhs of people who mostly belonged to the neighbouring rural areas. The relations between the mill owners and the workers were generally friendly. Gandhiji had some special reasons for establishing the ashram in the city of Ahmedabad. It was not only a center for producing mill cloth but also for handloom weaving and he thought the ashram would provide facilities for hand spinning and Khaddar which he wanted to revive. He also expected financial help for his ashram. But when he admitted the Harijans into the ashram one section of the mill owners who were orthodox objected and withdrew the payment of their donations. Gandhiji was not upset in the least. To him uplift of the Harijans was more important than getting donations. Luckily for him, a prominent mill owner, Ambalal Sarabhai, made a substantial donation to the Ashram. Gandhiji and Ambalal became intimate friends. Ambalal's sisters Anasuya Ben who went to England for higher education devoted her time on her return to the service of the labourers in the city of Ahmedabad and this brought her into contact with Gandhiji.

In the later part of 1917 plague spread in the city of Ahmedabad workers began to leave the city and go back to their villages creating acute labour scarcity. The mill owners raised the rate of wages by 75 percent to attract the labourers and to prevent them from returning to the villagers. Two months later the plague subsided and the mill owners declined to continue payment of the higher rate of wages. The workers however argued that because of the war there was an overall rise in the prices and it was impossible for them to work at the old rate of wages. They also pointed out that during the War import of cloth from Britain declined following which, cloth prices in the country went up resulting in huge profits to the mill owners. Consequently, they were in a position to pay higher wages. It was their demand that the wages should be raised by atleast 50 percent. The mill owners, however, turned this down. In that situation the labourers sought the advice of Gandhiji.

Gandhiji tried to persuade the mill owners to accept the demand. But they were adamant refusing to raise the rate by more than 20 percent. He then suggested a compromise formula under which the workers were to be paid at least 35 percent more than what they were getting before the outbreak of the plague. But the mill-owners stuck to their stand. Gandhiji then proposed the appointment of a mediator to decide what the reasonable rise in the wage should be and this should be binding on both the parties. In pursuance of this a mediator went into the problem and recommended a 35 percent rise. The mill-owners declined to accept the suggestion and thus broke the pledge they had given to abide by the mediator's decision. There upon Gandhiji asked the workers to resort to Satyagraha on the understanding that they would promise not to go back to work until the mill-owners conceded the 35 percent rise.

The Satyagraha they embarked upon differed from a strike in that the latter is quite often marked by violence and acts of destruction necessitating police intervention to preserve law and order. When the workers began the Satyagraha the police gathered in large numbers and took up positions in the city. But to their surprise the workers refrained from violence and behaved as a disciplined lot notwithstanding the fact that they found it difficult to ward off hunger as a result of unemployment. Every evening they were assembling in Gandhiji's Ashram where he taught them the virtues of non-violence's and the need to strictly abide by the pledge taken. Soon after the Satyagraha commenced, a few mills declared a lock out. But after some time they reopened there mills. Some of the workers by that time became tired of Satyagraha due to the economic suffering. They began to grumble that while they were starving Gandhiji was taking his food as usual, visiting Ambalal's house in his car and that he was unmindful of the suffering they were undergoing. Some of them wanted to go back to work notwithstanding the pledge they gave. Gandhiji to whose notice all this came saw that there was some justice in what they said about him and he undertook a fast declaring that it would continue until the mill owners agreed to raise the wages by 35 per cent.

The workers once again rallied around him. This fast of Gandhiji, the first of this kind which he undertook for promoting a public cause, brought about a change in the heart of not only Ambalal but several other mill owners. Many of them were Jains and it was painful for them to see a great saint like Gandhiji undertaking an indefinite fast. They held consultations among themselves and ultimately decided to abide by any compromise that Gandhiji might suggest. The fast was a great victory. He thought of a compromise which would prove honourable to both the parties. He suggested that the workers should return to work. On the first day they should be paid a wage of thirty five percent rise according to their pledge. On the second day they should be satisfied with a rise of twenty percent according to the views of the mill owners. But from the third day onward the rise of wages should be decided upon by a mediator and both the parties should abide by his decision. This compromise was accepted by both the parties. A professor in an Ahmedabad college was appointed as the mediator. He recommended a rise of thirty five percent, which was readily accepted, and cordial relations were established once again between the mill owners and the workers.

Gandhiji's Satyagraha in the dispute between the mill workers and mill owners in Ahmedabad city was unlike the Satyagraha in Champaran and Kaira. In Champaran Gandhiji alone went on Satyagraha. In Kaira only the peasant resorted to it. Gandhiji was of the firm view that the true leader was one who showed the way to the people by practicing what he preached. It is here he was different from the other leaders who were mostly satisfied with speech-making, debates and discussions, although there were exceptions to this as, for instance, Tilak.

Gandhiji attached great importance to compromise whenever any dispute arose. That is why he always insisted on the appointment of mediators whenever any disputes arose.

Significance of these Satyagrahas

The part which Gandhiji played in the Satyagraha in Ahmedabad made him the undisputed leader of the working class of the city. The Satyagraha in Champaran and Kaira made him the leader of the rural masses. And he endeared himself not only to the people in rural areas but also to those in urban centers. Although in the Satyagraha in Ahmedabad, the Government was not in the picture, it is of great significance since it further strengthened Gandhiji's claim to all India leadership. The sage of the three Satyagrahas which Gandhiji undertook in the year 1917–18 was the remarkable. Even those who did not agree with his ideas of Satyagraha had to recognize that he had a mass following in the country and little wonder they also accepted in due course his leadership though reluctantly. The Rowlatt Satyagraha was his next campaign which further raised his stature in the national context.

CHAPTER 14

THE ROWLATT SATYAGRAHA

The Nature of the Rowlatt Satyagraha

The three Satyagrahas which Gandhiji organised in 1917–18 were local in character in that they concerned themselves in the main with local issues. The Rowlatt Satyagraha which he organised in 1919 was the first All India Satyagraha. In addition to this, the issue involved in it was political and not economic as in the previous cases. It proved to be of crucial importance in making Gandhiji an undisputed leader and also resulted in strengthening among the masses a feeling of nationalism and hatred towards the alien rule.

The Rowlatt Satyagraha was so called because it was directed against the Rowlatt Act which the Government of India placed on the statue book on March 21, 1919. During the First World War the Government exercised arbitrary powers over the freedom of citizens and their movement under the Defence of India Act. But this Act was due to expire within six months after the War came to an end. The Government was however not in a mood to give up the powers it exercised once. It found an excuse for the continuance of its arbitrary power on the specious plea that militant revolutionaries (terrorists as they were called) were still active and that to put down their activities extraordinary powers were necessary. In order to draft a new Act which should take the place of the Defence of India Act, it appointed a committee under the chairmanship of Rowlatt, a British judge. The committee collected evidence on the seditious movement in India and made a number of recommendations in the report which it submitted. Among them were that power should be conferred on the police and magistrates to arrest any persons suspected of attempts to overthrow the lawfully established Government to try them in special courts and award any punishment on them including death, transportation and long term imprisonment. Suspected persons could also be taken into custody as undertrial prisoners for any length of time. It was open to the police and the magistrates to search the houses of persons without warrant to take possession of their property and to restrict their movement. To all these persons the ordinary law of the land would not apply nor the ordinary procedure laid down in the Penal code. It in effect substituted the rule of the police for the rule of law.

Protests were made against the recommendations by leaders irrespective of the party to which they belonged. They made representations to the Government and sent memoranda to take no action on the recommendations contained in the report. The Government did not pay any heed to them. In February 1919, two bills know as the Rowlatt Bills were introduced in the Central Legislature and after a heated discussion one of them was passed and placed on the statue book on March 21, in spite of the opposition of all the non-official Indians, both elected and nominated in the Imperial Legislature. Their voice did not count even though they were the representatives of the people. The official and non-official Europeans who commanded a majority and who represented no more than two lakhs of European residents in India were able to enact an arbitrary law in the face of the unanimous opposition of the Indian members. Even after the Act was passed, political leaders and associations sent representations to the Government to withdraw it but to no effect.

Gandhiji's Leadership

During this period as Gandhiji was seriously ill he did not participate in the protests against the report. By February 1919 he recovered and when he came to know that the Government was bent on introducing the Bills in the legislature, he gave notices to the Government and to the public that if the bills were passed into law he would organize a country wide Satyagraha on March 30, 1919. He convened a meeting of his followers at his Ashram in Ahmedabad. Many top ranking leaders like Swami Shradhanand of the Arya Samaj attended and most of them agreed with Gandhiji that as all constitutional weapons had failed, it was the duty of the people to offer Satyagraha. Gandhiji thereupon asked them to sign a pledge that they would resort to Satyagraha in case the bills were passed into Acts and they would continue the movement until they were repealed. He made it clear to them that the pledge once taken should not be broken. They agreed with him. It was at this meeting that he constituted a Satyagraha

Sabha consisting of those who signed the pledge and it was decided that Satyagraha should take the form of civil disobedience against the oppressive laws.

Gandhiji sent a communication immediately to the Viceroy on the decision of the Satyagraha Sabha. The Viceroy however paid no heed to this communication. Gandhiji thereupon organised branches of the Sabha in various cities and other important centers. Many of the leading citizens enrolled themselves as members. Thus Gandhiji was ready for starting a Satyagraha and as soon as one of the bills was placed on the statue book Gandhiji gave the green signal for the Satyagraha.

Gandhiji's Method of Associating the Masses with the Movement

Gandhiji however wanted to associate the people with the movement. But he did not want to them to take to civil disobedience like the members of the Satyagraha. His objective was that Governor should know that not merely educated and enlightened classes but also the ordinary people were opposed to the Act. The method which he chose for this purpose was unique. Gandhiji knew that any movement to which some religious significance was attached would easily attract the people. He said that on a particular day – the day first selected was 30th March 1919 and later it was changed to 6th April – all the people of the country should proclaim a hartal and suspended their normal business activities. They should fast and should offer prayers in temples, mosques, churches and places of worship. They should go in procession silently and hold public meetings at which resolution protesting against the Rowlatt Act should be passed. Fasts and prayer had a religious significance and a solemnity associated with them. It was not as if fasts are unknown. It has been the custom, for instance on the Sivaratri day. But observing a fast and offering prayers for a political purpose were new and unprecedented. Gandhiji understood the psychology of the Indian people and devised this unique from of protest.

As information about the change of date did not reach Delhi, March 30 was observed by the citizens as a day of fast, prayer and hartal. But in all other places it was April 6, that was observed as the day of protest against the Act. There were hartals through out the country. People fasted and offered prayers. They took out silent processions and passed resolutions. This was the first occasion when the people of the entire country expressed their feelings of protest against the alien Government as one man.

The day of protest was observed by and large in a peaceful and non-violent manner. Yet there were some centers where owing to the influence of a number of factors the people became violent.

Other Factors Responsible for the Satyagraha

A large number of people participated in the protest on the day fixed since to them Gandhi was a saint and a saviour of mankind. But this was not only factor which led to mass participation. We have to remember that acute economic distress prevailed throughout the country. People were impoverished, famines became frequent, unemployment mounted but Government did very little to improve the lot of the people. An atmosphere of discontent pervaded the whole country. A large majority of the people were not able to get even the essential of life like food and clothing. War increased further the burden of taxation. Officials resorted to measures to compel the people to subscribe to the war fund and to the war loans raised by the Government. In the outbreak of influenza in 1917 nearly six million people perished. Some of the provinces were ravaged by plague. The people were unable to give vent to their feelings of discontent. Gandhiji appealed to them to observe April 5 as a day of mourning and peaceful protest against the Rowlatt Act which gave them an opportunity to show their anger. People followed Gandhiji on this occasion more to show the economic discontent that prevailed among them. This was all the more so in Punjab when during the years of the War the people suffered most from the arbitrary rule of the Governor Sir Michael Odwyer who compelled the people to become recruits to the army and adopted severe measures to collecting the war fund and the war loans.

The other factor was the discontent that prevailed among the Muslims in particular. They were agitated over the Khilafat issue. The sultan of Turkey who was also a Caliph or religious and spiritual leaders was deprived of large part of his empire by the British and their allies as a result of the War because Turkey allied itself with Germany. In addition to this all the holy places which were under the control of the Caliph from the days of Prophet Mohammed came under the control of the British and their allies. This was resented to by the Muslims. Indian Muslims were also influenced by the course of events in West Asia and the treatment accorded to the Caliph and leaders like Mohammed Ali and Shoukat Ali began an agitation in favour of the restoration to the Caliph the political and religious status which rightly belonged to him. When their protest fell on deaf ears, they turned to Gandhiji who they knew was a friend of the Muslims. Like the Hindus they also accepted his leadership and they made common cause with the Hindus in observing the day fixed by Gandhiji as a day of protest, fast and prayers. They also opened their mosques to the Hindus in Delhi, Calcutta, Bombay and Several other places. From the platform of the mosques, many Hindus preached their sermons which were as eagerly listened to by the Muslims as the sermons of their own ulemas and moulvis. This was unprecedented in the seven centuries of Islam in India.

Thus in addition to the leadership of Gandhiji the two other important factors – economic distress of the people and the Khilafat issue – made a large majority of the people participate in the day of protest on March 30 in Delhi, and on April 6 in all other places. This indeed was the first occasion when the people of the entire country participated in a political movement.

The outbreak of violence in some places deserves explanation. Historians have gone into the subjects and attributed this to the influence of three factors – one was the psychology of he crowd or of the mob. People who are peaceful and non-violent individually participate in acts of violence when they are in a crowd or when they become part of the big mob. Crowds are often disorganized and they are easily excitable. So when on the day of the hartal they found that some persons did not close their shops they felt irritated and used violence to compel them to suspend business.

A second factor was the excessive use of force by the police and the military in dispersing crowds and in suppressing violence. This led to numerous deaths and injuries to a large number of people. The people grew further enraged and as an act of revenge against the police, the army and the Government which employed them and permitted them to use force, they attacked Government buildings, officials and took to various other violent activities.

A third factor which led to the outbreak of violence was the arrest of Mahatma Gandhi when he was only on his way to Delhi and Punjab to calm down the people. When his train came very near Delhi he was asked by the authorities to go back. He refused to obey the order and he was immediately arrested and forcibly taken to Bombay. The news of his arrest reached Delhi, Ahmedabad, Amritsar, Lahore and several places by April 10. And that was the signal for a mass upsurge. The violence which began on that day continued in some places because of the police excesses.

The Course of Satyagraha – Delhi

A reference to what happened in Delhi is relevant. It was on March 30 that they organised their protest against the Rowlatt Act. There was a general hartal in the city. But at the railway station the sweetmeat vendors did not suspend their business. The mob gathered there and compelled them to do so. A tussle then took place between them and the mob. The shop keepers refused to budge and sought the help of the station authorities who immediately took two persons into custody. On hearing this is a bigger mob gathered at the station and demanded that the two persons should be released. The authorities refused and called in the police who opened fire in which two persons died and several were injured. When this news reached the city a mob gathered at one of the most crowded localities in Delhi- Chandini Chowk – and here also clashes between them and the police took place and many lost their lives in firing and several were injured. The unwarranted firing by the police provoked the people in both the places. In the evening the Arya Samajist leaders, Swamy Shraddhananda addressed a public meeting appealing to the people to remain peaceful in spite of provocation by the police. While he was on his way back to his residence with his follower's one of the armed police pointed a gun at him. Immediately Swami Shraddhananda bared his chest asked him to fire if he had the guts. The policemen were dumbfounded and in the meanwhile a police officer appeared on the scene and prevented an outbreak of a violent clash. From that moment Shraddhananda became one of the most respected leaders of the city. The Muslims who earlier regarded him as their enemy followed him as enthusiastically as the Hindus did from then on.

Gandhiji wanted only a one day hartal, but the citizen of Delhi observed hartal on March 31 also in memory of those who died in the police firing. The bodies were taken in a big procession to the cremation ground and the leaders addressed an excited crowd. They were asked to be non violent strictly which they did. As some of the injured later died, the hartal continued for three more days. Similar processions were taken out on the following days. April 4 being a Friday thousands of Muslims gathered at Jumma Masjid, the most important mosque built by the Mughal Emperor Shahjehan. Hindu were invited to participate in the prayers, and Hindu leaders including Swami Shraddhananda were asked to sit by the side of the mullas and ulemas and address the gathering. This incident showed how in the days of the Rowlatt Satyagraha there was perfect understanding between the Hindus and the Muslims.

On April 5, the day of all India *hartals*, the citizen of Delhi also observed it. Nothing of significance happened during the following three days. Thousands of people went to the Delhi railway station to welcome Gandhiji on April 9, as he was coming at the invitation of the leaders to persuade the people to remain non-violent. But he did not arrive and they had to return disappointed. The next day came the news that Gandhiji was prohibited by the Government from entering Delhi and Punjab and on his refusal to obey the prohibitory order he was ordered to be taken to Bombay. This led to hartal in the city on April 10 and it continued for nine days. Leaders like Dr. Ansari, and Hakim Ajmal wanted the people to open the shops but by that time the leadership had passed into the hands of persons who were as easily excitable as the crowds themselves but there were no untoward incidents. Neither the Government not the leaders of the Satyagraha Sabha wanted the continuation of the hartal any more. When the shops were opened there was a police march through the streets. This created panic among the shop keepers who closed their shops immediately. On the 16th and 17th, twenty thousand jats from the neighbouring villages marched into Delhi with bamboo sticks and both the Government and the leaders grew alarmed. On the 18th the Seditious Meeting Act was proclaimed and meetings were prohibited. The military also were called in. It was then that the people found that it was no longer desirable for them to observe the hartal. They reopened their shops the next day and the hartal came to an end. That for nineteen days it should have been observed in the capital city of India was an eye opener to the authorities in making them realize the deep rooted hatred of the people towards them.

Bombay

There was a hartal in Bombay on April 6 which was peaceful on the whole. But when the news of the arrest of Gandhiji reached the people they not only observed a hartal but also indulged in violence, setting fire to shops and public buildings, and storming tramways. On 11 April, Gandhiji came to Bombay. He addressed the people and warned that he would have no alternative but to go on fast if the people did not observe strict non-violence. The police also exercised restraint unlike in Delhi. Both these factors restored peace in the city.

Ahmedabad

In Ahmedabad, the hartal on April 6 was peaceful but as the news of Gandhiji arrest reached there was an outbreak of violence. The labourers in the city were angered by the news of his arrest. They manhandled some of the Europeans. There were also rumours that Anasuya Ben was arrested. This was and additional cause of provocation. The police resorted to firing, and more than thirty people lost their lives and several were injured. Soon Gandhiji arrived in Ahmedabad, condemned the violence let loose by the people in the strongest terms and ultimately peace was restored in the city. The authorities were however bent upon teaching a lesson to the people as it were for what they did before the arrival of Gandhiji. A large number of people were arrested and tried. Some of them were sentenced to death and several more sentenced for long period of imprisonment though there was no justification for such a severe action. There were similar incidents in Kaira district.

The hartal in Madras, Calcutta and towns of Bihar and Uttar Pradesh was generally peaceful. In Calcutta Hindu leaders addressed gatherings in mosques along with the Muslim leaders. It was remarkable that except in a few places like Delhi and Ahmedabad the hartal was peaceful.

Its Suspension by Gandhi

On April 18 news of a tragic happenings in the Punjab reached Gandhiji who realized that he committed what he called a Himalayan blunder in calling upon the people to take the Satyagraha without preparing them for it. He suspended the Satyagraha. Many of his followers did not like the suspension but he told them that it was not his intention to abandon Satyagraha once for all and that he would resume it whenever he felt that the occasion demanded it. In July he said that he would himself undertake Satyagraha if no enquiry commission was appointed into the happenings in the Punjab. But he postponed it. He had some correspondence with the Viceroy. He felt that there would be no need for the resumption of Satyagraha. The frequent changes in his attitude were resented by most of his followers and gradually they lost their enthusiasm. They resigned from the Satyagraha Sabhas and in Delhi not only the Sabha was dissolved but also its records were destroyed.

Its Long Period Outcome

The Satyagraha may thus seem to have been a failure. It was undertaken to get the Rowlatt Act repealed. But the Government did not repeal it. Moreover the Satyagrahis took a pledge they would continue the movement until the Act was repealed but they abandoned it before they realized their objective. But from a long term point of view the Rowlett Satyagraha cannot be regarded as a total failure. It was the first occasion when there was an all India movement for a given objective. The hartal was observed simultaneously all over India. Secondly there was participation by the masses as well as the educated classes. Urban workers, peasants, shop keepers and in fact people engaged in diverse occupations participated in it. This was a visible sign of awakening among the masses. In the third place, it created unity between Hindus and Muslim and showed that such a unity was not an impossible task. It was during the Rowlatt Satyagraha that Gandhiji became an all India leader and this position he maintained all through. On the political views of Gandhiji also the Rowlatt Satyagraha exercised a great influence. To help him in the movement, a number of leaders came forward but many of them deserted him as they did not agree with his strategy. He, therefore, came to the conclusion that he should no longer rely on undependable individual leaders but should capture the Congress and use it as an instrument for carrying on his political work in future. During 1916-19, though he started and carried on many Satyagraha movements, he did not like to associate Congress with any of them. But the Rowlatt Satyagraha changed his attitude towards the Congress. He attended the Amritsar Session of the Congress in 1919 and took an active part in its deliberations. One section of the delegates led by Tilak and C.R. Das wanted to condemn the Montagu-Chelmsford reforms while another section led by Jinnah and Madan Mohan Malavya, wanted to give it a trial. Gandhiji shared the latter view and in a powerful speech supporting the reforms he declared he would undertake a nation wide campaign in its support. It was then that a resolution acceptable to both the sections was passed. This clearly proved that even men like Tilak and C.R. Das found that they should take Gandhiji's views into considerations and not ignore them. Though this did not yet result in making him the master of the Congress, it certainly was the first step in this direction and it became an accomplished fact at the Calcutta and Nagpur sessions in the following year. The Rowlatt Satyagraha indeed was an important stage in the politics of the country and in the history of the freedom movement.

The Causes of the Punjab Tragedy

The year 1919 witnessed the most tragic happenings in the Punjab. It was the making of the tyrannical rule of Michael O' Dwyer who became the Lieutenant Governor of Punjab in 1913. He had a total mistrust of the middle class intelligentia and alienated them completely by his measures which wrecked one of their leaders Har Krishan Lal and his financial concern. This led to heavy losses not only to Har Krishan Lal but also to the entire middle class in the Punjab and Delhi. During the War, he used force to get recruits to the army and to collect war loans and donations to the war fund. This alienated even the ordinary people of the Punjab. He did very little to arrest the phenomenal rise of prices during the period when even essentials of life became scarce. Nor did he take any relief measures when thousands of people suffered from influenza and plague. His primary aim was to prevent Punjab from coming under the influence of the Congress, Punjab was the province from which the British recruited the largest number of sepoys for the army, and if the people became politically conscious he feared it would adversely affect the recruitment process. It would not only weaken the army but also the hold of the Government over the people. This thinking motivated the tyrannical acts of Sir Michael O' Dwyer.

Lahore

Discontentment grew among the people as a consequence of his tyrannical rule. The Rowlatt Act gave an opportunity for them to give expression to this discontent. The people of Lahore met on February 4, 1919, even before Gandhiji's call for Satyagraha on the Rowlatt Act. They passed resolutions protesting against the Act. When the leaders heard of Gandhiji's call for Satyagraha on April 6, they were determined to respond to it on a large scale with the utmost enthusiasm. They had their preliminary meeting on April 2, and resolved to observe a hartal in a non-violent manner. The Muslims also joined the Hindus in a large numbers.

On April 6, there was a peaceful hartal in Lahore. In the evening, people took out a precession. Before they could participate in the public meetings the police tried to disperse the procession but due to the intervention of the local leaders this was prevented. At the meeting that took place in the evening a resolution protesting against the Rowlatt Act was passed, and the Government was urged to withdraw the Act immediately. These resolutions angered Sir Michael O'Dwyer. On April 7, at a meeting of the Legislative Council, he delivered a threatening speech in which he declared he would take action against the leaders if any untoward incident took pace on April 9. The Hindus invited the Muslims to participate in the Ram Navami celebrations. They responded favourably and in the evening the procession which was taken out ended in a public meeting at which once again the Rowlatt Act was critised and a resolution of protest was passed. Sir Michael O'Dwyer did not like the idea of Muslims joining the Hindus in processions or meetings and he grew ever more irritated in consequence.

On April 10, on hearing of the news of the arrest of Mahatma Gandhi who was on his way to Punjab and of Dr. Satyapal and Dr. Kitchlew, two of the leaders in Amritsar, the people of Lahore observed a hartal. The police fired on a peaceful procession leading to the death of nearly thirty persons. On April 11, too the hartal was continued. The Muslims invited the Hindus to participate in the Friday prayers in the famous Badshahi Mosque in Lahore. This was unprecedented. From the Pulpit of the Mosque, the Hindu leaders followed by the Muslim leaders addressed the gathering and immediately after the prayers were over, meetings were held outside the Mosque and a committee of fifty people was appointed to negotiate with the Government on behalf of the people. For the next four days the real Government in Lahore was in the hands of the People's committee.

The Government tried through landlords who were an influential community in Lahore to negotiate with the people's committee to bring the hartal to an end. But by then the landlords had lost all their influence and they could do little. There were however some who did not like the indefinite prolongation of the hartal and the suspension of business. The Government took advantage of this rift among the leaders. On April 12 it proclaimed the seditious meeting Act and banned the holding of meetings. In addition, the Governor called in the military, imprisoned important leaders and on April 14 introduced martial law in the city placing the administration under the control of Colonel Johnson though there was no warrant for this extreme step of making over the administration to the military.

For six weeks military rule continued in Lahore and the people were subjected to untold suffering. Curfew was strictly enforced and those who violated it were liable to be shot, flogged, fined or imprisoned. Shops were forcibly opened and goods were distributed free to the public. Lawyers and other professionals were ordered to register themselves with the authorities and forbidden to leave city without a permit. Martial laws notices were posted on the walls of private houses and inmates were punished if they were defaced or torn. Students had to report four times a day to the military authority. Motor cars and motor cycles owned by Indian were requisitioned for the use of the military and Europeans civilians. Fans and other electrical fittings were removed from Indian houses for the use of the British soldiers. The Europeans in the city applauded the Lt. Governor for all this, and at a farewell function organised when he left the city, he was praised as the protector of the poor and as the saviour of the British rule in India.

Amritsar

It was in Amritsar that events of the gravest consequence took place. On April 6 there was a peaceful hartal in the city. On April 10 when the people were provoked by the arrest of Dr. Satyapal and Dr. Kitchlew and Mahatama Gandhi, they took out a huge procession to the residence of the magistrate to find out why the leaders were arrested and deported. The procession though peaceful was attacked by the police. As a result of police firing two persons lost their lives. The people immediately turned violent killing five Europeans. A woman missionary was thrown out of the cycle she was riding. A number of buildings were set on fire and destroyed. On April 11 too a hartal was observed. A procession was taken carrying, the bodies of the martyrs to the place of the funeral. On April 12, General Dyer came to the city with a military contingent and though no martial law was proclaimed the administration was handed over to him.

He had a number of leaders arrested and issued a proclamation prohibiting the holding of meetings. But large sections of people were ignorant of the proclamation. On April 13, which was the Hindu New Year's Day, some 20,000 people assembled at Jallianwala Bagh at a public meeting. As soon as the meeting commenced General Dyer came with a military contingent of European soldiers and sepoys and ordered that within two minutes the people should disperse or else there would be firing. The venue of the meeting was surrounded by high walls on all sides and there was only a narrow exit through which the people could come out. It was hardly possible for them to leave the place within two minutes. As soon as the two minutes were over General Dyer ordered firing which went on till the ammunition was exhausted. He even said that he would have continued the firing if he had more ammunition in his hands. As a result of the firing thousand persons are believed to have lost their lives and at lest three thousand people were injured. Dyer imposed curfew in the city, and it became impossible for the relatives of the injured to provide them medical help. Dyer did not consider it necessary to provide medical relief to the injured.

On May 14, martial law was proclaimed in the city with Dyer as the administrator. There was no justification for the proclamation of martial law and yet the step was taken by Sir Michael O' Dwyer to punish the people of the Punjab. Water supply and electricity were cut off. Public flogging was resorted to on a massive scale. A "crawling order" was issued and all those who passed through the street in which the woman missionary was thrown out from the cycle were ordered to crawl. The issue of third class tickets on the railways was prohibited. Cycles were commandeered. People who closed their shops were forced to open them and prices of commodities were fixed by military officers. A public platform for whipping was erected and a number of triangles for flogging were also erected in various parts of the city. Indiscriminate arrests were made and of them 51 were sentenced to death, 46 to transportation for life and several to imprisonment. Whatever Dyer did was approved by Sir Michael O' Dwyer. General Dyer was questioned by the Hunter Commission whether all that did not amount to a form of a frightfulness, he replied "No it was not. It was a horrible duty I had to perform. I think it was a merciful thing.

I thought I should have shot well and shot strongly so that I, or, anybody else should not have to shoot again. It was quite possible to disperse the crowd without any firing but they would have come again and laughed and I would have made what I considered to be a fool of myself". It was with such brutality and callousness that he administered the martial law for a period of two months in Amritsar.

Similar was the administration of martial law at Gujaranwalla, Kasur, Sheekpura and other places. The officers issued curfews orders, prohibited traveling by Indians, ordered indiscriminate flogging, wholesale arrests and punishments by summary courts and special tribunals. In Gujaranwalla, the administrator resorted to aerial bombing leading to the death of hundreds of people in towns and neighbouring villages. It was only in a war that aerial bombing on civil population is resorted to. The martial law administrators seemed to treat Punjab as though it was an enemy country that should be destroyed.

The developments in Punjab sent shock waves all over the country though owing to strict censorship only meager information was available. Gandhiji did not express an opinion on these happenings till he had complete information. He even defended the passing of the Indemnity Act by the Central Legislature whose intention was to indemnify all the officials of the Punjab for their actions during the period of the military rule. Gradually he changed his attitude and he suggested that the government should appoint a commission of enquiry into the happening in the Punjab. All the other political leaders agreed with him in this respect. Even Montagu was convinced that such an enquiry should be instituted which was set up under the chairmanship of the Lord Hunter, consisting of five Europeans and three Indians. Neither Gandhiji nor the other political leaders and the All India Congress Committee were satisfied with the composition of the Committee. They set up a non-official committee. Though Gandhiji was not associated with it in the beginning, he was subsequently made a member and in the matter of collecting evidence and drafting the report he played a crucial role. The non-official committee suggested that if the Government agreed to certain conditions which it laid down, it would co-operate with the official committee but the government was not agreeable to it. The non –official committee examined 1,700 witnesses and on the basis of the evidence collected it published a report on March 20, 1920. It was only two months later, on May 20, that the Hunter Committee came out with its report. The report of the non-official committee was unanimous while the Hunter committee produced two reports, one signed by the European members and the other by the Indian members who were in a minority.

Among the findings of the non-official committee were (1) For the violent happenings on April, 1919, it was not the Rowlatt Satyagraha that was responsible but the tyrannical rule of Sir Michael O'Dwyer and the arrest of Gandhiji, Dr. Kitchlew and Dr. Satyapal. (2) when peaceful conditions were about to return, Sir Michael O'Dwyer's Government hastily and unnecessarily introduced martial law and prolonged it for two months though there was no necessity for it; (3) the massacre which was the outcome of General Dyer's firing at Jallianwala Bagh was most indefensible. It was done deliberately to create terror among the people and the same was the motive of all the martial law officers while administering the province during the two months of martial law. (4) it recommended that Sir Michael O'Dwyer, General Dyer and other martial law officers as well as Lord Chelmsford, the Viceroy, who approved of their misdeeds, should be deprived immediately of their offices as that was the minimum remedy for undoing the wrongs done to the people of the Punjab during the period of the martial law.

The majority and minority committee reports of the Hunter Committee expressed the view that the outbreak of violence in Punjab was the result of the Rowlatt Satyagraha but maintained that the firings resorted to by the police and army were defensible and the punishment like whipping, crawling were undefensible and that the conduct of the Central Government did not deserve condemnation.

The majority report expressed the view that the people revolted against the British Government, and that necessitated the proclamation of martial law and its prolongation for two months. Though General Dyer resorted to too much of firing at Jallianwala Bagh it was not done deliberately by him. The minority report, however, condemned the action of General Dyer and the introduction of martial law and its prolongation. In very many respects the minority committee agreed with the findings of the non official committee.

The Government of India approved completely the findings contained in the majority report. Montague however fully condemned the action of General Dyer and other martial law officers and also criticized the administration of the province by Sir Michael O'Dwyer.

As a result of the findings of the Hunters committee report General Dyer resigned his office. His conduct was condemned by the House of Commons. However the House of Lords and a large majority of the public in Britain praised him. In appreciation of his services they presented him with a jeweled sword and a purse of 25,000 pounds. The Anglo Indians in India subscribed liberally towards the amount and women especially contributed more than men. More than the conduct of General Dyer, it was the praise bestowed on General Dyer by the House of Lords and by the British public that roused the indignation of the Indians.

Nothing was done either by the Government of India or by the Home Government to redress the wrongs done to the people of the Punjab. Sir Michael O'Dwyer and Lord Chelmsford continued to remain in office. Those who were punished and kept in prison were not freed. Neither they nor their relations were given any compensation. More than all this the officials responsible for the misdeeds were pardoned for what they did. Even the moderate leaders were highly critical of the attitude of the Government towards the tragic happenings in the Punjab. The failure of the Government to remedy the injustice done to the people of the Punjab brought about a complete change in the outlook of Gandhiji. He came to the conclusion that it was sinful for him to co-operate with the Government any more and that a non-co-operation Movement for the purpose of getting rid of the alien rule was necessary. The Punjab tragedy indeed paved the way for the Non-co-operation movement of 1920–22 inaugurating a new chapter in the history of the freedom movement.

❖ ❖ ❖

THE BIRTH OF THE NON-CO-OPERATION MOVEMENT 1920–22

CHAPTER 15

The year 1920 saw the birth of Non-co-operation which formed the first stage in the history of the country's freedom movement under the leadership of Mahatma Gandhi. It was started initially to solve the Khilafat issue which agitated the Indian Muslims at that time. Later the remedying of the grievous wrongs inflicted, on the people of Punjab was included in the aims of the movement, and still later Swaraj was included as its decisive objective. Thus when the movement took shape in 1920 it had three aims before it.

The Khilafat Movement

We have noticed briefly the nature of the Khilafat movement. The Indian Muslims became alienated from the Government because of the treatment accorded to the Caliph, the spiritual head of the Muslims, who was also the Sultan of Turkey. The Muslims wanted that the Sultan should not be deprived of his possessions in the South East of Europe or in West Asia and Arabia, and that till the Muslims shrines in Mecca, Madina and Jerusalem should remain under his control. A Pledge to this effect was indeed given by Lloyd George, the British Prime Minister, during the War and it was a partly because of this the Muslims in the Indian army fight loyally on the side of the allies. The Muslims insisted that the pledge given to them should be fulfilled.

Gandhiji identified himself fully with the movement from the beginning. Apart from his attachment to the Muslim community from his South African days, he was against and pledge given by the Government to be broken. He also felt as a Satyagraha it was his duty to undo the injustice done to any community let alone the Muslims and he was convinced that in regard to the Khilafat, a great injustice was done to the Muslim community. Above all he thought that that was a good opportunity for bringing the Hindus and the Muslims together and restore amity between the two communities. He called upon the Hindus to actively co-operate with the Muslims to solve the Khilafat issue.

In March 1919 a Khilafat Committee was constituted in Bombay. Another committee was also constituted at Lucknow under the leadership of Abdul Bari, a religious leader, who was a guru of the Ali Brothers. Gandhiji associated himself with both committees. The two committees held a joint conference in Delhi on November 23 and 24 to which Gandhiji and a number of Hindu leaders were invited. Swami Shraddhananda suggested that Punjab should also be included in the movement to be started. But Gandhiji was keen to confine it only to the Khilafat issue. Informally the conference decided on non co-operation and as a first step, the celebration which the government proposed to hold to mark the victory in the First World War was to be boycotted. Accordingly there was the boycott of these celebrations which enabled the ordinary people of the country to become acquainted with the Khilafat issue.

Following the passing of the Government of India Act of 1919, all the political prisoners were released and among them were Mohammed Ali, Shoukat Ali, and Abul Kalam Azad. They attended the Amritsar session of the Congress and after it was over a conference of Hindus and Muslims was held. It was resolved to send a deputation to the Viceroy, and another to London to confer with the British Premier, Lloyd George. Accordingly on January 20, 1920, a deputation waited on the Viceroy but he said he could not make any promise as the matter (Khilafat issue) was entirely under the Control of the British Cabinet. The delegation which went to London was led by Mohammad Ali. Lloyd George told the delegation bluntly that the Sultan of Turkey could not receive better treatment than that accorded to the Christian powers like Germany and Austria, that the Sultan had no right to rule over the non-Turkish countries of Western Asia like Iraq, Syria, and others, and nothing could be done to meet the demands of the Indian Muslims. Moreover the issue was not one which the British alone could decide. They had to take into consideration the views of the French, the American and other allies.

This caused deep disappointment to the Indian Muslims. It was decided that March 1 should be observed as an all India Khilafat day when there would be complete hartal. Gandhiji associated himself fully with this idea and called upon all his followers to take part in hartal which indeed was a complete success.

On May 15 the terms of the treaty offered to Turkey were published by the allies which sealed fate of the Caliph.

On May 30, the All India Congress Committee met to consider the Hunter Committee report. It entirely disagreed with the views contained in the majority report and upheld the views of the minority. It passed a resolution that Lord Chelmsford should be recalled and that other officials who were involved in the Punjab tragedy should be removed. Gandhiji and some Muslims members raised the Khilafat issue and suggested Satyagraha to solve it. Though the members of All India Congress Committee showed sympathy towards the Muslims in the matter, there were differences of opinion on the appropriateness of a Satyagraha in this context. It was decided that a special session of the Congress should be held on September 4, 1920 at Calcutta to consider the matter. Meanwhile on June 1 and 2 a Khilafat Conference was held at Allahabad to which several Hindu leaders were invited. Motilal Nehru, Lajpat Rai and Madan Mohan Malavya were among those who opposed the idea of Non-co-operation. The conference finally decided inspite of their reluctance to appoint a committee with Gandhiji as the chairman to work out the details of the Satyagraha programme.

The committee decided that Satyagraha should be started on August 1 on the Khilafat issue. The programme consisted of the renunciation of titles, boycott of schools and courts and carrying on propaganda in favour of the boycott of legislatures also. Accordingly the Non-co-operation movement started with a bang on August 1. As a first step Gandhiji returned to the Viceroy all the medals and received from the British during the Boer war and the Zulu rebellion. He brought under his control the Khilafat committee which was an All India Organisation. Much earlier than this in April 1920, he also became the president of the Home Rule League started by Anne Besant and that gave him the leadership of another All-India Organisation. Both these were important factors in strengthening his leadership. From August 1 till September a heated debate went on in country as to the merits and demerits of Non-co-operation. By that time Mahatma Gandhi decided on including the redress of the wrongs done to the people to Punjab as an additional aim of the movement though he was originally opposed to it. It became clear to him at the

Allahabad conference that unless this was done the Hindus would not fully co-operate with the Muslims in the Khilafat issue and the Non-co-operation movement might not be successful. Moreover he felt that the extremists among Muslims constantly spoke of violence and war. Inclusion of a large number of Hindus would serve as a restraint upon them.

Before the September session of the Congress met, Gandhiji toured a number of provinces and saw it to that as many delegates as possible who were in favour of Non-co-operation attended the Calcutta session as delegates. He also made a special appeal to the Muslims to attend the session. Lajpat Rai was the first to suggest that legislatures should be boycotted though he subsequently withdrew it. Gandhiji, however, liked the idea and he decided on including it in the programme of Non-co-operation.

The Special Session of the Congress at Calcutta

The special session the Congress met in Calcutta in September, 1920, with Lajpat Rai as president. There was an appreciable number of Muslim delegates from different provinces. The atmosphere in Calcutta was not very much for Non-co-operation movement. C.R. Das, Bipin Chandra Pal, and others were against it. Motilal Nehru, Jinnah and Malavya too were opposed to it. There was, therefore, a considerable amount of dissension between those who supported the Non-co-operation and those who opposed it. In the election to the subjects committee, Gandhiji managed to secure a majority of members favourable to his view. It was a convention that the Congress approved the decisions of the Subjects committees. A resolution was passed by the committee on the suggestion of Motilal Nehru that among the aims of Non-co-operation the achievement of Swaraj should also be included. The programme of boycott of schools, courts, legislature, and foreign goods should be undertaken in addition to the renunciation of titles and resignation of government servants. Swadeshi should be adopted. The subjects committee approved the resolution of Non-co-operation as a mandate after a heated controversy for three days.

Acceptance of the Non-Co-operation Movement

Several factor influenced its decision. One was the vote of the large number of Muslim delegates. The second was the change that came over Motilal Nehru. He gave up the idea of opposing Non-co-operation as he was influenced to some extent by the Muslims on whose support he relied in his own province of Uttar Pradesh. The third was the important role played by the Marwaris of Calcutta and the businessman of Bombay in influencing the decision.

Gandhiji agreed that all the items included in the Non-co-operation movement need not be taken up immediately and they might be introduced one after another. Bipin Chandra Pal moved an amendment to the resolution which said that a deputation on behalf of the Congress should meet the Secretary of State for India, impress upon him the need to introduce a new Government of India Act granting full responsible government and that if he did not agree to it then alone should the country take to the programme of Non- co-operation and that, in the meanwhile, a committee should be appointed to examine in detail the programme of Gandhiji and carry on propaganda in its favour. C.R. Das seconded the amendment but when the vote was taken in the subjects committee 144 were in favour of Gandhiji's resolutions and 132 against it. It was a victory for Gandhiji. Between the special and regular sessions of the Congress in 1920 elections to the legislatures were held. All those who sympathized with the congress refrained from standing as candidates and also from voting. The non Congress parties like the liberals and the Justice Party in Madras secured a majority in most of the provinces and were able to form ministers. The boycott of legislatures by the congress did not lead to any political deadlock of the kind expected.

In the open session of the Congress the resolution was further discussed but in the end, 1855 delegates voted for it and 873 opposed it. An appreciable section of the delegates remained neutral. The special session of the Congress made Gandhiji the leader of the national organization.

Nagpur Session of the Congress and its Significance

Resolutions passed at the special session have to be ratified by the plenary session of the Congress before they could be put into effect. The session of the Congress was held at Nagpur from December 26 to 31 under the Presidentship of C. Vijayaraghavachari. C.R. Das had a contingent of 250 delegates from Calcutta to oppose Gandhiji's programme on Non-co-operation. Before the session met

Gandhiji undertook an extensive tour especially in the Hindi region of the Central Provinces and got Jamanalal Bajaj, one of his intimate friends and admirers, elected chairman of the reception committee. A large number of delegates came from Gujarat, Madhya Pradesh, Delhi and other provinces who were all disposed in favour of Gandhiji. In the election to the subjects committee, Gandhiji's followers got a majority. C.R. Das discovered that not much purpose would be served by opposing him though Jinnah, Kapardi, the Maharashtra leader, and Malavya (who did not actually attend the session but sent his views in writing) were determined to oppose him. Gandhiji entered into a compromise with C.R. Das and accepted several suggestion made by him including the one that all the items in the Non–co-operation programme should be put into effect immediately and not in stages, that one crore of rupees should be controlled for the Tilak Swarajya fund, a crore of members should be enrolled in the Congress and that a labour union should be formed to enable the working classes to associate with the movement. In this amended form, Gandhiji's resolution on Non-co-operation was moved by C.R. Das himself and carried by a big majority. Among the other resolutions passed at the session were that the ideal of the congress should be Swaraj instead of colonial self government, that the All India Congress committee should consist of 350 members elected by the Congress and that it should work as a subjects committee, that there should be working committee of 15 members to carry out the day to day work of the Congress, and that the Congress should establish branches in districts, talukas and villages.

These changes in the objectives of the congress and its organization gave a new dimension to the freedom struggle. Gandhiji's leadership of the Congress was established beyond doubt. The acceptance of his Non-co-operation programme by the Congress was a triumph for him. From then on Congress and Gandhiji became synonymous. The year 1920 truly witnessed the birth of the Non-co-operation movement.

THE COURSE OF THE NON-CO-OPERATION MOVEMENT

CHAPTER 16

The Programme of the Movement

The three ingredients of the Non-co-operation movement were constructive work, boycott and civil disobedience. Gandhiji gave primary importance to constructive work. It consisted of Swadeshi in the most comprehensive sense of the term and included hand spinning, production, sale and wearing of khaddar and the revival of cottage industries and traditional handicrafts. In his view this would solve the problem of unemployment and remove poverty. The second item was Prohibition which was the gateway to the economic improvement of the weaker section of the society and a better moral life. The third was the removal of untouchability. Its removal would make for national unity and enable the people to face more effectively the alien government. To Hindu-Muslim unity he attached great importance as he thought the communal tensions which became a feature of Indian politics from about 1870 were a source of strength to the alien government and amity between the two communities would strengthen the nation and make the fight for freedom easier and more effective. He felt that all these items should be put into practice to achieve Swaraj with a firm faith in truth and non-violence. An alien government can hardly withstand the opposition of such a people. After all, it was to solve the problem of poverty and create a better social order that Swaraj was necessary and constructive work would bring into existence all the fruits of Swaraj. In such a situation foreign rule would come to an end and even if there were still remnants of it, it was not a matter that should cause concern.

Progress of the Movement

In the scheme of boycott were included the renunciation of titles, boycott of courts and public services, educational institutions, foreign cloth and liquor. Those who participated in the non-co-operation movement were called upon to give effect to this programme without reservations. And yet there was only a limited response. The number of those who renunciated titles, for instance, was small. Most of the title-holders were loyalists and no wonder very few cared to renounce them. The boycott of courts was a little more successful but even here the total number of lawyers who gave up their practice was about 150 in the entire country. Although the number was comparatively small in relation to the total number of lawyers, it should be noted that among those who gave up practice were eminent leaders like Motilal Nehru, C.R. Das and Tanguturi Prakasam. The boycott of educational institutions was most successful. Thousand of students left them. National schools and colleges were established and by about the middle of 1921 there were 1246 of them. Students received education in their mother tongue. Many of them learnt Hindustani and some crafts. They joined the ranks of the Congress volunteers and it was through their efforts that the programme of non-co-operation was worked out. They took an active part in the picketing of shops dealing in foreign goods and liquor. They sold khaddar. They collected foreign cloth and made bonfires of them. The volunteers were in charge of arranging public meetings, maintaining order and distributing Congress literature to the public.

Very few gave up service under the government as they were not ready to face consequential unemployment. But among those who resigned office was Subhas Chandra Bose, a member of the Indian civil service. He joined the ranks of the non-co-operators and became one of the most eminent leaders of the freedom movement.

The boycott of foreign cloth was a great success. Many merchants joined the movements and stopped importing foreign cloth. Handspinning and production of khaddar were popularized. At a later stage the Congress Working Committee ruled that all Congressmen should wear khaddar which was regarded as the national apparel. Women too played a significant role in hand spinning and in the sale of khaddar.

The campaign against liquor was also successfully carried out due to organised picketing by Congress volunteers and by women. Many liquor shops had to close down. Volunteers also took special efforts to see that abkari sales which brought large revenue to the Government were boycotted by vendors in auctions. The result was that in some districts the Government's revenue from sale of liquor fell by seventy to eighty percent. It was the most successful part of the non-co-operation programme.

In several villages panchayats courts were established to settle civil and criminal disputes. Efforts were stepped up to remove untouchability. Members of the untouchable castes were enrolled as volunteers and they sat alongside of the so-called highcaste people at public meetings. This was the first step in the direction of the removal of untouchability in 1921–22.

One of the objectives of the non-co-operation movement was to find a solution to the Khilafat issue. The Muslims realized that unless they had the co-operation of the Hindus they would not be able to bring sufficient pressure on the authorities to realize their objective. The year 1921–22 witnessed tremendous unity between the two communities. Not that there were no communal riots at all, the most noteworthy being the rebellion of Moplah Muslim in Malabar.

For Gandhiji non-violence was a creed, even more important than the achievement of Swaraj. Some of his followers treated it as a matter of expediency. There were extremists among his followers who did not shun faith in violence and among them were the Ali Brothers, Mohammed Ali and Shoukat Ali. Occasionally they spoke about the need to resort to violence and that Muslims should support the Afghans if they invaded India. That was the time of war between India and Afghanistan. When Gandhiji interviewed the Viceroy in May 1921 the Viceroy pointed out to him the statement made by the Ali Brothers. Gandhiji assured him that such statements will not be repeated. He made the Ali Brothers apologise for what they said and communicated the apology to the Viceroy. At the Khilafat conference held in Karachi under the Presidentship of Mohammed Ali he stated that it was wrong and sinful for the Muslims to serve in the British Army and appealed to them to withdraw. Similar statements were also made by Shoukat Ali. Both of them were prosecuted and sentenced to imprisonment. Gandhiji reacted to this step and called upon his followers to repeat the statement made by the Ali Brothers at public meetings. He said that it was the elementary right of every citizen to appeal to the people not to serve under a foreign government. Government thought of arresting Gandhiji also. But Sir Tej Bahadur Sapru who was then a member of the Viceroy's Executive council told the Viceroy that most of the tragic happenings in Punjab during the days of the Rowlatt Satyagraha were the outcome of Gandhiji's arrest and that it would be unwise to take action against him when the non-co-operation movement was at its height. The Viceroy refrained consequently from taking any action against him.

Demand for Civil Disobedience

Meanwhile opinion was strengthening among the non-co-operators that neither constructive work nor boycott would bring Swaraj promised by Gandhiji by the end of the year. They forgot however the condition which Gandhiji laid down for achieving Swaraj, namely the completion of the constructive work and various items of Boycott. Leaders in the provinces were more enthusiastic about civil disobedience than constructive work or boycott. In some provinces such movements had already started as for instance, the Perala-Chirala struggle in Andhra under the leadership of Duggirala Gopalkrishanayya, the Satyagraha in Palnad, the defiance of forest laws as in Bihar, the refusal of labourers to work in the tea plantation owned by the Europeans in Assam and the refusal of tenants of zamindars and talukdars in Uttar Pradesh to pay rents. Some of these were not to the liking of Gandhiji. But he could not ignore the views and sentiments of local leaders who encouraged such movements as they appealed more to the masses than the distant goals of Swaraj and constructive work. So great was the pressure that at the meeting of the All India Congress Committee held in November 5, 1921 at Delhi a resolution was passed giving discretion to the provincial congress committees to start civil disobedience movements in any area within their jurisdiction provided the people were habitual wearers of khaddar, strictly followed the principle of truth and non-violence and worked for Hindu-Muslim unity. And with this resolution the movement entered the third stage.

Violence in Bombay During the visit of the Prince and Princess of Wales

Gandhiji said that he would himself undertake a No-tax campaign in Bardoli Taluk in Gujarat from November 23. All were eager to watch the course of the campaign under his personal supervision. But he postponed the campaign owing to the outbreak of riots in Bombay from November 17 to 21 in connection with the visit of the Prince of Wales. The Government of India invited the Prince and Princess of Wales to visit the country and it wanted to accord them a royal welcome in the belief that this would promote the loyalty among the people and turn them away from the non-co-operation movement. The Congress however passed a resolution in July that the visit of the Prince and Princess should be boycotted and that a hartal should be observed throughout the country on the day of their landing. Accordingly when they landed in Bombay on November 17, a hartal was observed in all parts of the country but while it was peaceful everywhere else violence erupted in the city of Bombay. Some non-co-operators attacked the Parsis, Europeans and Anglo Indians who participated in a reception to the royal guests by the Governor. Parsi women were the target of attack and this irritated all the three communities. From November 18 to 21 they used pistols and guns freely threatening the crowds, and the police also resorted to firing with the result that 53 persons lost their lives and more than four hundreds were injured.

Among those who were killed were 45 non-co-operators. These incidents horrified Gandhiji. He appealed in vain to the people to be peaceful. He got disillusioned with the trend of events and wondered why and how the message of non-violence which he preached for years had no effect on the people. He undertook a fast for three days to atone for calling upon the people to take to Satyagraha when they were not ready for it. He then postponed his no-tax campaign in Bardoli which he wanted to start on November 23.

This caused much disappointment to the leaders and the rank and file of non0co-operators. They wondered why the movement in Bardoli which was hundreds of miles away from Bombay should be postponed because of the happenings in the city. The Muslims began to feel that the postponement meant the unwillingness of Gandhiji to actively lead the Khilafat movement. Some of them even talked of resorting to violence to bring pressure on the Government and to carry on the movement without the help of the Hindus.

Government Policy of Repression

The Government kept a watchful eye on these developments. It was the policy of the Central Government during the non-co-operation movements not to allow the provincial Government to take arbitrary decisions. They did not want a repetition of the misdeeds perpetrated by Sir Michael O'Dwyer. But the outbreak of violence in

Bombay and the Moplah rebellion in Malabar brought about a change in the policy of the Central Government which gave a free hand to the provincial Governments to maintain law and order even by recourse to repressive measures.

The Bengal Government thereupon banned the volunteer organizations and placed innumerable restriction on the holding of public meetings and on the press. Similar action was taken in other provinces. The ban on volunteer organizations struck a blow to the non-co-operation movements since the political leaders mostly depended on the volunteers to carry on the movements.

C.R. Das decided to defy the ban in Bengal. He first sent his son and later his wife to work as volunteers and sell khaddar. The police arrested them and put them in prison. This roused the anger of the people of the entire province. More and more persons started defying the ban. The jails were filled with such persons and when there was not enough room for putting more men and women in jails, those who defied the ban were severely beaten up with lathis or taken to distant places in lorries only to be abandoned. On December 10, C.R. Das himself defied the ban and was sentenced to imprisonment. Soon Motilal Nehru, Lajpat Rai and other eminent leaders were put behind bars. The situation was getting critical and even the Moderates felt that it was wrong on the part of the Government to adopt a repressive policy. The Viceroy feared that even the Moderates might join the ranks of the non-co-operators and he therefore wanted to negotiate with them.

Another reason which prompted Lord Reading, the Viceroy, to think of negotiations was that the Prince and Princess of Wales were to visit Calcutta on December 24 and he did not want a repetition of what happened in Bombay. Through Malavya he sent word to C.R. Das who was then in prison that if the non-co-operation movement was called off and no hartal was observed on the day of the visit of the prince and princess to Calcutta all political prisoners would be freed and he would call a round table conference representative of political parties in the country to workout a scheme of reform to widen the scope of provincial autonomy. C.R. Das welcomed this proposal as a sign of victory of the non-co-operation movement. He consulted Maulana Azad who was also in prison, but before taking a final decision he wanted to consult Gandhiji. Correspondence went on for four days. Lord Reading grew vexed with this delay and called off the proposed negotiations. C.R. Das and others blamed Gandhiji for the dilatory tactics.

Ahmedabad Session of the Congress

The prince and princess visited Calcutta on December 24. The hartal was completely peaceful. In spite of this, the Government did not give up its policy of repression. It was in this atmosphere that the congress met for its annual session at Ahmedabad in the last week of December. C.R. Das was elected President but as he was in prison his place was taken by Hakim Ajmal Khan. The most important resolution passed was that the non-co-operators should resort to civil disobedience as that was the only way by which irresistible pressure could be brought on the Government.

The leaders of the other political parties were apprehensive of the outcome of the civil disobedience. They convened a conference in January at Bombay, and resolved that the Viceroy should reopen negotiations with the Congress leaders by holding a round table conference. Gandhiji who attended the conference as an observer said that he would postpone his no tax campaign at Bardoli which he wanted to start in accordance with the resolution passed by the Congress to February so that the Viceroy would have enough time to take a decision on the resolution passed by the All Parties' Conference. The Viceroy did not respond favourably to the resolution on the ground that Gandhiji did not call off the non-co-operation movement unconditionally and that he only postponed the no-tax campaign.

Gandhiji then wrote to the Viceroy informing him of his intention of starting the no-tax campaign in Bardoli. But at the same time he offered to give it up if the Viceroy agreed to the conditions which he proposed. But the Viceroy was in no mood to agree. Gandhiji, therefore, had no other alternative than to start the campaign on the day fixed by him. The entire country watched what the outcome would be.

Chauri Chaura Incident and Suspension of the Movement

On February 4 unprecedented violence took place at Chauri Chaura in Gorakhpur district, in U.P when a gathering of non-co-operators seized 22 policemen who fired at them and after confining them in a house set fire to it. All of them perished. This sent shock waves even amongst the non-co-operators in U.P. They appealed to Gandhiji that it was dangerous to continue the non-co-operation movement in such circumstances. Gandhiji felt stunned and thought that the country was not ready yet to carry on a non-violent campaign against the Government.

At the Ahmedabad session of the Congress held in December 1921. Gandhiji was given full authority to guide the movement. He used his discretionary powers not only to suspend the no-tax campaign but also the entire non-co-operation movement. The Congress Working Committee met at Bardoli a few days later to ratify the decision of Gandhiji and this was confirmed by the All India Congress Committee at the meeting in Delhi. The non-co-operation movement which commenced in 1921 ended in February 1922.

C.R. Das, Motilal Nehru, Lajpat Rai, and several others severely criticized Gandhiji for suspending the movement, and they wrote to him expressing feelings of vexation and disgust. This created a wide rift between him and the other political leaders. The Muslims also became completely alienated from him. At the meeting of the All India Congress Committee held at Delhi a resolution of no confidence in him was moved but it was lost. However all this led the Government to believe that he was no longer the popular leader he was in 1921–22.

Trial and Imprisonment of Gandhiji

The British Cabinet and some provincial Government in India for long wanted the Central Government to take action against Gandhiji. But nothing could be done as long as he commanded the confidence of the other political parties, the Muslims and the large mass of politically conscious people. Since the Government thought that there would be no risk any more in taking action against him Gandhiji was prosecuted for sedition on March 10, and the District Judge of Ahmedabad who tried him sentenced him to six years imprisonment as was done in the case of Bal Gangadhar Tilak. During the trial Gandhiji made a statement at once dignified and full of patriotic fervour which clearly revealed his basic political philosophy. It was listened to with great care by the District judge, by the jurors and by all the people assembled in the court. Many compared his trial to that of Socrates. Gandhiji himself requested the judge to impose on him the maximum punishment permitted by law and a punishment not less than that imposed on Bal Gangadhar Tilak. After the verdict he was taken to Yerrawada jail in Poona. Thus ended a glorious chapter in the history of the freedom movement.

Results of the Non-co-operation Movement

Ostensibly the non-co-operation movement was not a resounding success in as much as the three objectives for which it was started were not achieved. Neither the Khilafat issue nor the redressal of Punjab wrongs nor even the attainment of Swaraj was anywhere nearer a solution. A pessimistic view, however, is not warranted for we have to remember that winning freedom from alien rule is not a matter that could be accomplished overnight. Did not the Americans fight for seven long years with Britain for achieving independence? The Italians had to carry on wars for nearly half a century from 1820–70 to achieve final liberation from Austrian rule. In these and other cases those who fought for independence secured considerable foreign help also. The freedom movement in India was then only a year old and little wonder the British, who at that time owned nearly one fifth of the world could not be thrown out.

The movement did produce number of positive results which helped the revival of the freedom movement later on a much larger scale. The masses took and active part in every part of the country to give it a popular character. The people lost all fear of the Government, of the police, jails, and even of the armed soldiers. Women played and important role alongside of men. It is no insignificant gain that there was a tremendous political awakening in the country.

There was also a great upsurge in rural areas which were hitherto untouched by the political movement. Besides, the organizational superiority of the Indian National Congress was confirmed as a result of the movement. Unlike the previous Satyagraha, Gandhiji carried on this movement under the auspices of the Congress. And from then on the Congress became the leading political body in the country and the Government was obliged to conduct political negotiations only through the Congress. All other organizations paled into insignificance except, of course, the Muslim League which was revived later.

The leadership of Gandhiji was accepted by the masses and any setback to his popularity was no more than temporary. He continued to remain the leader of the movement all through the struggle.

❖ ❖ ❖

THE DEVELOPMENT FROM 1921–28

CHAPTER 17

Disillusionment over the Montagu–Chelmsford Reforms

The period between 1921 and 1928 witnessed a number of momentous developments in the country besides, of course, the non-co-operation movement which shook the entire sub-continent. Among them the Montagu-Chelmsford reforms which came into operation in January 1921 stand foremost though they caused considerable disillusionment. Even the Liberal Party and the Justice Party which formed ministries felt that real power was not transferred to them but continued to be retained by the members of the Indian Civil Service and the Governor of the Provinces. Though under Dyarchy the ministers were empowered to deal with the departments transferred to them the rules and regulations were so framed under the Government of India Act that they enabled the Secretaries to exercise real control over them. The Secretaries were empowered even to appeal to the Governors whenever they differed from the views of the ministers and in several cases the Governors overruled the ministers contrary to all established norms of parliamentary form of Government. Finance being a reserved subject the Ministers were not able to introduce the improvements they thought desirable because they had absolutely no hold over the purse. They could not get adequate finances for improving education, agriculture, industries, etc. which were under their control. Governors overruled ministers at Cabinet meetings. Though the elected members were in a majority in the provincial legislature they did not constitute a single homogenous party. Some of them were in opposition to the Ministry of the day. But the ministers were able to continue with the support of the nominated and official members.

Their excessive reliance on the nominated and official members also made them subservient to the Governor depriving them of the independent status which they should have enjoyed in any scheme of responsible Government. As these defects became more and more pronounced even the parties which were enthusiastic in the beginning about Dyarchy became thoroughly dissatisfied with it and began to agitate for reforms that would end Dyarchy, make the legislative council wholly elected to give substance to the system of responsible Government.

With the imprisonment of Gandhiji, the Congress became a divided house –one section believing in the revival of civil disobedience at the appropriate time and in carrying on constructive work in the meanwhile so that it might serve as a preparation for such revival. They did not want any change in the strategy or tactics of non-co-operation movement. In this category was C. Rajagopalchari and they came to the known as no-changers. The other section led by C.R. Das, Motilal Nehru and Vithalbhai Patel wanted a change in the Strategy of the Congress. They thought that the Congress should abandon the boycott of elections to the legislative council, participate in the elections of 1923, enter the legislature and carry on non-co-operation from within the legislatures. They came to be known as pro-changers.

The All India Congress Committee set up a civil disobedience enquiry committee to tour the country to report on the possibility of reviving the civil disobedience movement and also to gather opinion on Council entry. The committee reported that the masses were not for a civil disobedience movement and their enthusiasm for constructive work had wanted. But on the question of Council entry they could not make a unanimous recommendation, opinion of the members being equally divided.

The Rise of the Swarajya Party

Congress politics too was pressing through notable developments. The all India Congress Committee met in November to consider this report. But it left the final decision on Council entry to the Congress plenary session to be convened in December, 1922 at Gaya. The Gaya Congress met under the Presidentship C.R. Das. In his address he strongly supported the Council entry programme. But the Congress did not share his view, and led by C. Rajagopalchari the majority passed a resolution against Council entry. C.R. Das thereupon resigned from the Congress Presidentship and formed the Swarajya Party in co-operation with Motilal Nehru. The aim of this party was to participate in the elections to be held in 1923, and to fight the Government from within the legislatures. The Swarajya Party did not however leave the Congress.

The year 1923 once again witnessed a heated debate on Council entry between the No-Changers and the Pro-Changers. Maulana Azad felt that a split would only weaken the Congress. He wanted to bring the two sections together, and on his advice a special session of the Congress was held in September 1923, at which a resolution was passed permitting Congressmen who had no conscientious and religious objection to participate in the election to stand as candidates for the legislatures and to exercise their franchise. He called upon Congressmen not to carry on a hostile campaign against the pro-Changers. The Swarajya Party's stand was thus vindicated and the resolution was confirmed at the regular session of the Congress held at Kakinada in December under the Presidentship of Mohammed Ali.

In the elections the Swarajyists won 48 seats in the Imperial Legislature. They also won a majority of seats in the legislature in C.P and became the largest single party in Bengal. They secured some strength in Assam, Uttar Pradesh and Punjab. In Orissa and Madras, however, their showing was very poor. The success of the Swarajyasists in the elections to the Central Legislature was indicative of the support for the Congress and its policies.

The Work of the Swarajya Party in Central and Provincial Legislatures

The Swarajyists formed only a minority in the Central Legislature which consisted of 145 members. But 24 members who belonged to the party of Jinnah agreed to co-operate with them and this enabled the two parties to work together to defeat the Government on a number of occasions. Several Bills could not be passed because of the adverse vote. The two parties together formed what was called the Nationalist Party. Many cut motions were introduced to the Budget and passed. The Governor General had therefore to exercise his power of certification frequently thus demonstrating that even after the passing of the 1919 Act the people's representatives had very little say on the policy formulations. It was precisely to draw attention to this the Swarajyists entered the legislature and they certainly did succeed in this attempt.

The Swarajyists also introduced a number of resolutions on matters of public interest and got them passed much to the consternation of the Government. In February 1924, Motilal Nehru moved a momentous resolution demanding an amendment of the 1919 Act with a view to introducing full responsible Government. For this purpose a round table conference representative of all political parties was urged to be convened for framing a new constitution which should be put before a new legislative assembly elected for the purpose and if passed by it, it should be sent to the British Parliament for automatic approval. The object of the resolution was to ensure that it was for the people of India to decide what form of Government they would prefer to have. Inspite of bitter opposition from the Government the resolution was carried in the Central Legislature. It was a triumph for the supporters of the Council entry programme.

Instead of accepting the resolution the Government decided to appoint a committee under the chairmanship of Sir Alexander Muddiman, consisting of five official members and four non-official members, to suggest changes in the Act of 1919. The report of the committee was not unanimous. While the majority report suggested a few alternations in the Act of 1919 and was signed by the official members the minority report of the four non-official members recommended that Dyarchy should be done away with and all power should be transferred to minister responsible to the Legislature and that, even at the Centre, Dominion Government should be introduced. When the report came up for consideration by the Central Legislature the Government proposed that the majority report should be approved. Motilal Nehru introduced an amendment that the recommendations of the minority should be approved and that further examination of these recommendations should be left to a Round Table Conference or to some other kind of a representative conference. The legislature threw out the resolution proposed by the Government and supported by a large majority the amendment introduced by Motilal Nehru. This was also a big victory for the Nationalist Party.

Yet another success achieved by it was in regard to the recommendation of a commission appointed to enquire into the future of the Indian Civil Service under the chairmanship of the Lord Lee. These recommendations proposed to raise the salaries and allowances of the members of the Indian Civil Service and their privileges. Government placed the report before the legislature and wanted its approval. But Motilal Nehru proposed an amendment that in future the members of the Indian Civil Service should be recruited not by the Secretary of State for India in Britain but by the Government of India and that subject to rules made by the legislature a Public Service Commission should be appointed in India for the purpose of holding examinations for admission into the civil service. In spite of the opposition of the Government this amendment was passed by the legislature. These stand out as the achievements of Congressmen and their supporters in the legislature.

In actual practice however all this victory was infructuous because of the powers of certification the Governor General had. There was no way of compelling the Government to implement the resolutions which received the support of the legislatures. There were also occasions when Jinnah's party did not co-operate with the Swarajyists. This created considerable disappointment in the rank of Congressmen. They began to feel that Council entry was not after all that effective they thought it would prove to be. The Swarajyists were in dilemma. Some of them wanted to go further, accept ministership if they commanded a majority in the provincial legislature. In course of time that views became predominant in C.P. and the Maharashtra part of Bombay Presidency. Those who were in favour formed the party of responsible co-operators on the line originally suggested by Tilak that selective co-operation should be extended to the Government when useful and Government should be opposed only when such opposition was called for. Persons like Madan Mohan Malaviya and Lajpat Rai started the Hindu Mahasabha to safeguard the interests of the Hindu community as against the Muslim League which was revived in full strength in 1924 and which pursued sectarian policies as a whole. This division in the ranks of the Congress considerably weakened it and at the session of the Congress held at Kanpur in December 1926, a resolution was passed that the Congress members should walk out of the legislature and participate in its deliberations only when it was absolutely necessary. In the elections held in the later part of 1926, the Swarajyists got only a few seats in the legislature. The split in the Congress ranks and the formation of other parties opposed to the Swarajyists were mainly responsible for this. This held to disillusionment in regard to the programme of Council entry.

During the years 1924–26, the Swaraysists had majority in the Legislative Council of U.P. They however refused to form a ministry when invited by the Governor. When the non-Swarajyists Government was formed they passed a vote of no confidence against it and compelled the ministry to resign. The result was that the transferred subjects were taken over by the Governor. They also rejected the budgets in 1924, 1925 and 1926 and the Governor had to use the certification power to pass them as well as several other bills voted down by the Swarajya party. The party's main objective was to emphasise that the Montagu Chelmsford reforms were a sham and they did not transfer any real power to the elected members of the legislature or the ministers responsible to them.

In Bengal the Swarajyists under the leadership of C.R. Das constituted the single largest party in the legislative council. They too refused to form the ministry when invited to do so. When non-Swarajyist ministries were formed, he succeeded in throwing them out of office. The Governor had to administer all the transferred subjects. Bills which were highly repressive in character placing restraints on the freedom of persons, speech, association and the press were passed by the exercise of the certification powers by the Governor. C.R. Das thereupon threatened to carry on a province-wide agitation. The Government grew panicky. Both the Viceroy, Lord Reading, and the Secretary of State, Lord Birkenhead, thought it prudent to come to some understanding with C.R. Das who was prepared to reciprocate. At a number of public meetings under the provincial conference held at Ferdipur he condemned the acts of terrorism by the revolutionaries and stated that if the political prisoners were freed and the repressive laws and the regulations of 1918 repealed he was ready to enter into a compromise with the Government. It was generally held that better political conditions would prevail not only in the province but throughout the country by coming to such an understanding. Unfortunately C.R. Das died in June 1925 and with his death both the Viceroy and the Secretary of State gave up all idea of an understanding with the Swarajyists and the Congress.

Role of Mahatma Gandhi after his Release in 1924

The role played by Gandhiji in the politics of the Congress after his release due to illness in April 1924 before the expiry of the full term (and not because the Government was morally convinced of his innocence) is a matter of great significance. He decided not to take an active part in politics till the full period of six years was over, but he made a few exceptions to this rule. He disliked the split in the Congress between the Pro-Changers and the No-Changers and though he was personally against the Council entry he did not want to oppose the Swarajya party on this issue especially because the special session and the regular sessions of the Congress of 1923 passed resolutions in favour of Council entry. He, therefore advised the No-Changers not to criticize the Council entry programme but concentrate their attention on constructive work in respect of which it was possible for both the groups to work together.

At the Patna meeting of the All India Congress Committee held in the latter part of 1924, a resolution was passed at his instance under which all the political work of the Congress was handed over to the Swarajyists and autonomous bodies like the All India Spinners' Association of the Harijan Sevak Sangh were set up to carry on constructive work. He came to terms with Motilal Nehru and C.R. Das who did not have much faith in the Non-co-operation movement and it was agreed that the movement should be formally abandoned. A resolution to that effect was passed by the All India Congress Committee. The movement which was only suspended in 1922 after the Chauri Chaura incident was given up.

Gandhiji presided over the Belgaum session of the Congress in December, 1924 at which these resolutions were confirmed. From then on thought he attended the meetings of the Congress committee as a special invitee he gave up his connection with the Congress. Till March 1928 he devoted himself to constructive work and extensively toured the country to carry on propaganda in favour of Swadeshi, the removal of untouchability and Hindu-Muslim unity.

Growth of Hindu Muslim Tension

Meanwhile the rift between the Hindus and the Muslims widened after 1922. It was the Khilafat issue brought the two communities together and after the Non-co-operation movement was suspended by

Gandhiji in 1922, there was not much a possibility of the two communities working together on this issue. More over the political revolution in Turkey in 1924 resulted in the abolition of the post of Sultan and Caliph and led to the establishment of a republican form of Government. It automatically put an end to the Khilafat issue. These factors accentuated the differences between the two communities in the country. Several communal riots took place. The Muslim League which was none too active during the days of the Khilafat movement was revived and Jinnah took over its leadership. The communal riots led to a worsening of the political situation in general and efforts were initiated to bring about unity between the two communities. For this purpose Mohammed Ali, President of the Congress, convened a meeting in Bombay of all leaders of important political associations. The conference appointed two sub-committees one to frame a new constitution for the country and another to suggest a solution to end the tension between the two communities. The first committee did the work entrusted to it but the other committee was not able to arrive to any solution for the communal differences. As a result, the first committee's report also was put in cold storage. As tension continued Gandhiji undertook a fast for 21 days in Delhi with a view to resorting communal unity. Though everyone sympathized with his motives no acceptable solution was forged. Gandhiji ended his fast without being able to bring the two communities any nearer.

Revival of Muslim League and Jinnah's Demands

During the year 1924 Jinnah as the President of the Muslim League formulated certain constitutional proposals which in his view would bring about political unity between the two communities. Among them were . . .

1. that the future constitution of India should be federal in character with maximum autonomy to the provinces. He preferred such a system because though the Muslim were in minority in the country as a whole, there was a Muslim majority in provinces like Bengal, Punjab and Sind and provincial autonomy under a federal system would enable them to exercise power independent of the Hindu vote. It was in this scheme of Jinnah that the word federal came to be used almost for the first time.

2. that Muslims should get weightage in the Central Legislature and in the legislatures of all the provinces where they were in a minority.
3. that until adult suffrage was introduced they should be guaranteed a majority of elected seats in legislatures of provinces where population-wise they were a majority
4. that Muslim representative should be elected in separate electorates and
5. that the British Parliament should pass a new Government of India Act introducing full responsible Government in India.

It should be noted that all the parties were agreed on the need to introduce full responsible Government. The Hindu Mahasabha was not in favour of weightage being given to the Muslim community in the legislature. It was also opposed to separate electorates and consequently the political stalemate continued.

Political Stalemate in the Country by 1927

By the middle of 1927 political activity came to a standstill as the Congress itself was split into a number of parties – Swarajyists, the party of responsive co-operation and the Hindu Mahasabha. There was no agreement between the Muslims league and these political parries on the political issues. Government took advantage of the situation and refused to budge an inch in the direction of transferring more power into the hands of the people's representatives.

The stalemate was however sought to be broken by the appointment of the Simon Commission in November 1927. Such a Commission was to have been appointed in 1929–10 years after the passing of the Government of India Act of 1919. The Tory Government which was in power in Britain feared that in the general election of 1929, the Labour Party might come to power and it might appoint a commission which would be favourable to the Indian demands. Lord Birkenhead wanted to preempt this move by appointing a commission two years in advance.

❖ ❖ ❖

THE CIVIL DISOBEDIENCE MOVEMENT OF 1930—THE GENESIS

CHAPTER 18

Country Wide Boycott of Simon Commission

It was remarkable indeed that all political parties exhibited a rare sense of unanimity in deciding to boycott the Simon Commission. Three factors influenced them to adopt this attitude. One was that it consisted entirely of Britishers and there was not one Indian representative on it. The members had no first hand knowledge of the conditions in India and all political parties were convinced that the recommendations made by it were bound to fall short of their expectations.

Secondly by then people had realized that Swaraj was their birth right and there was no question of any Commission enquiring into the fitness or otherwise of the people of India for Swaraj. To co-operate with the Commission was inconsistent with national self-respect. It was a denial of the right of the people to rule themselves.

Thirdly, the Central legislature had already passed resolution that the culture Constitution of India should be settled by a Round Table Conference representative of all the political parties in the country, and the appointment of a Parliamentary Commission for the purpose went against such resolutions. And it was not surprising that all the political parties including the Liberals and the Muslim League resolved to boycott the Commission. This added a new dimension to the politics of the Country.

The Madras Session of the Congress

The Congress met in December, 1927 at Madras under the Presidentship of Dr. Ansari. Two of his resolutions which were passed were of great importance. The first was that the Simon Commission should be boycotted and a hartal observed in all parts of the country on the day of its landing in Bombay and also on the day of its visit to any place. The second resolution was that the subjective of the National Congress was the establishment of complete independence, and severance of all connections with the British Empire and not mere colonial self-government. In passing the resolution, younger leaders like Jawaharlal Nehru played an important part. Nehru had visited Russia and was influenced by the revolution which took place in that country in 1917 and by the political, economic and social programmes which it carried out. He became a confirmed Socialist. His ideas on the ties between Britain and India also changed. Many others like Subhas Chandra Bose agreed with him and this was responsible for the passing of the resolution on Independence as the goal of the Congress. There was not much opposition to it as Gandhiji did not attend the Madras Session of the Congress.

The year 1928 was a momentous one in the history of the freedom movement. It witnessed the boycott of the Simon Commission the drafting of a constitution for India by a committee under the chairmanship of Motilal Nehru appointed by an All Party Conference. Opinion also began to crystalline in favour of starting the civil disobedience movement in the case the British refused to respond to the demands of the Indian Nationalists.

The Simon Commission landed in Bombay on February 3. Hartal was observed on the day of its landing throughout the country and public meetings were held in protest against it and voicing the demands of the people. The Central legislature also passed a resolution expressing want of confidence in the Commission. Though the hartal was peaceful, the police resorted to unwarranted firing to disperse the processions especially in the cities of Madras, Lucknow, Calcutta, and Lahore. In Madras, Tanguturi Prakasam, the Andhra Leader, came to the scene of the firing and wanted to see the body of a victim. The police threatened to shoot him. He then laid bare his chest and asked the police to fire at him if they had the courage. The policeman became dumbfounded and withdrew the gun. At Lahore Lajpat Rai was severely wounded in the course of the firing by the police and succumbed to the injuries later. In Lucknow and Calcutta also the firings led to many killings.

The commission which was in India for a month came back a second time in October 1928 and stayed on till April 13, 1929. Hartal was observed in every city that it visited. The boycott resulted in the

Commission relying on the evidence of a few loyalists and its findings were such as not to enthuse the more important political parties.

Lord Birkenhead, the Secretary of State of India, more than once declared that if an agreed Constitution was formulated by the political parties in India he would take it as a basis of future constitutional reforms. Like most Britishers, he believed that in a country torn by dissensions the framing of a Constitutional agreeable to all parties was an impossibility. But the Indian political parties accepted the challenge. The Congress took the initiative in the matter at its session in 1927 and authorized Dr. Ansari, the President, to get such a Constitution prepared. He convened a meeting of the representatives of all important political parties, and the conference appointed a committee under the chairmanship of Motilal Nehru to prepare a Constitution and submit it by August, 1928.

Nehru Committee Report on Future Indian Constitution

The committee completed its labours by the date fixed. It recommended that India should have Dominion Status, that the Constitution should be federal, that the residency powers should be located in the Centres, that there should be adult suffrage and that a responsible ministry should carry on the Government at the Centres as well as in the provinces. It recommended that Muslim representatives should be elected in mixed electorates and their representation in the Center and the Provincial legislatures should be on the basis of the population.

Jinnah's Demands – His Separalist Policies

The constitution was approved at a meeting of the All parties Conference. But Jinnah, as president of the Muslim league, proposed certain amendments in regard to Muslim representation and urged that the residuary powers should be located in the provinces and not in the center. Though several were agreeable to the amendments proposed by him, the members of the Hindu Mahasabha opposed them and the question of Muslim representation remained unsolved. All parties were agreed at the conference that India should have Dominion Status and a federal Parliamentary form of government.

Jinnah, however, was upset that his amendments on Muslim representation were not accepted by the conference. This made him a staunch communalist supporting the separatist interest of the Muslim community.

Calcutta Session of the Congress

The Congress met at its annual session in Calcutta in December, 1928. Jawaharlal Nehru, Subhas Chandra Bose and others were particular about India severing all connections with the British Empire and they strongly opposed Dominion Status proposed by the Nehru Committee. Gandhiji in a compromise formula urged that for the time being Dominion Status should be accepted as the goal of the Congress and that the British Government should be given a year's time to take a final decision on the grant of Dominion Status, and if it failed to concede the demand within the year India should declare complete independence as its final objective and adopt civil disobedience as the method for achieving it. Jawaharlal Nehru and others saw that nothing would be lost by waiting for one more year and the compromise plan suggested by Gandhiji was accepted. It was thus made clear that Civil disobedience would be resorted to once again if the demands of the people were not compiled with by the Government.

The Government was greatly disturbed at the trend in favour of complete independence and it was equally alarmed with the reentry of Gandhiji into politics and by the resurgence of terrorism in certain parts of the country. The eminent revolutionary Bhagat Singh shot at Saunders, the police officer, who was thought responsible for the injuries received by Lajpat Rai during the visit of the Simon Commission to Lahore. The killing of Saunders was to avenge the death of Lajpat Rai. A little later Bhagat Singh and one of his colleagues threw a bomb inside the Central legislature when it was holding its meeting on April 8, 1929. He and his colleagues were arrested and kept in prison. It was about this time that Jatindra Das, a noted revolutionary, undertook a fast unto death. He died after fasting for 63 days. An attempt was also made to plant a bomb to destroy the train by which the Viceroy was traveling from south India to Delhi. The entire country was surcharged with emotion and the authorities were shaken to the core.

The year 1929 witnessed world depression and India too was affected by it. The prices of raw commodities fell and those of imported goods rose. There were strikes in factories and on the railways. The Communist party though banned infiltrated into the Socialists party and the Congress and promoted labour agitation.

Labour Government in Britain

It was during the days of the depression that general elections were held in Britain. The Labour Party was returned as the largest party in the House of Commons and a Ministry under Ramsay Macdonald was formed. The new government wanted to take steps to smoothen the relations with India, and the Viceroy, Lord Irwin, was summoned for talks. He went to Britain and after his return he issued a declaration on October 31, 1929 that it was implicit in the announcement made by Montagu in August, 1917 that India would have Dominion Status and that the British Cabinet proposed to convene a conference representative of all parties in India and Britain to settle the future form of Government and the Parliament would take into consideration the points of agreement, arrived at such a conference in settling India's constitutional future. As the Viceroy's declaration contained a reference to Dominion Status and to a representative conference Indian leaders welcomed it. They, however, wanted further clarifications but before they could meet the Viceroy there was an uproar in British Parliament against the idea of Dominion Status. The British Cabinet knew that it could not go ahead with constitutional reform unless it had the support of the Conservative Party and it, therefore, assured the Conservatives that Dominion Status was not the immediate objective but only the ultimate goal.

When Gandhiji, Jinnah and other leaders met the Viceroy on December 23, 1929 and asked him whether the representative conference would frame a Dominion Constitution for India he told them that he could not commit himself to it and that everything would depend upon the nature of the agreement reached at the proposed conference.

Viceroy's Unsatisfactory Declaration on Dominion Status

This clarification of the Viceroy disappointed them. It was clear to the leaders that Dominion Status was still a far cry and that unless pressure was brought to bear upon the Government the nation's demand would never be conceded.

Lahore Session of the Congress – Resolution on Independence and Civil Disobedience

It was under these circumstances the Congress met for its annual session at Lahore on December 29 under the Presidentship of Jawaharlal Nehru. Even at the end of one year the time given to the British Government, no decision in favour of immediate grant of Dominion status was taken. The congress thereupon declared itself in favour of complete independence and resorting to civil disobedience for achieving it.

Gandhiji was authorized to work out the details of the programme of civil disobedience in consultation with the Working Committee and the All India Congress Committee. And this precisely was the genesis of the civil disobedience movement in December 1929.

CHAPTER 19

THE COURSE OF THE CIVIL DISOBEDIENCE MOVEMENT

Declaration of Independence – January 26, 1930

Almost the first step that was taken to initiate the Civil Disobedience movement was the drafting of a declaration by the Congress Working Committee announcing India's determination to attain complete independence. The pledge was to be read at the public meetings in the whole country on 26th January 1930. It was a momentous as the American declaration of Independence. The declaration said:

"We believe that it is the inalienable right of the Indian people as of any other people, to have freedom and to enjoy the fruits of their toil and have necessities of life, so that they may have full opportunities of growth. We believe also that if any Government deprives a people of these rights and oppresses them the people have a further right to alter it or abolish it. The British Government in India has not only deprived the Indian people of their freedom but has based itself on the exploitation of the masses and has ruined India economically, politically, culturally and spiritually. We believe, therefore, that India must severe the British connection and attain Purna Swaraj or complete Independence.

"India has been ruined economically. The revenue derived from our peoples is out of proportion to our income. Our average income is seven pice (less than two pence) per day, and of the heavy taxes we pay 20 percent raised from the land revenue derived from the peasantry and 3 per cent from the salt tax which falls most-heavily on the poor.

"Village industries such as hand-spinning, have been destroyed, leaving the peasantry idle for atleast four months in the year and dulling their intellect for want handicrafts and nothing has been substituted, as in other countries, for the crafts thus destroyed.

"Customs and Currency have been so manipulated as to heap further burdens on the peasantry. British manufactured goods constituted the bulk of our imports. Customs duties betray clear partiality for British manufactures and revenue from them is used not to lessen the burden on the masses but for sustaining a highly extravagant administration. Still more arbitrary has been the manipulation of exchange ratio which has resulted in millions being drained away from the country.

"Politically, India's status has never been so reduced as under the British regime. No reforms have given real political power to the people. The tallest of us have to bend before foreign authority. The rights of free expression of opinion and free association have been denied to us and many of our countrymen are compelled to live in exile abroad and cannot return to their homes. All administrative talent is killed and the masses have to be satisfied with petty village offices and clerkships.

"Culturally the system of education has torn us from our moorings and our training has made us hug the very chains that bind us.

"Spiritually compulsory disarmament has made us unmanly and the presence of an alien army of occupation, employed with deadly effect to crush in us the spirit of resistance has made us think that we cannot look after ourselves or put up a defence against foreign aggression, or even defend our homes and families from the attacks of thieves, robbers and miscreants".

"We hold it to be a crime against man and God to submit any longer to a rule that has caused this four fold disaster to our country. We recognise, however, that the most effective way of gaining our freedom is not through violence. We will, therefore, prepare ourselves by withdrawing so far as we can all voluntary association from the British Government, and will prepare for civil disobedience, including non-payment of taxes. We are convinced that if we can withdraw our voluntary help and stop payment of taxes without doing violence, even under provocation, the end of this in human rule is assured. We, therefore, hereby solemnly resolve to carry out the Congress instruction issued from time to time for the purpose of establishing Purna Swaraj".

The Independence Day was celebrated throughout the country on January, 26. The declaration was read at hundreds and thousands of meetings and the people took the pledge in solemn silence that they would stand by it under all circumstances and make the sacrifices required for the purpose of making the country independent. It was glorious day in the history of the freedom movement and January 26 continues to be the most sacred day for the Indian people.

A few days later Gandhiji wrote a letter to the Viceroy in which he enumerated eleven points for the Government on which to take immediate action stating that if there was favourable response he would abandon the idea of civil disobedience. This caused surprise among Congressmen that he should have referred to a number of points other than Swaraj for the achievement of which the Lahore session of the Congress decided on starting the movement. But the real intention of Gandhiji was to test the sincerity of the authorities, whether even on points for minor importance they were willing to modify their attitude. No satisfactory reply was received from the Viceroy. Civil disobedience was seen to be inevitable and the only question to be decided was what from it should take. Although it was originally resolved that, only those who believe in non-violence as a creed should participate in the movement the All India Congress Committee permitted all Congressmen to participate in it to impart to its character of a real mass movement. It gave complete authority to Gandhiji to decide its form and its programme.

Gandhiji's Decision to Break the Salt Law

Gandhiji finally hit upon the highly ingenuous and unique plan of disobeying the salt law under which it was illegal for individual to manufacture salt. Government had a monopoly over its manufacture and it also levied a duty on salt. Many people ridiculed him for having chosen the defiance of the salt law for overthrowing the mighty British but subsequent event showed the practical wisdom of this step. Salt was an article of common consumption. Defiance of the salt law had a telling impact on every man and woman. Defiance of salt law was simple and yet effective in as much as the manufacture of salt by the common people was well within their competence needing no expertise. This naturally made it easy for the people to join the Satyagraha in large numbers with an active sense of participation in the movement. On March 2 Gandhiji wrote to the Viceroy informing him of his decision to break the salt law and set in motion the civil disobedience campaign.

Dandi March

It was on March 6 that he undertook, accompanied by seventy-nine inmates of the Sabarmati Ashram, the new famous historic march to Dandi in Surat District. He walked through the villages even as thousands of men and women witnessed the march with great enthusiasm and profound dignity. He conveyed his message to them and appealed to them not to defy the salt law until he himself did it. He reached Dandi on March 12. Early in the morning, he and his followers had a sea bath after prayers and picking a handful of salt on the coast by boiling sea water, Gandhiji symbolically broke the salt law.

Congress Carries on the Movement

Ever since the Jallianwala Bagh massacre the week from April 6 to 13 was being observed as a National Week in the country. Significantly enough Gandhiji called on the people to break the salt law during the National week. For the benefit of those who were far removed from the coast and were in the interior and, therefore, not in a position to break the salt law as such, Gandhiji conceived of an additional programme of civil disobedience. It consisted of peaceful picketing of shops dealing in sale of foreign cloth and liquor, abkari sales which fetched large revenue to the Government and the cutting of spathes of palmyra and date trees. Gandhiji also called upon them to carry on in a more intensive scale the programme of constructive work especially hand spinning, weaving of khaddar, removal of untouchability and promotion of Hindu-Muslim unity. It was with this comprehensive programme that the salt Satyagraha was launched in 1930. Even in places far from the coast salt water was brought and salt manufactured to defy the law.

The "illicit" salt that was thus prepared was neatly packed in small quantities. The satyagrahis held them in their hands refusing to part with them even as the police mercilessly inflicted severe lathi blows on them. In the clashes that ensued between the satyagrahis and the police, the former suffered serious injuries but that did not dampen their enthusiasm.

Picketing was also systematically on at cloth shops and there was a perceptible fall in the imports of foreign cloth. The police wielded the lathi and also fired on peaceful crowds resulting in several fatalities besides serious injuries to a vast number of people. Removing Gandhi caps and the national flags hoisted in public places and even in private houses by the police was an occurrence gleefully executed.

Even as the jails became overcrowded police resorted more frequently to cruel suppression by the use of the lathi and firing. Women were carried in lorries to distant places and left there to fend for themselves.

On May 5 Gandhiji wrote to the Viceroy that with his followers he would raid the salt depot at Dharsana in Surat district. Immediately thereafter he was arrested and lodged in the Yerrawada jail in Poona. The entire country observed hartal to voice their protest against the action taken on Gandhiji. In fact Bombay observed a five days hartal and entire business came to a standstill. There were instances of persons resigning from Government service. All this created considerable impact not only in India but elsewhere as could be seen from the fact that a group of missionaries in America sent a written plea to the Indian Government to entire into negotiation with Gandhiji who was carrying on a non-violent struggle. They also wanted an end to the violence unleashed on peaceful crowds.

The satyagrahis made three raids on the salt depot at Dharsana on May 22 and 25. The police encircled them leading to a clash between them and the satyagrahis who suffered the indignities perpetrated on them in a strictly non-violent manner. And yet the police fired upon innocent people unmindful of the fatal consequences.

An American Press Correspondent, Well Miller, and a British Journalists, Slocombe, were witness to these gruesome happenings in which brutal force was used by the police against the satyagrahis whose behaviour throughout was exemplary. From every part of the world letters were sent to the press in India admiring the non-violent fight against the British. All this had an impact on public opinion. The Programme of picketing continued. It was in Bombay that the boycott of foreign cloth was organised on a massive scale. The mercantile community fully co-operated while Congressmen succeeded in sealing all the godowns in which foreign cloth was stored. At the same time the merchants agreed not to import any more and this brought about a standstill in the trade of foreign cloth.

Civil disobedience took diverse forms in different States depending on local conditions. Leaders were naturally interested in taking up issues of immediate interest to the people. In Bombay and C.P. for example, there was large scale disobedience of forest laws. There was a no-tax campaign at Bardoli and Midnapur of Bengal as well as in some places in Bihar and Karnataka. Ryots defied the Government and the zamindars by refusing to pay taxes and rents. The mass resignation of village officers added to the intensity of the campaign. Gradually, the scope of the boycott was enlarged to include British banks, insurance corporations etc. All this led to a marked fall in the business transaction of the British-owned firms.

Simultaneously, the demand for khadi and mill-made cloth registered an increase. Mill yarn producers agreed to sell yarn at low prices to the weavers of handloom cloth. These were indications that the movement was going apace in the right direction.

Government Policy of Repression

The reply of the Government to all this was repression and more repression. A number of ordinances were promulgated giving powers to the police and the magistrates to take whatever action they liked against the satyagrahis and their sympathizers. Curbs were placed on the press and on the holding of public meetings. Several newspapers had to be closed. Since meetings could not be held there was a set-up of underground activity. Congress committees and similar organizations were banned. The premises in which they were located were forcibly taken possession of and furniture, photographs of national leaders and records were seized along with all the belongings only to be destroyed. By about the end of the year a lakh or more Satyagrahis were in jails leading a miserable life. They were also subjected to all kinds of brutalities. In Peshawar, Sholapur and Bardoli the military took over the administration and virtual martial law prevailed reminiscent of the harrowing days of the Jallianwala Bagh tragedy of 1919.

The Government had on their side the zamindars, the Muslims and other minorities. To the Muslims they gave the assurances that no reforms would be introduced without their approval. These section therefore remained loyal although the tactics employed by the Government did not a weebit weaken the freedom movement.

Report of the Simon Commission

The Simon Commission published its report in the later part of 1930 at a time when the country was in a state of political turmoil and the people were carrying on a defiant battle braving odds against the British. The Commission's recommendations were reactionary. There was no reference to dominion status nor did it suggest any change in the structure at the center in the direction of full responsible Government. In the provinces it is recommended the abolition of Dyarchy and transfer of all departments to responsible ministers. At the same time it recommends provision which would enable the governors to overrule the decision of the ministers. Even the Moderates were, therefore, not satisfied with the recommendations. Lord Irwin, too, was not particularly enthused because it did little in the direction of conciliating the Congress party or the informed public opinion in the country. He wrote to the labour Government that a Round Table Conference, representative of all the Indian parties, should be convened. The British Cabinet agreed to the proposal and a Round Table conference was called to meet in London in 1930. As a result of its deliberations, it was agreed that India should have a federal system in which the British Indian provinces and the Indian states should be participants that there should be responsible Government at the Centre in some measure that diarchy should be abolished in the provinces and the special powers of the governors should be reduced to the minimum. On the Hindu-Muslims and the members of the Hindu Mahasabha who attended the conference.

On the concluding day, Ramsay Macdonald, the British Prime Minister, made an announcement that he would take action on the proposal agreed upon. But on the Hindu-Muslim question he appealed to the parties concerned to come to some understanding so that he might not be put to the necessity of forcing a decision on them.

The real snag was the non-participation of the Congress and it therefore appeared to the Viceroy and the British Cabinet that all these decisions were unreal. The Congress was the only party which commanded the confidence of a large section of the people. It was also the party fighting for freedom and the authorities were aware that any proposal for constitutional reforms which did not receive its approval would find no validity. It was also realized that there was no let-up in the Civil Disobedience movement. In the light of this thinking, the British showed statesmanship in releasing Gandhiji and the other leaders who were in prison. Immediately after their release the Congress Working Committee met and passed a resolutions disapproving the decision of the round table conference and resolving to continue the movement. When this news reached Sapru and Jayakar who were in London they urged Gandhiji not to take any hasty step till they returned to India. Gandhiji responded favourably and the two leaders entered into talks with him and the members of the Congress working committee and convinced them that India's interests would be best served by Gandhiji meeting the Viceroy and holding discussions with him. Gandhiji wrote to the Viceroy requesting for an interview which was granted on February, 17, 1931. The discussions continued till March 5 when an agreement was reached.

Gandhiji-irwin Pact

Gandhiji agreed to suspend the civil disobedience movement and the Viceroy to free all political prisoners not accused of violence and permit the manufacture of salt by individual for their private consumption as also the peaceful picketing of foreign cloth and of liquor shops. Apart from these which formed the core of the pact Gandhiji agreed to Congress participation at the Second Round Table Conference.

That Gandhiji should be invited to carry on discussions with the Viceroy was itself a recognition of the leading role of the Congress in the politics of the country. Several Congressmen including the members of the Working Committee criticized Gandhiji for having come to an agreement with the Viceroy which made no mention of Independence. But Gandhiji assured them that he would take it up at the Round Table Conference. He further clarified that civil disobedience was not given up, but was only suspended and that it would be open to the Congress to resume it if they found there was no change in the attitude of the British Government. The congress Working Committee thereupon gave its approval to the agreement.

Meanwhile Lord Willingdon who had very little Sympathy with Indian aspirations succeeded Lord Irwin as Viceroy. The members of the I.C.S. were unhappy with Lord Irwin who recognized Gandhiji as his equal and even entered into an agreement with him. Neither the new Viceroy nor the British Officials showed any preparedness to hounour the pact. Repression continued as before and in the United Provinces where the peasants were unable to pay taxes because of a bad harvest, it was the highest. In Peshawar and other parts of the North-West Frontier Province, the military still dominated. There were difficulties also in Bardoli where the negotiations between Sardar Vallabhbhai Patel and the officials had to be a snapped because the latter were unwilling to abide by the terms of the Gandhi-Irwin agreement. Restrictions were also placed on the manufacture of salt by private individual and on peaceful picketing. Gandhiji was in a dilemma as to whether he should attend the Round Table Conference under the Circumstances.

The Viceroy, however, was keen that Gandhiji should participate in the conference and assured him that the Government would adopt a conciliatory attitude. This prompted Gandhiji to proceed to London. He was quite conscious that lord Willingdon was cast in a different mould from that of Lord Irwin and that the general attitude of the Government and the bureaucracy was not very much different from what it was prior to the Gandhi-Irwin pact.

Karachi Session of the Congress

The Indian National Congress held its plenary session in March 1931 shortly after the conclusion of the Gandhi-Irwin Agreement. The leftist forces were slowly asserting themselves in the Congress while the extremists were opposed to the agreement itself. There was considerable dissatisfaction with Gandhiji when he arrived in Karachi to attend the session. This was further intensified as Bhagat Singh and his two other associates who were sentenced to death were hanged six before the Congress session. His critics were up in arms against Gandhiji for not being able to halt their execution. Gandhiji had actually pleaded with the authorities for their pardon but to no avail. Bhagat Singh was an idol of the people and many Congressmen were of the view that Gandhiji did not work hard enough to save Bhagat Singh and his companions from the gallows. It was in this surcharged atmosphere that the congress session met in Karachi under the Presidentship of Sardar Patel. Gandhiji made an impassioned speech to secure the approval of the party to his agreement with Irwin and participation in the Round Table Conference.

Although under the terms of the agreement the Congress was entitled to send delegates in proportion to its political status and importance, Gandhiji desired that he should be the sole delegates. This indeed was a mistake on his part. He should have taken along with him a number of other leaders of the party including a nationalists Muslim of the stature of Dr. Ansari. Although he spoke eloquently at the conference he could not single handed carry the conference with him. Further, the presence of nationalist Muslims on his side would have blunted the importance of the other Muslim delegates who pleaded special privileges for their community. In retrospect it was felt that Gandhiji had to bear too heavy a burden.

And yet the Karachi session of the Congress will be remembered long for enunciating certain fundamental rights that should be embodied in any future constitutions of India and thus for the first time ushered a new concept of socialism. This satisfied to some extent progressive sections of the party including Nehru. A resolution was also adopted praising the heroism and patriotic fervour displayed by Bhagat Singh and his colleagues though it was apparent that Gandhiji was not very enthusiastic about such a resolution.

THE RESUMPTION OF CIVIL DISOBEDIENCE

CHAPTER 20

Gandhiji's Disappointment with the Results of the Second Round Table Conference

Following the agreement with Lord Irwin, Gandhiji attended the Second Round Table Conference in the hope it will yield the positive results. But he was disappointed. The situation had undergone sea change in the meanwhile with the fall of the Labour Government and the coming into power of a new coalition Government in Britain. Although Ramsay Macdonald continued to be the Prime Minister he had to the line of his Conservative supports. This proved a limitation in making his influence felt fully in the cabinet. The conservatives did not want the decisions of the Round Table Conference to guide the policy of the British Government. It was their intention to make the Simon Commission Report the main basis of constitutional reforms. Further, the new British Government encouraged the Viceroy, Lord Willingdon, to pursue a policy of repression and to see that the Congress was suppressed and the people's resistance crushed. The Round Table Conference was used by the Conservative Party to drive a wedge between the Congress and the leaders of the Muslims and other minorities. The idea of a separate state for Muslim already surfaced even at the time of the first Round Table Conference. Though the Conservative Party encouraged the Muslims to demand a separate state the thrust of Gandhiji's exhortations was to impress on the British authorities that the Round Table Conference was intended to come to grips with the constitutional problem and not to accentuate bitterness between the different communities in India. This according to him, it was purely a domestic problem and could be solved only by mutual discussion among the representatives of the different communities.

The efforts to bring about some agreement between the Congress and the minorities failed miserably because the Muslims hoped that even if they did not get a separate state, they could win the special concession they wanted from the British and therefore the question of coming of an understanding with the Congress was as irrelevant as it was unnecessary. The representatives of the European mercantile community at the Conference also encouraged them to stick to their separatists' policies by promising a number of commercial concessions to them. These reactionary forces were active and a memorandum was presented to the Prime Minister by the representatives of the minorities at the conference pressing for special representation and for separate electoral constituencies not only to the Muslim but also to Harijans, Europeans in India, Indian Christian, Sikhs and Anglo-Indians. None of these interests cared to look at the problem from and all India point of view. Gandhiji got disgusted with this development and before he left for India, he made it clear that if the untouchables were given special electorates, he would be compelled to undertake a fast unto death. In his opinion the injection of the virus of separate electorates was calculated to disrupt the Hindu community without affording any advantage to the depressed classes. It was this view that made him undertake such a fast when the Communal Award of Ramsay Macdonald was published conceding separate electorates to the Harijans.

Willingdon's Policy of Repression

Gandhiji returned to India on December 28, 1931 with all hopes dashed. During his absence, the policy of repression was resorted to by the Government on a large scale and a reign of terror was let loose. Almost all the terms of the Gandhi-Irwin agreement were given a go-by. Though it was one of the articles of the agreement that the question of Bardoli peasants should be settled by a committee consisting of Sardar Patel and Government representatives, the latter refused to co-operate with Patel with the result that negotiations through the committee had to be given up. In the North West Frontier Province, Abdul Gaffar Khan, Frontier Gandhi as he was called, was jailed along with a number of his colleagues and the province was administered under military rule. No relief was given to the peasants in the United Provinces which was going through an acute famine that year and a Congress committee which investigated into the question requested the authorities to suspend the collection of land revenue till the investigation was over. The Government however, declined to accede to this following which the people started a no tax campaign. In Bengal repression was resorted to in a ruthless form and police raj became the order of the day. A few days before the return of Gandhiji, Nehru and other leaders were sentenced to imprisonment.

Resumption of Civil Disobedience

Soon after Gandhiji landed in Bombay, leaders from all provinces met him and acquainted him with the happenings in the country. He did not want to make up his mind about the future course of action without ascertaining the Government version as well on matters at issue. He, therefore, requested the Viceroy to grant him an interview but the Viceroy in a stiff reply made it known that he was not prepared to discuss with him the pros and cons of the Government policy. Gandhiji felt disappointed. The Congress Working Committee decided on resuming the civil disobedience movement from January 4, 1932. Gandhiji wrote again to the Viceroy seeking an interview to clarify his position as well as that of the Congress. The Viceroy bluntly refused to meet him on the specious plea that no Government could do so when a threat of civil disobedience movement was being flaunted. And with all the doors of negotiations closed, the Congress had no alternative but to stick to its decision to resume the civil disobedience campaign.

Character and Course of the Movement

At midnight on January 3, Gandhiji and all the prominent leaders of the Congress party were arrested and sent to prison but this did not deter the people from carrying on the movement. They had experience since they had already seen similar movements in 1921 and 1930. They, therefore, knew exactly what to do even in the absence of their trusted leaders. They strictly adhered to non-violence. Their programme consisted of defiance of as many laws as possible. Thousands of people participated in the Satyagraha and jails soon became full. Camp jails and temporary structures were put up but even these were inadequate considering the large number of people who were sentenced to imprisonment. Rather than send them to jails the police used force against them.

The satyagrahis then turned their attention to deprive the Government of its revenue. This precisely was the object in picketing British goods. A reduction in imports would necessarily entail a colossal loss of revenue normally due from import duties. The satyagrahis also picketed liquor shops and organised boycott of abkari sales which drastically brought about a fall in the income from these two sources. In some provinces no-tax campaigns were organised while in others the ryots stubbornly refused to pay land revenue. They even declined to remit the grazing fee for their cattle. There were also instances of non-payment of the chowkidari tax which was collected as a local tax.

National symbols which have an emotive value were the next targets of attack by the authorities. For the satyagrahis the national flag, the Gandhiji cap, khadi and the singing of Vandemataram constituted the national symbols. Flags were flown on all buildings and other public places. Even as the police made a persistent effort to pull down the flags, the satyagrahis resisted these attempts with all their might remembering at the same time not to indulge in violence. The police also arrested people wearing khadi and Gandhi caps. This inevitably led to clashes between the two sides. The singing of Vandemataram at public meetings and while taking out processions was banned by the Government. Yet the satyagrahis defied the orders and suffered willingly the humiliation inflicted on them by the police.

A plethora of ordinances – as many as twelve in number – were issued by the Government to curb the civil disobedience movement. Innumerable kinds of restraints were placed on the Press. The satyagrahis managed to issue hand bills and through typed and cyclostyled sheets carried on their propaganda without let up. The movement was thus continued with unbridled enthusiasm. There was an arrangement for observing special days, as for instance, January 4 as the all Indian Prisoners' Day, to mark the day on which Gandhiji was arrested. Likewise, the day on which there was firing in Peshawar became the Peshawar Day. A National week was also observed and each day in the week had a special significance.

An important event in 1932 was the annual session of the Congress in Delhi. The Government did everything within its power to prevent the session from being held. But 500 delegates from all over the country succeeded in reaching the venue and the session took place under the Presidentship of Ranchod Das Amrit Lal, an eminent citizen of Ahmedabad. The annual report reiterated that independence was the goal of the Congress. The resumption of the civil disobedience movement was formally approved. There was also a reaffirmation of the people's faith in Gandhiji's leadership. By another resolution the session paid glorious tributes to the thousand of people who participated in the non-violent struggle.

Just as the delegates left the meeting, the police came to realize what had happened. Having realized their failure to prevent the session from being held they arrested some delegates who were still around and produced them in court. They were promptly sentenced to imprisonment.

In 1933, a session of the Congress was held in Calcutta. Pandit Malaviya who was to have presided was arrested in the train itself while he was on his way to Calcutta and was sent back to Allahabad. The session was held under the Presidentship of Mr. Sengupta. The police were determined to break the session. They entered the pandal and tried to disperse the gathering by attacking the delegates with lathis. Meanwhile, the delegates who were in a defiant mood succeeded in passing the scheduled resolutions. The Delhi and the Calcutta sessions were proof positive of the grim determination of the people to carry on their fight in the true spirit of non-violence.

Government Policy of Repression

The government adopted highly questionable methods and repressive tactics to suppress the movement. This action taken by the Government was more stringent than ever before. The ordinance curtailed the freedom of the people in more ways than one. Severe restraints were placed on the freedom of the Press, of association, on the free movement of people and on holding of public meetings. The severity of the ordinances was most conspicuous in Bengal on the supposed plea that terrorists were active in the region. Persons were taken into custody on mere suspicion and kept in prison without trial. The Government requisitioned all modes of conveyances and forcibly took possession of even residential buildings without paying rent. House arrests became the order of the day. The services of non-official were requisitioned under police regulations to assist the police. Punitive policeman were stationed in many towns and the expenses incurred on them were collected arbitrarily from the residents. Collective fines were also imposed. To try the arrested persons special courts were established without providing a right of appeal to the High Court. The whole country virtually became a vast prison house. During 1932, and important event took place when a delegation of the Indian League in Britain of which Bertrand Russell was the president visited India. V.K. Krishna Menon was among the four members, the other three being Britishers. The team toured the length and breadth of the country meeting official and non-official. They visited jails and collected evidence especially from those who came out of prison after serving their sentence. The members of the team were also eye witness to the clashes between the satyagrahis and the police. A report was prepared embodying the findings of the team soon after it returned to England. Bertrand Russell in his preface said that the atrocities committed by even the Nazis in Germany paled into insignificance before the police brutalities perpetrated on innocent people to suppress the non-violent satyagraha.

Ramsay Macdonald's Communal Award and Gandhiji Fast

While the movement was in full swing the British prime Minister announced the communal award under which not only the Muslims, the Indian Christians, Europeans, Anglo Indians and the Sikhs but also the Harijans were given special representation in the legislatures to be constituted under a new Government of India Act. Gandhiji was in prison at that time and he threatened to go on fast unto death unless the provisions for separate electorates to the Harijans were revoked from the Communal Award. According to him, the Harijans were an integral part of the Hindu Community and it was a sin to separate them from the rest of the Hindus. The British Premier, however, promised to revise the Award if there was an arrangement on the question between Gandhiji and the Harijans leaders. Gandhiji started his historic fast unto death. Malavya and other prominent leaders thereupon convened a high level conference of representatives of the caste Hindus and Harijans including Dr. Ambedkar, the most outstanding of them all. As a result of the deliberations Dr. Ambedkar agreed to a compromise and it was embodied in what was called the Poona Pact. Gandhiji broke his fast and the Communal Award was accordingly revised. Under this Award, the number of seats reserved for the Harijans in the legislature was considerably enhanced much above the number reserved for them in the Communal Award.

Secondly, the Harijans representatives in the legislature were to be elected in two stages. For every seat reserved for them, four candidates were to be chosen by separate Harijan constituencies. One of these was to be finally elected by a joint electorate consisting of caste Hindus and Harijans.

Subsequent Course of the Movement

Gandhiji's fast was instrumental in the reassurance that the Harijans were an integral and inseparable part of the Hindus. It was also the first major offensive against untouchability. At the conference convened by Malavya, resolutions were passed urging caste Hindus not to practice untouchability and that when Swaraj was obtained, it would be completely abolished. In the meanwhile public wells, roads, and other places of public resort including temples should be thrown open to the Harijans. Action was taken in many States to implement the resolution, especially that part relating to temple entry. This was yet another significant step in the removal of untouchability which was rightly considered as the darkest blot on the Hindus social system.

After the Poona Pact, Gandhiji's interest in the civil disobedience movement slowed down somewhat and he concentrated his attention on tackling the Harijans problem. He found that there was yet no real change in the general attitude of the Hindus toward the untouchables. He undertook a fast for 21 days in May 1933. The Government released him from prison but Gandhiji scrupulously avoided politics and continued his efforts to promote the welfare of the Harijans with redoubled vigour. This created an adverse reaction among those who were keen on the continuance of the civil disobedience movement. They even tried to persuade Gandhiji to once again lead the movement, but he was not enthusiastic about it mainly on the ground that during the years 1932-33 many satyagrahis went underground and resorted to secret activities and they did not strictly adhere to the tenets of Satyagraha. He advised the then president of the Congress, M.S. Aney, to suspend the movement for six weeks in the first instance and later it was extended by another three months. He was however persuaded to seek and interview with the Viceroy to discuss measures that would bring an end to the rule through ordinances and to stop repression since the Satyagraha movement was suspended. Lord Willingdon refused to grant and interview and this naturally angered the Congressmen. It was then resolved that instead of a mass civil disobedience individual satyagraha should be resorted to in pursuance of which Gandhiji and 34 of his Ashram inmates were getting ready for it with the target date as August 1. But on the night of July 31, he and his followers were arrested and sent to prison. An order was passed that he should be confined to Poona. Gandhiji refused to obey the order and he was again arrested and sentenced to one year's imprisonment. Many Congressmen resorted to individual Satyagraha.

Gandhiji wanted to carry on Harijan work from prison but his request was turned down. Gandhiji therefore decided to go on fast from August 16 following which the Government released him unconditionally. But he was reluctant to resume political work until the one year to which he was originally sentenced to imprisonment was over. He devoted his entire attention to Harijan Welfare and this brought to an end the individual civil disobedience.

Calling Off of the Movement

As observed by Dr. Pattabhi Sitaramayya in his History of the Indian National Congress, people had lost the zest for the movement by that time. Those who were freed from jails were unwilling to court arrest. Those who wanted to go to jails were not taken into custody and instead lathi blows were administered on them mercilessly. The movement which was started on Januray 4, 1932, having lost momentum came to an end by about May 1934. At the meeting of the All India Congress Committee held in Patna on May 18 and 19, a resolution was passed formally calling off the movement.

In the movement of 1932–34 several lakhs of people participated. According to official figures 67,991 men and 3,462 women were sent to jails but this was considered by the Congress as a colossal under estimate. According to the Congress atleast 12,000 Muslims offered Satyagraha most of whom were from the North West Frontier Province. The fines levied on the satyagrahis were collected by using force from their relatives though they were no way concerned with the movement. People who had the remotest connection with the movement and even bystanders were rounded up and sent to prison. In trying to suppress the movement the police resorted to all kinds of cruel methods. It was not surprising therefore that quite a few satyagrahis suffered from life long illnesses.

Its Results

Superficially it might appear that the movement had failed since it did not bring Swaraj straightway. But it is not as though the suffering through which the people willingly passed was in vain. The desire for Swaraj was further entrenched in the people who only wanted a little respite to start all over again with renewed vigour. It was conclusively proved that the Government lost its moral right to rule. The achievement of independence has all over the world been an arduous process and a long drawn out affairs. The Vandemataram, Home Rule, and the civil disobedience movement should be regarded as significant steps in the triumphant march to freedom. Each stage brought the people nearer the goal, the determination to realize it becoming keener and stronger than ever. The readiness with which the people responded to the Quit India Movement in 1942 was ample proof of this.

In this movement all sections of the people played their role with a sense of purpose and dedication. They were prepared to suffer any hardship arising out of the highly repressive policies of the Government. An unexpected consequence was that the common suffering brought about greater cohesion among the people. The movement also led to the emancipation of women. They came out of their purdah to boldly face the consequences. Taken as a whole, the civil disobedience movement could be regarded as a great step forward in the historic march to freedom.

THE REVOLUTIONARY MOVEMENT

CHAPTER 21

The Origin of the Revolutionary Movement in Bengal

By 1905 political activity in the country assumed three main forms. There were the Moderates whose objectives was colonial self-government and who were bent on following purely constitutional methods for achieving it. They were mainly influenced by the developments in Britain. The nationalists were in the second stream and their ideal was Swaraj. They believed in passive resistance and they were more influenced by political movements in the Continent of Europe than by British historical events. Finally there were revolutionaries (the terrorists as they were called by the British). They wanted Swaraj but they had no faith either in constitutional agitating or in passive resistance. According to them, only an armed rebellion could achieve the purpose, namely, throwing out the British from India. Since, however, conditions were not propitious yet for a massive armed revolt they resorted to selective assassination of British officials and their Indian associates. They drew inspiration from the Nihiles of Russia and the Sinn-Fenn movement in Ireland. They believed that the killing of official instrument in committing atrocities on Indians would strike terror into the hearts of the British authorities who, it was thought, would then be compelled to yield. They had no difficulty in procuring the necessary arms to carry out their objective. They secured money by looting Government treasuries and the richer classes. They gave the assurance to the latter group that the money would be returned to them on the achievement of Swaraj. Besides, they seized arms from police stations and from the chowkidars in the zamindari estates. The sailors who visited the Calcutta harbour were also reported to have given them arms. Through their friends employed in foreign firms engaged in arms imports, they were able to collect such material while in transit from the port to the firms. In addition, they had set up underground factories to manufactures bombs for which they acquired expertise by sending youngmen to foreign countries for training.

Most of the revolutionaries came from the educated ranks of the lower middle class in Bengal. They were frustrated because, of the growing unemployment and the acute economic distress that prevailed. Their activities assumed serious proportions following the partitions of Bengal which was carried out in spite of the unanimous public opinion against it. They were convinced that the continuance of the British rule would deal a death blow to Hindu religion and culture. Tilak, Aurobindo and other nationalist leaders inspired them with zeal and fervour. The movement was started mainly by those who obtained training in samithis that were set up all over Bengal to give physical training to the young and to teach them the true meaning of nationalism. The Anusilan samiti of Calcutta was the most prominent in this regard. Although their original intention was not really to train the young in armed rebellion, a few of those who were trained in these institutions pursued such a course of their own accord. The training they received in the samithis such as wrestling, sword-fighting and wielding of the lathis was of immense help to them, The British were known to have thought of the Bengalis as a timid people and that for them the pen was mightier than the sword. It was to disprove of this that the samitis came into being with all their stress on physical training to the youth. Quite often the Englishmen went out of their way to shower insults on Indians and even cause physical injury to them knowing full well that even if they were tired by the judicial officials they would suffer no punishment. The Bengalis, therefore, took law into their hands and did not hesitate to attack individual Europeans. In addition to physical training the samitis were responsible for inculcating in them a love for the history and religion of the country. They became centers, as it were, of national education. They secured the co-operation of the intellectuals who spoke at the meetings organised for the benefit of the trainees. The Ramakrishna Mission who also helpful in this direction. Sister Nivedita deserves special mention. The youth also received lessons in the Bhagvad Gita, while the speeches and writings of Vivekananda were an integral part of their studies. All this kindled in them a spirit of patriotism and an earnest desire to liberate the country. The Gita drove home the point that a righteous war was justified to get rid of evil and that there was nothing wrong in taking to arms for this purpose. The message of the Gita was the soul was imperishable, that it was only the body that perished and, therefore, there was no need to fear death. The doctrine of rebirth had a profound influence on the revolutionaries.

Almost all of them took to Brahmacharya. Women were not permitted to participate in the revolutionary activities. When the revolutionaries broke into the houses of wealthy individuals, they spared the women inmates and did not touch their jewellery. They were essentially a disciplined lot.

As has been noted, although the samitis did not impart special training to the youth in armed rebellion, they believed it was the only way by which they could liberate the country from foreign yoke. Aurobindo, who was working as a Professor in the Maharaja's College in Baroda around 1900, supported the revolutionary movement. He deputed his brother Birendra Kumar to organize a movement in Calcutta. A little later Aurobindo himself came to Calcutta and became a close associate of the revolutionaries. Birendra Kumar was instrumental in organizing an underground factory in Calcutta to manufacture bombs.

This indeed was the beginning of the revolutionary movement in Bengal. Newspaper like Yugantar, Sandhya and Vandemataram gave every encouragement to the movement. Among the daring acts of the revolutionaries, mention should be made of the attempt made by Khudiran Bose and Prafulla Chauki to murder the magistrate by name Kingsford who gave harsh sentences on those accused of sedition. The magistrate who subsequently transferred to Muzzaffarpur to save him from a possible attack by the revolutionaries. These two young men, however, proceeded to Muzaffarpur and attempted to kill him by throwing a bomb into a coach in which they thought the magistrate was traveling. It turned out to be a case of mistaken identity. Two European women who were in the coach were hit by the bomb and they succumbed to the injuries. Khudiram Bose fell into the hands of the police while Prafulla Chauki committed suicide. Khudiram Bose was tried and sentenced to death. Handsome tributes were paid to him by the nationalists and newspapers described him as a hero and a martyr to the cause of liberty. Tilak who wrote in praise of Bose in his paper was charged with sedition, sentenced to six years' imprisonment and was sent to suffer the term in a Mandalay jail. It may be noted that political murders had begun much earlier in Poona than in Bengal. In 1897 the two Chapekar brothers murdered Major Rand known for his dictatorial methods in dealing with Indians even under unfortunate circumstances like the plague which broke out in Poona. His associates were also done to death. It was in connection with the developments that Tilak suffered imprisonment for the first time.

Alipur Bomb Case

The Alipur Bomb conspiracy case was a landmark in the revolutionary movement in Bengal. The police discovered a bomb manufacturing plant in Calcutta. Aurobindo and his brother Birendra Kumar were closely associated with it. Aurobindo had to be released after he spent a year in jail as an undertrial prisoner as the police could not produce enough evidence to implicate him. But the others including his brother were sent to Andamans. A few suffered long periods of imprisonment in Bengal jails. During this case one of the accused turned approver but the other accused smuggled a revolver into the jail and shot him dead. Two persons who were arrested and tried for this were sentenced to death. They were hailed by the nation as heroes in much the same way as khudiram Bose. The people in general were highly proud of the revolutionaries.

Revolutionary Movement in Maharashtra

Maharashtra too was a center of revolutionary activity. The Savarkar brothers – Ganesh and Vinayak – started a revolutionary organization and worked intensely for the spread of revolutionary ideas in Maharashtra. Ganesh Savarkar was involved in an assassination case and he was sentenced to transportation to Andamans by Jackson, the magistrate of Nasik. By then Vinayak Savarkar had left for England for higher studies where he became a close associate of Shyamji Krishnavarma, a revolutionary in London. They made the India House a center for their activities. Fearing arrest by the authorities, Varma left London and stayed with Madame Came and other who were engaged in revolutionary activities. Savarkar carried on the revolutionary work with India House as the base. He even managed to send arms to Maharashtra. The revolution in Maharashtra murdered Jackson. Simultaneously, M.L. Dhingra killed Sir Curzon Wylle, an official in the India office, London as a reprisal against the severe punishment inflicted on the revolutionaries in India by the British magistrates. During his trial in London, Dhingra told the magistrate in his statement, "I admit the other day I attempted to shed English blood as a humble revenge for the inhuman hangings and deportations of patriotic Indian youth.... I believe that a nation held in bondage with the help of foreign bayonets is in a disarmed race I attacked by surprise. Since guns were denied to me I drew forth my pistol and fired. As a Hindu I feel that a wrong done to my country is an insult to God. He concluded by saying. "The war of independence will continue between India and England so long as the Hindu and English races last and the present unnatural relation does not cease". All this seemed to have evoked the admiration of even Winston Churchill and Lloyd George and the British Emperor too felt that there as something wrong about the state of affairs in India. A little later Savarkar was arrested under dramatic circumstances. When the ship in which he was being brought to India reached Marseilles in France, Savarkar in a daring escape bid leapt out of the ship, swam across the waters and reached the French soil. But the British police gave a chase and brought him back to the ship even though such an arrest contravened international law. After he was taken to India he was tried in connections with the Nasik conspiracy case and was sent to Andamans where his brother was already undergoing a sentence.

Revolutionary Activity in Punjab

Yet another center of revolutionary activity was Punjab. Hardayal was its most prominent figure. Anticipating arrest he fled to the United States for refuge. Rasbehari Bose, a Bengali revolutionary, was next only to Hardyal in importance. He left Bengal for U.P. when the Alipur Bomb case was instituted. He managed to secure the confidence of the police authorities who were not aware that he was carrying on revolutionary activities. In fact, he was responsible for the throwing of a bomb into the car in which Lord Hardinge was making a ceremonial entry into Delhi in 1912 as the Viceroy after the shifting of the capital from Calcutta. Rasbehari Bose managed to escape although he was implicated in the Delhi conspiracy case. He first left for Bengal and later migrated to Japan. It may be recalled that in the formation of the Indian National Army in Singapore during the Second World War he played a significant role.

The Ghadar Movement in the U.S.A

The next phase of the revolutionary movement originated during the First World War. Hardayal organised a party called Ghadar consisting of the Sikhs who migrated to the United States Ghadar means mutiny and the objectives in the formation of the party was to organize the Sikhs and others in the united States to start an armed revolution in India. When the First World War broke out a number of Indian revolutionaries in Europe also war broke out a number of Indian revolutionaries in Europe also organised an association to negotiate with the German authorities the possibility of shipping arms to India via the United States. Hardayal was in close contact with this association. The British Government had him arrested in the United States but he managed to escape to Europe where he joined the revolutionary organization. The Ghadar movement was active as ever and finally persuaded the German authorities to send arms to India in two ships from the United States, the first one to land on the coast of Bengal and the second at Balasore in Orissa.

Jatin Mukherjee, the leader of the revolutionary movement in Bengal, went to Balasore to receive the arms but to conceal the real purpose he opened a cycle shop. He spent most of his time in a village away from Balasore to evade the police. Meanwhile British authorities came to know of the shipment of arms and they promptly intercepted the ships on the high seas – a fact which the revolutionaries were not aware of. The police also came to know of the activities of Jatin Mukherjee, went to Balasore and made a serious attempt to round him up and his associates. There was a pitched battle between Jatin Mukherjee and the police. The revolutionary was joined by his followers who bitterly resisted the police. It resulted in the death of one person. Jatin himself was severely injured and he succumbed at the Balasore hospital. Jatin Mukherji was truly a great leader of the revolutionary movement in Bengal and is held in the highest esteem even to this day. His death marked the beginning of the collapse of the revolutionary movement in Bengal.

It was about this time the Sikhs, who constituted the main element of the Ghadar party, decided to return to Punjab after the commencement of the first World War to start on armed rebellion to India. During 1914 and 1915 they returned in several batches touching various sea port towns on the eastern and the south eastern coasts of Asia where they contacted the Indian residents and persuaded them also to come back to India to take part in the uprising. They met the leaders of the sepoy regiments stationed in those areas and appealed to them to rebel against the British authorities.

Komagatamaru Incident

Of equal importance is another event which took place in 1914 a party of Sikh residents of Hong Kong and a few sea towns in East Asia hired a Japanese steamer by name Komagatamaru and set sail to Vancouver on the west coast of Canada to settle there as immigrants. Although they took care to observe all the rules and regulations imposed by the Canadian Government the authorities refused them permission to land when they actually reached the destinations. They had therefore to return by the same steamer to India and landed at Budge. Budge near Calcutta. The government of Bengal suspected them to be members of the Ghadar party did not want them to enter Calcutta. A train was, therefore, arranged to take them to Punjab but on their refusal to oblige the authorities violence was used against them. In the resultant clash which took a serious turn, twenty persons died. Sixty of them were however forced to get into the train. This brutal behaviour of the British was strongly resented to by the Sikhs in Punjab and this strengthened the determination of the Ghadar Party to stage a revolt. (it may be noted that the campus where the session of the Congress was held in 1976 in Punjab was named Komagata Nagar in memory of those who lost their lives in the tragic incident).

The members of the Ghadar party expected arms from Germany. They also planned a course of action in pursuance of which they looted Government treasuries, cut off telephone and telegraph wires and damaged railway bridges. With the help of Rasbehari Bose they established contacts with the revolutionaries in Bengal obtained bombs and came into touch with some of the sepoy regiments in Punjab. But the biggest weakness of the party was the lack of a cohesive organization. Unlike the revolutionaries in Bengal who were well organised the Ghadar party did not have proper leadership. Moreover, they did not observe strict secrecy in carrying on their work. Men of the intelligence service infiltrated into their ranks and carried information regularly to the police authorities. They also did not get the arms which they expected through the Germans in U.S.A.

February 21, 1915 was the day fixed for the armed uprising and for the revolt of the sepoy regiments. As this information was leaked out the date was changed to February 19, 1915. But even this was not kept a secret and the authorities promptly disbanded the sepoy regiments suspected of treason, tried the sepoy under martial law and sentenced a large number of them either to death or to long terms of imprisonment. They also arrested many persons suspected of conspiracy to raise the revolt. Ras Behari Bose escaped arrest and fled to Japan. The Ghadar party was thus silenced and as a result, the revolutionary movement in Punjab suffered an eclipse. In addition to the repressive laws on the statue book, the Defence of India Act was passed. Under these acts, the Lahore conspiracy case was passed. Under these acts, the Lahore conspiracy case was instituted in which 28 were sentenced to death and many to long terms of imprisonment or transportation to Andamans.

The Results of the Revolutionary Movement

The revolutionary movement led to thousands of people being sentenced to imprisonment and torture while in prison in the most inhuman manner. Many of them committed suicide or suffered from life long illness. But they bore all this suffering willingly. It was in this heroic spirit that they carried on the movement inspite of the various atrocities perpetrated on them. They, however, had the satisfaction that they were highly praised by great leaders like Tilak, Aurobindo, Lajpat Rai and other eminent Indian educationalists like P.C. Roy and Meghnath Saha. Ballads were composed in their honour and were sung by the common people.

It is often asked whether the movement yielded any beneficial result at all. Birendra Kumar Ghose answered the question in 1909. He said that he revolutionaries were fully aware that by merely assassinating individual officials it would not be possible to overthrow the mighty British Empire but the real purpose of the movement was entirely different. It was to politically awaken the people by their acts of heroism and self sacrifice and make them conscious of the evils of foreign rule and the need to liberate the country from foreign yoke. He also said that another purpose of the movements was to make the people lose the fear of the police and the military and face them boldly and with courage irrespective of the consequences. Both these purposes were admirably served by the movement. When in 1921 the call came from Gandhiji, the masses participated in the non-co-operation movement with great enthusiasm. That indeed was proof of the political awakening of the people.

With a view to restoring normalcy in the country, the Government set at liberty most of the political prisoners immediately after the passing of the Government of India Act, 1919. The revolutionaries gave up violence and sincerely believed in taking part in the non-violent struggle for freedom started by Gandhiji. When Gandhiji suddenly abandoned the non-co-operation movement, it caused great disappointment among them and this was the reason why they renewed their activities.

Activities of Mahendra Pratab

The activities of Raja Mahendra Pratab, a prince belonging to the small principality of Hathras, which was taken away by the British deserves mention. He was much influenced by the boycott Swadeshi and national educational movements started in 1906, He attended the Congress Session in Calcutta in 1906 and started and educational institution at Brindavan in Mathura and trained youngmen in the service of the nation. After the outbreak of the First World War, he proceeded to Europe and joined the Indian revolutionary association there. He went to Berlin and had an interview with the German emperor who gave him letters of introduction to the Sultan of Turkey, the Amir of Afghanistan, the Maharaja of Nepal and several princely rulers in India. His object was to stage and armed rebellion in India. Some of his associates came to Kabul. The Amir gave him permission to make Kabul the base of his operations. He formed a provisional national Government with himself as the President, Brkatulla as the Prime Minister and Obeidullah as the Minister in charge of foreign affairs. At that time, some of the prominent Muslims leaders in the country were in West Asia and they tried to get the help of the Sultan and Turkey to wage a war of independence in India. They also contacted several Indian sepoy regiments fighting in West Asia. But the efforts of Raja Mahendra Pratab and the Muslim leaders failed because they got no response from the Indian princely rulers. Their secrets also leaked out and the British authorities took prompt suppressive actions. Frustrated, Mahendra Pratab went back to Europe and returned to India only after the country became free in 1947. He was later to the Lok Sabha.

Rivival of the Movement After 1923

The revolutionary movement after 1923 differed from that of the earlier period. It was better organised both in Bengal and in Northern India. In Bengal a Hindustan Republican Association was started under the leadership of Surya Sen. He did not think that the assassination of individuals was the sole means to win freedom and he wanted to carry on guerrilla warfare against the British. Similarly the revolutionaries in U.P organised a Hindustan Socialist Republican Association, and Chandrasekhar Azad became its leader. Among some of the incidents which happened in Bengal reference has to be made to the attempt on the life of Sir Charles Tegart, the Inspector General of Police, Gopinath Saha, who was deputed for the purpose fired at Day, another European official by mistake and he succumbed. Saha was tried and sentenced to death. He became as famous as Khudiram Bose. C.R. Das moved a resolution in the Bengal Provincial Conference expressing admiration for his heroism and had it passed. At about the same time Surya Sen raided the railway station in Chittagong and was able to escape with a large amount of money. Several assassinations took place in 1924–25 the most sensational of them being that of the police superintendent which took place while he was on a visit to the Alipore jail in 1925.

Activities of Surya Sen in Bengal

Many revolutionaries participated in the Calcutta Session of the Congress in 1928 as volunteer under the direction of Subhas Chandra Bose. It was shortly after this that Surya Sen thought of a simultaneous attack on police station and armoury in Chittagong, Meymansing and Barisal on April 19, 1930. He and his followers raided the armoury in Chittagong in a daring act, killed two persons who were keeping watch on the armoury, captured fire arms and finally set fire to the armoury. They destroyed the telephone exchange, later went to the police station and proclaimed the establishment of a national Government under his Presidentship. A little later, a strong police force surrounded them and they were compelled to flee to the hills at Jalalbagh where they rearranged their forces. The armed police surrounded them there too, and a keen fight ensued for three hours in which eleven revolutionaries lost their lives and 64 were killed in the Government side. This battle created a new confidence in the possibilities of an armed uprising against the British.

Several women also joined the movement. In the month of May, clashes took place between the revolutionaries either lost their lives or were captured by the police. Surya Sen escaped and went underground for some time. In Calcutta also a strategy was evolved by the Yugantar Party to simultaneously attack the police stations, Europeans clubs tanks and other places. Two young girls attempted to murder the Governor of Bengal. An Inspector – General of Police and a Police Superintendent were killed. Some of the revolutionaries entered the secretariat in Calcutta and killed a few officials. Murderous attacks were made on three districts collectors, a district judge and a police Superintendent.

After the Chittagong raid, Surya Sen continued his activities for nearly three years. Conspiracy cases were initiated against many of his followers and fourteen of them were transported to Andamans. In 1932 the police surrounded Surya Sen when he with some of his followers was hiding in a village. But he and two other managed to escape. One of the girls, Pratilata, organised a raid on the European club for killing an European woman and injuring many others. Pratilata was fired at in return but she escaped along with some of her associates. Later she committed suicide by taking poison.

In February 1933, the police tried to apprehend Surya Sen who was hiding in a village. He offered resistance, escaped and took refuge in a tank nearby when he was betrayed to the police by a Gurkha sepoy. The police captured Surya Sen and he was later sentenced to death. The Gurkha sepoy who betrayed him was killed by the revolutionaries. Although with the death of Surya Sen the revolutionary movement lost its momentum in Bengal, revolutionary ideas continued to dominate the youth. There were revolutionary cells in almost every educational institution. Hatred of foreign rule pervaded the whole atmosphere till it bore fruit in the Quit India Movement in 1942.

Kakori Railway Incident – Activities of Bhagat Singh

In Northern India too there were equally important happenings during the second phase of the revolutionary movement. The Kakori railway incident, under the leadership of Ramprasad and nine others, attracted wide attention. They boarded a train on the Shaharamour – Lucknow route, pulled the alarm chain as the train was reaching the Kakori station, entered the guard van, seized all the money amounting to several lakhs and fled. The authorities traced them and in the conspiracy case instituted against them and 31 others, four of them were sentenced to death and the others to varying terms of imprisonment in a trial that lasted one year. Chandrashekhar Azad, who assumed the leadership of the movement in North India, made it clear that the object of the revolutionaries was to establish a socialistic order after Swaraj was won. A number of strikes took place in 1928–29 in Bombay, Kanpur and Calcutta and this strengthened the revolutionary forces in the country. Several officials were assassinated but the murder of Saunders, the police official who was responsible for the lathi charge against Lajpat Rai in 1928 during the visit of Simon Commission, was the most notable of all. Bhagat Singh was the hero who performed this daring act and escaped arrest. As a consequence of this police repression increased in an around Lahore and many innocent people had to suffer. The people began to grumble that while the revolutionaries who were responsible for the assassination escaped, they were made to suffer the consequences of their deeds. Bhagat Singh felt immensely hurt and wanted to show that he was prepared to undergo any ordeal for the sake of the country. He and two of his associates entered the Legislative Assembly Hall on April 8, 1929. An important Bill which tried to check the activities of trade unions under the Communists was then under discussion, and considering this a most opportune time, they threw a bomb into the Assembly Hall. There was a tremendous stir in the House and though it was easy for them to escape, they continued to sit in the gallery and threw leaflets published by their association into the Hall. The police arrested them. Their trial which began on May 7, 1929 ended on June 12 and they were sentenced to transportation for life. During their trial they made open statements that their object was not the mere overthrow of the British rule but also to establish socialism and promote the welfare of the ordinary people. The police discovered a factory in Lahore and another in Shaharanpur where raw materials were stored to manufacture bombs. The police arrested a number of people following the discovery. Some of those who were arrested revealed to the police the secret activities of their Association and in addition to this they also disclosed that it was Bhagat Singh who killed Saunders. Thereupon Bhagat Singh and two of his associates were tried in what had come to be known as the Lahore Conspiracy case. In the course of the trial they claimed that as political prisoners they should be accorded special treatment and when that was refused, they undertook a fast in which they were joined by a few other political prisoners. The fast was abandoned soon after though Jitendar Das, a youngman continued his fast for 63 days and died. His body was taken to Calcutta, the place of his birth and on the way thousands of people gathered at every railway station to pay him homage. In Calcutta six lakhs of people joined the funeral procession. All this shows the great sympathy which the people in general had towards the revolutionaries and their administration for the heroism and courage displayed by them.

During their trial Bhagat Singh and his associates refused to be carried to the court. The police found it difficult to carry them Government then passed an ordinance under which the courts were empowered to try criminals even during their absence. On October 1930 Bhagat Singh, Sukhdev and Rajguru were sentenced to death and Tiwari and Bijoy Kumar Sinha to transportation for life and several others to long terms of imprisonment. Several of his friends advised Bhagat Singh to escape from the jail for which they made the necessary arrangements. He, however, refused to do so preferring death in the cause of the country. During the negotiations proceedings Gandhiji-Irwin Agreement, Gandhiji tried in vain to secure the Viceroy's pardon for them. Bhagat Singh and his associates were hanged on March 23, 1931, six days before the Karachi Session of the Indian National Congress.

The police bluntly turned down the request to handover Bhagat Singh's body to his relatives who were keen to arrange his funeral according to traditional rights. The police did the cremation on the banks of the river Ravi but before the body was completely burnt they threw it into the river and left the place. Thereupon, Bhagat Singh's admires rescued the body and cremated it according to traditional rites, collected the ashes and immersed them in the sacred river.

Dr. Pattabhai Sitaramaya has rightly said that Bhagat Singh's name was at that time as popular as that of Gandhiji. The people admired the sacrifices of the revolutionaries in the same way as they admired the sacrifices of the non-violent fighters. A resolution was passed at the Karachi session of the Congress placing on record the heroism displayed by Bhagat Singh.

Activities of Chandrashekhar Azad

After the Lahore conspiracy case the revolutionary movement lost its momentum. Almost all its leaders, except a few – Chandrashekhar Azad being one of the exceptions - fell into the hands of the police. Azad managed to continue his activities and even the police. Azad managed to continue his activities and even arranged to place a bomb on the railway track on which the train carrying the Viceroy was to run. Though the bomb caused damage to the train the Viceroy escaped unhurt. In July 1930 Azad raided a shop in Lahore and carried away a large booty. Some of those who were arrested revealed that Azad was responsible for the looting of the shop. A second Lahore conspiracy case was brought against him and some of his colleagues. But Azad escaped arrest. On February 27, 1931 a police party discovered him in a public park in Allahabad. The police could not secure his surrender and in the encounter that followed two policemen lost their lives before he was shot dead. With this the revolutionary movement in North India ended. Some of the revolutionaries joined the Congress while a few others the Communists Party.

Bombay, Central provinces, Madras and Rajputana too had their share of revolutionary activities. Factories for manufacturing bombs were started in Bombay and Ahmedabad. In 1930 an unsuccessful attempt was made to kill the Governor of Bombay while he was on a visit to the Ferguson College.

The Place of the Movement in the Freedom Struggle

The revolutionaries were dubbed as terrorists and murderers. But it was not for any personal gain that the revolutionaries resorted to killings. It was conceived as a part of their planned action for liberating the country and for establishing a socialist society. It was not a resounding success no doubt, but then even the non violent struggle launched by Gandhiji should, in terms of immediate results, be regarded as having failed. One has to take a broader and long range view of the historic developments to be able to make a proper assessment of the revolutionary activities. The British soon realized that it was no longer possible for them to exercise undisputed sway over India. From this angle the revolutionary movement should be accorded a high place among the factors that led to withdrawal of the British and the achievement of freedom.

CHAPTER 22

THE DEVELOPMENT FROM 1929–39

We have to trace the more important developments in the country in the period from 1929 to 1939 which had a momentous effect on the freedom movement; this may be regarded as an important decade in the history of the country as well as of the freedom movement. Among the developments special reference has to be made to the steps taken by the British Government to place on the Statue Book the Government of India Act of 1935. Secondly, the decade also witnessed a distinct change in the course of Muslim politics with communalism on the ascendancy. A third development related to the changes in the attitude of the Congress towards the working of the new Government of India Act – its participation in elections, the formation of Congress ministries in eight province and the subsequent resignation of the ministers, there were also changes in the internal politics of the Congress in relation to these developments.

The British adopted two distinct lines of policy in dealing with the political situation. One was that of repression – to put down the nationalist movement and the other was the policy of constitutional reform by creating a split among the Nationalists and winning over the Moderates, the Muslims and other minorities by meeting their separatist interests. We have noted the repressive policy adopted to deal with the Satyagraha and the civil disobedience movements led by the Mahatma Gandhi and the revolutionary movement. We now refer to the policy of constitutional reform which culminated in the passing of the Government of India Act of 1935.

The first step in the direction of constitutional reform was taken with the appointment of the Simon Commission in 1927 by the Conservative Party in Britain which was in office. It was the desire of that party that the new constitutional reforms should be based on the recommendations of the Commission. But the boycott of the commission in India, the resolution passed by the Lahore session of the Congress in favour of complete Independence followed by the Salt Satyagraha convinced the Labour party which meanwhile came into office that in the formulation of constitutional reforms, the view of the Indian representatives should have to be taken into consideration. That was the genesis of the Round Table Conference which held its first session in 1930.

These deliberations enabled the Labour party to gauge the views of Indian political parties on the shape of the future Government of India. But as the Congress did not participate in the Conference, the discussion appeared to be unreal and therefore efforts were mounted to bring the Congress at least to the second session of the Conference in 1931. Reference has already been made to the events which led to the participation of the Congress which Gandhiji as its sole representative in the second session of the Conference. But by that time the labour party went out of office and a coalition Government with the dominant support of the Conservative came to power. Though Ramsay Macdonald continued to be the Prime Minister, the Conservative party did not want to attach to the Round Table Conference any importance. It had already taken important political decisions that 1) the Government of India Act should be placed on the Statute Book and 2) that it should be based as far as possible on the recommendations contained in the report of the Simon Commission. In view of this the Conference lost all its importance and though a third session was held in 1932, the Conservative Government having made up its mind by that times as to what the nature of the future Government of India should be the Conference practically played no role in the shaping of the constitutional reforms.

The Communal Award of Ramsay Macdonald was a pointer to the shape of things to come. The British always believed that the Indians did not constitute a nation in the accepted sense of the term and they were made up of a number of communities with varying and divergent interests. The Communal Award clearly emphasized this point of view and it was decided that special representation should be given to Muslims, Sikhs, Backward Classes, Indian Christians, Anglo Indians, Chambers of Commerce, and Universities and that representatives of these bodies should be elected in separate communal constituencies with weightage as far as possible. An attempt was made in the Award to separate the Harijans from the Hindus but this had to be abandoned because of the fast unto death undertaken by Gandhiji and the ensuing Poona Pact. Subject to this exception, communal representation became a feature of the Government of India Act of 1935.

After the publication of the Communal Award, the British Government issued a white paper on Indian constitutional reforms. It provided broadly for a federal political system, for a form of Dyarchy at the Centre which was to come into effect along with the federal system, the abolition of Dyarchy in the provinces and the transfer of all power to ministries responsible to the legislatures which were all to be wholly elected subject to certain powers reserved to the Governors of the provinces to safeguard special interests like those of the minorities, the European mercantile community etc.

Indian Public opinion, especially represented by the Congress, the Muslim League led by Jinnah, and even the Moderates strongly condemned the reactionary provisions contained in the white paper. Even the Central Legislature passed a resolution disapproving of the white paper. The Conservatives cared little for Indian opinion and it referred the White Paper to a joint committee of both the houses of Parliament. A number of Indian witnesses appeared before the joint committees and submitted memoranda suggesting alternations in it. Ultimately the joint committee endorsed on the whole the main features contained in the white paper and submitted its report.

The Provisions of the Act

On the basis of this report, a bill was prepared which was passed by both Houses of parliament. It received Royal assent in 1935 and came to be known as the Government of India Act of 1935. It may be noticed that it took eight years for giving shape to the Act. But the result was not commensurate with the time taken to formulate it. It did not satisfy any of the political parties. It was put into effect in 1937. It was in operation for only a decade since by 1947 the country had become free and at no time the whole Act was implemented. The Centre continued to function under the Government of India Act of 1919 partly because the Government of India Act contained a condition that the federal system at the Centre should not come into effect until after a certain proportion of Indian princes agreed to enter the federation. Though at the first Round Table Conference, the princes welcomed the federation they subsequently changed their mind and they went on pressing for special privileges and status even after parts of the Government of India Act came into effect in 1937. Negotiations with them by the Government were not over by the time the Second World War broke out. The Government then decided that during the period of the war, there should be no changes at the Centre. The result was that the Central Government continued to function on the basis of the Act of 1919. The only new institutions created at the Centre were the Federal Court, the Federal Public Service Commission and the Federal Railway Board, but their impact on the constitutional set up was minimal. As a result of the act, Dyarchy was abolished in the provinces and all power was transferred to ministers responsible to the legislature. Legislature also became wholly elected. The franchise was widened and the number of voters under the Act was four times as large as that under the Act of 1919. The provinces became autonomous. The Act provided for a division of functions and powers between the Centre and the provinces. There was an enumeration of the powers allotted to the provinces and they included subjects like Public order, Justice and Courts, Education, Local Self Government, Land Revenue and Public Health.

There was also a separation in regard to finances. Certain taxes and sources of revenue were exclusively allotted to the provinces and they consequently acquired a modicum of financial autonomy. There was provision for grants from the Central Government to provincial Government to supplement their revenues.

Muslim Politics – Jinnah's Fourteen Points

The decade witnessed a further development in Muslim politics. Efforts made to bring about closer unity between the Hindus and the Muslims were sabotaged partly by the British Conservative Government and partly by the communalistic sections in India.

We have already noticed that attempts at unity made with the recommendations of the Nehru Committee of 1928 were under discussion. Jinnah, however, wanted alterations in the recommendation of the committee to safeguard the Muslim interest. This was not agreed to mainly by the representatives of Hindu Mahasabha. As a result he became even more communal minded. Even then he did not abandon his original nationalism. In 1929 he formulated a scheme for a new Indian constitution containing fourteen points to be the basis for unity between the communities. These points were –

1. The future constitution of India should be a Federation with all residuary powers located in the provinces;
2. That all provinces should have a uniform system of autonomy;
3. In the central and provincial legislature and in all other elected bodies the minorities should have adequate representation. In provinces where they were in a majority their representation also should be in conformity with it;
4. In the central legislature the Muslims should have one third representation, even though they constituted twenty four percent of the total population in the country;
5. All representative of minorities should be elected in separate and not mixed constituencies unless the minorities agreed to the mixed system;
6. If at any time the provinces were to be reconstituted the Muslims should remain a majority in Bengal, Punjab and North West Frontier provinces;
7. All communities should have complete religious freedom;
8. No Bill should come for discussion in any legislature if it were to be opposed by 3/4 of the representatives belonging to any community;
9. Sind should be separated from Bombay and constituted into a province;
10. Beluchistan and N.W. F. Province should have the same kind of autonomy as in other provinces;
11. Muslims should have separate representation in all public offices and in local bodies;
12. There should be constitutional guarantee for the protection of Muslim culture, education, religion, personal law and charitable institutions. They should have an adequate share in all grants made by the Government.
13. In all the ministries formed at the Centre or provinces, Muslims should be given atleast 1/3 of the seats and
14. No changes should be made by the Central legislature in the constitution without the approval of the provinces.

Hindus generally were agreeable to all these points except communal constituencies. Before a consensus could be reached on this, Jinnah left for London and did not return in India until 1934. The Leadership of Muslim politics passed during his absence into the hands of politicians who were totally communal minded.

Among them was Fazl-I-Hussain of Punjab. He became member of viceroy's Executive council and held that office during the session of the Round Table Conference. His view was that political power in India should be shared by the Hindus and Muslims and the six Indian provinces – Sind, Punjab, Beluchistan, N.W.F. Province, Bengal and Assam should be treated as Muslim majority provinces and U.P., Bihar, Bombay, Orissa, C.P. and Madras should be the six Hindu majority provinces and it was only then that power could be equally divided between the two communities.

As a member of the Executive Council, he tried hard to thwart the steps being taken by Sapru and Jayakat at the first session of the Round Table Conference and by Gandhiji as its special session to bring about a consensus on the question of electorates and he also prevented any nationalist Muslim like Dr. Ansari from being sent as a delegate to the Round Table Conference.

Shortly after the publication of the Communal Award, some of the National Muslims like Shaukat Ali and Maulana Azad convened a Hindu-Muslim Conference at Lucknow and had resolutions adopted in favour of joint electorates with reservation of 32 per cent of the seats in the Central legislatures. Just at that moment the section led by Fazl-I-Hussain condemned these resolutions and the then Secretary of State of India also announced that in the new constitution to be framed, the Muslims should be granted one third of the seats in the Central legislature and that Sind should be constituted into a separate province.

The Idea of Pakistan

The efforts unity thus came to nought. At about the time of the first Round Table Conference one Rahmat Ali a Muslim student of the Cambridge University, moved the idea for the first time that Muslim majority provinces should be constituted into a separate state to be called Pakistan. The proposal was taken up by the British Conservative Party though it was not given any serious consideration by the Muslim delegates at the conference. A little later at the annual conference of the Muslim league, the famous poet and Philosopher, Iqbal, pressed the same idea and from that time on it began to attract the attention of leading Muslim politicians. Gradually the idea caught up until in 1940 at the Lahore session of the Muslim League, a formal resolution that India should be divided into two separate States and that one of them Pakistan should be made over to the Muslims was passed it is thus clear that during the decade under reference, the separatist tendencies among the Muslims grew strong and they gained further strength as a result of the acute difference of opinion which arose between the Congress and Jinnah in the formation of the ministries after the elections in 1937.

Meanwhile, the Swarajya Party once more came to the forefront and it decided on participating in the elections to be held for the Central Legislature in 1934. There was however a split within the Congress between the two sections. One section led by Malavya wanted the Communal Award of Ramsay Macdonald should be condemned. The other section did not favour total condemnation. It was of the view that though the Congress was representative of all categories of people the Muslims were one distinct section recognized by the Communal Award and it was not advisable for the congress to totally reject it. As a result of these differences of opinion, Malavya and his supporters organised themselves into a Congress Nationalist Party and fought the elections held in 1934 as a separate party though remaining in the Congress. In the elections the Congress gained 44 elected seats in the Central legislature and the Nationalist party 11. By that time Jinnah returned from England, assumed the leadership of the Muslim league and was able to gain 22 elected seats. The congress –Nationalist Party agreed to work with the Congress inside the legislature. Jinnah also did the same and the results was that 77 members of the legislature constituting a majority of the total strength became a mighty opposition, voted against the budget and most of the Bills introduced by the Government and made it incumbent on the Governor General to frequently exercise his powers of certification, demonstrating thereby that the people of the country had no faith in the Government of the day.

The Growth of Leftism

During these years leftist ideas gained a foothold and were spreading their influence. Socialistic and Communistic thoughts were current. As the communists Party was banned, most of its members infiltrated into the congress ranks. At the Lucknow Session of the Congress held in April, 1936, Jawaharlal Nehru as President of the Session put forward views more or less akin to those of the Communists. He, Subhas Chandra Bose and a few younger members of the Congress constituted themselves into what may be regarded as the left wing. Gandhiji, though he was not a member of the Congress, was still its guiding star from behind the scenes as most of its prominent members had full confidence and faith in him. Under his influence, the Congress was opposed to any kind of Communism. Jawaharlal Nehru understood this and when he presided over the Faizpur session of the Congress at the end of 1936 he made no reference to Communism. Gandhiji's control over the Congress organization was near total and he held the view that its main duty was to fight for the freedom of the country and not to interpose ideological issue like communism which were certain to create a split and weaken the very progress of the freedom movement. Though leftism influenced sections of the Congress, it did not make any worthwhile impact.

Elections Under The Act of 1935

The Congress decided to participate in the elections to be held early in 1937 under the Government of India Act of 1935. The elections were, however, held for only the provincial legislatures Congress achieved a majority in U.P, Orissa, C.P., Bihar and Madras and it formed the largest single party in Bombay, N.W.F. Province, Assam and Bengal. Though the Muslim League participated in the elections under the leadership of Jinnah it was not able to secure an appreciable number of seats in Muslim majority provinces like Punjab, Sind and N.W.F. Province. The problem which the Muslim faced in these provinces were different from those in provinces like Madras and Bombay where they were in a minority. In the former, there was no fear of the Hindus dominating provincial politics. This was precisely the reason for the league not being able to cash in on its propaganda that Islam was in danger in the majority Provinces. It demonstrated that, as yet, the League was not in a position to claim that it was the sole representative of the Muslims in India. On the other hand, the Congress could claim to speak on behalf of all the non-Muslims in the country without being challenged.

Although the Congress was in a position to form ministries in several of the provinces, there was a controversy among the leaders as to whether this should be done at all. The sections led by Nehru. Was against such information, but the other sections supported in on the ground that as the Congress had participated in the elections it should stand to reason that they must accept office. It was also argued that through the formation of ministries the Congress would be able to undertake legislations and implement policies which promote the welfare of the people. Ultimately the pro-acceptance section gained around but the final decision was left to the all India Congress Committee. The Committee considered the issue in depth and resolved to form ministries provided the Governors gave an assurance that they would not interfere in any way with the functioning of the ministries. The Governors were not prepared to give such an assurance. But on further consideration, the Governor General came to the conclusion that the only alternative to the formation of popular ministries would be for the Governors themselves to assume powers of administration and such a course would be contrary to the spirit of the Act of 1935. He, therefore, made it clear that the Governors should not interfere in the exercise of the power granted by the Act of 1935 to the ministries.

The All India Congress Committee was satisfied with this assurance and it resolved that the Congress should form ministries in all the provinces in which it commanded a majority in the legislatures. Congress ministries were ushered in seven provinces in July 1937.

Rift Between the Congress and the Muslim League

A more serious problem had to be faced by the Congress in the formation of the ministries. It was incumbent on the Governors of provinces to see that the minorities were given due representation in the ministries. The Muslims were the most important of the minorities. The problem before the Congress was whether the Muslim to be included in the ministries should be from their party or belong to any non-Congress parties like the Muslim League. The question became highly controversial in the united provinces. The congress was of the view that only a Muslim belonging to the Congress party should be included in the ministry. It argued that it was only then that the ministry could work as a single team, but it was only then that the ministry could work as a single team, but Jinnah did not agree with the view. He held the opinion that only Muslims who were elected under separate Muslim constituencies were the real representatives of the Muslim Community. They alone would be in a position to safeguard the interest of the Muslims. Therefore, it was only those Muslims that should be included in the ministry. He also pointed out that in the United Provinces, especially, 26 out of the 64 Muslims members of the legislature belonged to the Muslim League and constituted the largest single Muslim group and that it was entitled to be included in the ministry. What he wanted was the formation of a coalition ministry consisting of the Congress and Muslim League.

The Congress laid down certain conditions before such a ministry could be formed. One was that in the legislature, the League Should not function as a separate unit but merge itself in the Congress. Jinnah was totally opposed to this. To him it appeared to be a suicidal policy. From 1905 onwards the League functioned as a separate unit. That it should now be merged in the Congress for the sake of one or two seats in the ministry was most unwelcome to him. He, therefore, rejected the conditions laid down by the Congress since such a step according to him would not lead to justice to the Muslims at the hands of the Congress. It was a parting of Ways between him and the Congress. This was the precursor to the passing of the resolution by the Muslim League on Pakistan.

The Work of the Congress Ministries

The Congress ministries remained in office for 28 months from July, 1937. The Congress had made a number of promises to the people in the election manifesto. But it was not possible to take immediate action on all of them. Elaborate preparation was called for before any action could be taken. The people on the other hand were impatient. In certain provinces like U.P. and Bihar, the peasant rose in revolt refusing to pay the rents due to the Zamindars. This created an acute law and order problem. Elsewhere the Communists encouraged strikes among the factory labourers as in Bombay, Ahmedabad and other cities. This also resulted in the outbreak of violence. It became necessary for the ministries to call in the police on a large scale for the purpose of maintaining law and order. Governors and the members of the Indian Civil Service were not sure if the Congress ministries would adopt a firm policy in matters like these. But the ministries rose to the occasion and they even secured proper guidance from Gandhiji and the Congress Working Committee in regard to the policies they should follow. The result was that they proved themselves to be efficient administrators though before they assumed office they were only trained to be participants and agitationists in non-co-operation campaigns. Congressmen showed they could be good at governance if they were given the opportunity and not mere critics of the British rulers.

Among the more substantive achievements of the Congress ministries were the measures to give relief to tenants in zamindari areas and generally to the weaker sections who were overburdened with debt. In several provinces, free and compulsory education was introduced. Schemes of basic education sponsored by Gandhiji were implemented and attempts were made to spread adult education. Steps were taken to remove untouchability, secure the entry of Harijans into temples and provide them with land and house sites. Yet another achievement was the introduction of Prohibition. Before they could accomplish more, the ministries had to resign following the outbreak of the Second World War.

THE PRELUDE TO QUIT INDIA MOVEMENT

CHAPTER 23

The Quit India movement of 1942–44 is the most significant landmark in the history of the freedom movement, heralding the final stage. The independent struggle which commenced in 1920 reached its conclusion with this movement. Then followed a period of negotiations which culminated in the final withdrawal of the British in India in 1947.

The Second World War

The Quit India movement is regarded as an offshoot of the Second World War and the reluctance of the Government to settle the national issue through negotiations. The war resulted in certain other developments which had a bearing on the freedom movement. It was during the Second World War, for instance, that the Indian National Army organised by Subhas Chandra Bose in Singapore and Malaya raised the banner of revolt. It was again during this period the conditions were created which enabled Jinnah to make the Muslim League the sole representative of its community and practically compelled the British to concede the demand for Pakistan. Above all it dealt a fatal blow to the British as an imperial power, for, by the end of the war it lost all its naval superiority as well as its overall military strength. Further, its financial resources were fully depleted. Britain practically became a bankrupt nation and worse, a satellite, as it were, of the United States of America. The Labour Government which came to power in Britain at the end of the war realized that in the face of the continued opposition of the Indian people it could no longer hold sway over them and it would be prudent to voluntarily abdicate power and grant freedom.

It should be noted that the British supremacy in India was not merely the outcome of wars they carried on here in the eighteenth century and the first half of the nineteenth but also the victory it achieved in the other wars waged with the Portuguese, the Dutch, the French and the Russians who were its close rivals in the quest for imperial ascendancy in India and in the other countries of Asia and Africa. It was not until after overcoming the resistance of the Portuguese, the Dutch and above all the French in Europe by waging successful wars against them that the British took the plunge and fought battles with the Marathas, the Sultans of Mysore, the Sikhs and other rulers in India. If therefore it was the wars of an earlier period that made Britain the ruler of India, it was the world wars that produced exactly the opposite effect in that Britain lost the Indian Empire. It was true that the British vanquished their enemies but it was a Pyrrhic victory that it ultimately achieved.

With the rise of Hitler to power in Germany in 1933, the alarm bells for the Second World War Started sounding ominously. The Congress seriously began to consider what its attitude should be towards Britain if war really broke out. At the Lucknow session of the Congress held in April 1936, Jawaharlal Nehru in his presidential address made it abundantly clear that India could never consent to be a party to an imperialistic war and that India could not come to the aid of Britain. In the Congress election manifesto this point was stressed beyond doubt, and the significance of the fact that the Congress was returned to power in eight provinces securing massive popular backing cannot be lost sight of. It was a sign that the people too shared the view that India should not participate in an imperialistic war. At the Haripura session of the Congress in 1938 as well as the Tripura session the year after, formal resolutions were passed to this effect.

The Resignation of the Congress Ministries

Just before the outbreak of the World War the Government of India Act of 1935 was amended by Parliament conferring more powers to the Central Government to exercise stricter control over the provincial governments in the eventuality of a war. This was done without any reference to the Indian Central legislature or to the popular ministries which held power in the provinces or to Indian public opinion. This was naturally resented to by the Congress and at the meeting of the All India Congress Committee held in August, 1938 a resolution was passed that unless the British introduced a truly democratic form of Government, India should not lend support to the war effort even though it might be claimed by the British that it was being fought for the preservation of democracy. On September 3, the war broke out with England, France and Poland on one side, Germany and Austria on the other. Immediately a proclamation was issued by the Viceroy that India as part of the British Empire automatically became a party to the war and that all the people should actively help the Government in the prosecution of the war. This unilateral declaration was strongly resented to by the Congress. The Princes, the liberals, the Justice party and the party of the Harijans led by Dr. Ambedkar and a few other organizations decided on giving full support to the British during the period of the war. Subhas Chandra Bose who by that time had left the Congress to form a new political party called the Forward Bloc declared that not only should aid not be given to the British, but also that the satyagraha campaign should immediately be started to compel the British to part with power. He campaigned vigorously to press this view in the country which led to his immediate imprisonment.

The congress, however, could not arrive at any firm decision in regard to its attitude though all along it passed resolutions against participating in an Imperialistic war. Differences of opinion cropped up among the leaders after the war broke out. Gandhiji wedded as he was to non-violence was averse to giving aid to the British in a violent war. At the same time, he felt that it was inconsistent with the principles of Satyagraha to start a movement when the enemy was in difficulty and thus aggravate the crisis. Nehru on the other hand saw in the war a struggle between the forces of democracy for which Britain and France stood and the forces of fascism led by Hitler and that in such a war it was the moral duty of the people of India to aid the former in its bid to wipe out fascism. The Congress Working Committee met on September 15 and passed a resolution calling on the Government to declare its war aims and agreeing to wait till such a declaration was made before it took a decision. On October 10 the All India Congress Committee met and passed a resolution calling on the Government not only to declare its war aims but also make it clear that its aim was to grant complete independence to India, and that some steps would be taken in this direction.

The Muslim League under the leadership of Jinnah met on September, 18 and resolved that no constitutional reform should be introduced unless it was approved by the league and that the league should be recongnised as the only body representative of the Muslim community as a whole and that if the Government accepted these two propositions, it would extend all the support it demanded.

The Viceroy meanwhile consulted several other leaders. On October 17 he made an announcement stating:

1. that it was the ultimate aim of the British to confer Dominion Status ;
2. that it was not either desirable or practicable to take any steps in that direction during the period of the war;
3. that till the end of the war the Government should be carried on in accordance with the provision of the Act of 1935;
4. that at the end of the war the Government would bring about a new Government of India Act after consulting the leaders in the country and the minorities like the Muslims and
5. that an advisory committee consisting of the representatives of the princes and of the important political parties should be constituted to give advice to the government during the period of the war.

In this announcement there was no definition of war aims or of any steps that would be taken in the direction of independence as demanded by the All India Congress Committee. On October 22, the Congress working Committee met and resolved that as there was no change in the attitude of the British Government and they had the least desire to part with political power the best course for the Congress was to non-co-operate with the Government and consequently the Congress Ministries in the eight provinces where they held office from July, 1937 should resign rather than co-operate with the Government in its war activities. Accordingly by about November 15 all the ministries resigned.

There was a sharp difference of opinion among the informed sections in the country as to whether the resignation of the ministries was at all a wise step. There were some who genuinely believed that had the ministries continued they could have influenced the policies of the Governments to some extent and that they had lost such an opportunity by quitting office. As it became clear that no co-operation would be forthcoming from the Congress, the British began to lean more and more on Jinnah and the Muslim League for support for carrying on the war and for running the normal administration. Jinnah took advantage of this situation, and within four months after the resignation of the Congress ministries, he got a resolution passed at the

Lahore session of the League held in March, 1940 demanding the creation of a separate state for Pakistan as the only solution to the Hindu-Muslim problem. The government seemed to be in a mood to give favourable consideration to such a demand.

It was difficult for the Congress to decide on the further course of action. The resignation of the ministries could not by itself be a final answer to the burning issue before the country. The matter came up for discussion at the session of the Congress held in March, 1940 at Ramagarh under the Presidentship of Maulana Azad. It was resolved that nothing short of Independence would satisfy the aspirations of the people, that the representative of the people alone had the right to frame a constitutional and that if the Government did not take immediate steps in the direction of granting Independence, the Congress would be obliged to resort to civil disobedience.

Gandhiji's Opposition to Mass Civil Disobedience

And yet there was considerable hesitation to launch a civil disobedience movement immediately. Gandhiji was not very much in favour of resorting to it on moral grounds. He was also of the view that the masses had not become completely non-violent and therefore mass civil disobedience could well lead to violence. He was afraid that the Muslims would keep out of such a movement and that communal riots might ensue if the congress gave the call for civil disobedience. Jawaharlal Nehru also was against such a movement as he thought that it would weaken the course of democracy. Hence the Congress resolution in favour of the civil disobedience movement could not be immediately put into practice.

From April 1940 the war situation in Europe took a serious turn. Hitler brought under his control Denmark, Norway, Sweden and France. The German airforce bombed cities and industrial centers in England. German submarines continued to sink British ships carrying food and raw materials from distant parts of the world to Britain. It appeared as if Hitler might invade England and subjugate it. This created a painful dilemma for the Congress leaders. Several held the view that they should actively help the British and put a stop to the further progress of Hitler and his Fascism. They were even prepared to ignore Gandhiji in this regard.

The Congress Working Committee met in July 1940 at Poona and passed a resolution that the British should immediately issue a declaration that their ultimate aim was to grant independence to India and that they should establish at the Centre a National Government responsible to the legislature and if this was done the Congress would give all support to the war effort. The All India Congress Committee endorsed the resolution knowing fully well that Gandhiji was opposed to lending support to a violent war. Gandhiji, there upon, renounced his leadership of the Congress.

On August 8, the Viceroy, Lord Linglithgow, announced British policy in response as it were to the resolution of the Congress and of the Muslim League. He stated that 1) some more Indians would be appointed to his executive council, 2) that an advisory body would immediately be constituted.3) that under no circumstances would the British undertake any kind of constitutional reform which would not secure the approval of the minorities and especially of the Muslims and 4) that at the end of the war a constituent Assembly representative of all sections of the people would be convened to frame the future Constitution of India.

But this announcement did not satisfy the Congress. What is wanted was a responsible Government at the Centre and not a mere addition of some more members to the executive council which was responsible only to the Viceroy. The third item in the announcement was in contradiction to the fourth. Any constitution framed even by a Constituent Assembly was made subject to the approval of the Muslim minority. This meant that a minority representing only about 25 percent of the population had the right to veto the decision of seventy-five percent of the people. This, it was held, was only in conformity with the British policy of "Divide and Rule". The Muslim League was fully satisfied with the announcement while the Congress felt firmly that it was most undemocratic.

The Congress Working Committee which met from 18th to 22nd August appealed to Gandhiji to assume the leadership of the Congress once again. Gandhiji agreed to it. By that time it was clear that all attempts at the negotiated settlement were of no avail. The question was whether the resolution of the Ramgarh Congress that civil disobedience should be resorted to should be followed up by matching action.

Individual Civil Disobedience

While Gandhiji was still opposed to mass civil disobedience he could not any more resist the pressure from Congressmen that civil disobedience should be resorted to. It was then decided on what came to be called "individual civil disobedience" as distinct from "mass civil disobedience". It was only a few individuals selected by Gandhiji that should offer Satyagraha. Its object was not so much to secure straightway the freedom of the country as to assert the individual's right to freedom to speech. Everyone who was permitted by Gandhiji to resort to it was asked to proclaim that the war undertaken by the British was an unrighteous war and that Indians should not participate in it. Such a public declaration was considered seditious by the Government, and all those who did so were sentenced to imprisonment.

Among the first to offer individual satyagraha was Vinoba Bhave. Then came the turn of the members of the Congress Working Committee, including Nehru, Patel and Rajendra Prasad. Gandhiji gave permission to a large number of Congressmen for participating in the movement. Till about the end of 1941, 25,000 persons were in different jails. The British were unmoved by the satyagraha. In August 1941, Churchill and Roosevelt issued what became the famous Atlantic Charter promising self-government to all subject nations on the Ground that every nation had an inherent right to independence. Several Indians thought that the Charter would apply to India also. But in September Churchill made a categorical statement in the House of Commons that the Charter had reference only to people subjugated by Hitler and not to India or the other British dependencies. This made it clear that the individual civil disobedience movement had no visible impact on the British policy towards India. Gradually the enthusiasm for the movement dwindled and by December 1941 it almost came to an end.

Course of Muslim Politics

In October, 1937 the Muslim League met at a conference in Lucknow under the Presidentship of Jinnah and passed a resolution demanding equal partnership between Hindus and Muslims in the Government of the Country, that in all elected bodies 50 percent of the seats should be reserved to the Muslims and the Government should recognize the Muslim League as the only body representative of the Muslim community. Punjab leaders who were till then kept aloof from the league had now accepted the leadership of the league and of Jinnah and the ulemas who were generally opposed to the secular policies of Jinnah also supported him. This was the great triumph for him, he insisted that the Congress was prepared to negotiate with him, he insisted that the Congress should declare itself to be a purely Hindu organization and among the Congress representatives appointed to negotiate with him there should be no Muslim. This meant that even eminent Nationalist Muslims of the order of Maulana Azad should not join in any team to negotiate on behalf of the Congress. Acceptance of this demand was bound to be a suicidal move in as much as the Congress was a national body from the very beginning and representative of all communities including the Muslims.

In December 1938, the League met at Patna and decided that it should resort to direct action to assert Muslim rights against alleged abuse to powers by the Congress ministries. But before effect was given to this resolution the Congress ministries resigned and Jinnah felt that there was no need for any direction action. On the other hand, he issued a directive to the Muslims that they should observe the day of the resignation of the Congress ministries as a day of victory for the Muslims and many Muslims did respond.

Meanwhile the Government too veered round to his point of view, and announced that in all matter affecting the Muslim community, it should only consult Jinnah and his league. It was at this stage that the Muslim League held its session in March 1940 at Lahore and passed a resolution urging that all the Muslim majority provinces in the North West and North East parts of India should be constituted into a separate State of Pakistan. By that time, Jinnah was fully convinced that in a united India there could be no sharing of political power between the Hindus and the Muslims and that it was only when the country was partitioned that the Muslims would be in position to exercise political power independently of the Hindus.

And yet the creation of Pakistan was no real solution to the Hindu-Muslim problem. Pakistan would only be of advantage to Muslims in provinces where they were in a majority like Punjab, Sindh and Bengal. The fact was that in these provinces, there was no fear of Hindu domination and the creation of Pakistan was not going to make any difference to their position either. Nor Pakistan was going to be of any help to the Muslims in provinces where they were in a minority. In such provinces, they would have to live alongside of the Hindus. But, Jinnah apparently had little concern for the Muslims in these provinces. Moreover even after the creation of Pakistan the idea was not to exterminate Hindus, Sikhs and Christians. There would still be a

Hindu-Muslim problem in it and the problem of Non-Muslim minorities in Pakistan was bound to persist. In spite of serious defects lie these Jinnah stood by the Pakistan resolution, and it became a one point programme in his policy during the next seven years when the British actually partitioned the country and handed over power to two separate Dominions – India and Pakistan – on August 15, 1947. The movement gained ground mainly because the professional middle class among the Muslims gave support to it as it was felt that they would then be able to get jobs and improve their economic condition without having to compete with the educated Hindus in a united India. Several sections of the British gave their active support to it. They felt that was the most effective way of "punishing" the Congress and the Hindus who were bitterly opposed to British Rule.

From the middle of 1941, the war situation proved even more critical for the British. Hitler invaded Soviet Russia and quickly marched into the interior of the Country and was knocking at Moscow. Large parts of Russia were occupied by his forces. It was the biting cold that halted his advance. But he was certain that after the winter was over, he would be able to bring South-Eastern Russian under his control and even march to the borders of India via Persia. Mussolini also had entered the war by that time. Both he and Hitler arranged to invade Northern Africa with the object of occupying Egypt and cutting off the Suez route to India. Hitler also succeeded by the end of the year in occupying the island of Crete, Greece, Rumania, and Hungary and Bulgaria became allied to him. All this meant the choking of the passage of British ships through the Mediterranean to India.

America and Japan enter the War

More serious than this was the entry of Japan into the war in alliance with Germany and Italy. In December 1941, it suddenly attacked the American ships in Pearl Harbour in the Pacific causing large-scale destruction. The Americans were drawn into the war as a consequence, but it took time before they could stem the onward march of the Japanese forces. Within four months the Japanese were able to occupy the Phillipines, Hong Kong, Indonesia, the entire Indo-China, destroy the British ships in the Singapore harbour, bring Singapore and Malaya under their control and even invade Burma. The British were compelled to evacuate their possession on the other side of Bay of Bengal and it appeared to be only a question of time when the Japanese would invade India.

This added a new dimension to the problem before the Congress. What was to be done in case the Japanese invaded the country? What was to be done in case the Japanese invaded the country? Would it be possible for the battered British to defend India? Would they also evacuate large areas of India in the face of Japanese invasion? It was the view of Gandhiji that in case Japan invaded the country, the people should resist them in a non-violent way according to the principles of satyagraha. But this did not appeal to his followers. In the later part of December, the Congress Working Committee met at Bardoli and passed resolutions offering active help to the Government if the two conditions on which it insisted earlier – 1) and immediate declaration in favour of India's independence, and 2)the installation of the representative National Government responsible to the Central Legislature were fulfilled. It was only on behalf of such a National Government that the people would enthusiastically fight.

On January 2, 1942 Sapru and eleven other leaders belonging to the Liberal and other parties also appealed to the British Premier that he should accept the conditions imposed by the Congress. But neither the resolution of the congress Working Committee nor the appeal of Sapru had the desired effect. The Government of India and the British Cabinet strictly stood by the Viceroy's announcement of August 8, 1940. In February, Chiang Kai Shek, the head of the Chinese Government, visited India. He had been engaged in a war with the Japanese since 1936, mostly with the help of the arms from the British and the Americans through Burma and North Eastern India. If the Japanese invaded India, the supply route to China was bound to be snapped. So his object in visiting India was to study the India situations at first hand and to bring about an understanding between the British Government and the Congress. He was quick to realize that without the support of the Congress it would not be possible for the British to defend India and also to mobilize men and materials to help him. He met Gandhiji, Nehru, and prominent political leaders and also responsible British officials. He thereupon appealed to the British Premier to come to terms with the Congress. But his appeal fell on deaf ears.

It was now the turn of President Roosevelt. He understood right that India occupied a key position from the strategic point of view in the war against Japan. In his opinion Japan constituted a source of greater danger to the Allied cause then even Hitler. It was necessary according to him that the British Cabinet should accept the conditions laid down by the Congress and secure its co-operation in mobilizing the resources of the country for fighting the Japanese. He wrote to the British premier and also instructed America's Ambassador in London to convince Churchill about the need to conciliate the Congress.

Cripp's Proposals

Since Britain depended on American help for carrying on the war, the British could not brush aside the meaningful appeal made by Roosevelt. The British Prime Minister had perforce to make a move in the direction suggested by the President. The British Cabinet met, drafted proposals for the purpose and deputed Sir Strafford Cripps, a prominent member of the Cabinet, and a personal friend of Nehru to negotiate with the Congress on the basis of these proposals. Cripps arrived in India on March 23, 1942.

The proposals which he bought consisted of two parts. The first dealt with the future constitutional set-up of the country and the second with the immediate reconstitution of the Central Government in India. There were four proposals in the first part. 1) the first laid down that India would become a Dominion by the end of the war with the right to secede from Britain if it wanted; 2) that a Constituent Assembly would be convened consisting of the representative of the people and the constitution drawn by the Assembly would form the basis of the future constitution of India; 3) that any province or group of provinces which were unwilling to accept such a Constitution would be free to become separate Dominions; 4) that as the British gave assurance from time to time to the minorities in India, the Dominion Government of the future would enter into a treaty with Britain to enable the British to give effect to those assurances and also to safeguard some other essential interests of Britain.

The second part which dealt with a new Central Government emphasized that as long as the war lasted, the defence of India should be the sole responsibility of the British Government. The Governor General and his Executive Council would continue to carry on the Government. This meant that there would be no responsible Government at the Centre during the war.

The Congress did not evince much interest so far as the future set-up was concerned. It welcomed the first two proposals in the first part, but it was opposed to the third proposal which favoured the setting up of more than one Dominion in the country and conceding the demand by the League for Pakistan. The reason for the Congress not evincing much interest in the future set-up was that in the past many promises were made by the British only to be broken. And there was no guarantee that the promises contained in the proposals brought by Cripps would be implemented. What it wanted was the establishment immediately of a responsible Government at the Center. It was only then that the people would feel that the Government was theirs and they should do every thing possible to help in defending the country. As a result of the discussions which Cripps had with Maulana Azad, the Congress president, Nehru and other Congress Leaders he was personally convinced that there should be a responsible National Government at the Centre and assured them that the Governor General's Executive Council in future will work as a responsible ministry and that the Viceroy will occupy the same position in the Government of India as the King did in England.

The Congress leaders were hopeful that a settlement on these lines would be approved by the British Cabinet though it was not in conformity with the proposals which Cripps brought along with him. But there was considerable opposition on the part of the Viceroy and the members of the Executive Council to such a settlement. Cripps did not take the Viceroy into confidence while carrying on negotiations with the Congress leaders. The Viceroy felt hurt and he wrote to Churchill that under no circumstances should be responsible government be installed at the center during the period of the war. Churchill agreed with the Viceroy and he vetoed any settlement on the lines proposed by Cripps. Cripps was helpless in the face of the veto of the British Premier and the Cabinet. The emissary of President Roosevelt who was specially sent to India to mediate between Cripps and the Congress tried his best to prevail on Cripps to stick to the Congress point of view. But he also failed. The Congress was upset at the withdrawal of the assurance given by Cripps.

Just before the departed from India, Cripps made the astounding statement in a broadcast that the proposals which he brought from Britain and his mission failed because of the obstinate attitude of the Congress Working Committee and of Gandhiji's faith in his creed of non-violence. When Roosevelt came to know of the intended departure of Cripps, he wanted Churchill to delay it so as to carry on further negotiations. But Churchill replied that Cripps had already left, and that in the face of the obstinacy of the Congress no purpose would be served by further negotiations. Thus ended the mission of Sir Stafford Cripps. It should be noted that Jinnah's Muslim League also rejected the proposals of Cripps on the ground that there was no reference to Pakistan in it.

Even before the departure of Cripps, the congress made it clear that what it wanted was a National Government representative of all political parties in the country and not just a government dominated by the Congress alone. Though it was against a coalition Government in 1937, it now felt that the Muslim League and Jinnah should be accommodated and a resolution on these lines was passed by the Congress working Committee on April 10. Cripps who was well aware of this made an untrue statement in India as well as in the House of Commons later that the Congress wanted to dominate over the Government of the Country without regard of the minorities and that was the main reason for the failure of his mission.

Quit India Resolution of the Working Committee

The failure of the Cripps' Mission convinced Gandhiji that the British were not willing to part with power at all. The only solution to the Indian problem was that the British should quit India immediately after transferring power in an orderly manner to a national Government. He wrote a series of articles in the "Harijan" on the subject of Quit India and made it clear how it would not adversely affect the interest of Britain and her allies in carrying on the war against Japan. The points on which he placed emphasis were :

1. India belongs to the people of the country. The British have no right to rule over it.
2. It was because the British ruled over India that the Japanese wanted to invade the country. If the British transferred power to the Indian people there would be no danger of a Japanese invasion.
3. Even if Japan invaded the country after the British withdrawal the India people were ready to make all sacrifices for safeguarding their newly acquired independence. There was no question of the Indian people ever collaborating with the Japanese. Even if the

British did not withdraw from the country, the Indians would not seek the co-operation of Japan in driving them out.

4. The new national Government to be formed in India after the withdrawal of the British would permit Britain, America and their allies to station their forces in the country, occupy military bases for the purpose of carrying on the war with Japan. It is not the desire of the Indian people that Britain, America, China, or Russia should be defeated in the war. There would, therefore, be no obstacles in the way of the allied forces carrying on their operations against the Japanese even after the withdrawal of the British forces.
5. The new National Government in India would be representative of all parties and it would have the necessary strength and capacity to organize the defences of the country and to carry on the day administration. If even anarchy were to follow after the withdrawal of the British it was preferable to the imperial sway of Britain. But there was no danger of any such anarchy.

On July 14, the Congress Working Committee met at Wardha and passed the following resolution:

1. Britain should immediately quit India. This is necessary not only in the interests of India but also in the interests of world peace and the overthrow of fascism, imperialism and all other forms of dictatorial and racial domination.
2. There can be no solution to the Hindu-Muslim problem as long as a third party like the British continued to rule the country. It is the policy of divide and rule adopted by the British that has all along stood in the way of a solution to the communal problem.
3. As soon as the British withdrawal a national Government representative of all parties will be formed and a Constituent assembly will be duly convened to frame a Constitution agreeable to all sections of the people.
4. Permission will be given by the new national Government for stationing of allied forces in the country to carry on operations against Japan.
5. The Congress, therefore, appeals to the British to accept the resolution that they should quit India and transfer power immediately into Indian hands.
6. In case the British refused to quit the country, the Congress would be compelled to resort to civil disobedience and utilize all the

non-violent strength at its disposal to bring pressure upon the Government and to achieve freedom.

7. As the subject is of very great importance the final decision should be left to a meeting of the All India Congress Committee to be convened in Bombay on August 7.

In the interval between the meeting of the Congress Working Committee and the All India Congress Committee in Bombay, the Muslim League passed a resolution condemning the move for civil disobedience on the ground that it was intended to establish Hindu rule over the country. The liberals and political parties like the Hindu Mahasabha too disapproved the idea of civil disobedience. But as subsequent events had shown a majority of the people of the country were in favour of the stand taken by the Congress Working Committee.

AICC Meeting in Bombay

The All India Congress Committee which had its momentous session in Bombay discussed the issue for two days. A resolution was passed on August 8, endorsing the decision of the working committee and authorizing Gandhiji to work out the details of the civil disobedience movement in case it was launched.

It was not the objective of Gandhiji that civil disobedience should be immediately started. He was still hoping to get an interview with the Viceroy to discuss the matter with him before taking the eventual step. He thought all this would take several weeks and that was why he did not lay down and set guidelines for the movement incase it was to be carried on. The Viceroy, however, moved swiftly to take action against Gandhiji and other Congress leaders. On August 9, early in the morning, Gandhiji was arrested and kept in the Aga Khan palace. All the Members of the Congress Working Committee were also taken to custody and lodged in Ahmednagar. In the next two or three days provincial and district congress leaders were also rounded up. Simultaneously, all Congress committees were declared unlawful. Congress meetings were also banned. In short, the Government did everything within its power to deprive the people of leadership. The masses were left with nobody to guide them and yet there was a thrilling popular upsurge. The desire for freedom was entrenched firmly in the minds of the people who carried on the movement with tremendous zeal and enthusiasm. The Quit India movement made rapid strides.

❖ ❖ ❖

CHAPTER 24

THE COURSE OF THE QUIT INDIA MOVEMENT

The Nature of the Quit India Movement

The Quit India Movement was qualitatively different from the satyagraha movements of 1921–22, 1930–31 and 1932–34. In the first place, it was not only Congressmen but also those who belonged to the Forward Block the Revolutionaries and other extreme leftists participated in it. It was verily a mass movement. Even though all the prominent leaders were in jail the people carried on the movement. This was a source of irritation to the Government because it thought that when once the people were deprived of leadership, the movement will automatically collapse. In the second place, the movement was not strictly non-violent in character. Many of those who believed in violence as the only method for getting rid of foreign rule participated in it. Some Congressmen also began to feel that there was nothing wrong in resorting to violence. This was illustrated by the fact that in 1940 and 1941 the Congress working committee passed resolution informing the Government that the Congress was ready under the leadership of Gandhiji and the creed of non-violence not withstanding, to help the Government in carrying on the war provided it agreed to certain conditions. The Quit India Movement assumed the character of the revolutionary movement of the kind witnessed elsewhere in other parts of the world. Moreover Gandhiji only stipulated they should be prepared to make any sacrifice and undergo any amount of suffering in the cause of the country's freedom. The one directive he gave to the people was "Do or Die". The participants interpreted this each in his own way and the results was violence on a large scale which could not be avoided.

The Course of the Movement

People also resorted to violence to match the use of the force by the police and by the armed forces when they observed hartal. They organised actually peaceful processions on the 9th and the 10the August in protest against the arrest and imprisonment of their leaders. As a result of the repressive measures unleashed by the authorities many people lost their lives and several were injured, and this provoked the people to resort to violence. In the absence of any specific guidelines from Gandhiji, provincial Congress committees laid down their own plans for carrying on the movement. Cutting off of telegraph lines and telephone wires, destruction of railway track, attacks on railway stations and interfering with all lines of traffic by which the police and the military force were moved from place to place occupied a prominent place in the action programme. Among those who advocated violence was Jaya Prakash Narayan, the leader of the Socialist Party. He established branches of his party in the country with the object of collecting arms from places like Goa, manufacturing bombs and explosives, setting fire to petrol tanks and destroying all means of transport. Revolutionary cells were established in different parts of the country by other parties also. They carried on underground activities which became violent. Railway stations were attacked by crowds, the equipment in the stations was destroyed, rails were removed, trains were stopped forcibly at stations and railway wagons were set on fire. Deep pits were dug across the roads to dislocate transport. In some parts of the country, trains came to a dead stop and for a number of days Bengal for instance was cut off from the rest of the country.

The movement was most intense in the eastern parts of U.P., Bihar and Bengal. In these areas the people were able to establish even parallel government. In Midnarpore especially such a government lasted from December 1942 to August 1944. But the masses who indulged in violence did not have the capacity to assert themselves nor did they have any experience in administration. The leaders were all thrown into prison and there was no central organization to coordinate the activities of the people in different areas. Though revolutionary fervour of the highest order was displayed no decisive results could be attained in the end.

Suppression of the Movement

Moreover, the Government ruthlessly suppressed the movement. It used the massive force at its command to terrorise the people. In the indiscriminate firings that followed a large number of persons lost their lives. The police wielded the lathi on every conceivable occasion. Undertrial prisoners were served no food and starvation deaths were not uncommon. The prisoners were also subjected to torture and women prisoners were made to suffer indignities of the worst form. Even children were not spared. In villages houses were set on fire. Collective fines were imposed. The country looked as if it was under military occupation what with the deployment of armies everywhere. The British Prime Minister even admitted that the army was concentrated to the maximum extent possible in India.

Students played a prominent role in the struggle. They abandoned their studies to participate in the activities connected with the Quit India movement. While there are no exact estimates of the number of people who either lost their lives or were permanently maimed or sent to jail official figures had it that the arrests between August 9 and December 1942 were 60,229. Those who were sent jail after trial numbered 26,000 and 18,000 persons were kept in jail without trial. The number of persons who were killed was 1,090.

On the whole the people showed exemplary courage and grim determination to carry on by subjecting themselves to suffering willingly. It was expected that workers would go on a general strike, but it did not materialize since most of the factory labourers were under the influence of the communists party which kept aloof from the movement.

Result of the Movement

The Quit India movement was not a total failure as some critics seem to imagine. The determination of the people to get rid of foreign rule and free the country became even more deep-rooted as a result of the movement. It also indicated that they would participate wholeheartedly in similar movements when the occasion arose. The Government also realized that though it was able to suppress the movement the last word on it was not said. It also had to reckon with the fact that the movement would not necessarily be non-violent and that the people were ready for guerilla warfare.

To suppress a whole nation such circumstances would be impossible. This was the reason why from about the end of 1944 the British thought seriously of entering into negotiations with the Congress to secure a peaceful settlement of the political issue. That it was also possible to bring about this qualitative change in the attitude of the British is a distinct gain and the Quit India movement cannot by any count be regarded as having failed. It created positive conditions which were conducive to the achievement of freedom much earlier.

Though the movement was suppressed by the Government it blamed Gandhiji for all the violence that broke out and the Congress party which was wedded to non-violence was held to be really behind all the violence that characterized the movement. In a series of letters which he wrote to the Viceroy, Gandhiji tried his best to show that neither he nor the Congress as such was responsible for what had happened. Though the resolution in favour of "Quit India" and the starting of civil disobedience was passed on August 8, it was never his intention, he said, to start it immediately. He thought of meeting the Viceroy and carrying on negotiations with him. He was denied opportunity to do this. Moreover all Congress leaders were thrown into jail and the people were left leaderless. The Quit India movement was thus a spontaneous one and it was not carried on under his direction or under the direction of the Congress. If he had been free, he would most likely have suspended such a movement as on previous occasions, keeping his options open, the moment there was even the least violence. But he was given no opportunity this time, and he argued it was wrong on the part of the Government to accuse him or the Congress.

The Viceroy was not convinced of Gandhiji plea. Moreover the British Premier went on repeating that only Gandhiji was responsible for all the violence but also Congress itself was a small party and its demand for self-government was opposed by as many as nine crores of Muslims, five crores of untouchables and another nine crores of people in Princely states. The Congress, therefore, spoke only for a minority of 16 crores out of a total population of 39 crores. No change was discernable in the general attitude of the British towards the Indian political problem. Gandhiji, therefore, felt that he should prove his earnestness by undertaking a fast from February 10, 1943 to March 3. During the period of the fast, all political parties in the country except the Muslim league appealed to the Government to release him from prison. Prominent Americans also made a similar appeal. But the Government paid little heed. As a protest three Indians members of the Viceroy's Executive Council resigned. Gandhiji successfully went through the ordeal. Within a few months after this, the private secretary passed away followed by the death of Kasturba, his life partner. Even them the Government was not inclined to release him. It was only on May 5, 1944, when he fell seriously ill that the government set him free. By that time the war took a favourable turn and this was also one of the factors that led to the release of Gandhiji.

The quit India Movement may have failed to achieve the final objective inspite of the heroic sacrifices made by the people. It must be noted that the British suppressed it with all the might at their disposal. Those who participated in it were no match to the authoritarian regime and in fact people in one part of the country did not know exactly what was happening elsewhere. There was no machinery for co-ordinating their activities. The large majority of them had very little political sense. The leaders who could have guided the students, the illiterate peasant and the large mass of people were in jail. Yet the participants showed remarkable enthusiasm and endurance, but the main constraint was they could not channel their activities in a positive and constructive manner. A mere negative approach of the kind that was witnessed, significant as it was, did not prove to be adequate for the purpose on hand. But in the long run the movement was really productive. It strengthened among the people the desire to free the country from alien rule. The British were aware that the next movement might not be non-violent and that the chances of a guerilla warfare for achieving their objective could not be ruled out. Therefore they veered round to the view at the end of the Quit India movement that the right thing would be to initiate negotiations with the political parties. The Quit India movement could thus be regarded as epoch making in India's freedom struggle.

OTHER DEVELOPMENTS DURING THE QUIT INDIA MOVEMENT

CHAPTER 25

American Report on the Incapacity of Britain to Defend India

Even as the Quit India movement was in progress there were other significant developments which exercised considerable influence on the freedom movement itself. The first was the view entertained by the representative of President Roosevelt who came to India that the British were in no position to defend the country if the Japanese attacked it. They seemed to corroborate the views of the Congress and the consequential demand that British should quit immediately. The demand of the Congress for British withdrawal stemmed from the firm conviction that in case of a Japanese attack the British in India would evacuate the country, just as they evacuated Singapore, Malaya, and Burma leaving the country defenceless. It therefore urged that they should handover power immediately to a national Government which alone could mobilize all the resources available for defending the country. Its point of view was that the British should evacuate the country in an orderly manner so that there will be time for new national government to organize defence on efficient lines. It is remarkable that the representatives of the American President conveyed to Roosevelt a general impression that the British had neither the strength nor the will to defend the country against the Japanese invasion. They made it clear that most of the regiments in the Indian army were away fighting in West Asia and North Africa and the few regiments left in India were too weak to fight the Japanese. They also observed that the sepoys were mere mercenary soldiers fighting for the sake of money. The Britishers who commanded the Indian army were of low caliber and they were sent to India as they were not competent to fight battles in Europe or North Africa. The Commander–in-Chief, Lord Wavell, though a man of great ability was too old to organize the defence on proper lines. The British, it was pointed out were sure that the Americans would be able to defeat the Japanese ultimately and in that eventuality they would give back to Britain all the possessions they had lost. It was this confidence that made them indifferent to India's defence. It was, therefore, pointed out that the American President should prevail upon Churchill to come to an understanding with the Congress and if that was not possible, to send more American forces especially airplanes to India for warding off a Japanese attack. Though Roosevelt felt that the British should negotiate with the Congress he was not particularly keen to exercise pressure on Churchill for fear that it might create a split between Britain and America which was not exactly desirable at that stage of the war.

The Bengal Famine

The years 1942–44 witnessed a steady deterioration in the economic situation in the country. As a result of the war, prices spiralled and even essential goods like food and clothing became scarce. India which was self-sufficient at one time in food had to import from abroad. Burma was one of the main sources of food supply. But owing to the Japanese invasion these supplies were cut off. The British insisted on a scorched earth policy under which the cultivators in Bengal which was a border province threatened by Japanese invasion could not cultivate land in certain areas. Whatever supplies were available were requisitioned by the Government to feed the army. Controls also were placed on the movements of grains into Bengal, and also inside Bengal. The League Government which came to power in the province entrusted the distribution of grain to a few Muslim monopolists and, in collaboration with officials, they created artificial scarcity which further increased the prices. The problem became serious because a large number of refugees migrated to Bengal from Burma. The boats plying in the rivers of West Bengal were requisitioned by the Government. The city of Calcutta into which thousand of people from all corners of the province shifted became a vast slum. It was under these conditions the most serious famine broke out in Bengal. The Government was in no position to take steps to give any relief to the famine-stricken people and conservative estimates put to death toll at three million. Little wonder the Economic distress which this created deepened the political discontent as well, and the people lost confidence in the British and in their ability to repel a Japanese attack.

Jinnah's Objectives and their Realisation

These years also saw the rise of Jinnah as the undisputed leader of the Muslims. He had two objectives before him. One was the creation of Pakistan which was his ultimate ideal. The other was the establishment of ministries controlled by the Muslim League in all the Muslim majority provinces – Bengal, Sind, Punjab and North West Frontier and Assam, if possible. The clause in the Cripps proposal which stated that any province or group of provinces which were unwilling to accept a constitution framed by the Constituent Assembly might become separate dominions almost conceded the demand for Pakistan, Jinnah took the credit for this. For none of the Chief Ministers of Bengal, Sind, Punjab or the North West Frontier was in favour of Pakistan, The Chief Minister of Punjab pointed out, for instance, that if Pakistan was created, the Hindu and Sikhs where they were in a majority would secede and Punjab would lose all the importance it possessed. Similar objections were raised by the Premiers of Sind and Bengal. Even the Viceroy and Lord Wavell, the Commander- In-Chief, were opposed to the idea of Pakistan. In spite of all this the British Cabinet conceded the demand and it was a feather in the cap of Jinnah.

Jinnah's immediate object, however, was to have League ministers installed in the Muslim-majority provinces. The League did not command a majority in the legislature of these provinces and he knew it was only through the help of the Governors that he could achieve his objective. To carry the favour of the Governors, he called a meeting of the Muslims League soon after the working committee of the Congress passed the Quit India resolution in July 1942. The league in a resolution said they would have nothing to do with such a civil disobedience movement as its intention was to establish Hindu rule in India. Naturally this was welcomed by the British and a little later Jinnah called another meeting of the League and it passed several resolutions the main thrust of which was that if the British yielded to the Congress demands, the Muslims would be compelled to resort to direct action to safeguard their interests and that the Muslims regiments in the army would rebel against British authority. This also had its effect on the British. In Bengal the Governor compelled the

Chief Minister, Fazlul Huq to resign and a league ministry was installed. In Assam, several Congress M.L.A.'s were jailed and a contrived majority was created for the League and a League ministry was installed. In Sind, the Chief Minister, Alla Baksh, was a nationalist who swore by Hindu-Muslim unity. He even renounced the titles conferred on him by the British. This irritated the Governor. He dismissed him from office and a League ministry was installed. In the North West frontier too, Abdul Gaffar Khan and his followers were put in prison making it easy for a league Ministry to be formed. A similar attempt was made in Punjab. Many followers of Sir Syed Sikandar Ayat Khan, the Chief Minister, joined the League. But even then it was not possible for the League to secure a majority and Sikandar Hyat Khan continued to be Chief Ministers though his position was precarious. It is noteworthy that to please Jinnah the Governors were ready to install League ministries. Jinnah thus became the sole leader of the Muslim community and the Muslim League the representative of its interests.

The Indian National Army under Subhas Chandra Bose

Yet another development during this period was the organization of the Indian National Army by Subhas Chandra Bose and the invasion of India which he undertook in 1944 with the help of the Japanese forces. Bose had actually proposed a civil disobedience campaign as soon as the Second World War broke out. But Gandhiji and Nehru among others were against it. He left the Congress and formed the Forward Bloc. When the War broke out he stated a civil disobedience campaign in Bengal. Bose was immediately jailed along with his trusted followers. But he embarked on a fast and the Government released him although he was kept in house custody. But he managed to stage a dramatic escape and after a series of thrilling experiences packed with adventure he finally reached Berlin. He met Hitler and urged facilities to broadcast from Berlin radio to the people of India campaigning against the British rule. He wanted to raise a regiment comprising the India sepoys captured by Germans in the war, and attack the British on the borders of India. He appealed to Hitler to help India become independent. Hitler accepted the first two suggestions but not the third. When the Japanese entered the war, Bose thought that he would be able to secure Japanese help and wage a war of India's independence. With the help of the Germans, he managed to go to Tokyo in 1943.

By that time the Indians residents in Japan, Hong Kong. Indonesia, Thailand and other countries of South East Asia were planning an armed rising in India. They first met at Tokyo and later at Bangkok and with the help of the Japanese, they raised an army of nearly 15,000 composed mainly of prisoners captured by the Japanese in Singapore, Malaya and other places. Rashbehari Bose became the head of the Indian Army, but at the same time he successfully persuaded Subhas Chandra Bose to assume the command of the army. After he reached Tokyo, Bose met the Japanese Prime Minister who promised to give him help and co-operation in his efforts. Bose then went to Singapore and managed to raise strength of the Indian National Army to 40,000. He established a provisional Indian Government with himself as the president and other Indians as Cabinet Ministers. He made Hindustani the official language and the language for carrying on military drill. The tri colour Congress flag was adopted as the National Flag. The Japanese handed over to him the Andamans which they had already occupied. It became the first Indian territory under the INA's political control. His idea was to invade India with the help of the Indian National Army. The Japanese were at first opposed to it as they did not have enough confidence in the ability of the sepoys that they would come out successful. The Japanese suggested that they themselves should attack and hand over to him all the territories they might occupy. This was not acceptable to Bose since it was his desire, that the Indians themselves should overthrow the British rule. Ultimately the Japanese veered round to his view and his February 1944 Subhas Chandra Bose and his Indian National Army left Rangoon towards India with some Japanese forces accompanying them.

In the Course of their marches the National Army defeated the British regiments in two places and ultimately entered Indian territory and took possession of Mowdok. In the battle many Britishers were killed. Others left the battle field leaving a large number of weapons and ammunition. Meanwhile, the other regiments of the Indian National Army in combination with the Japanese forces entered Nagaland and hoisted the Indian National Flag in Kohima. Another regiment entered Manipur and occupied Imphal. But by that time the Japanese met with severe reverses in the Pacific. The Americans reoccupied the Phillippines and territories subjugated by the Japanese and the Japanese withdrew their forces from the borders of India. This affected the fortunes of the Indian National Army. Without the help of the Japanese air force it was impossible for the army to continue fighting with the British forces in India. By June 1944, they evacuated the places already occupied and returned to Burma. By the end of 1944 and the beginning of 1945 the British armies invaded Burma and occupied Rangoon. The remnants of the Indian National Army were captured and once again they became prisoners of war thus ending the historic armed rising under the stewardship of Subhas Chandra Bose and the Indian National Army. But even the Bose did not want to abandon his attempts. He flew with another Indian and reached Formosa on August 18, 1944, with the object of going to Tokyo and getting help from the Japanese. The plane carrying him caught fire and Bose died under tragic circumstances. The national Government after India became independent appointed a commission to enquire into the circumstances of his death and confirmed the incident although there are still many who believe he is alive.

I.N.A.'s Role in the Freedom Struggle

Subhas Chandra Bose occupied a pivotal place among the freedom fighters. The Indian National Army's exploits convinced the British that the Indians were ready to fight back to get rid of their rule. More important than this was the realization that they could no longer take the Indian sepoy for granted. The sepoy regiments which recaptured Rangoon in 1945 praised the courage displayed by the Indian National Army and this did not go unnoticed by the British officers as well. For two centuries it was only with the help of the Indian sepoys the British ruled the country. The British began to realize that they could no longer hold on after what they had seen. They increasingly recongnised that their suzerainty was coming to an end especially after the grim determination displayed by the men of the Indian National Army to free the country from foreign domination unmindful of the risky hazards involved. In 1946 three I.N.A. Generals – a Hindu, a Sikh and a Muslim – Who commanded the regiments of the Indian National Army were tried at the Red Fort in Delhi. The trial created bitter resentment all over the country. Eminent persons like Sapru, Bhulabhai Desai and Jawaharlal Nehru in their capacity as advocates defended the accused. Donations to meet the expenses involved were willingly paid by the people. Although the tribunal pronounced them guilty of treason, the Government thought it prudent to grant them pardon. In the process the I.N.A.'s prestige shot up. The Indian National Army proved that the Indian Soldier was not merely a mercenary but was a volunteer willing to sacrifice his life for the cause of the country. The officers of the Army demonstrated their ability to lead independently and gave convincing evidence of their resourcefulness in meeting difficult situations. Above all the I.N.A. was a symbol of communal harmony and comradeship. The Britishers saw in the I.N.A. a significant portent that non-violence did not deplete the armoury of the struggle for independence.

CHAPTER 26

THE PERIOD OF NEGOTIATIONS

After the Quit India Movement came to and end, the period of negotiations commenced. In the first stage the negotiations took place even as the British were busy with the Second World in its last phase. The second stage was reached after the war came to an end.

Release of Gandhiji

In many 1944 Gandhiji was unconditionally released. Though he did not want to enter into any negotiations with the British without consulting the members of the Congress Working Committee who were still in prison, he was very much agitated over the political stalemate and much more over the deterioration in the economic condition of the people. Shortly after his release in an interview with a correspondent of one of the influential newspapers in Britain Gandhiji spoke of the conditions which might help in putting an end to the political deadlock. Gandhiji was convinced that the cause would be served better by his writing to the viceroy. In his letter he informed the Viceroy that there was a need to put an end to the deadlock. He suggested certain conditions that Britain should declare that India's Independence was the goal of her policy, that immediately as a first step in giving effect to this policy a Government responsible to the legislature and representative of all political parties should be set up, but this Government would not interfere in the conduct of the war which would entirely be the responsibility of the Viceroy and the Commander-in-chief, that it would concern itself only with the other aspects of the administration and that if the above conditions were agreed to, he would advised the Congress working committee to formally abandon the civil disobedience campaign and that he should be given and interview with the Viceroy to explain to him in detail the implications of his letter.

Gandhiji's Unsuccessful Attempt to Negotiate a Settlement

In his reply the Viceroy stated that the time for granting Gandhiji an interview had not come yet, that the conditions which he laid down were not practicable while the war lasted, and even after the war any constitutional reform was possible only when there was complete agreement between the Hindus and the Muslims and other minorities. This meant that not only during the period of the War but also later there would be no fundamental changes agreement on constitutional reform between the Hindus and the Muslims, Gandhiji's efforts to enter into negotiations with the Viceroy proved a non-starter.

Gandhiji-Jinnah Talks on Pakistan – Their Failure

Gandhiji next made an attempt to come to terms with Jinnah. He knew that an understanding would not be possible unless the demand for Pakistan was conceded. In this context C. Rajagopalchari evolved a formula and obtained Gandhiji's consent for it with a few alterations. Gandhiji proposed to Jinnah that there should be talks between them on the basis of the formula. Jinnah agreed and the talks went on for three weeks in the latter half of 1944. The formula accepted by Gandhiji included:

1. The Muslim League should co-operate with the Congress in the achievement of the country's freedom and Pakistan should be created after the country became free.
2. Those areas in Bengal and Punjab which had a majority of non-Muslims should be excluded from Pakistan. This meant the exclusion of the districts in East Punjab where the Hindu and Sikhs were in majority and the districts in West Bengal which had a Hindu majority.
3. Before Pakistan was established, the views of the people inhabiting the areas to form part of its should be ascertained through a plebiscite.
4. Even after the creation of Pakistan and Hindustan there should be a treaty between the two States on matters relating to the defence of the whole country, communication and other essential matters of common interest.

Jinnah, however, insisted that Pakistan should be created before the Muslim League co-operated with the Congress in the efforts to gain freedom. This was because he was doubtful of the Hindus agreeing to the formation of Pakistan when once the British withdrew from the country. Secondly, he insisted that Punjab and Bengal should be included in Pakistan in their entirety. Thirdly, he also objected to any plebiscite in regard to the formation of Pakistan. He knew that large number of Muslims in the Punjab and Bengal were opposed to it and in a plebiscite they and the non-Muslim population might join together to vote against its formation. Finally, he wanted Gandhiji to accept that the Hindus and Muslims were to separate nationalities. Gandhiji was totally opposed to this since he felt it would be dangerous for Hindustan if Muslims felt that they were a separate nation and for Pakistan if the Hindus and Sikhs in it felt that they were a separate nation. He held the view that the difference in religion should never constitute a people into different nations.

The talks which failed enhanced the importance of Jinnah. Gandhiji's acceptance of Pakistan as the basis for talks also enhanced Jinnah's Stature.

Lord Wavell's Attempt to Negotiate a Settlement

Lord Wavell who became the Viceroy of India in October 1943 was keen that the political stalemate should be brought to an end primarily because of the growing economic deterioration in the country. He felt that in this task the help of the political parties should be sought and a Central Government representative of these parties should be formed. He carried on correspondence with the British Cabinet on the matter. He proceeded to England in March 1945, held discussion with Churchill, the Secretary of state fro India and members of the British Cabinet and obtained their consent to open negotiations with the Congress and the League on the issue of forming a Central Government consisting of an equal number of representative of the Congress and the League though not fully responsible to the legislature. He returned to India on June 14 and announced on June 25 that a conference would be held in Simla, representative of the Congress, the League and other political parties for arriving at decisions on certain important issues namely the Hindu-Muslims problem, the formation of a Central Government with Indians as its members and with only the Viceroy and the Commander-in-chief as the non-Indian members. The Central Government would conduct the war and carry on the day to day administration of the country and decide by what method the future constitution of India should be framed. He also announced that the members of the Congress Working Committee would be immediately released and the ban on Congress bodies would be lifted. Effect was given to this immediately.

The Simla Conference and its Failure

The Congress Working Committee met on June 21 and agreed to participate in the Simla Conference. The Muslim league also decided to participate.

The Conference met at Simla on June 25, 21 delegates belonging to the Congress, the League and a few other political parties participating. The Viceroy requested the Congress and the League to send to him separately a list of the names of not less than eight persons and not more than 12 out of whom he would select those who should be in the proposed Central Government. Accordingly the Congress submitted 12 names. But Jinnah declined to do so unless the Viceroy accepted two conditions –that all the Muslims in the proposed Central Government should be members of the Muslim League and that the interests which affected the Muslim community should not be decided by a majority vote in the Government. There should be a special committee for taking decisions on these matters. This meant that even so staunch a Muslim nationalists as Maulana Azad could not join the Central Government.

The Viceroy did not accept Jinnah's conditions. He selected five Muslims, four of whom belonged to the Muslim League and Sir Sikhander Hayat Khan, Chief Minister of Punjab who belonged to the Unionist Party. Jinnah refused to accept the names suggested by the Viceroy. He was encouraged to do so by some prominent members of the Indian Civil Service who never made secret of their hostility to the nationalist aspirations. They were bitterly against Congress participation in government. They encouraged Jinnah to stand firm. The Viceroy referred the matter to the British Cabinet. The Cabinet too was opposed to anything being done against the wishes of Jinnah and the Muslim League and, therefore, asked the Viceroy not to proceed further in the matter.

Labour Party comes to Power in Britain

At the meeting held on July 14 the Viceroy declared that the Simla conference failed one he took the blame for it on himself though every one knew that it was Jinnah and the British Prime Minister that stalled a settlement. From the very beginning the Conservatives in Britain led by Churchill were against any concessions being given to the Congress. Within ten days of the Simla Conference general elections took place in Britain. Churchill and the Conservative's party were defeated. The Labour Party was returned with a large majority and two days later, a Labour Government with Mr. Attlee as the Prime Minister was formed. This sudden development gave a new turn to the entire course of events in India. Negotiations were started and within two years the British withdrew from the country. The war too came to an end on August, 1945 Japan having surrendered.

Labour Government Decides on Withdrawal from India

That the negotiations were bound to succeed was evident from the determination of the Labour Government under Attlee to withdraw from India and transfer power to Indians hands. The Labour Party favoured withdrawal even earlier. It was in this respect that it differed from the Conservatives. The devastating results of the World War, though the British Won lent urgency to the policy of the Labour Party to withdraw from India. The war depleted Britain's resources completely. Its military strength was crippled badly. Before the war it was a creditor nation, but as a consequence of the war, it became heavily indebted to the United States and other countries. As its industrial establishments suffered total damage in the war, all its resources were spent on re-establishing them and on reconstructing her economy. Under such circumstances, the Labour Government felt that the country had neither the human nor the material resources for maintaining her imperial rule over India. The Indian National Army demonstrated that even the sepoys on whose loyalty it depended could not be relied upon any more. The rule over India under such circumstances was considered to be a heavy and an unnecessary burden.

And yet the Labour Party would not have come to a decision to withdraw from India had it not been for the determination of the people of the country to undergo all sacrifices for forcing the British to quit as was shown by the various non-co-operation movements from 1920 to 1944. It was also recongnised that the movement might not always be non-violent and if it turned violent as it did during the Quit India movement. It would be difficult to suppress it. There was also a realization that the policy of "divide and rule' would not any more be a success. After all, the Muslims constituted only 24 per cent of the population. Their help would not be decisive in the force of the opposition of the vast majority of the people. Except in the movement of 1921–22 the Muslims kept aloof from the non-co-operation movements but this did not deter the majority from carrying on the struggle for freedom against the British. By 1945, even the Muslims wanted an independent Pakistan. These developments also convinced the British that it would be unwise for them to hold on to India any more. Unlike the French or the Dutch the British were pragmatic enough to realize that it would be a waste of effort to attempt to practice colonialism any more. The Labour Party's decision to withdraw from India was entirely an outcome of the situation resulting from the war as well as the internal developments in the country.

The first indication of the Labour Government's mind was evident in the King's speech delivered at the joint session of the two Houses of the British Parliament soon after the new Government was formed. In it the King stated that it was the intention of the Government to take steps to give independence to India at an early date.

Premier Attlee's Statement on August 21, 1945

The Labour Government soon began to consider the question to whom, power should be transferred. It felt that it should be decided on the basis of elections to be held for the Central and Provincial legislature. On August 21 an announcement was made to this effect. A week earlier, Lord Wavell, the Viceroy, was invited to Britain and discussion took place between him and the Cabinet till September 16. On the latter date, as soon as he returned to India, Wavell stated that a constituent Assembly would be convened early, that there would be discussion in regard to the relation between India and Britain after the British withdrawal from the country and that elections would take place in December 1945.

Elections to the Legislatures

The Congress well as the Muslim League decided to participate in the elections. In the elections to the Central Legislature, 91.3 percent of the voters in the general constituencies voted for the Congress which secured 57 seats being a majority of the elected seats in the legislature. In Muslim communal constituencies 86.6 percent of the electorate voted for the candidates set up by the Muslim League and it secured all the 37 seats for which it set up candidates. Besides them 5 independents, 2 Akali Sikhs and 8 Europeans were elected. Of the 102 elected seats, it is noteworthy that the Congress got a majority thus showing that the general electorate was solidly behind the Congress and its policies. Similarly, the elections revealed that the Muslim voters were behind the Muslim League. If the British were to carry on negotiations, it was not apparent that it should be with the Congress and the League.

In the elections to the provincial legislatures in all the Muslim majority provinces, except in the North-Western Frontier Province, the Muslim voters voted for Muslim candidates. But the Muslim League was not able to secure a majority in all of them except in Bengal where a league Ministry was formed. In the North-West Frontier province, the Congress formed a ministry. In Punjab a Unionist ministry consisting of Muslims, Hindus and Sikhs was formed under the leadership of Sir Syed Hayat Khan. In Sind, the Governor intervened in the formation of a ministry and a League ministry was installed in office. In all the other provinces Congress ministries came into power.

Cabinet Delegation to India

After the elections, Lord Wavell thought of carrying on negotiations with the leaders of the Congress and the League and conveyed his views to the British Cabinet. But in view of what happened earlier in the Simla Conference, the British Cabinet was not very much in favour of the Viceroy carrying on the negotiations. Even as the correspondence was going on between the Viceroy and the British cabinet, a naval mutiny broke out in Bombay, Vishakapatnam and other ports towns. The mutiny was an eye opener to the British Government. The sepoys were already suspect in the British eye. And now it began to doubt the loyalty of the naval ratings also. On February 14, it made an announcement that a delegation consisting of three persons—Lord Pethick Lawrence, Sir Strafford Cripps and Mr. H.V. Alexander—would visit India to carry on negotiations with the Congress, the League and other political parties and interests. Accordingly the Cabinet Delegation arrived in Delhi on March 24 to hold discussion which lasted three weeks. It found that all the parties barring the League were in favour of maintaining the political unity of the country.

Jinnah was adamant that nothing would satisfy the League except the creation of Pakistan. He convened a meeting of 400 Muslim legislators on April 10 at Delhi. It passed a unanimous resolution in favour of Pakistan. On April 16, the Cabinet Delegation met Jinnah and placed two alternatives before him. The first was the creation of Pakistan from which the areas where the non-Muslim were in a majority like East Punjab and West Bengal would be excluded. The other was that the Muslim majority provinces would be constituted into a sub-federation within an All India Federation in which the Central Government would have powers only over Defence, External affairs and Communications. Jinnah chose the second alternative. Even after that he raised some other controversial issues. The Cabinet Delegation finally announced its plans in the light of the discussion held. This came to be known as the Cabinet Mission Plan on May 16.

Cabinet Delegation Plan of May 15

According to this plan (1) an All India Federation Consisting of the provinces in British India and the princely States would be formed; (2) The central Government in such a Federation would have powers only over three subjects – Defence, External Relations and Communications; (3) all the other powers would be located in the provinces. This should enable the Muslims in the Muslim majority provinces to shape their future without any fear of Hindu domination; (4) All the Hindu majority provinces would be grouped in Section A; the Muslim majority provinces in North-West India – Sind, Punjab, North-West Frontier and Beluchistan would be grouped into Section B; the two provinces of Bengal and Assam in Eastern and North Eastern India would be grouped into Section C; each of these section if the corresponding provinces wanted would be a sub-federation and exercise any power that might be delegated to them; (5) The future constitution would be decided upon by a Constitutional Assembly to which members would be elected on the basis of one for every million people. They would be elected by the provincial legislatures, the members voting in general, Muslim and Sikh constituencies. Representation also would be given in the same proportion to the Princely States and question as to how they should be appointed would be settled through negotiations with the princes. The Constituent Assembly thus formed would at its first meeting elect its President and other office bearers and appoint advisory committees to recommend the safeguards for the minorities and also fundamental rights; (6) After this the Assembly would meet in separate sections and these sectional meetings would take decision on the form of provincial government and of the government of the sections; (7) After the provincial constitutions and sectional constitutions are framed the Constituent Assembly would meet in full session and draft the Constitution of All India Federation. What is noteworthy in this procedure is that the Constituent Assembly as such has no say in shaping provincial or sectional constitutions; (8) The constituent Assembly also would determine the kind of treaty for regulating the future relations between India and Britain, (9) As it would take some time for the new constitutions to be framed an Interim Government would be formed to exercise all powers and it would be representative of the Congress, the League and contain a representative of the Sikhs, the Indian Christians and the Parsis.

Attitude of the Congress and the League Towards the Plan

The plan formulated by the Cabinet Mission represents an ideal compromise between the views of the Congress which wanted to maintain the integrity of the country and of the Muslim League which wanted a division. The All India Federation proposed would maintain the unity of the country and the sectional groupings would give to the Muslims most of the power which they wanted to enjoy through Pakistan. It would, therefore, have been appropriate if the Congress and the League had accepted the Cabinet Mission Plan especially because the right to participate in the Interim Government was to be given only to the parties which accepted the plans as a whole. The Cabinet Mission was keen on the formation of such an Interim Government before it left the country.

Controversy Regarding the Interim Government

The Muslim League gave its approval to the Cabinet Mission Plan on June 6 and authorised Jinnah to carry on negotiations with the Viceroy in regard to the composition of the Government. The Congress approved the Plan on June 25, but declined to join the Interim Government. The controversy centred round the choice of Muslims in the Interim Ministry and the number of Muslims, Sikhs, Indian Christain and Parsis to be appointed. As on agreement was reached on these matters between the League and the Congress, the Viceroy announced on June 16, with the consent of the Cabinet Mission, that an Interim Government would be formed with six members belonging to the Congress (of whom one would be from the schedule castes) five belonging to the Muslim League, one Sikh, one Indian Christian and one Parsi – 14 in all, and he asked the Congress and the League to join the Interim Government on that basis. He also stated that if the Congress and the League declined he would form an Interim Government consisting of members of parties which approved the Cabinet Mission plan. Even before the Congress made known its decision, the Viceroy gave certain other assurances to Jinnah and thereupon the Congress refused to join the Interim Government. Under these circumstances the Cabinet delegation thought that no purpose would be served by continuing its stay in India and left the country on June 29.

The Viceroy did not go ahead with the formation of an Interim Government according to his earlier promise. Jinnah got furious that though he was willing to join the Interim ministry, the Viceroy did not move in the matter. On July 6, the All India Congress Committee met under the Presidentship of Jawaharlal Nehru who in the meanwhile succeeded Maulana Azad and approved the Cabinet Mission Plan. After the meeting Nehru issued a statement in his personal capacity that the meeting of the Constituent Assembly in sections was not binding and that the Assembly was free to carry in its proceedings as a full sovereign body. There was nothing new in his views. From the very beginning the Congress was opposed to sectional grouping as well as to Assam which was a Hindu majority province being included with Bengal in Section. But Jinnah took a serious objection to the views of Nehru. He called a meeting of the Working committee of the League on July 27, in which a resolution was passed urging that the creation of Pakistan alone would satisfy the League and the Muslims should be prepare to take to direct action to enforce its demand. In the interval, the Viceroy once again appealed to the Congress and the league to co-operate with him in the formation of an interim Government. As the League now changed its view on the Cabinet plan and insisted on the creation of Pakistan he decided on an interim Government even without the League being represented in it. This marked a change in his attitude brought about by the deteriorating political and economic situations in the country. On August 6, he invited Nehru to join the Interim Government. On August 8, the Congress Working Committee met and approved the Cabinet Mission Plan without any reservation which was given expression to by Nehru and authorised him to join the Interim Government. Before forming the Government, he invited Jinnah to nominate the representative of the League in the Interim Government and Jinnah declined to do so. Sardar Vallabhbhai Patel, Dr. Rajendra Prasad, Asaf Ali, C. Rajagopalachari, Sarat Chandra Bose, John Matthai, Sardar Baldev Singh, Covesji Hormusji Bhaba, Jagjivan Ram, Dr. Shafat Ahmed Khan and Syed Ali Zaheer formed the interim ministry. Two seats were left vacant for the Muslim League if they cared to join. On September 2, the members of the Interim Government took the oath of office.

Muslim League "Direct Action Day"

Jinnah gave a call to the Muslim to observe August 16, as the "Director Action Day" to which they responded. The day was marked by large scale riots in Calcutta and in other parts of Bengal. The Chief Minister Declared August 16 as a holiday and when the riots broke out he instructed the police not to intervene, no did he care to seek the help of the army to restore peace and order. Unprecedented riots broke out in which 5,000 people lost their lives in what came to be known as "the Calcutta killings", and 15,000. If the Congress direct action in 1920–22, 1930–31 and 1932–34 was by and large non-violent, the direct action observed by the League led to brutal killing of Hindus and Muslims on a massive scale.

This created an atmosphere of civil war between the Hindus and the Muslims throughout the country. It caused anguish to Gandhiji, and he advised the Congress Working Committee to take immediate steps to come to an understanding with the league and pass a resolution to recognize the Muslim League as the sole representative of the Muslim community. The Working Committee passed the resolution accordingly though it offended the fundamental concept that the congress was a national body and not a mere Hindu organization. Thereupon the Viceroy and Nehru again invited Jinnah on the Strength of this resolution to join the Interim Government. By that time Jinnah was in more chastened mood. He did not like the idea that the Congress alone should lead the Interim Government. He thought that might prove detrimental to the Muslim interest. But Nehru insisted that before joining the Government, Jinnah should rescind the resolution passed on July 29 rejecting the Cabinet Mission Plan. The Viceroy assured Nehru and Jinnah had promised to get it rescinded and therefore wanted to permit the League to join the Interim Government. With the confidence that Jinnah would fulfil his promise, Nehru allowed five members nominated by the Muslim League (of which one was a schedule caste) to join the Interim Government. To make room for the Muslim League representatives, he asked Sarat Chandra Bose, Shafaat Ahmed Khan and Syed Ali Zahir to resign and an Interim Government consisting of the congress and the League representative began to function from October 26, 1946.

What Jinnah wanted was only League representation in the Interim Government. He did not get the resolution of July 29 rescinded. The representative of the Muslim League refused to accept the leadership of Nehru or to work as a single team. The Government became divided into two groups. This had an adverse impact on the quality of administration. All officials from the highest to the lowest ranks were vertically split into a Muslim and a non-Muslim section. The two sections worked at cross purposes even in regard to such a vital matter as the maintenance of peace and order. One of the League's representatives became Finance Minister and he presented a budget which adversely hit the merchants belonging to the Hindu Community.

Riots in Bengal

Tension grew between the Hindus and the Muslims and this led to large scale massacre of Hindus in Naokali and Tippara in East Bengal where the Hindus were in a minority. The Hindus in a retaliatory move killed Muslims in Bihar. Nehru and others proceeded immediately to Bihar and initiated measures to give protection to the Muslims, and peace was restored in the province without much delay. It was then that Gandhiji went to Naokali and Tippara, Spent two months visiting village after village in a bid to restore harmony between the two communities.

While these unfortunate developments were taking place new problem arose. According to the Cabinet Mission Plan, the future Constitution of India was to be framed by a Constituent Assembly for which elections were already held. Nehru and the Congress were anxious that the Assembly should meet early but it would not meet unless Jinnah and the Muslim league rescinded the resolution passed on July 29 rejecting the Mission plan. Jinnah was not prepared for this and proposed on the other hand that the meeting of the Constituent Assembly should be postponed. Nehru did not agree to this proposal. Lord Wavell agreed to issue notices to the members elected to the Assembly so that it could meet on December 9. Immediately Jinnah called upon the Muslim league members elected to it to boycott the meeting.

Formation of the Interim Government by Nehru

Nehru demanded that under these circumstances the Muslim league members in the Interim Government should be removed from office. All this perturbed the British Cabinet and to settle the differences between the league and the Congress, Nehru, Jinnah, Baldev Singh, the Sikh representative and Lord Wavell were invited to London for talks. Nehru was not willing and on December 6 the British Cabinet issued a declaration on the controversial issues. It laid down that the meeting of the sectional groups and the inclusion of provinces in the different sections according to the plan were unalterable and they should be strictly adhered to. This was the bone of contention between the Congress and the League all along. The Congress proposed that the interpretation of this part of the plan should be referred to the Chief Justice of India and all parties should abide by his decision. The Cabinet said it had no objection to such a reference but it could not compel the League to abide by the opinion of the chief justice if it went against the Contention of the League. Secondly, the Cabinet made it clear that in case the Muslim League members refused to participate in the deliberations of the Constituent Assembly and if the Assembly framed a Constitution in their absence, the British would not be prepared to force such a constitution on the League. These decisions were a boost to the Muslim League and this encouraged Jinnah to stand firm in regard to the Muslim League boycott of the Assembly.

The Assembly met on December 9. It elected Dr. Rajendra Prasad as its President, appointed an advisory committee to report on the safeguards to be granted to the minorities and on fundamental rights. Nehru moved a resolution on the aims and objectives of the Assembly but no discussion took place on it in the absence of the League members. The Assembly was adjourned to meet on January 20. The assembly did meet again as scheduled, but the league members continued to boycott it. The resolution on the aims and objectives was discussed and passed but no further business was transacted.

Nehru and all the members of the Interim Government other than those representing the Muslim league demanded that the League members should be removed from it. The Viceroy, however refused to do so since it was the League's contention that even the Congress did not accept the Cabinet Mission Plan unconditionally and the League members had as much right to be in the Interim Government as the congress members. Thereupon, Nehru and other members sent in their resignations. The resignation of the Congress members could prove as disastrous as the removal of the League members.

Atlee's Announcement of February 20, 1947

The British Cabinet, therefore, wanted to take a decision which it thought would given the Indian leaders a last chance to come to an agreement. On February 20, 1947 the British Premier made a historic statement in the House of Commons which contained the following clauses.

1. The British would withdraw from India on a date not later than June 1948;
2. If by that time, the Constituent Assembly framed a Constitution approved by all the parties and a new Government was installed according to it, it would transfer power to that government :
3. If no such Constitution was framed, the British would transfer power to the various Government that might then be holding office in the provinces; and
4. if for any reason even this was not possible it would transfer power to any other institution which would be most beneficial to the people of India.

Its Significance

The announcement once for all removed any doubts the Indian politicians harboured about the bonafides of the intention of the British to quit the country. The British thought this would bring the Indian political leaders closer and the Congress and the League would come to some understanding to enable them to take advantage of the transfer of power.

The announcement made by the British Premier was indeed a notable one. There are hardly any precedents of a voluntary withdrawal by an imperial power. The British, however, did so in respect of India which is statesmanlike even though there were compelling circumstances that were responsible for the historic step.

The announcement also declared that Lord Mountbatten would succeed Lord Wavell as Viceroy and he would be entrusted with powers to take the necessary measures for the transfer of power into Indian hands before June, 1948.

❖ ❖ ❖

THE ACHIEVEMENT OF FREEDOM

CHAPTER 27

Reaction of the Congress Working Committee and Muslim League to Attlee's Announcement

The Congress Working Committee which met on March 6, 1947 welcomed the announcement of Lord Attlee and at the same time invited Jinnah to hold discussions on the future course of action. It also passed a resolution that in case partition of the country became inevitable. East Punjab and West Bengal should be excluded from Pakistan. Jinnah declined the invitation of the Congress Working Committee. According to the announcement, power would be transferred to the Congress ministries in eight provinces in which it was then holding office. The league, however, was holding office only in Bengal and Sind. Jinnah was keen to bring Punjab and the north West Frontier provinces also under the control of the League at the time of British withdrawal. He called for direct action in Punjab and the North West Frontier Province. This led to violent communal riots. Sir Sikander Hayat Khan, the Prime Minister of Punjab, tried his best to control the riots. But neither the Governor nor the members of the civil service and the members of the Muslims League in the Interim Government extended their help to him. On the other hand, they gave all encouragement to the followers of the League. In disgust, Sir Sikandar Hayat Khan resigned. But as there was no majority in the Punjab legislature for the Muslim League, a League Ministry could not be formed and the Governor took over the administration. A similar situation prevailed in the North-West Frontier Province.

Lord Mountbatten's Decision to withdraw British Rule by August 15, 1947

Lord Mountbatten became Viceroy and Governor General on March 24, 1947. He immediately held consultations with the leaders of the Congress and the League and some important politicians. He summoned a conference of Governors whose assessment was that the situation was grave and Punjab and the North-West Frontier Province were in a state of civil war which could quickly spread to the other parts of the country. Lord Mountbatten was therefore not confident that under the circumstances the British could carry on even till June 1948. They were handicapped by lack of resources in men and material to rule the country. Nor was there co-operation between the members of the Congress and the League in the Interim Government. The Services from the highest to the lowest were similarly divided. The police could not be relied upon in the matter of controlling the law and order situation. The army alone could perhaps restore peace, but Lord Mountbatten was not certain about this either. He felt that the Government of the country should be handed over to the representatives of the people by August 15, 1947. He convinced the British Cabinets of this.

Therefore he engaged himself in formulating a plan for the transfer of power in consultation with his advisers who had specially come from Britain. He held that partition of the country was unavoidable. At the same time he wanted that East Punjab and West Bengal should not be part of Pakistan and the district of Sylhet in Assam which had a Muslim majority should be included in Pakistan.

Lord Mountbatten made a plea to the congress leaders to agree to his scheme of partition. They accepted it in the belief that in the ultimate analysis it was the lesser evil. In the atmosphere of civil war generated by the direct action of Jinnah, Sardar Patel felt that it was impossible to work in a harmonious manner in the Central government of an undivided India. What was happening in the Interim Government was enough indication that the League and the Congress could not work together as a team. It was on this ground that Sardar Patel was inclined to accept the proposal for partition. Rajendra Prasad and Nehru also agreed because the idea of an all India federation in terms of the Cabinet Mission proposal seemed to them to be unworkable. When once Pakistan was created, the Constituent Assembly of India could go ahead with the drafting of a constitution with a strong Centre.

Gandhiji ultimately agreed to partition when he found that important leaders like Nehru, Rajendra Prasad and Patel were not opposed to it. His personal views apart, he called upon the All India Congress Committee which met on June 14 to agree to partition.

The Muslim League objected to Partition with East Punjab and West Bengal excluded from Pakistan. Mountbatten overruled it and the League had no alternative but to accept a Pakistan which Jinnah characteristics on a different occasion as "moth-eaten."

The plan which Mountbatten prepared was not revealed to the Congress leaders in all its details. He forwarded it to the British Cabinet which approved it with minor modifications. But when Nehru looked into the details, he found several defects and he protested against such a plan. Mr. V.P. Menon who had been the Constitutional Adviser to the Government of India since the days of Wavell intervened and advised Nehru and Patel that all the defects in the Plan could be removed if they agreed to India and Pakistan becoming Dominions within the Commonwealth instead of becoming completely independent. In his opinion connections with British would be of great help to India in the coming years. They agreed to this suggestion of Menon even though in the past they preferred complete independence to Dominion Status. Mountbatten had no difficulty in accepting Menon's suggestions. The new plan according to which India and Pakistan would become Dominions within the British Commonwealth was approved by the British Cabinet.

The Indian Independence Act

In accordance with this plan, the British Parliament passed on July 18, the Indian Independence Act. According to the Act: 1) India and Pakistan should become two Dominions within the British Common wealth from August 16, 1947; 2) to each Dominion the King should appoint a Governor General, but the same person might hold office of the Governor General in both the Dominions; 3) the legislatures in each Dominion should have full power in all matters of internal and external policy and no legislation enacted by the British Parliament or orders issued by the British Government would have any applicability in India or Pakistan; 4) there would be two Constituent Assemblies, one to frame a Constitution for India and another for Pakistan and until the new Constitution was framed and brought into effect, the Government of each Dominion would be carried on in accordance with the Government of India Act 1935 with appropriate alternations as India and Pakistan became Dominions;

5) the Constituent Assembly of each Dominion would also be its legislature until a legislature came into existence under the new constitution; 6) Britain would have no rights of paramountacy over the Indian princely states. They would be free either to remain sovereign or accede to India or Pakistan according to their convenience.

Even before the Indian Independence Act was passed, the legislature of Punjab and Bengal met in two separate sections. The legislators in West Punjab met in one group and in another met the legislators of East Punjab. Similar meetings were held in West Bengal and East Bengal separately. They were asked to vote whether they would join Pakistan or India or the Indian constituent Assembly or the Pakistan Assembly. The legislators from West Punjab and East Bengal voted in favour of Pakistan and its Constituent Assembly. Those of east Punjab and West Bengal voted for India and the Indian Constituent Assembly. A plebiscite was held in the district of Sylhet in Assam and the majority voted in favour of joining Pakistan. A plebiscite was also held in the North-West Frontier province. It was, however, boycotted by the followers of Khan Abdul Gaffar Khan and the result was a majority voted to join Pakistan. All this meant that the partition of the country in all its details was approved by the people themselves.

On August 11, Jinnah was elected President of the Pakistan Constituent Assembly. It was expected that Mountbatten would become the common Governor General of India and Pakistan. But Jinnah Became the Governor General of Pakistan.

The constituent Assembly of India met at midnight on August 14-15 under the Presidentship of Rajendra Prasad to herald the achievement of Freedom. Nehru, the Prime Minister-designate, in an inspiring speech called upon the members of the Assembly and the people of India to dedicate themselves to the service of the country. The following day Mountbatten assumed the office of the Governor General of India. It was day of rejoicing for the people of the country. Meetings were held to celebrate the momentous event which was the culmination of a long struggle.

A new era of independence thus began. The people were henceforth free to shape their destiny as they liked.

General Character of the Movement

The history of the freedom movement in India deserves to be inscribed in letters of gold. It was a people's movement. Almost all classes of people, the English educated, those in urban areas and the illiterate masses in rural areas enthusiastically participated in the various, critical phases of the struggle. Women played a glorious role. It was Gandhiji that led the movement. Again it was not confined to any one region, but was an all India movement. It resulted not in the freedom of any one or two parts of the country but of the country as whole. In this respect also it differed from all the previous movements.

Even from the point of view of movements which took place in other parts of the world, it had certain unique characteristics. History tells us that the Dutch in the 16th and 17th centuries, the Americans in the 18th century, the Italians in the 19th century and many other people of Asia and Africa in the 20th century carried on movements for the sake of freedom from alien rule. But all these were regular armed risings. The movement in India was on the whole non-violent. This was due to Gandhiji's leadership. Whenever it took a violent turn, he made it a point to suspend it. It is true that there were certain exceptions to this general character. There was violence during the Quit India Movement. The revolutionaries in Bengal, Punjab and Maharashtra too indulged in violence and they believed that only through an armed rising it would be possible to get rid of the alien rule. They contributed to the success of the movement in some measure. There was also the Indian National Army under the command of Subhas Chandra Bose. But we have to regard these as exceptions to the general rule.

The movement in India, unlike the movements in the Western world, were led by the English-educated intelligentsia. It was they that spread the ideas of nationalism and democracy. Even in the West, intellectuals like Voltaire, Rousseau and Mazzani were responsible for ideas relating to national freedom and democracy. But it was the bourgeois, the commercial and industrial classes that were mainly responsible for carrying on their movement to a successful conclusion. In India, however, there was no indigenous bourgeois to do this on a large scale. Some of them gave monetary help to Gandhiji. But they did not actively participate in the movement.

Almost all the leaders of the Indian national movement – Tilak, Arabindo, Bipinn Chandra Pal, Lajpat Rai, Gandhiji, Patel. Nehru, C.R. Das, Prakasam, Gopala Krishnaya, C.Rajagopalachari and several other belonged to the Class of intelligentsia. They not only created ideas but also put them into effect.

From the time Mountbatten got the approval for the second plan, committees were appointed to work out the details regarding the division of assets and liabilities, bank balances, civil servants and the army between India and Pakistan. A Boundary Commission was also appointed under the chairmanship of Lord Radcliffe, a British Jurist, with representatives of the League and the Congress to aid him. As there was no agreement of any matter between these representatives, the chairman had to bear the entire responsibility of fixing the boundaries of East and West Punjab and of East and West Bengal. The boundaries which he decided upon especially as between East Punjab and West Punjab resulted in a large numbers of Sikhs leaving their sacred shrines in West Punjab and their rich colonies. The Sikhs were dissatisfied with this boundary. It was their aim to make the Chenab the boundary between the two Punjab's. Communal riots consequently broke out. Muslims in Western Punjab were determined on getting rid of the Sikhs and the other Hindus appropriating their lands and property. Millions of Sikhs and the other Hindus had to flee to East Punjab as refugees. The same thing happened to Muslims in East Punjab and Delhi. They had to flee to West Punjab as refugees. In the course of this six hundred thousand people perished and twelve million people had to leave their ancestral homes. Though freedom from British rule was achieved without much violence, it was unfortunate that the partition of India was preceded and followed by unprecedented violence.

India Becomes Free

Atleast the day of freedom dawned on both India and Pakistan. Jinnah left India on August 7 to Karachi, the capital of Pakistan.

The Freedom Movement in India received tremendous impetus because of the deliberate impoverishment of the people under the British Rule. It was economic misery and suffering that made the masses participate in it with enthusiasm and perseverance. Though this was the root cause of the movement, political factors too played a crucial part in its origin and growth. The spread of English education was responsible for the growth of nationalism. The political unity established by the British, the uniform system of administration introduced by them, and the means of transport and communication to which they paid a great deal of attention created a feeling among the people that they all belonged to one nation, that Swaraj was their birth-right and that they must undergo all sacrifices to achieve it. Reformers like Raja Ram Mohan Roy, Keshav Chandra Sen, Dayananda Saraswati, Vivekananda and Annie Besant contributed to the growth of Nationalism.

Economic distress by itself does not lead to revolutions. It must be properly channelised and this was done in India by the English educated classes, by religious and social reformers and even by those who carried on research in the history of the past and wrote about the glories of ancient and medieval India. A variety of factors were ultimately responsible for the growth and success of the freedom movement. It was unfortunate that certain sections of the Muslims community kept aloof from the movement, and this led to the division of the country in the end. But all Muslims were not a party to it. As has already been shown, many of their leaders were opposed to the creation of Pakistan. But the British took up the cause of the extreme communalists and sectionalists, helped in early days Sir Syed Ahmed khan who was the first to put forward the two nation theory and Jinnah later on. It was this policy of "Divide and Rule" adopted by the British much more than the separatist tendencies promoted under the British that led to the division of the country. In spite of all this, the freedom movement was a success. The freedom movement in India has many unique characteristics not present in similar movements in the past and qualitatively and dimensionally different from movements in other parts of the world.

APPENDIX – I

FREEDOM MOVEMENT IN ANDHRA

CHAPTER 28

Nature of the Movement

The freedom movement in Andhra was essentially an integral part of the national movement. Its course was more or less the same. The classes which participated in it and the political activity that followed were also similar. What is important to note is that Andhra was not a separate province like Bengal or Bombay. It was part of the composite Madras Presidency and it was more backward than the region where the Tamil-speaking population was in majority. The capital city was also predominantly Tamil speaking though at one time the Telugu-speaking people were numerically dominant. English education spread more widely and quickly in the Tamil-speaking area. Christian missions were active there much earlier than in the Telugu area. The Government also established more educational institutions in that part of the presidency than in the Telugu region. Madras being the capital, the Tamil-speaking people benefited much more from the educational institutions in the city than the Telugus. It took a long time for English education to spread in the Telugu area. As it was the English educated section that all progressive movements in the country in the 19th century, political activity in Andhra was a belated phenomenon as compared with other parts of Madras. The position could be compared with Bihar and Orissa which were part of the province of Bengal until 1911.

Popular Discontent – The Cause

All revolutionary movements, the freedom movements in Andhra not excluding, have their root in economic and social discontent. Such discontent spread fast in the days of the Company's rule in Andhra and continued even after the Government was taken over by the Crown. British rule on the whole was different in that its ideology was not the same as that of the previous governments. The latter interfered very little in the economic and social life of the people. They were mainly interested in collecting land revenue and other taxes from the people. So long as the people paid the dues regularly they did not bother to interfere with their other activities. But the British in their country had a distinct political system. Legislation played an important part in regulating the lives of the people in Britain. Under the Company administration various laws were enacted in India to change the system of land revenue and to introduce the right of private property in land. In the northern districts of Andhra the zamindari system was introduced and the zamindars became the owners of the land from which they merely collected the land revenue previously. In other districts, the ryotwari system was introduced and the cultivators became the tenants of the Government, though proprietary rights over the land they cultivated were conferred upon them. In the ryotwari areas where the revenue was directly collected by the Government, there was no regular system of survey and settlement for a long time and the revenue collected was arbitrary and often burdensome. In the zamindari areas the position was much worse as the zamindars were free to collect whatever they liked from the cultivators. Revenue had to be paid in cash and not in kind as in the olden days. When prices fell as they actually did in 1834, the tax burden became heavier. The Government also collected revenue systematically and did not allow arrears to accumulate. The cultivators who were unable to pay the land tax had to borrow at heavy rates of interest from the money lenders by mortgaging their land to them. When they were unable to repay the debt, they were forced to part with their lands.

There was a steady decline in industries like weaving, ship-building iron, manufactures of weapons like swords and daggers from the 1760s because of the Industrial Revolution in England. Masulipatnam, Tuni, Nellore among other places were famous for the fine cloth they manufactured and exported to foreign countries. The East India Company too carried on extensive trade in these textiles during seventeenth and the eighteenth centuries. As a result of the Industrial Revolution such goods began to be imported into Indian from Britain at much cheaper prices. People preferred them to Indian goods. Factories began to set up and this also led to a decline of crafts and industries. As a consequence the pressure on land increased. Agriculture became the main occupation of the people and very little was done in the days of the

Company to promote irrigation (except the building of the anicuts across the rivers Godavari and Krishna) or to introduce any improvements in agriculture as was done in Britain and West Europe in the nineteenth century. Agriculture became less productive. Famines were more frequent and occurred with greater severity taking a heavy toll of human life besides loss of cattle. All this led to greater economic discontent among the people.

Even after the Crown took over, conditions did not very much improve. In addition to these economic causes, other factors like the attempts made by the Chrristian missionaries to convert Hindus increased the discontent. From about the 1820s Christian missionaries went to several parts of Andhra and established educational institutions but their main object was not so much to spread literacy as to use these institutions as places for carrying on conversions. They succeeded to an extent in this. They also extended their activities to rural areas, and in times of famine they were able to convert the poorer classes, especially the untouchables. This created considerable indignation among the more enlightened sections of the community. With the spread of English education after 1850, these sections grew in number and they gave vivid expressions to their anger.

In1858 the Crown took over the Government. The Proclamation issued by Queen Victoria gave many assurances such as treatment as equals of the citizens of the British Empire, throwing open all higher offices on an equal basis to Indians who were educationally qualified and the strict observance of religious neutrality, but in practice these pledges were honoured more in the breach. Racial arrogance was the order of the day and the British treated in Indians as an inferior and uncivililsed race. Government officials gave encouragement both directly and indirectly to Christian missionaries and this was totally against the pledge of religious neutrality. The admission of Indians to the higher offices was not put into effect, and this was a source of disappointment to the English educated classes. The period between 1858 and 1885 is verily a period of broken pledges by the Government.

Beginnings of Political Activity

The system of survey and settlement which was introduced did not result in reducing the hardship of the ryots who had to pay land revenue. Their debts increased and many of them became landless and unemployed. In the earlier stages there were no organizations through which people could express their grievances and make representations to the Government. It was through political associations that this was done by the English educated classes in Bengal and Bombay. In Andhra however there were no such associations till after 1885 when the Indian National Congress was founded. Earlier there were political associations only in the city of Madras and Andhra leaders in the city participated in their activities. They were of little use for the people in the districts. The situation changed to a great extent after 1885. The Congress attracted the attention of the English educated sections in Andhra too. Several Andhras made it a point to attend the annual sessions of the Congress. The table below gives an idea of Andhras who attended the annual sessions from 1887.

Year	*Place of Session*	*No. of Andhra Delegates*
1887	MADRAS	100
1888	ALLAHABAD	45
1889	BOMBAY	151
1890	CALCUTTA	22
1891	NAGPUR	43
1892	ALLAHABAD	17
1893	LAHORE	14
1894	MADRAS	336
1896	CALCUTTA	16
1897	AMARAOTI	21
1898	MADRAS	208
1899	LUCKNOW	14
1902	AHMEDABAD	9
1903	MADRAS	143
1904	BOMBAY	37
1905	BENARAS	29

It was these delegates that awakened the political consciousness of the people. Through public meetings they conveyed the message of the Congress and the significance of the resolutions passed to the people. They started district associations which in turn held district conferences on the model of the annual sessions of the Congress, passed resolutions on various local issues suggesting solutions to be presented to district and provincial authorities. Although the activity started late, it was as eventful in Andhra as in the other parts of the country.

Influence of Newspapers

Newspapers also played an important role in the general awakening of the people. By the close of the country there were as many as 20 newspapers, mostly weeklies, fortnightlies and monthlies. Almost all of them were bilingual – Telugu and English. They contributed much to the general awakening of the people, to consolidate the movement of social and religious reform and to the growth of political consciousness. Like the English educated classes, those who started the papers were moderates in their political outlook. Although they criticized the policies of the Government they did not lay too much stress on freedom or Swaraj. But the criticism of the policies provoked the people to take interest in political problems. The indifference to politics which characterized the people earlier gradually disappeared and they began to realize that their progress rested ultimately on what the government did. Later on they took a prominent part in the freedom struggle under the leadership of Mahatama Gandhi and the Indian National Congress. It was this awakening that was brought about by the spread of the English education, the growth of political associations like the district associations and the work of the newspapers that was mainly responsible for the prominent part they played in the movement.

It is worthwhile noting the causes championed by the newspapers. The extreme poverty of the people, the burden of heavy taxation, the extravagant expenditure incurred on the army and civil administration, corruption among officials, neglect of education of the masses and lack of medical relief, the growth of crime and lawlessness and the inability of the police to maintain order were highlighted. Among other items to which attention was focused were the high price of salt, the excise policy of the Government and the indifference of even the lowest ranks of Government officials towards the people, the non-employment of Indians in the higher ranks of civil services, the vesting of executive and judicial authority in the hands of the district collectors and the partiality shown by the courts to Europeans accused of crime. In the period between 1885 and 1905 there was also the complaint about the discrimination between the Hindus and the Muslims, and between certain Hindu caste and others. It is also pointed out that when communal riots took place officials showed partiality to the Muslims. There were also adverse comment on the activities of the missionaries in using school and hospitals maintained by them for conversion of the people of Christianity and the encouragement given to them by the authorities in a variety of ways including grants on large areas of land at nominal prices. It was suggested by almost all paper that instead of employing Europeans on high salaries it would be less expensive to employ Indians who were equally efficient. All this is important to show how newspapers still in an infant stage contributed to a great deal to the political awakening of the people.

Role of Religious and Social Reform Movements

In Bengal and Bombay, religious movements were to a great extent responsible for the growth of nationalism and the general awakening of the people. In Andhra however their influence was only marginal. The Brahmo Samaj came late to Andhra. Veeresalingam Pantulu and Venkataratnam Naidu who led it began their activities in the last decade of the nineteenth century when the movement had lost much of its original strength. It had only a few followers in Andhra. The Arya Samaj did not have branches in Andhra and its activities were confined to the city of Hyderabad and its neighbourhood. The Ramakrishna Mission also did not spread its activities in Andhra till about the second decade of the twentieth century. The Theosophical Society had several branches, but membership was not substantial. On the whole therefore it may be said religious movements did not influence the people in Andhra to the same extent as they did in the rest of the country.

On the other hand, the social reform movement was quite persuasive. Veeresalingam Pantulu wrote extensively on the social evils specially affecting women. He carried on a crusade against the disabilities of women and popularized the idea of re-marriage of widows. He also started homes to educate windows so that they might live as respectable members of the society. He promoted the cause of women's education by starting schools and encouraged others to do the same. He also took up the cause of the untouchables. In course of time there was an appreciable improvement in the status of women.

Role of Literature

Men of letters also contributed substantially to the growth of nationalism and patriotism among the people. Chilakamarti Lakshminarsiham took the lead in writing patriotic poetry and stories and novels which depicted the heroism of the Rajputs in the wars against the Turks, Afghans and Mughals. The lead was followed by other eminent writers like Gurazada Appa Rao, Duvuri Rami Reddy. Vedula Satyanarayana Sastry, Mangipudi Venkata Sarma, Rayaprolu Subba Rao, Vishwantha Satyanarayana, Tummala Sitarama Murthy among others. Their writings were in two channels – an all India theme pertaining to the country as a whole and the other referring to Andhra in particular. Whatever be the idea, their purpose was to make the public nationalistic and patriotic minded. In the 1920's when the Non-co-operation movement was started many inspiring ballads calling upon the people to sacrifice their lives if necessary for the freedom of their motherland were composed and they were sung at all public meetings even in rural areas. More than 500 ballads were composed and among them top priority should be given to the balled composed by Garimella Satyanarayana which began with the words "we do not want the white man's rule". It became a household utterance, more popular than even the Vandemataram song.

By about the beginning of the twentieth century the Andhras had become highly political with a zeal for patriotism and fully national minded prepared to do anything to uphold the cause of the nation. They were only too ready to take an active part in the solution of economic, social and political problems. In doing this they wanted to act in concert with the people in other parts of the country. This political awakening was further strengthened by the tour of Bipin Chandra Pal in Andhra in 1907.

Influence of Vandemataram Movement

Even before Pal undertook his tour, the people of Andhra had responded to the Vandemataram movement. In the City of Madras, a national fund and an industrial association were started with a view to encouraging Swadeshi in the Madras presidency of which Andhra was then a part. In the public meeting held in the city on March 29, 1906, Gadcherla Harisavothama Rao who was then a student of Madras Christian College made a stirring speech exhorting his countrymen to take to Swadeshi. He was followed by Adipudi Somanatha Rao, an eminent Aryasamajist and a social reformer of Andhra, who compared India to a house only rented to the British. He made frequent references to the industrial and political progress of Japan. Many students of the city – and there were several Andhras among them – enlisted themselves as members of the Industrial Association. A Swadeshi League was also started and its members deputed Nyapathi Subba Rao Pantulu, the well-known Congress leader, to tour Andhra to popularise Swadeshi. C.Y. Chintamani who was then assistant secretary of the India Industrial Conference joined Nyapati Subba Rao Pantulu, and both of them extensively covered the Telugu districts holding meeting in all the important towns. In the meetings addressed by both, resolutions were passed urging people to start industrial concerns and organize an industrial wing in all the district associations. When the news of the arrest of Surendra Nath Banerjee at the Barisal conference in Bengal came to be known to the people of Andhra, protest meetings were held and the action of the Lieutenant Governor of East Bengal was strongly condemned. In this way the Vandemataram Movement influenced the Andhras. Several Andhras also attended the Calcutta session of the Congress held in December in 1906 under the Presidentship of Dadabhai Naoroji and brought along with them the message of Swaraj, Swadeshi, Boycott and National Education. From then on the Vandemataram song became a favourite with the people of Andhra. Even little urchins began to sing Vandemataram at the sight of Europeans who used to feel annoyed. The Andhra region was thick with Vandemataram when Bipin Chandra pal visited the area.

Pal's Tour

Bipin Chandra Pal visited Vizianagaram and Vishakapatnam and addressed large gatherings and from there went to Kakinada. He addressed similar meetings and found adequate response to his message of Swaraj, Boycott, Swadeshi and National Education. He next went to Rajamundry stayed there for five days and delivered lectures on these subjects. Besides political leaders and writers like Chilakamarti Lakshmi Narsimham, students took a prominent part in these meetings. As instructed by him they wore Vandemataram badges while attending their colleges. Many of them had already become members of Bala Bharat Samiti, a quasi-political association in the city. Harisarvothama Rao who was then a teacher-trainee in the

Government Training College was active in welcoming Pal at all the meetings which he addressed. From Rajamundry pal went to Vijayawada, Masulipatnam, and finally to Madras where he delivered a series of lectures on Swaraj and other subject intimately associated with it. This was a triumphant tour and in all the towns he visited he was able to convey to the people his message. As in the case of Bengal, people in Andhra too felt that Swaraj should be their objective, and the programme of Swadeshi, Boycott etc. should be followed in the same way as the Bengalis did. Swadeshi stores were opened in all towns and the Bengalis did. Swadeshi stores were opened in all towns and in villages. Donations were collected to send young men to Japan to get trained in small scale industry like the making of pencils, candles etc., National schools sprung up. One such school was started by Nyapati Subba Rao Pantulu in Rajamundry. More important than this was the Andhra Jateeye Kalasala the foundation stone for which was laid by Pal in 1907. It started working in 1911 under the principalship of Kopalli Hanumantha Rao who gave up his practice as an advocate and dedicated himself to national service under the influence of Pal. He received active co-operation from Dr. Pattabhai Sitaramayya and Konda Venkatappayya.

While these were the known advantages secured as a result of Pal's tour it also influenced the people in an emotional way and even Europeans were amazed at the transformation brought about by Pal's visit. A Christian missionary working in and around Rajamundry wrote to the Government; "There is no immediate danger on hand but Pal no doubt had sown a powerful seed which has fallen on fertile ground and is beginning to grow to some places more rapidly than one is inclined to think". The Krishna Patrika wrote: "The respect and hospitality with which the people entertained him and the eagerness with which they listened to his speeches are not signs of temporary rise of feelings but convey a special meaning underlying them all. They are the indications of a desire for independence and a longing for changes lurking in the hearts of the people. The new spirit teaches a lesson to the westerners who have a mania for extension of dominions and who wield terrible swords. The lesson will be taught not by arms, not by war but by a bloodless sacrifice." These were found choicest expression in other papers in Andhra.

Rustication of Students in Rajamundry

Two significant incidents are associated with the visit of Pal. The first one concerned the students of the two Government Colleges at Rajamundry—the Arts Colleges and the Training College—for both of which Mark Hunter, a well known educationist was the principal. He resented the activities of the students in connection with Pal's visit – their cry of Vandemataram and their membership of the Bala Bharta Samiti. In defiance of his orders the students of the Arts College began to wear a medal or a paper ticket on which the word Vandemataram was printed. He ordered them to remove the medals and badges. While some obeyed his orders, many refused to do so. He then ordered all such students to leave the college. He reported the matter to the syndicate of the Madras University. Ultimately with the approval of the Government 133 students of a total strength of 222 were rusticated. A more serious action was taken against Harisaarvothama Rao, the teacher trainee in the Training College. He was dismissed from service and the Government issued an order debarring him entry into any branch of public service. As a result of this he became a wholetime national worker and played a distinguished role in various capacities – journalists, freedom fighter, member of the legislature and as a front rank worker in the field of adult education and library movement.

Kakinada Riot

The second incident in the wake of Pal's visit took place in Kakinada. It had its origin in one Captain Kemp, the district medical officer, manhandling a boy of 17 who gave a full-throated Vandemataram. The boy received injuries when Captain Kemp dragged him to the police station nearby, and left him unattended and uncared for. This roused the indignation of the people and a mob of 300 attacked the European club in the town causing heavy damage to the building. Captain Kemp was then dining in the club. The Collector of the district who came to know of this attack arrived at the club immediately to disperse the crowd. The rioters hit him on the forehead and made good their escape. The Europeans in the incident though it was apparent that it was entirely the outcome of the misbehaviour of Captain Kemp. The Collector and the Government fell in line with this view. The police arbitrarily arrested 50 people as they did not know who the real culprits were. They also imposed a collective fine on the town and stationed a punitive police force at the expense of the inhabitants.

The arrested persons were tried and a good many of them including one A.L. Narasimha Rao, a graduate, and the owner of a local swadeshi store were convicted. They all appealed to the District Court and the District Judge discharged most of them but confirmed the sentence on 13 persons. Leading citizens of Kakinada held a public meeting to express loyalty to the Government but declared that the riot was not the outcome of any political conspiracy. Gradually the Government withdrew the punitive police.

The impetus given to Swadeshi and Boycott at the time of Pal's visit continued to sway the public in Andhra during the years 1907-1909. Although most political leaders belonged to the school of moderates which dominated the Congress after the Surat split in 1907, propaganda in favour of Swaraj, Boycott and Swadeshi was steadily carried on and it was reported that the influence was felt even in the rural areas which were hitherto unaffected by politics. The credit for this should go to the students who were rusticated by Mark Hunter. It was during this time that Chilakamarti Lakshmi Narsimham composed a few of his patriotic poems. Books were written encouraging people to dedicate themselves to the cause of freedom.

Imprisonment of Harisarvothama Rao

The year 1908 was a year of repression all over the country. It was the year when Tilak was sentenced to six years imprisonment in Mandalay. In Andhra, Harisarvothama Rao who was connected with a Telugu paper –Swarajya –was prosecuted for sedition and through the District court sentenced him to simple imprisonment of only six months, the Government preferred to appeal to the High Court which enhanced the sentence to three years rigorous imprisonment. The policy of repression continued in the year 1909 also. Action was taken against people on mere suspicion that they were manufacturing country bombs. The Tenali bomb case took place in 1909. On the whole, however, there was not much of terroristic or revolutionary movement in Andhra.

Kotappa Konda Riot

In 1909, the Kotappa Konda riot took place. Kotappa Konda is a hillock with a temple of Siva. As was usual thousands and people assembled there on the Sivaratri day when a tussle took place between one Chinnappa Reddy and the police. The number of police constables was small and in the riots that followed the mob set fire to the temporary police station and injured the district superintendent of police. They also tried to attack the sub-collector who appeared long after the riot. Not having enough police force he left the scene immediately. The crowd also dispersed after the festival was over. Later the Government arrested a number of people for participating in the riot. Twenty one persons were convicted while Chinnappa Reddy was sentenced to death. He was regarded as a true hero and martyr who had the courage to defy the police. Many ballads were composed recounting his heroic deeds and they are in vogue to this day. The riot has hardly any political significance.

In 1910 there was little political activity in Andhra. This was mainly due to the domination of the Moderates. The Nationalists had no active leaders among them and no organization to pursue their activities. In 1911, the Vandemataram Movement in Andhra ceased with the annulment of the partition of Bengal.

The Andhra Movement

Political activity took a different form between 1911 and 1916. There were the years when the Andhra movement was carried on by leaders of all parties with a view to persuading the Government to constitute the Telugu districts into a separate province. Conferences were held and resolution passed in favour of a separate Andhra province. Meanwhile, the First World War brought in its wake new problems that required serious and urgent attention with the result the Andhra Movement occupied a low priority.

In 1916, the Home Rule Movement attracted the attention of the political leaders. Even so conferences were held year after year in which resolutions urging the creation of a separate Andhra province were passed. But nothing tangible took place until 1953, seven years after freedom was won when under extraordinary circumstances, the Government of India had to concede the demand.

THE HOME RULE MOVEMENT IN ANDHRA

CHAPTER 29

Activities of Besant

From 1914 the course of political events in Andhra as in the rest of the country was affected by the First World War. At all the conferences held during these years – the Andhra conferences, the provincial conferences, and the district conferences – resolution were passed assuring the Government of the loyalty of the people to the allied cause, and help to the Government in men and materials and donations to the war fund. At the same time the resolutions requested the Government to lift the ban imposed after the great revolt of 1857-58 against the recruitment of the Telugus to the army. It was forcefully pointed out that Telugu sepoys played a significant role in the wars fought in the days of the Company and that it was a mistake to regard them as non-military race and impose a ban on their recruitment. This apart, resolutions were also passed requesting the Government to introduce liberal constitutional reforms.

Fresh impetus was given to the demand for constitutional reforms when Annie Besant, President of the Theosophical Society, with its headquarters at Madras entered politics in 1914. She became a member of the Congress and started two newspapers—the Common Weal and New India to plead for immediate introduction of Home Rule in India. She started a Home League in 1916. Five months earlier Tilak also started a similar League and both of them agreed to work in close-co-operation. Besant concentrated all her efforts in popularizing the idea of Home Rule. After the Calcutta Session of the Congress in 1916, she toured coastal Andhra and spoke on Home Rule. Moderates also joined her league with as much enthusiasm as the nationalists to the utter indignation of the Government. Besides this she started a separate branch of the league to cover the Andhra district, and placed it under Harisarvothama Rao who was appointed its secretary. He wielded a powerful pen and issued a large number of pamphlets in Telugu, popularizing the demand for Home Rule. The activities of the Andhra Branch spread to the rural areas too and the Government grew panicky.

Besant's Internment

The Government in Madras proposed to deport Besant to put a stop to her activities but the Government of India did not agree to this. The Provincial Government then tried to restrain her activities by demanding a heavy security but this did not adversely affect her activities. She used other channels for carrying on her work. She organised a citizen's league in Madras, started a boy scouts movement to enlist the co-operation of the youth and prepared a scheme for Home Rule for the country. All this provoked the Government ultimately to take action against her. She was told either to leave India and go back to England or to be prepared for internment. She rejected the first alternative and she was consequently interned with two of her colleagues.

Its Effects

The Government action became counter productive in that the Home Rule Movement became more popular. A large number of local branches were established in Andhra and they numbered as many as 52 at the end of 1917. At the various district conferences and meetings resolutions were passed protesting against her interment and demanding her release. Harisarvothama Rao took an active part in all these meetings and recruited a large number of enthusiastic for the Home Rule movement. The members of the Theosophical Societies in Andhra too started taking keen interest in Home Rule and actively worked for it. A proposal for a passive resistance was made and the Madras Provincial Congress Committee passed a resolution supporting it as the only effective method of getting her released and for activating Home Rule.

Her Release

That especially was a period when the British felt that need for the help of Indians in prosecuting the war. The British Cabinet thought it expedient to grant constitutional concessions to India and this precisely was the reason for the famous announcement made by Montagu on August 20, 1917 in the House of Commons. The release of Annie Besant and her Colleagues in September was a sequence to this.

Annie Besant continued her Home Rule activity even after the August announcement. The Andhra Public supported her and resolutions were passed at all districts and provincial conferences demanding Home Rule. The government tried to drive a wedge between different communities with a view to halting the progress of the movement. The Brahmin – Non-Brahmin controversy was capitalized by the Government and it began to encourage, the Justice Party which was the spokesman of the non-brahmins who were bitterly opposed both to the Home Rule movement and the Congress. All this was done to impress on Montagu who visited India in 1917 that the demand for Home Rule came from a very small sections of the people in Andhra and the majority comprising non-brahmins were opposed to it.

The year 1918 witnessed a number of protest meetings against the report on Indian constitutional reforms formulated by Montagu and Chelmsford. This sums up the political activity in Andhra in 1918. By the end of the year of the Home Rule movement lost its momentum in Andhra and it was Gandhiji who was held as the leader by the Andhras too with his unique technique of Satyagraha as an effective means to achieve the national objective of freedom.

Outcome of the Movement

Gandhiji's entry into politics electrified the entire atmosphere in Andhra and the people were ready to participate in any movement organised by him. The preparatory stage for the Andhras to actively engage themselves in the freedom movement organised by Gandhiji has truly been reached.

Rowlatt Satyagraha

In 1919, Gandhiji gave a call to observe April 6 as a day of national mourning in protest against the Rowlatt Act which was passed against the unanimous wishes of the political leaders in the country. The public in Andhra responded to the call. In accordance with his directive, Andhras observed 6th April as a day of prayer and fasting. There was complete Hartal – the first of its kind in towns and in villages. There was community bathing in the morning, followed by "Sankirthan" parties singing devotional and patriotic songs, offering of prayers in places of worship, stopping of work in factories, business houses and shops, holding mammoth meetings in the evenings and passing resolutions calling on the Government to repeal the Rowlatt Act. The day passed off peacefully in Andhra. This is a remarkable testimony to the people's faith in the leadership of Mahatma Gandhi.

THE NON-CO-OPERATION MOVEMENT IN ANDHRA

CHAPTER 30

Programme of the Movement

After the Rowlatt Satyagraha in 1919, Mahatma Gandhi gave a call for Non-co-operation with the three-fold objective of bringing pressure on the Government to settle the Khilafat issue in accordance with the wishes of the Muslims in India, to obtain redress for the wrongs done in the Punjab, and for winnings Swaraj. The special session of the Congress held in Calcutta in September 1920 approved his programme and it was also ratified by the regular session held at Nagpur in December, 1920. Many eminent Andhra Leaders attended the two sessions though a few of them including Venkatappayya were not very much in favour of the movement. They ultimately decided to throw their lot with Gandhiji. The people in Andhra responded to the call with great enthusiasm.

As demanded by Gandhiji they boycotted the elections to the legislative councils held in the later part of 1920 under the Government of India Act 1919. Only a small percentage of voters exercised the franchise and those belonging to the Justice Party alone took part in the elections. There were instances of empty ballot boxes being returned. The enthusiasm of the people increased when All India Congress Committee met a Vijayawada on 31st March 1921. Nearly two lakhs of people gathered there from different parts of Andhra singing patriotic ballads. They heard with rapt attention the speeches delivered by great leaders like Gandhiji, Motilal Nehru, C.R. Das, and Ali Brothers, and decided that they should participate effectively in the movement.

Boycott

The three items in the Non-co-operation movement were boycott, constructive work and civil disobedience. Boycott included surrendering of titles, boycott of courts and of schools managed by the Government or receiving aid from the Government and boycott of foreign cloth and liquor. The constructive programme related to the establishment of panchayat courts, national schools and colleges, hand spinning and khaddar, removal of untouchability, and Hindu-Muslim unity. The civil disobedience movement encompassed defiance, in a non-violent manner, of laws enacted by the Government and the refusal to pay taxes.

The number of persons who surrendered titles in Andhra was not very large. This was only to be expected since most of the title-holders were loyalists. The boycott of courts had a better response. Though the number might not appear to be appreciable some 103 lawyers joining the boycott-it is worthy of note that among those who gave up practice were lawyers like Tanguturi Prakasam who occupied a position in the Bar similar to that of Motilal Nehru and C.R. Das in their respective provinces of Uttar Pradesh [and Bengal. Several thousand of students boycotted schools and colleges and among them was Kala Venkatarao who was to become a leading public figure later. Students enrolled themselves in the volunteer corps raised by the Congress and they took a leading part in picketing shops dealing in foreign cloth, unmindful of the lathi blows showered on them. The vaisya merchants of Guntur and other places took a pledge that during the movement they would not impart of sell foreign cloth. It was, however, in regard to boycott of liquor that Andhra topped. Leaders and volunteers persuaded the bidders in abkari sales which usually fetched large revenues to the Government not to take part in the biddings. Their efforts succeeded remarkably in many districts. The excise revenue fell by 50 percent to 70 percent. In Nellore district no more than a mere Rs. 102 could be collected on account of abkari sales – a fact which attracted the attention of the entire country and of Gandhiji.

Constructive Work

As regard constructive work, hand spinning, production of khadi and its sale were the pivotal points which attracted attention. In this women played a prominent role among with men. Centers like Ponduru in Srikakulam which were famous for weaving this finest varieties produced more khadi than during any previous period. Andhra Khaddar became famous throughout the country. It was the most successful part of the constructive programme. Mention should be made of panchayat courts established in about hundred villages, and they decided many civil and criminal disputes. The most successful court was in Mattapalam in Naraspur Taluk of Godavari district. National schools and colleges too were established in many places and by June, 1921, there were 44 of them with a total strength of 2,729. The leading place as occupied by the National College established at Eluru. It was opened in 1921 by Gandhiji himself with zamindar giving an endowment of one lakh of rupees. Several of those who joined the Non-co-operation movement served as teachers and principals in the National schools and colleges. The students in these colleges enrolled themselves as volunteers.

The session of all India Congress Committee held in Vijayawada on 31st March, 1921, resolved that one crore rupees should be collected for the Tilak Swarajya Fund, that one crore new members should be enrolled in the Congress and that 30 lakh charkas should be introduced. A quota for each province was fixed. The quota in respect of the first and the last items was more than fulfilled in Andhra by the targeted date. Serious attempts were also made to remove untouchability. Gandhiji made it a condition for civil disobedience that in the concerned area untouchability was not practiced. Those who were keen on civil disobedience had to pay attention to this item and in the early part of 1922 the committee which was appointed by the Congress to enquire into the conditions prevailing in Pedanandipadu firka which embarked on a no-tax campaign was convinced of the removal of untouchability in that area and was also convinced that this evil had been eradicated in Guntur and other districts.

Among the items of constructive programme the establishment of ashrams though not emphasized by Gandhiji attracted the attention of workers in Andhra. The Pinakani Ashram in Nellore district and the Sita Nagaram Ashram in Godavari District deserve mention. They took a prominent part in constructive work and in spreading the philosophy of non-violence.

Civil Disobedience

The Andhra leaders were much more interested in a civil disobedience movement than in the programme of boycott and constructive work. They wanted to defy the Government by refusing to obey its laws and pay taxes to erode governmental authority and pave the way for the establishment of Swaraj. It was believed this would also help in mobilizing the masses to disobey the Government fearlessly. Moreover to attract the local people, the leaders felt that local issues should be taken up more actively than the constructive programme. It was only in November 1921 that the Congress gave formal permission to the provincial Congress committees to start the civil disobedience whenever the conditions laid down by Mahatma Gandhi were fulfilled.

Dugirala Gopalkrishnayya

Among the movement started in Andhra three of them attracted the attention of the country. The first was the Chirala-perala event led by Duggirala Gopalakrishnayya. He took his Master's degree from the Edinburgh University and was considered an intellectual. After his return to India he served for sometime in the Government College at Rajamundry and at the National College at Masulipatnam. He was, however, not satisfied with the education imparted in these colleges. After attending the Calcutta Congress in 1920 he was inspired by the programme of non-co-operation and decided to dedicate himself to the course of Swaraj as a first step he raised a disciplined band of soldiers, thousand in number and named it Ramadandu – the followers of Rama, the patron God of the Andhra. It was a well-trained corps and he pressed them into service at the All India Congress Committee session in Vijayawada on 31st March, 1921 and on 1st April, 1921 to maintain order at the meetings. All the leaders were impressed by the effective role and played by the Ramadandu and the spirit of dedication displayed by the volunteers.

Chirala and Perala Episode

Chirala and Perala were two contiguous areas in Guntur district with a population of 15,000. The Government for reason of its own decided in 1920 to have a common municipality for the two towns. But the people resented the moves as the new dispensation would only mean more taxes without any corresponding benefit. And yet the municipality was constituted and even the new ministry of the Justice Party which came to power in Madras did nothing to meet the people's wishes. It was just then that Gopalakrishnayya assumed the leadership of the people in the area. As a protest against the government's decision all the elected councilors resigned. But the Government carried on the administration under the control of a salaried chairman. In January 1921 the people refused to pay the municipal taxes. A number of them including a woman were prosecuted, tried and sentenced to imprisonment. After the All India Congress Committee session concluded in Vijayawada, Gandhiji came to Chirala. Gopalakrishnayya asked him for advice as to the future course of action to be taken by the people of the unwanted municipality. Gandhiji suggested two alternatives. The first was the continuation of the no-tax campaign in a non violent manner and the other was the mass exodus of the people to the vacant areas beyond the municipal limits. The second course would automatically result in the municipality ceasing to exist. At the same time Gandhiji made it clear to Gopalalkrishnayya that whatever course the people adopted, the Congress would take no responsibility and they should stand on their own legs. Gopalakrishnayya had enough confidence in the people and in his ability to carry them with him. He finally persuaded the people to move to the sandy area outside the municipal limits and create there a temporary town which he called Ramanagar.

This was an unprecedented step. For eleven months the people living in Ramnagar in thatched huts braved the elements undergoing severe hardship. Their morale was kept high by Gopalakrishnaya and his Ramadan. His aim was to establish a parallel Government in Ramanagar to demonstrate how Swarajya as conceived by him would work. He set up an Assembly composed of members elected by all castes and even established an arbitration court. As his biographer put it, "doubts disappeared in his presence, fears vanished before him and life became a new joy to the subject of Gopalakrishna Raj". Samkirtans and bhajans, in which he was versatile because of his vast learning in Sanskrit and Telugu, kept high the morale of the people. He had to face financial difficulties and to collect money he went to Berhampur where a session of the Andhra conference was being held. He was prohibited by the Government from addressing public meetings but he defied the order following which he was arrested, tried and sentenced to one year imprisonment. He was sent to the Trichinoploy jail. There was none who could take his place in Ramanagar. The Government pursued a policy of severe repression against the people for having built thatched sheds on government land. Heavy penalties were imposed as a result of which some of the people deserted the camp. In the end all the people returned to their homes in the new municipality. Although the civil disobedience movement which lasted eleven months did not succeed, the courage and fearlessness displayed by the people stood them in good stead and they were able to play a significant role in the subsequent Satyagraha movements. In the municipalities of Repalle and Vijayawada also a similar agitation was witnessed though not on the same scale but the Government relented and yielded to popular pressure by taking action in conformity with the wishes of the people.

Forest Satyagraha in Palnad

The next incident which attracted wide attention was the forest satyagraha or the riots of Palanad in Guntur district in the middle of 1921. The peasants in the area were being oppressed by the levy of heavy fees collected from them for grazing their cattle in the forests. And as the crops also had failed during that year they were unable to meet the demand for payment of the grazing fee. They therefore decided not to pay fees and were fully prepared to meet the consequences. As a preliminary to this they resorted to social boycott of government officials and refused to supply to them even the necessities of life. The sub-Collector who was camping in the area found it impossible to get milk, eggs and other essentials. The social boycott did not however produce the expected change in the official. The forcibly drove out the cattle from the forests, confined them in the village pound and refused to free them unless the fees were paid. This led to clashes between the owners of cattle and the armed police. To disrupt the Satyagraha movement, the police resorted to firing as a result of which one of the leaders Kannuganti Harumanthu was killed. Meanwhile Gandhiji called of the non-co-operation movement owing to the untoward incidents in Chowri Chowra and with this the Palnad satyagraha also ended abruptly.

No Tax Campaign in Pedanandipadu

A much more important event was the no-tax campaign undertaken by the ryots in Pedanandipadu Firka of Bapatla Taluk in Guntur District. As a first step the village officers were persuaded to resign. No land revenue could be collected without the help of the village Karnams who maintained the records or of the village munsiff who actually collected land revenue. There was a difference of opinion between the local leaders like Konda Venkatappayya and Mahatma Gandhi on the starting of the no-tax campaign. Gandhiji wanted that he should first try the experiment in Bardoli in Gujarat before a similar campaign was launched elsewhere. The local leaders however tried to convince him that all the condition for starting such a campaign laid down by the Congress working Committee were met and that the ryots were very keen on starting it. Gandhiji then reluctantly gave them permission. It was in January 1922 the month when the first instalment of land revenue was to be collected that the campaign began. The revenue officials were unable to collect even five percent of the revenue. The campaign was under the leadership of Parvataneni Veerayya Chowdari. He succeeded in keeping high morale of the people in the face of repressive measures. The properties of the people including movables, cattle and lands were attached by revenue officials for non-payment of taxes. But the Government totally failed in its efforts to sell them as no one was forthcoming to buy. To terrorise the people they moved the military into the area. But even this was of no consequence. The Congress volunteers worked round the clock to maintain order among the people and see that violence did not break out. Government felt helpless. It was at that stage the non-co-operation movement was called off. Gandhiji and the local leaders abandoned the no-tax campaign and paid the taxes.

End of the Movement

Though Guntur was the most active center of the civil disobedience movement in Andhra, there was equal enthusiasm in the other coastal districts. There were the most affluent districts in the region. People were literate and they had efficient leaders. The officials felt that the non-co-operation movement might pose a danger to governmental stability and they adopted all sorts of repressive measures to put an end to the movement. These measures did not deter the politically conscious sections of the people. The movement came to an end not so much as a result of demoralization among the people in Andhra as the decision taken by Mahatma Gandhi and the Congress Working Committee. The local leaders generally followed the dictates of the All India leaders and this was the main reason why the movement could not be further carried on.

THE DEVELOPMENTS IN ANDHRA FROM 1922–29

CHAPTER 31

The Swarajya Party in Andhra

With the imprisonment of Mahatama Gandhi in 1922, there was no united leadership at the national level in the congress. Nor was there agreement among the leaders as to what course of action should be pursued. At Bardoli the non-co-operation movement was suspended but not completely abandoned. There was a controversy between the No-changers like C. Rajagopalachari and Rajendra Prasad and Pro-Changers like Motilal Nehru and C.R. Das. The division was also present among the leaders in Andhra. The No-changers wanted to revive the mass civil disobedience movement when the time was ripe for it and in the meanwhile to concentrate attention on the various items of constructive work like khaddar, removing untouchability etc. The pro-changers wanted to take part in elections to be held in 1923 and enter the Councils Central and Local and to carry on non-co-operation from within. The controversy between the two sections continued for more than two years. Meanwhile the pro-changers organised the Swarajya Party with a view to contesting the elections. In Andhra also the Swarajya Party was organised by Vemavarapu Ramadas Pantulu, K.V.R. Swamy and Unnava Lakshminarayana, among others.

On the whole, however, the vast majority of Congressmen in Andhra were No-changers. T. Prakasam too was in the beginning a No-changer but later advocated participation in elections. The civil disobedience enquiry committee appointed by the Congress to report whether there was any immediate prospect of reviving civil disobedience movement was of the view that conditions were not ripe for it. In spite of this the No-changers continued to adhere to their view and called upon the Congressmen to concentrate their attention on constructive work. In 1922 and during the larger part of 1923 they were able to make some headway. They did propaganda for khaddar and by about the middle of 1923 Andhra occupied a leading place in the production of khaddar especially of the finer varieties. This was an encouraging aspect but equal success was not achieved in regard to the other items like temperance, national schools, removal of untouchability, establishment of panchayats and Hindu-Muslim unity.

The Swarajya Party came to believe that the time was propitious for contesting the elections and Ramadas Pantulu was elected to the Council of State. A good number of them were elected to the Madras Legislative Council. We are not here exactly concerned with the work of the Swarajyaists either in the Central Legislature or in the local legislatures. Even in the latter, where they were elected in large numbers, they were not able to create constitutional deadlocks which was really the object of Council entry. The annual session of the Congress held in December 1923 in Kakinada was a unique event. A few months earlier Konda Venkatappayya was elected acting president of the Congress and Duggirala Gopalakrishnaya its Secretary. This was considered a great honour to the Andhra and Duggirala Gopalakrishnayya played an important role in the special session of the Congress held in 1923 at which a resolution was passed urging that freedom should be given to those who wished to enter the legislatures and no propaganda should be carried on by the No-chargers against them. This was confirmed by the regular session held at Kakinada. By that time elections were over and though the controversy between the Pro-changers and the No-changers continued even after that, it ceased to evoke much interest. After his release, Mahatma Gandhi favoured a compromise between the two wings, and step by step he yielded to the Swarajyists. In 1924 he presided over the Belgaum session of the Congress and got a resolution passed by the All-India Congress Committee early in 1925 to hand over all political power in the Congress to the Swarajya Party. The Swarajyists ultimately won.

In the elections held in 1926, the Swarajyists were not returned to the Central Legislature in large numbers owing to a variety of circumstances but were returned with substantial strength to the Madras legislature. They were in a position to form a Ministry but the Congress was against office acceptance. This restriction was relaxed when C.V.S. Narsimharaju, a member of the Congress party, was given permission to stand for the Presidentship of the Madras Legislative Council and he was duly elected to that office. Even after that the controversy did not end creating bitterness between those who wanted to accept office and those who were opposed to it. All this had its effect on the course of the freedom movement. There was really no such movement between 1922 and 1926. Several Congressmen in Andhra were tired of the stalemate. Bulusu Sambamurthi tried to keep up the enthusiasm by bringing the new idea that the Congress should declare itself as a body aiming at complete independence and the severance of all connection with the British. Under his influence and that of others, resolutions were passed at some of the district conference held in the years 1924-26 in favour of a change in the objectives of the Congress from Swaraj to complete independence. These were the main aspects of the activities of the freedom fighters between 1922 and 1927 after which the situation entirely changed as a result of the visit of the Simon Commission. Politics became much more lively and eventful from then no leading finally to the Salt Satyagraha in 1930.

Alluru Seetharamaraju

We have to refer to the revolt led by Alluri Seetharamaraju between 1922 and 1924 in the Agency areas of Godavari and Vishakapatnam districts. These areas were inhabited by the tribals. Raju became their leaders and organised them to fight against the British. Significance is attached to this revolt because it was unlike the previous tribal revolts in the days of the East India Company. The revolt led by Seetharamaraju was essentially political in character. He was influenced by the ideal of Swaraj enunciated at the Calcutta session of the Congress in 1920. He firmly believed that in the light of what happened in 1920–22, Swaraj could not be achieved by mere non-violence. There was nothing unrighteous and unethical about resorting to violence to achieve the objective and he cited Hindu scriptures and writings bearing on Hinduism in support. He wanted to try it in the tribal areas partly because the terrain was most hospitable for the purpose. Guerilla tactics were ideal in a region with jungles and hills. Further, the tribals were simple-minded and they admired a person who could even tame wild animals and proficient in Hindu mythology as well as astrology-the qualities which Sitarama Raju possessed in abundance. The tribals were also dissatisfied with the conduct of the British officials. Several restrictions were placed on the shifting system of cultivation which was the traditional mode followed by the tribals. There were curbs on grazing rights and catling of timber and collecting forest produce which were their customary occupation. Corruption was rampant among officials and the contractors engaged by them failed to pay the wages that were due to the tribal people working under them.

Sitaram Raju took note of these malpractices indulged in by the concerned persons to oppress the tribals and took up their cause by organizing a revolt against the authorities. Raju was born in a Kshatriya family in 1897 in Moggalu village in West, Godavari district. He did not show much promise at school but he was proficient in horse riding and other activities with which Kshatriyas were traditionally associated. It is said he became a sanyasi and wandered in the tribal areas. He came into close contact with the people and was anxious to promote temperance among them. He also tried to settle their disputes through panchayat courts. The officials were suspicious of him as his programme was similar to the one advocated by the non-co-operators in the plains. Restrictions were placed on his movements but he was able to convince the officials that he was not actuated by any political motives. Having thus established his bonafieds he was really preparing for a rebellion which began in August 1922. At the outset he organised raids on police stations in the area to acquire firearms. The first such attack was made on August 22, 1922 and a few arms were seized. He continued similar raids successfully because the police forces at the stations were small in number and inefficient too. Raju steadily built up a good collection of arms. During one of these raids he rescued one Veerayya Dora who was in prison. The Dora became his trusted lieutenant along with the Gam brothers-Gam Mallu Dora and Gam Gantam Dora.

The authorities woke up to the realities of the situation and dispatched a police force on September 3 to intercept him but he succeeded in humbling them. The prestige of Raju shot up. Then he went from village to village collecting food and other essential requirements. The police attempted to attack him when he was engaged in Kali worship on top of a hill but they did not succeed. This further enhanced his reputation as one possessing divine powers.

Raju had another successful encounter with the police. This made the authorities sit up and devise more effective steps to suppress the rebellion initiated by him. In October a special contingent of the Malabar police arrived on the scene but it did not make much difference to the situation. In all these encounters his targets were Europeans and not Indians.

Raju also had a well trained corps of spies who critically watched the movements of the authorities and the police. In November he made a number of raids in different places and collected a lot of booty. In December he tasted his first defeat in a skirmish in which some of his followers were killed. This was followed by yet another attack which proved disastrous for him. Consequently, Raju's popularity slumped somewhat. The authorities offered a reward for his capture and that on the Gam brothers and Veerayya, He envaded the police for months wandering in the hills.

Early in May the Government appointed Rutherford who was considered to be an efficient member of the Civil services as a special commissioner. Rutherford issued warrants against tribals whose deportation was considered necessary and also arrested about two hundred people. On May 6, 1924, the police accidently came upon Raju's force which was 50 strong. In the encounter that followed, the police killed two rebels, wounded several and captured Aggiraju, a right hand man of Raju.

May 7 proved to be a bad day for the heroic Raju. The police secured information about Raju's hideout and a special force marched to the spot. It was a coincident that a person with a beard was just then located and the police rightly held him to be Seetharamaraju, chased him and fired at him. He fell on the ground and was captured. Raju made a futile attempt to escape but he was killed by gun shot wounds. He was formally identified by the Deputy Tahsildar of the place and his body was cremated on the morning of the 8th, though some believed that he was transported to the Andamans and that he was not really shot dead.

With his capture, the rebellion subsided. The efforts were continued by the police to clear the area of small gangs. Villagers also assisted the Government. Gantam Dora lost his life and by September 1924 no rebel was left and the Government reestablished its authority.

Men of his them have failed to understand the political character of Raju's revolt. Some of them especially in the Congress did not like the violent methods which he pursued. As the Andhra Patrika a leading Telugu daily put it, the Rampa fituri is a good example to illustrate that the adoption of violent methods like rebellions and fituris not only prove self destructive but also prove very harmful both to the people and to the country. Very few showed in those days sympathy for Raju and the revolt he led. It was only two or three years later that sections of the youth in Andhra began to speak highly of him and of his heroic exploits. He became a leader of hallowed memory and anniversaries were celebrated from 1927. On the occasion of the celebration in 1929, messages were received from Subhas Chandra Bose and Jawaharlal Nehru and it became customary for Andhra leaders to pay tributes to him. Though Raju's rebellion did not have a decisive effect on the course of the freedom movement in the country, his example became a source of inspiration to others and it thus acquired significance in the freedom movement in Andhra.

Lull in Andhra Between 1925–27

In the years 1925–27, there was little political activity in Andhra though the merits and demerits of the Council entry programme versus civil disobedience, the role of the Congressmen in the legislatures, and on the ultimate goal of the Congress – Whether it should be Dominion Status or complete Independence were hotly debated. As a result of the advice for Mahatma Gandhi the All India Congress Committee decided to handover the political work of the Congress to the Swarajyists. In spite of their continued opposition, Congressmen participated in the elections in 1926. Vemavarapu Ramdas Pantulu was elected to the council of State and the Swarajyists were elected as the single largest party to the Madras Legislature. But the Congress was opposed to the acceptance of office and consequently the Swarajyists did not form the ministry when they were invited by the Governor of Madras. They remained in opposition though they were undecided as to whether they should oppose or support the ministry taking into account the circumstances and the nature of the questions that came up for discussion in the legislatures. The more radical minded among the Congressmen like Bulusu Sambamurthy wanted to change the ideal of the party to complete independence under which India would have nothing to do with Britain. Resolution to this effect were passed in district conferences as well as in the provincial conference held in 1927. it was worthy of note that this was done even before the Madras session of the Congress held in December, 1927 passed a resolution in favour of complete independence. But all these debates and controversies did not lead to any fresh political activity.

Attention was paid to constructive work on which Gandhiji was keen. He did not want to take part in the any political activity as he felt that he was sentenced to six years imprisonment in 1922 and though he was freed two from prison in 1924, it was his moral duty not to participate in political activities until the period of six years was over. He therefore concentrated on khaddar, the removal of untouchability and other items of the constructive programme. But even in this regard spectacular progress was not achieved in Andhra. There was non-co-operation with the Government.

Simon Commission Visit to Andhra

The situation changed as a result of the appointment of the Simon Commission in 1927. The Andhras fell in the line with the people in the rest of the country in deciding to boycott the all white Statutory Commission. They declared that the British had no right to enquire into whether Indians were fit for Swaraj because Swaraj was the birthright of every nation and resolution in favour of Independence had already been passed at some of their conferences. They suggested the boycott of the commission even before a resolution to that effect was passed by the Congress. From the beginning of 1928 propaganda was carried on by the leaders to create public opinion in favour of boycott. Municipal councils also passed resolutions in this regard and they decided to close all educational institutions on the day the Commission landed in India. And on February 3, 1928, accordingly there was total hartal in all important towns and villages. The hartal was peaceful. In the city of Madras, however there was violence when the police resorted to firing against a procession which resulted in one person losing his life, and several being injured. Tenguturi Prakasam, the Andhra Leader, visited with his followers the scene of the firing and he wanted the permission of the police to see the body of the person who lost his life. Not only was he refused permission but also an armed policemen pointed his gun against him. Prakasam displayed exemplary courage when like Swami Sharddhananda in Delhi, he bared his chest and asked the policeman to fire at him. The police as dumb-founded. The daring act on the part of Prakasam attracted the approbation of the public, and from them on he came to be known as Andhra Kesari –the lion of Andhra.

The Commission visited Madras on February 26. Orders were issued prohibiting all propaganda in favour of boycotting the Commission. There were two congress committees in the city-one for the Andhra and another for the Tamil – speaking section. The Andhra Committees was in favour of disobeying the prohibitory order, but the other committee did not share the view. As a consequence of this no propaganda was carried on, but a total hartal was observed. The boycott was successful.

The Commission programmed to visit Guntur and Ongole in Andhra. Earlier they went to Calcutta and it was from Calcutta they undertook their journey to Andhra. The Andhra leaders and the public had already passed resolutions urging the boycott of the Commission. When the train in which the members of the Commission traveled halted at the Vijayawada Station a striking incident took place. Kaleswara Rao, municipal chairman of Vijayawada, had the boycott resolution of the council typed and another sheet of paper on which was written in bold letters the words, "Go Back Simon", was got ready and both of them were put in a sealed cover. It was then sent to the railway station through a municipal daphedar to be handed over to Sir John Simon. The daphedar managed to reach the compartment in which Simon along with his colleagues was seated and handed over the sealed cover to him. Simon opened the cover ad passed it on to the collector who was standing on the platform. The ingenuity of Kaleswara Rao and his daphedar attracted countrywide attention.

During the Commission's visit to Guntur there were black flag demonstrating both at the Tenali and Guntur railway Stations. Guntur towns observed hartal. The Commission could not interview any persons. Their programme consisted of visiting a neighbouring village where they saw a Harijan school at work.

The year 1928 was significant for the report on constitutional reforms by the Nehru Committee. It advocated Dominion Status as the goal of India and prepared a constitution for such a Dominion. The report came up for discussion in Andhra too, and although there were some who stood for complete independence the Andhra provincial conference as well as district conferences approved the report of the committee.

In 1929, the Simon Commission visited Madras a second time before it finalized its report. On this occasion both the Andhra and the Tamil Leaders worked together to carry on propaganda in favour of boycott. On February, 18 the day of its visit, Andhra leaders in Madras were taken into custody and were let off only late in the night. In spite of this the hartal was successful.

In April and May 1929 Gandhiji undertook a six week tour of Andhra. By that time the period of his self-imposed political inactively came to an end. He visited a number of towns and though he spoke mostly on Khaddar, the uplift of Harijans and other classes and constructive work, he was actually preparing the people for the next stage of the freedom struggle.

His tour was truly educative and proved to be an important factor in their participation in the Salt Satyagraha in March, 1930.

❖ ❖ ❖

SALT SATYAGRAHA

CHAPTER 32

The Decision of the Andhra Leaders to Break the Salt Law

After passing resolution demanding complete Independence at the Lahore session of the Congress on December 21, 1929, and undertaking a Non-violent Satyagraha to achieve it, Gandhiji began to give thought to the way in which the campaign should be carried out. He decided ultimately on defying the law against the manufacture of salt. When he was on his march from Ahmedabad to Dandi in February –March, 1930, several Andhra leaders met him and he told them that he relied very much on the enthusiasm of the Andhras for the success of his campaign and advised them as to what they should do. After their return to Andhra, the leaders met in a conference to work out the details of the programme they decided to raise a band of volunteers, to appoint Konda Venkatappaya as director of the campaign for the entire province and to appoint similar dictators for each districts. They also decided as per the advice of Dr. Pattabi Seetharamayya to start the campaign for manufacturing salt in different centers and not at only one center. He pointed out that if it was started at different centers the Government would find it more difficult to tackle it. It was left to each District Congress committee to select the places where it should be started in the district as also the other details of the programme. It was resolved that the campaign should begin during the National week between April 6 and 13.

The Course of the Movement

In accordance with these decisions, breaches of the Salt Law were observed in the centers selected in each district. Sea water was boiled and salt manufactured. Volunteers collected the small packets containing the salt and undertook to sell them in the market. The police tried to compel the volunteers to hand over the packets to them but on refusal they used force against them by showering lathi blows on them. The volunteers were not prepared to part with the salt packets. The packets were sold in auction and the people purchased them at fabulous prices. This went on for a number of months in the province. After some time the people wanted to raid the salt depots as did the volunteers in Bombay province who raided the Dharsana depot. Attempts were made to raid the depot at Naopada in Ganjam, at Balacheruvu in Vishakhapatnam District and at Kanuparti in Gntur District. The raid at Naopada could not be carried out because of the concentration of a large police force. For carrying on the raid Balacheruvu the volunteers in the Sibiram of Vishakapatnam consisting mostly of woman made the preparations. But the sibiram was surrounded by the police and the inmates were not allowed to come out. Hence no raid was possible. The raid on Kanuparti was successful. Volunteers including well-known women leaders like Unnava Lakshmibayamma participated but they were forcibly put in lorries, carried to long distances and let off. The Provincial Congress Committee resolved on suspending raids on June 10 as the atrocities committed by the police especially on women were atrocious.

In the beginning the Madras Government was averse to arresting leaders and putting them in jails. But the district collectors were against this kind of inactivity as it affected, in their view, the prestige of the Government. Consequently, the Government gave them discretion in the matter, and by the end of April all the leaders were put in prison. In spite of this the people carried on the campaign with enthusiasm.

In several places, the police brought down the National Flag hoisted in prominent places. This led to clashes between them and the public. The people would not allow them to pull down the flag and they resisted the attempts of the police in this direction. The incidents related to this aspect in Masulipatnam, Karavadi in Guntur District and Nuzvidu in Krishna District assumed importance throughout the province. The police also resorted to severe lathi charge even on persons who met in peaceful gatherings. The police action on the villages of Angaluru in Krishna District and at Eluru in Godavari District became notorious. They also attacked the sibirams of volunteers as they constituted the main centers for the whole movement and the attacks of sibirams at Rajamundry and Guntur took a serious form. The Volunteers were taken into custody, building destroyed and the furniture and records taken possession of. A ban was imposed on the wearing of Gandhi caps and the police beat up persons wearing such caps, and started removing them. Even those who wore Khadi were manhandled. Jails were overcrowded. The prisoners protested against the food given to them. But the only answer to these protests was lathi charge inside the prison. As time went on the Government found that there were not adequate number of jails and, therefore, avoided the imposition of imprisonment as a punishment and made more severe use of the lathi. In the case of women they were bundled in lorries to be carried to distant places to be left there. Repression continued in all conceivable forms but id did not make a dent on the tempo of the campaign.

Gandhi – Irwin Agreement and After

On March 6, 1931 the Gandhi-Irwin Agreement was concluded and the campaign was suspended. Among the conditions of the agreement were that all political prisoners should be released, permission should be given to individuals to manufacture salt for their private use and volunteers should be allowed to carry on the picketing of foreign cloth and liquor as they did during the campaign. But the authorities did not strictly adhere to the terms of the agreement. Lathi charge continued even after the conclusion of the agreement in places Nellore, Guntur and Peddapuram. In Vadapalli in East Godavari District a procession during the car festival was forcibly dispersed as the portraits of Mahatma Gandhi and other national leaders were displayed. There was a similar incident in the Srikakulam car festival. All political prisoners were not released. Some were kept in prison on the ground that they indulged in acts of violence and restrictions were also placed on the manufacture of salt by private citizens and on picketing by volunteers. All this was brought to the notice of the Government but to no avail.

Not much of political significance happened in the year 1931. On December, 31 Gandhiji returned from London after attending the Second Round Table Conference empty-handed as it were. Lord Willingdon who succeeded Lord Irwin was bent upon curbing with an iron hand anti-Government activities and he took recourse to severe repression for this purpose while Gandhi was away in London. On his return Gandhiji found that the political situation had deteriorated and that many prominent persons like Jawaharlal Nehru were out in prison. He attempted to have discussions with the viceroy on the various political issues but the Viceroy would not even grant him an interview and therefore the Satyagraha campaign which was suspended as a result of the Gandhi-Irwin agreement was resumed on January 4, 1932.

Resumption of Civil Disobedience

The resumed campaign was carried on in Andhra with rare enthusiasm and persistence in spite of the police resorting to excessive force. The emphasis was now on civil disobedience – disobeying not only the law regarding the manufactures of salt, but several other laws as well as the new ordinances issued by the Government to deal with the renewed campaign and the orders issued by the districts authorities. People were only too ready to suffer the penalties imposed on them in a spirit of non-violence. All those who were asked to furnish security for good behaviour declined to do so. In defiance of police orders they marched in the streets holding national flags, singing national songs and wearing Gandhi cap and khaddar. They conducted public meetings in defiance of prohibitory orders. This was the general pattern of the campaign. Almost everyday for two to three months many persons courted arrest and were sent to prison for disobedience of the official orders. Against several others, prohibitory orders were issued under Section 144 of the Indian Penal Code. Distribution of anti-government pamphlets became an integral part of the campaign. Picketing of foreign cloth shops, liquor shops and abkari sales was pursued with vigour. Frequent clashes between satyagrahis and the people became inevitable.

Government repression took a more severe form in 1932 than in 1930-31. That became a regular feature of Governmental policy of Lord Willingdon. Lathi charge was resorted to even where there was no need for it. The police were given special training in the use of the lathi. House searches were systematically carried on. There were raids on Congress offices, Khadi depots and co-operative institutions which were under the management of Congressmen. The police seized furniture, records and everything on which they could lay their hands on. There were regular raids on the sibirams of volunteers and ashrams. The wearing of Gandhi caps was looked upon as a crime.

Even though the High Court declared that one had a right to wear it, the police removed forcibly Gandhi caps from any one, whom they saw wearing them. In some cases even those who wore khaddar were beaten up. The police seized and destroyed the portraits of national leaders. Many were punished for providing lodging or boarding facilities to volunteers. Under the provisions of the press law many printing presses were closed. The publication of many newspapers was banned. Books also were proscribed. In this campaign, as in 1930-31, women played a prominent role. The police humiliated them in a very many cases they put them in lorries, carried them to distant places only to be abandoned there uncared for and unprotected.

The cruelty inflicted on prisoners took a more severe form during the campaign. There were lathi charges in jails also on the ground that prisoners rebelled against the quality of food that was supplied and that they disobeyed rules of discipline. It is difficult to list all the names of those who underwent brutal treatment at the hands of the police. But special mention should be made of the treatment accorded to Bulusu Sambarmurti and Khasa Subbarao. False charges were brought against Venneti Satyanarayana and Dr. Subramanyam of Rajamundry. The district judge who tried them found them not guilty and pointed out in the course of the judgement that the police officials like the Deputy Superintendent of Police concocted evidence against them. It was quite obvious that the rule of law gave place to policeraj.

Inspite of the suffering inflicted on them, the satyagrahis continued their campaign with grim determination. When newspapers were banned they got cyclostyled papers circulated. Volunteers in West Godavari and in Krishna were especially active in this regard. Though the Congress and its committees were banned, Congressmen in Andhra held a provincial conference at Tenali and district conferences without the police knowing about them. This was done by them in the same way as the Congress session was held in Delhi in 1933. It is noteworthy that most of these conferences were presided over by women. It was much after the event that the police came to know of the meetings and several persons were prosecuted and sent to prison.

The tempo of the movement declined in 1933 although the struggle was not given up when Gandhiji undertook his fast in

Yerrawada jail at Poona. Sympathetic fasts were undertaken by Congress leaders in Andhra. In many places there was a big qualitative change in the attitude towards Harijans and this was indicated by the throwing open of public and private wells to them. They were admitted into temples as well.

Gandhiji was released on May 1, 1933, and for various reasons he was compelled to opt for individual civil disobedience in the place of mass civil disobedience. He felt that the masses were not yet completely non-violent and that was an important reason for resorting to this kind of satyagraha. In response to his call many Andhra took part in individual civil disobedience and suffered imprisonment. When the movement was called off on May 30, 1934 the campaign in Andhra also came to an end.

The Nature of the Movement

In the campaign of 1930–34 it was the coastal districts of Andhra that were active. They were rich in resources and a large class of well to do middle class peasant—the Reddis of Nellore, the Kammas of Guntur and Krishna, the Kshtriyas of Godavari, who joined the political movement. These years were also noted for the rise of various organizations outside the Congress. Gandhiji himself established a number of such associations like he Harijan Sevak Sangh, All India Spinners' Associations and made them autonomous so that they might carry on their work without being involved in politics. Similar associations were also started by local leaders. There was the ryots association and a peasant association started by Prof. N.G. Ranga. They ran a number of summer schools and carried on a vigorous campaign against the zamindari system. Ranga toured the districts to spread his message of peasant uplift. He had radical ideas and he gave expression to them in his summer schools as well as in the course of his tours. As the Communists party was banned, the communists could not propagate directly. They started labour associations in districts and they carried on their work through them. There was also the Andhra Socialist Party. Leaders like Tenneti Viswanatham and N.G. Ranga played an important role in its work. The communists also joined the party and tried to get control over the organization. Besides these there was the intelligentsia consisting mostly of lawyers and journalists who participated in the movement. The vaisyas also joined in appreciable numbers due in some cases to the fact that Gandhiji was a vaisya. They gave up for some time the sale of foreign cloth. The movement was thus not confined to any one particular class or community. It was broad based and national in character. As a class the zamindars kept themselves aloof from the movement.

The years 1934–37 witnessed a number of controversies among Congressmen. Except a small minority all were anxious to take part in the elections held in 1934 and many swarajyists were returned to the Central legislature and they formed the largest party in the Madras legislature. The Governor called upon them to form the ministry but they declined because of the Congress ban on the acceptance of office. C.S. Narasimharaju was, however, permitted become the president of the council. There was a controversy whether when the Act of 1935 came into being Congressmen should participate in the elections and accept office or not. Opinion in Andhra was divided.

Kakinada Bomb Case

In addition to all these, youth associations were started by leaders like Madduri Annapuranayya. They had extremist ideas and they managed to hold conferences in various districts from 1935. Though there was not much of terrorism in Andhra a bomb was exploded in Kakinada on April 15, 1933. Nine persons were charged with being members of a revolutionary organization, one of them being Orgunti Ramachandriah, a student of Andhra University, and who was later to become a professor of history in the University. They were charged with having conspired to collect arms, commit dacoits and robberies and assassinate government officials. The case was tried by the committing magistrate from May 11, 1933 to December 9, 1933 and by the session courts of East Godavari upto April 21, 1934. In the sessions courts the accused were found guilty and were sentenced to imprisonment and fine. The high Court set aside the conviction and sentences against seven of the accused and they were set at liberty. The conviction of the remaining two for the offence of conspiracy was set aside but their conviction on other grounds was upheld. The period of imprisonment was reduced and the court ordered that the fines if paid should be refunded.

The Formation of Congress Ministry in Madras

The elections to the legislatures were held in the early part of 1937 under the Act of 1935. Congressmen were voted in large number to the central legislature and to the eight of the Provincial legislatures. They constituted the majority in the latter, and they were in a position to form ministries under the New act. In Madras, C. Rajagopalachari was elected leader of the Congress Legislature Party and he was asked to form a ministry. But as the Congress demanded certain assurances from the Governor before accepting office and as they were not given, Rajagopalchari declined the offer and an interim ministry was constituted with K.V. Reddy Naidu as the Chief Minister.

Negotiations were carried on between Government and the Congress in the following months, and ultimately an understanding was reached which led to the formation of a Congress ministry in Madras with C. Rajagopalcharis as the Chief Minister. Among the Andhras who joined the ministry were Tanguturi Prakassam, V.V. Giri, B. Gopala Reddy, Kaleswara Rao, Tenneti Viswanatham B.S. Murti and M. Bapineedu Bulusu Sambamurti was elected speaker of the Assembly.

July 14, 1937, the day on which the Congress assumed office was observed throughout Andhra as a day of rejoicing. It marked a partial triumph of the freedom fight carried on especially in the years 1930–34. Processions were taken out and public meetings held welcoming the formation of the Congress ministry.

The ministry remained in office for 28 months till October 29, 1939. One of the resolutions that was passed by the Madras Assembly was that the Government of India Act of 1935 was unsatisfactory, and that it should be replaced by a new Constitution to be enacted by the people themselves. Such a demand as previously made by the congress and other organizations in their non-official capacity. By passing this resolution the demand was given expression to by a duly constituted legislative body. This made it clear that though the Congress accepted office it was determined to carry on the fight till its ultimate goal was achieved.

The Congress in Office

During the 28 months the Congress was in office the ministry took steps to carry out some of the ideals for which the Congress stood. As a testimony to this, it released the political prisoners from jails, refunded the deposits taken from the printing presses and newspapers and wrote off arrears of fines levied on those who took part in the movement of 1933-34. It withdrew the orders issued by the previous government prohibiting the hoisting of the national flag on the buildings of local and municipal bodies. The concessions granted under the Gandhi-Irwin pact which were subsequently cancelled were restored and the restrictions placed on the holding of meetings and taking out processions were removed. The ministry passed an Agriculture Relief Act which provided liberal scaling down of debts and arrears of rent due from cultivators.

A committee was appointed under the chairmanship of T. Prakasam, the Revenue Minister, to enquire into the Zamindari system and make recommendations for its abolition. After an exhaustive study the committee recommended the abolition of the system completely. But before legislations could be enacted to this effect, the ministry resigned and it was only after the country became free in 1947 the system finally abolished.

The ministry took the first step to introduce prohibition. The Madras prohibition Act was passed in 1937 and by time the ministry resigned it was in force in four districts. Legislation was also undertaken to improve the social and economic condition of the Harijans. A number of Acts were placed on the Statue book to enable Harijans to gain admission into temples. Provision was also made to grant lands and housing facilities to them on a liberal scale.

Steps were taken to put into effect Gandhiji's scheme of basic education. Improvements were introduced in the field of adult literacy, local-self government, co-operation, cottage industries, public health, and famine relief. All these measures clearly demonstrated that the congress was a body devoted to constructive work for prompting the general welfare of the community. The ministry resigned in October 1939 as a result of the decision taken by the All India Congress Committee.

THE QUIT INDIA MOVEMENT IN ANDHRA AND ACHIEVEMENT OF FREEDOM

CHAPTER 33

Lifetist Activity

After the resignation of the Congress ministries there was little political activity in Andhra as Gandhiji was against civil disobedience. Some Andhra Leaders like Prakasam even expected that the Government would come to an understanding with the Congress and that a Congress ministry would again come to power in Madras and continue the work which was left unfinished when it resigned in 1939. But this expectation was not fulfilled. There was activity on the part of the leftists in the province like the Forward Bloc led by Madduri Annapuranayya, the Kisan Party led by Prof. N.G. Ranga and the Socialist Party. The Communist Party was banned but the members of the party managed to get into the Congress and the Socialist Party. Subhas Chandra Bose toured certain areas of Andhra in 1940, addressed meetings at Rajamundry and Eluru among there towns calling upon the people to take advantage of the situation created by the War and start a civil disobedience campaign. This plea was taken by the Leftist which also advocated the starting of such a Campaign. Anti British and anti-war slogans calling upon the people not to enlist themselves in the army or contribute to the War fund and the war loans were raised by them. Many leftists were arrested and sent to prison.

Individual Civil Disobedience

We have already seen that Gandhiji was pressured to start the individual Civil Disobedience movement in November 1940. Andhra took a prominent part in it. All the leaders who happened to be the members of the Congress committees participated in it and were sent to prison. In several cases the magistrates were reluctant to issue orders of arrests and fill the jails with the Satyagrahis. Gandhiji suggested that these who were not arrested should march to Delhi but on reaching the borders of the Madras province and the Central provinces, they were forced to go back. By about the close of 1941 the movement came to an end. It is not known exactly how many Andhras went to jail during the Individual Civil Disobedience movement. According to a press not issued on March 1941, the total number of arrests in the country expect in the Punjab was 4, 749 and out of them the Andhra share was 882. But in this respect it stood second among the provinces, the first place going to the United Provinces which contributed 4,995. Andhra however, headed the provinces in the matter of fines imposed, the figure being Ts. 76,533 out of Rs. 2,96,630 for the country. By 1942, Congressmen in Andhra became alive to the dangers of a Japanese invasion of the country. District Congress Committees met and appointed peoples projection committees to meet any invasion threat by Japan. They also fell in line with the views of Gandhiji who wrote in the columns of his paper that the British should immediately quit. Such a view became firmer when in April the Japanese bombed Vishakapatnam. Many Andhras attended the All India Congress Committee meeting in Bombay on August 7 and 8, 1942 when the Quit India Resolution was passed.

Quit India Movement

On August 9 the news of the arrest of Gandhiji and other prominent leaders of the Congress reached Andhra. For three days from August 9, there were hartals in all towns and villages. Public meetings were held and resolution passed condemning the arrests. Peaceful processions also were taken out. The police used lathis to disperse the processions. They also resorted to firing as a result of which many people lost their lives. Even those who undertook peaceful picketing of toddy shops and shops dealing in foreign cloth were not spared. Shops were forcibly opened and shop keepers were compelled to sell the articles. All this and the arrest of the leaders infuriated the people and this was responsible for the outbreak of violence in Andhra from August 12.

The Andhra Circular

Even before the Quit India resolution was passed by the All India Congress Committee on August 8, the Andhra Provincial Congress Committee drew up a plan of action if the movement had to be inevitably started and carried on. The plan was embodied in what come to be called as the Andhra circular. The text of the plan did not become available to the Government but parts of it came to be known and these were pieced together. It was on this basis that the Government accused Gandhiji and the Congress later on of having planned violent campaign in advance. In the records of the Kurnool District Congress Committee is available a plan which was similar to the Andhra circular and this may be regarded as a copy of the original circular.

According to this circular, the movement was to be carried on in six stages. In the first stage all prohibitory orders should be disobeyed. Salt should be freely manufactured. Even when an organization like the Congress committee was declared unlawful, members should move about openly. In the second stage, lawyers are to give up their profession, students should boycott schools and colleges, and assessors and jurors should not respond to the summons issued to them. Village officers and Government officials should resign their jobs. In the third stage workers employed in the railways and factories should be induced to resort to strikes. In the fourth stages shops dealing in foreign goods, toddy shops and foreign companies should be picketed. In the fifth stage alarm chains in railway compartments should be pulled and trains stopped. People should be encouraged to travel without tickets. Telegraphs and telephone wires should be disconnected. Date and palmyra trees should be destroyed. Forest satyagraha should be started. In the sixth and the final stage there should be a non-tax campaign and the payment of all taxes excepting municipal taxes should be stopped. Recruiting Offices should be picketed as well as sepoy battalions. Congress flags should be hoisted on all the Government buildings as a sign of the success of the movement. There were also instructions as to how prisoners in jails should disobey the prison regulation, how to safeguard the honour of the Congress flag and other related matters. As the news about the Civil disobedience movement might not be published in the newspapers, Congressmen should bring out hand bills giving out important news. The plan stressed that non-violence should be strictly observed.

But when the movement actually commenced these stages were not observed. Persons in each locality adopted their own plan of action. In all cases the main emphasis was on disrupting the means of transport like railways and the means of communication like telegraphs and telephone. This was done as it would prevent the sending of the police and the military from one part of the country to another to curb the movement. What happened in the course of the movement is evident from some of the incidents.

Attack on Tenali Railway Station

On August 12, a large crowd attacked the railway station at Tenali. The Station master and the staff were asked to vacate the premises. The crowd then demolished the booking office, set fire to the station master's room and the refreshment room and record and furniture. It also set fire to the train examiners' office in which oil was stored. The passenger trains in Madras were stopped outside the station and the signals tampered with. Passengers were asked to get down and some of the bogies were set on fire. With great difficulty the station masters managed to send a message to the local police. The district magistrate and the superintendent of police arrived with a party of police reserves. They found that the crowd could not be dispersed even by repeated lathi charges. They then opened fire, which resulted in six being killed, and eleven injured. The damage to railway property was estimated at Rs. 2, 50,000.

Incidents in Chirala

On this same day a procession of 500 students marched to the court of the sub-magistrate in Chirala and asked him to close the court. After causing damage to the building the crowd raided the office of the sub-registrar and the sales tax office and stoned the police station. It then proceeded to the railway station, attacked it from all sides and caused damage to a train on the platform. Then it attacked the cabin, cut the telephone and signal wires and set fire to the station building. There were other incidents of a similar character at the station. The crowd dispersed only after the arrival of the police and the civil guards. The damage caused was estimated at one lakh of rupees.

Incidents in Guntur

On August 13, a crowd of 2,000 consisting mostly of students gathered in front of the Hindu College, Guntur. They resorted to stone throwing at the cars passing by and at the police. A number of them proceeded towards the Gandhi Park opposite to the College. The police followed them and suddenly opened fire and several among those who were merely listening to the radio programme in the park were wounded and two persons died. The Bar Associating held a meeting the next day and passed a resolution condemning the action of the police. Educational institutions had to be closed for a week.

Incidents in Bhimavaram

Worse was to follow at Bhimavaram in West Godavari District. On August 17 a crowd of more than 2,000 entered the court of the stationary sub-magistrate, and asked him to close the court. After he told them that he would do not work that day they moved towards the district munsif 's court. The court was not sitting then. The crowd next proceeded to the revenue divisional office, and it asked the officer to resign. He was made to hold a Congress flag and march some distance with them. The crowd then set fire to the building and the records. They next burnt down the office of the deputy inspector of schools. The crowd then went to the police station. The sub-inspector seeing that the rioters were rushing to seize the fire arms in the station opened fire. Meanwhile police regiments came and opened fire. As a result three were killed and five injured. In the meantime a part of the crowd proceeded to the police lines and set fire to them.

Incidents in other places were more or less of this pattern. In their hostility towards the alien government the people behaved in a reckless manner with every justification for much of what they did.

Government Repression

In addition to lathi charge and firing Government took other measures against those who were suspected of having participated in the movement. In addition to arrests, collective fines were imposed. Such fines were generally imposed on villages which were in the neighbourhood of the railway track and roads which suffered damage. The fines amounted to much more than the estimated cost of the damage. Government held the view that the fines should be collected from residents who belonged to the land owning community and to the communities of vaisyas, Brahmin and the intelligentsia. Muslims, Harijans and backward classes were exempted from paying them though the officials knew that members of those communities also participated in rioting Collective fines were imposed in seven of the ten districts of Andhra. They were Anantapur, Cuddapah, West Godavari, Guntur, Krishna, Kurnool and Nellore. The highest amount of Rs. 3,21,681 was collected in the Guntur District.

Though a large number of people were arrested all of them were not sent to jails. Some were let off after fines were imposed on them. This explains why the number sentenced to imprisonment in 1942 was not in proportion to the intensity of the struggle. Gandhiji also advised Congressmen not to court imprisonment unnecessarily.

The struggle reached the climax in August and the first half of September, 1942. The tempo then slowed down, several persons continued the struggle not only in 1942 but also in 1943. In 1943 there was an increase in the use of explosive and bombs. Cases of combustible material being thrown into post boxes were noticed. The Government continued its policy of repression. As a matter of fact it became more intensive in 1943 than in 1942. Many more were taken into custody in the latter year. Obstacles were placed in the way of celebration of the Independence Day on January 26, 1943. In spite of this the Day was celebrated in most places and processions consisting mostly of students were taken out and demonstration organised.

Gandhiji's Fast

From February 10 to March 3 Gandhiji undertook a fast in vindication of his stand that he was unnecessarily and unreasonably accused of responsibility for the violence. In Andhra sympathetic facts were observed. Hartals were organised and processions taken out. Gandhiji survived the fast and the Andhras felt greatly relieved.

Movement Ends

An attempt was made to hold a session of the Andhra Mahasabha to demand a separate Andhra Province. The Government refused permission in the first instance, but it was given after an assurance that there would be no political speeches. There were fewer incidents on 1944. August 9, the day on which Gandhiji was arrested was an occasion for political observance. But Gandhiji advised Congressmen not to undertake demonstrations. He also appealed to all Congressmen who went underground to report themselves to the police. Among these who did so was Nivarti Venkata Subbiah, Secretary of Kurnool Congress District Committee. He was tried but was left off.

Incidents After 1944

In 1944 district assemblies were formed in place of the District Congress Committee which was banned. They concentrated their attention on constructive work. In 1945, the Andhra watched with great interest the outcome of the Simla Conference convened by Lord Wavell. Its failure caused disappointment to them and Congressmen attributed it more to the weakness of Wavell than to the obstinacy of Jinnah. The latter part of the year was devoted mostly to election campaigns for the Central Legislature and the Provincial Legislatures. Congress set up large number of candidates. The campaign was undertaken by leaders like Prakasan, Pattabhi Sitaramayya, Kala Venkata Rao and Sanjeeva Reddy. Congressmen were returned in large numbers to the Central and the Provincial Legislatures. While the election campaign was going on the I.N.A. trials took place in Delhi. Demonstrations against the Government were held in Andhra area too and contributions were made for the fund raised for the defence of the I.N.A. men under trial.

The year 1946 is memorable for the naval mutiny in Bombay. This had its impact in Andhra too when Naval ratings came out of ships stationed in the harbour of Vishakapatnam and the people in the city and its neighbourhood showed their admiration for the mutineers.

Achievement of Freedom

In the elections that took place in March 1947 to the Madras legislatures the Congress secured a majority. A ministry was formed with Prakasam, the Andhra leaders, as the chief minister. He remained in office only for a short time. He was succeeded by O.P. Ramaswamy Reddiar. The years 1945-47 were a period of political negotiations. We have already seen that these negotiations ended successfully after Lord Mountbatten became the Viceroy. The Indian Independence Act was passed in July, 1947, and on August 14, the British withdrew from the country and freedom was achieved. August 15 was a day of universal rejoicing for the people in Andhra as it was in other parts of the country. Andhras were happy that the sacrifices they made in the cause of freedom bore fruit in the end. At the public meetings they paid tributes to those who participated in the struggle for freedom and above all to Gandhiji who led them to victory. The national flag was hoisted all over Andhra and like the rest of the countrymen, the Andhras stepped into a new period.

❖ ❖ ❖

APPENDIX–II

THE FREEDOM STRUGGLE IN TELANGANA

CHAPTER 34

Nature of the Struggle

Telangana is today a part of Andhra Pradesh. Prior to 1948 it was in the state of Hyderabad under the Nizam. The revolt here was not so much for freedom from alien rule as from the despotism of the Nizam. He allowed no political activity in the state, and in this respect there was a great contrast between the British rule in Andhra and the Nizam's rule in Telangana. There was no freedom of speech, freedom of association, freedom to hold meetings or publish newspapers. The people here were, however, influenced by the political development in Andhra where political associations were started and newspapers were published. The people had little political awareness and it took several years before they asserted themselves. In the earlier stages the movement was directed towards achievement of civil liberties. As time passed, the demand was for responsible Government and finally when India became free, pressure was brought to bear on the Nizam to accede to the Indian Union.

From 1883 attempts were being made by leaders like Agor Nath Chatopadhaya, father of Srimati Sarojini Naidu, who was employed in the Nizam's educational service to initiate people into political activity. When the Indian National Congress was started in 1885 some of them became its members, and attended its annual sessions as delegates. One or two newspapers were also established like the Hyderabad Record in Urdu. But they were soon proscribed because they criticized the policy of the British Residents in Hyderabad and occasionally the Nizam too. There were correspondents of "The Hindu" published from Madras and of the "Pioneer" published from U.P. and it was from the reports in these papers people out side the State came to know of what was happening in Hyderabad State.

Literary and Cultural Renaissance

As in British India, political activity in Telangana was preceded by literary and cultural renaissance, first among the Telugu speaking people and then the Marathi speaking people in Marathawada which formed the western part of the Hyderabad State and the Kanarese speaking people in the southern part.

A branch of the Arya Samaj was established in Hyderabad in 1892. It also contributed to the cultural awakening of the Hindus. Ganapathi Festival was celebrated on the lines indicated by Balagangadhar Tilak.

Cultural activity amongst the Telugus began with the starting of the Krishnadevaraya Andhra Bhasha Nilayam in 1901 through the efforts of K.V. Lakshmana Rao, the diwan of the Raja of Munagala, and Ravisetti Ranga Rao. The Nilayam was a center of activity and literary meetings were organised in the library from time to time. A little later another library was started in Secunderabad in 1904, and at Hanumakonda in 1905. The library movement gradually spread and it contributed to the cultural and literary renaissance of the Telugu-speaking people. Lakshmana Rao was also responsible for the establishment of the Vignana Chandrika Mandali for the publication of books in Telugu on modern subjects. The headquarters was shifted to Madras in 1907 since the Government of the Nizam grew suspicious of its activities.

The Maharashtrians also followed the example of the Telugus and started in 1908 the Vivekavardhani Pathasala and the Vivekavardhani Educational Society. In Karnataka area also, educational activities were started with Gulbarga as the center.

The Swadeshi and boycott movement of Bengal and of the terrorist movement of Maharashtra began to spread their influence in Hyderabad too. The Osmania University was founded in 1919. There was also social reform activity. A society was formed for the uplift of the Harijans and improving the status of women. Telugu papers like Golconda Patrika and Nilagiri Patrika and papers in Urdu were started.

Influence of the Non-co-operation and Khilafat Movements

The Non-co-operation movement started by Gandhiji in 1920 and the Khilafat movement closely associated with it had its repercussions in Hyderabad. It brought the Hindus and Muslims together on the same platform and speeches were made denouncing the policy pursued by the British towards the Sultan of Turkey. Students from Hyderabad pursuing courses in Aligarh, Poona, and Bombay gave up their studies to work for the political awakening of the people of the state.

The Andhra Jana Sangh

In 1921 the Andhra Jana Sangh was founded. Eminent persons like Madapati Hanumantha Rao were actively associated with it. The cultural and social uplift of the Telugu speaking people was its main objective. It started libraries and reading rooms and schools with Telugu as the medium of instruction. It published several books in Telugu. It helped the merchants who were harassed by the officials to form merchants' associations in Hyderabad. It agitated against compulsory labour in rural areas. This induced the Nizam's Government to abolish it. It started also a girl's high school in Hyderabad with Telugu as the medium of instruction.

Andhra Maha Sabha

In 1930 its name was changed to Andhra Maha Sabha. Annual conferences were held under its auspices. Women's conferences were also held along with it. It carried on political activity, passed resolutions in favour of elected local bodies and the spread of primary education. Government was suspicious of its activities. Special permission had to be taken from the Government before it held meetings and conferences. In consequence of this, conferences were held outside the State in places like Kakinada, Poona and Bombay. This had its effect on the Government of the Nizam, and in 1937 a committee was appointed under the chairmanship of Aravamuda Ayyangar, a leading advocate, to suggest constitutional reforms.

Andhra Maha Sabha too underwent changes. Till 1941 the moderates dominated the sabha but gradually the communists led by Ravi Narayana Reddy swelled the ranks of the Maha Sabha. This led to a split, and from 1944 the Andhra Maha Sabha began to hold two separate conferences, one under the control of the moderate section, and the other under the control of the Communists. Similar associations were started also by the Maratha and Kannada speaking sections of the people.

State Congress and Satyagraha Movements

In 1946 the State Congress came into existence by a merger of the then existing associations. This was done partly because the associations were accused by the Government of being communal and they thought that as the Congress was a national body the formation of a state Congress and the merger of separate associations in it would eliminate the charge that they were communal.

From 1938, a new epoch began in the politics of the State. Satyagraha was undertaken by a number of organizations in protest against the restriction placed on their activities. The Arya Samaj suffered most from these restrictions. Nearly 12,000 people participated in the Satyagraha started by it, most of them entering the State from Outside. All of them were arrested and jailed. The treatment accorded to them was inhuman. It was while he was in jail in connection with the Satyagraha movement that Vandamataram Ramachandra Rao became prominent. During prayers in jail, he used to sing the Vandamataram song. This was prohibited by the jail authorities but he persisted. He was subjected to severe flogging but he never gave up. It was for this reason that he came to be known as Vandemataram Ramachandra Rao and he played a prominent part in the public life of the state. It is said that it was he who conveyed to K.M. Munshi, the Agent General of the Union Government in Hyderabad in 1948, the secret negotiations which the Nizam was then carrying on for the purchase of Goa from the Portuguese. Satyarahas were started by the Hindu Mahasabha and Praja Mandala in the state. Border camps were set up in order to establish contacts between the political bodies in British provinces and the Hyderabad State.

Osmania University Incidents

In the Osmania University, for the Hindu students residing in the hostels, Vandemataram was a part of their prayers schedule. This was prohibited by the university authorities. But the students persisted. This spread to colleges in the city, and to educational institutions outside. The authorities took severe action against all such students. Quite a few of them were admitted by the Nagpur University as its students.

Ramananda Tirtha and Hyderabad State Congress

It was in 1938 that Ramananda Tirtha decided on starting a Hyderabad State Congress. He formed an executive committee of 15 members under his Presidentship and enrolled 1,200 primary members. He wanted to call a meeting of the general body in September1938) to discuss the details. The Government banned the executive committee as well as the general body on the ground that through the Congress appeared to be a non-communal body, it was really communal in character and had affiliation with an outside body like the Indian National Congress. These charges were denied by Ranmananda Tirtha and his followers. They felt that they had no other alternative but to offer satyagraha. On the advice of Gandhiji the satyagraha was however suspended and yet the ban continued. Then the Congress agreed to call itself the Hyderabad Conference. Even then the government considered it as communal. Individual satyagraha was resorted to in 1940 on line of the movement started by Gandhiji.

Activities of Itihad-ul-mussalman

It was then that the Itihad-ul-Mussalman a Muslim political body established in 1927 became active. It warned the Nizam that under no circumstances should democracy and responsible government as demanded by the state Congress be introduced and the privileged status which the Mussalmans enjoyed for more than two centuries should be preserved. The Itihad even proclaimed that the Nizam himself should be subject to its dictates if he wanted to preserve his sovereignty.

Reaction to Cripp's Proposals

It was just about this time that Sir Strafford Cripps visited India with his new constitutional proposals. The Nizam put forward his claim to complete independence in case the British withdrew. This view was hotly contested by the state Congress. The Nizam and the Itihad were one in urging an independent Hyderabad State.

Reaction to Quit India Movement

During the Quit India movement a similar campaign was started by the followers of the state Congress. Their demands were that the

Congress should be recognized as a lawful body, that civil liberty should be granted to all the citizens in the state and that responsible government should be introduced. A number of people were arrested and put in prison.

Razakar Movement

During the negotiations with the Cabinet Mission, the Nizam reiterated his claim for independence. Meanwhile the Communists started their anti-federal struggle in the districts of Nalgonda and Warangal. The All India State Peoples Conference which was led by Congress leaders like Nehru and Dr. Pattabhi Sitaramayya evinced interest in the affairs of the Hyderabad State. As a result of the Communists movement coupled with the pressure from the State People's Conference the ban on Congress was lifted in April, 1946. Throughout the state, tension prevailed. The Itihad also organised a parallel military force which came to be known as the Razakars. More than 20,000 men were enrolled. All the ranks were supplied with weapons like swords and daggers. Those in command had fire arms. The Razakars were closely associated with the regular army of the Nizam and with the police and obtained arms from them. They committed atrocities especially in the rural areas. The people had to suffer the terrorism let loose by the Razakars and the communists. The Nizam did not care to intervene.

Visit of Jaya Prakash Narayan

On May 7, 1947, Jaya Prakash Narayana addressed a mammoth public meeting in Hyderabad at which he made and impassioned plea that the people should with one voice urge accession of Hyderabad to India when once the British withdrew. He was to deliver his second speech the next day, but in the meanwhile he was externed. This created resentment among Congressmen and the trade unionists and workers. Meetings were organised by them and once more the demand for the immediate introduction of responsible government was put forward. Satyagraha also followed. The police arrested the leaders and jailed them. The mob grew excited. They burnt buses and caused damage to public property in and around Hyderabad city. Communal riots also broke out with all their disastrous consequences.

Nizam Proclaims his Independence

On August 15, 1947, India became Independent. The Nizam issued a declaration that from that day onwards he was also an independent ruler of his State. The Congress and other bodies protested against it and they started what was called the "Join India Movement" which went on till 1948. Committees for the purpose were established outside the state. Border camps were also set up. Satyagraha was started again by Ramananda Thirtha. Many of them were arrested and jailed. From outside the state, Congressmen supplied funds for carrying on the Join India Movement. Jaya Prakash Narayana took an active part in this connection. The movement gradually assumed a mass character. More than 20,000 people participated in it. The Congress flag was hoisted in several places.

Join India Movement

The worsening conditions inside the Hyderabad State which was geographically at the centre of India perturbed the Government of India. Mr. Nehru's Government made it clear to the Nizam that it would not allow the continuance of such conditions which were a threat not only to the peace and order inside the State, but also affected the neighbouring States. Lord Mountbatten too felt concerned. Under pressure from the Ithihad and the Razakars whose strength had increased to 50,000 under Kasim Razvi's leadership the Nizam could not come to any decision. He sent delegation after delegation to Delhi to carry on negotiations with the Government. Ultimately on October 19, 1947, the delegation agreed to conclude a Standstill Agreement with the Government of India. The Agreement had to be taken back to Hyderabad for the signature of the Nizam. The Razakars and the members of the Ithihad prevented the delegation from proceeding with the Agreement. There was considerable uncertainty for a numbers of days. It was only on November 20 that the standstill Agreement was signed by the Nizam according to which he handed over to the Government of India control over Defence, External relations and Communications. Shortly after this, the Congressmen who were jailed were set free. Ramananda Thirtha proceeded to Madras, Bombay and finally to Delhi to consult the leaders as to the future course of action, and on their advice he once more demanded the introduction of responsible government and accession to the Indian Union. On the Nizam's refusal Satyagraha was started.

Meanwhile, in violation of the terms of the Standstill Agreement, the Nizam strengthened his army, started negotiations with Pakistan, established ammunition factories, accumulated large number of vehicles of all varieties and placed an embargo on the use of Indian currency and functioning of Indian banks in the State and prohibited trade in gold and silver.

It was in January 1948 that K.M. Munshi came to Hyderabad as the Agent General of the Government of India. The Razakars opposed his occupying the Residency buildings or any other building in the city and he had to occupy a Government of India building in Bolaram. Reports were reaching him of the atrocities committed by the Razakars, of their looting, arson and attacks on border villages inside India. He reported these matters to the Government of India, and conveyed the message that unless the Razakars were disbanded there could be no security to the people of the State and peace on the border areas. Thereupon the Government of India wrote to the Nizam that the Razakars should be disbanded.

The Indian Government took the further step of asking the Nizam to convene a Constituent Assembly and hold a plebiscite to decide the question of accession. The Nizam replied that he was a sovereign ruler and was free to do what he liked. The Razakars continued their atrocities, attacked trains between Bombay and Madras, and between Madras and Delhi as they passed through the Nizam's territory. There were regular clashes between them and the Kissan Dals organised by the Congress. There were also clashes between the Indian regiments and the Razakars. Razvi's speeches became more and more provocative. He said the Nizam represented the Mughals who were the rulers of India before the coming of the British and that he would see that the flag of the Nizam was hoisted on the Red Fort in Delhi. The Government of India again wrote to the Nizam to ban the Itihad and to disband the Razakars and take a decision on the question of succession. Lord Mountbatten tried to advice the Nizam on these matters and his efforts failed. He was in fact the only friend that the Nizam had in the Government of India. But he left the country on June, 21, 1948. The Nizam, thereupon, appealed to Lord Attlee, the British Prime Minister, and to the American President to intercede with the Government of India on his behalf. But they declined. Finally, he decided on taking his case to the United Nations and sent an official to New York for this purpose.

On September 10, the Government of India issued an ultimatum to the Nizam and on September 13, it was followed by what has come to be know as the "police Action" against the State. Sardar Patel was then the Home Minister. Two columns of the Indian Army entered the state, one from Sholapur to Hyderabad, and another from Vijayawada. Other regiments were to follow in course of time. Within two days the Hyderabad forces were subdued and on September 17, the Nizam surrendered.

The Security Council admitted the case field by the Nizam on September 16, but after his surrender he formally withdrew the case on September 23. General Chowdary took over the administration of the states as the military Governor and in 1950 a civilian government was established with M.K. Vellodi, a member of the Indian Civil Service as the Chief Minister, and with a number of popular ministers. In 1952 elections to the state Assembly took place and a full responsible ministry under Dr. B. Ramakrishna Rao assumed office. The freedom struggle in Telangana came to an end with the surrender of the Nizam on September 18, 1948. Reference is made to subsequent events so as to bring out how after his surrender democratic government was introduced in the state.

SELECT / DOCUMENTS

I

A " HIMALAYAN MISCALCULATION"

BY M.K. GANDHI

[The first nationwide Civil Disobedience Campaign was launched by Gandhiji on April 6, 1919 in protest against the Rowlatt Act. It was called off on April 18 as he thought the people needed further training to practise Satyagraha. The Jallianwala Bagh massacre took place on April 13]'

NEWS WAS RECEIVED that the Rowlatt Bill had been published as an Act. That night I fell asleep while thinking over the question. Towards the small hours of the morning I woke up somewhat earlier than usual. I was still in that twilight condition between sleep and consciousness when suddenly the idea broke upon me – it was as if in a dream. Early in the morning I related the whole story to Rajagopalachari.

"The idea came to me last night in a dream that we should call upon the country to observe a general hartal. Satyagraha is a process of self-purification, and ours is a sacred fight, and it seems to me be in the fitness of things that it should be commenced with an act of self-purification. Let all the people of India, therefore, suspend their business on that day and observe the day as one of fasting and prayer. The Musalmans may not fast for more than one day; so the duration of the fast should be 24 hours. It is very difficult to say whether all the province would respond to this appeal of ours or not, but I feel fairly sure of Bombay, Madras, Bihar and Sindh. I think we should have every reason to feel satisfied even if all these places observe the hartal fittingly."

Rajagopalachari was at once taken up with my suggestion. Other friends too welcomed it when it was communicated to them later. I drafted a brief appeal. The date of the hartal was first fixed on the 30th of March 1919, but was subsequently changed to 6th April. The people thus had only a short notice of the hartal. As the work had to be started at once, it was hardly possible to give longer notice.

But who knows how it all came about? The whole of India from one end to the other, towns as well as villages, observed a complete hartal on that day. It was a most wonderful spectacle. . .

Needless to say the hartal in Bombay was a complete success. Full preparation had been made for starting civil disobedience. Two or three things had been discussed in this connection. It was decided that civil disobedience might be offered in respect of such laws only as easily lent themselves to being disobeyed by the masses The salt tax was extremely unpopular and a powerful movement had been for some time past going on to secure its repeal. I therefore suggested that the people might prepare salt from sea water in their own houses in disregard of the salt laws. My other suggestion was about the sale of proscribed literature. Two of my books, viz., Hind Swaraj and Sarvodaya (Gujarati adaptation of Ruskin's Unto this Last), which had been already proscribed, came handy for this purpose. To print and sell them openly seemed to be the easiest way of offering civil disobedience. A sufficient number of copies of the books were therefore printed, and it was arranged to sell them at the end of the monster meeting that was to be held that evening after the breaking of the fast.

On the evening of the 6th an army of volunteers issued forth accordingly with this prohibited literature to sell it among the people. Both Shrimathi Sarojini Devi and I went out in cars. All the copies were soon sold out. The proceeds of the sale were to be utilized for furthering the civil disobedience campaign. Both these books were priced at four annas per copy, but I hardly remember anybody having purchased them from me at their face value merely. Quite a large number of people simply poured out all the cash that was in their pockets to purchase their copy. Five and ten rupees notes just flew out to cover the price of a single copy of fifty rupees! It was duly explained to the people that they were liable to be arrested and imprisoned for purchasing the proscribed literature. But for the moment they had shed all fear of Jail-going.

It was subsequently learnt the Government had conveniently taken the view that the books that had been proscribed by it had not in fact been sold, and that what we had sold was not held as coming under the definition of proscribed literature. The reprint was held by the Government to be a new edition of the books that had been prescribed, and to sell them did not constitute an offense under the law. This news caused general disappointment.

. . . I proceeded to Ahmedabad. I learnt that an attempt had been made to pull up the rails near the Nadiad railway station that a Government officer had been murdered in Viramgam, and that Ahmedabad was under martial law. The people were terror stricken. They had indulged in acts of violence and were being made to pay for them with interest.

A police officer was waiting at the station to escort me to Mr. Pratt, the Commissioner. I found him in a stage of rage. I spoke to him gently, and expressed my regret for the disturbances. I suggested that martial law was unnecessary, and declared my readiness to co-operate in all efforts to restore peace. I asked for permission to hold a public meeting on the grounds of the Sabarmati Ashram. The proposal appealed to him, and the meeting was held, I think, on Sunday, the 13th of April, and martial law was with drawn the same day or the day after. Addressing the meeting, I tried to bring home to the people the sense of their wrong, declared a penitential fast of three days for myself, appealed to the people to go on a similar fast for a day, and suggested to those who had been guilty of acts of violence to confess their guilt.

I saw my duty as clear as daylight. It was unbearable to me to find that the labourers, amongst whom I had spent a good deal of my time, whom I had served, and from whom I had expected better things, had taken part in the riots, and I felt I was a sharer in their guilt.

Just as I suggested to the people to confess their guilt, I suggested to the Government to condone the crimes. Neither accepted my suggestion.

The late Sir Ramanbhai and other citizens of Ahmedabad came to me with an appeal to suspend Satyagraha. The appeal was needless, for I had already made up my mind to suspend satyagraha so long as the people had not learnt the lesson of peace. The friends went away happy.

There were, however, others who were unhappy over the decision. They felt that, if I expected peace everywhere and regarded it as a condition precedent to launching satyagraha, mass satyagraha would be an impossibility. I was sorry to disagree with them. If those amongst whom I worked, and whom I expected to be prepared for non-violence and self-suffering, could not be non violent, Satyagraha was certainly impossible. I was firmly of opinion that those who wanted to lead the people to Satyagraha ought to be able to keep the people within the limited non-violence expected of them. I hold the same opinion even today.

Almost immediately after the Ahmedabad meeting I went to Nadiad. It was here that I first used the expression of "Himalayan miscalculation" which obtained such a wide currency afterwards. Even at Ahmedabad I had begun to have a dim perception of my mistake. But when I reached Nadiad and saw the actual state of things there and heard reports about a large number of people from Kheda district having been arrested, it suddenly dawned upon me that I had committed a grave error in calling upon the people in the Kheda district and elsewhere to launch upon civil disobedience prematurely, as it now seemed to me. I was addressing a public meeting. My confession brought down upon me no small amount of ridicule. But I have never regretted having made that confession. For I have always held that it is only when one sees one's own mistakes with a convex lens, and does just the reverse in the case of others, that one is able to arrive at a just relative estimate of the two. I further believe that a scrupulous and conscientious observance of this rule is necessary for one who wants to be a Satyagraha.

Let us now see what that Himalayan miscalculation was. Before one can be fit for the practice of civil disobedience one must have rendered a willing and respectful obedience to the state laws. For the most part we obey such laws out of fear of the penalty for their breach and this holds good particularly in respect of such laws as do not involve a moral principle. For instance, an honest respectable man will not suddenly take to stealing, whether there is a law against stealing or not, but this very man will not feel any remorse for failure to observe the rule about carrying head lights on bicycles after dark. Indeed it is doubtful whether he would even accept advice kindly about being more careful in this respect. But he would observe any obligatory rule of this kind, if only to escape the inconvenience of facing a prosecution for a breach of the rule. Such compliance is not, however, the willing and spontaneous obedience that is required of a Satyagraha. A Satyagraha obeys the law of society intelligently and of his own free will, because he considers it be his sacred duty to do so. It is only when a person has thus obeyed the laws of society scrupulously that he is in a position to judge as to which particular rules are good and just and which unjust and iniquitous. Only then does the right accrue to him of the civil disobedience of certain laws in well defined circumstances. My error lay in my failure to observe this necessary limitation. I had called on the people to launch upon civil disobedience before they had, thus qualified themselves for it, and this mistake seemed to me of Himalayan magnitude. As soon as in entered the Kheda district, all the old recollections of the Kheda Satyagraha struggle came to back to me, and I wondered how I could have failed to perceive what was so obvious. I realized that before a people could be fit for offering civil disobedience, they should thoroughly understand its deeper implications. That being so, before re-starting civil disobedience on a mass scale, it would be necessary to create a band of well-tried, pure hearted volunteers who thoroughly understood the strict conditions of Satyagraha. They could explain these to the people, and by sleepless vigilance keep them on the right path.

With these thoughts filling my mind I reached Bombay, raised a corps of Satyagraha volunteers through the Satyagraha Sabha there, and with their help commenced the work of educating the people with regard to the meaning and inner significance of Satyagraha. This was principally done by issuing leaflets of an educative character bearing on the subject.

But whilst this work was going on, I could see that it was a difficult task to interest the people in the peaceful side of satyagraha. The volunteers too failed to enlist themselves in large numbers. Nor did all those who actually enlisted take anything like a regular systematic training, and as the days passed by, the number of fresh recruits began gradually to dwindle instead of to grow. I realized that the progress of the training in civil disobedience was not going to be as rapid as I had at first expected.

II

NATIONAL WEEK

By Jawaharlal Nehru

The SIXTH of April was the first day of the National week, which is celebrated annually in memory of the happenings in 1919, from Satyagraha Day to Jallianwala Bagh. On that day Gandhiji began the breach of the salt laws at Dandi beach, and three or four days later permission was given to all Congress organization to do likewise and begin civil disobedience in their own areas.

It seemed as though a spring had been suddenly released; all over the country, in town and village. Salt manufacture was the topic of the day, and many curious expedients were adopted to produce salt. We know precious little about it, and so we read it up where we could and issued leaflets giving directions; we collected pots and pans and ultimately succeeded in producing some unwholesome stuff, which we waved above in triumph and often auctioned for fancy prices. It was really immaterial whether the stuff was good or bad; the main thing was to commit a breach of the obnoxious salt law, and we were successful in that, even though the quality of our salt was poor. As we saw the abounding enthusiasm of the people and the way salt making was spreading like a prairie fire, we felt a little abashed and ashamed for having questioned the efficacy of this method when it was first proposed by Gandhiji. And we marveled at the amazing knack of the man to impress the multitude and make it act in an organized way.

❖ ❖ ❖

III

SPEECH AT THE PLENARY SESSION OF THE SECOND ROUNDTABLE CONFERENCE IN LONDON

BY M.K. GANDHI

I DO NOT THINK that anything that I can say this evening can possibly influence the decision of the Cabinet, probably the decision has been already taken. Matters of the liberty of practically a whole continent can hardly be decided by mere argumentation, or even negotiation. Negotiation has its purpose and has its play, but only under certain conditions. Without those conditions negotiations are a fruitless task. But I do not want to go into all these matters. I went as far as possible to confine myself within the four corners of the conditions that you, Prime Minister, read to this Conference at its opening meeting......

Although you have invited the Congress, you distrust the Congress. Although you have invited the Congress, you reject its claim to represent the whole of India. Of course, it is possible at this end of the world to dispute that claim, and it is not possible for me to prove this claim; but, all the same, if you find me asserting that claim, I do so because a tremendous responsibility rests upon my shoulders.

The Congress represents the spirit of rebellion. I know that the word "rebellion" must not be whispered at a Conference which has been summoned in order to arrive at an agreed solution of India's troubles through negotiation. Speaker after speaker has got up and said that India should achieve her liberty through negotiation, by argument, and that it will be the great glory of Great Britain if Great Britain yields to India's demands by argument. But the congress does not hold quite that view. The Congress has an alternative which is unpleasant to you.

I heard several speakers – I have tried to follow every speaker with utmost attention and with all the respect that I could possibly give to these speakers – saying what a dire calamity it would be if India was fired with the spirit of lawlessness, rebellion, terrorism and so on. I do not pretend to have read history, but as a school boy I had to pass a paper in history also, and I read that the page of history is soiled red with the blood of those who have fought for freedom. I do not know an instance in which nations have attained their own without having to go through an incredible measure of travail. The dagger of the assassin the poison bowl, the bullet of the rifleman, the spear and all these weapons and methods of destruction have been up to now used by, what I consider, blind lover of liberty and freedom. And the historian has not condemned them. I hold no brief for the terrorists . . . for the sake of liberty people have fought, people have lost their lives, people have killed and have sought death at the hands of those whom they have sought to oust.

The congress then comes upon the scene and devises a new method not known to history, namely, that of civil disobedience and the Congress has been following up that method. But again, I am up against a stone wall and I am told that is a method that no Government in the world will tolerate. Well, of course, the Government may not tolerate, no Government has tolerated open rebellion. No Government may tolerate civil disobedience, but Governments have to succumb even to these forces, as the British Government has done before now, even as the great Dutch Government after eight years of trial had to yield to the logic of facts. General Smuts is a brave General, a great statesman, and a very hard taskmaster also, but he himself recoiled with horror from even the contemplation of doing to death innocent men and women, who were merely fighting for the preservation of their self-respect. Things which he had vowed he would never yield in the year 1908, reinforced as he was by General Botha, he had to do in the year 1914, after having tried these civil resisters through and through. And in India lord Chelmsford had to do the same thing; the Governnor of Bombay had to do the same thing in Borsed and Bardoli. I suggest to you, Prime Minister, it is too late today to resist this, and it is this thing which weighs me down, this choice that lies before them, the parting of the ways probably. I shall hope against hope, I shall strain every nerve to achieve and honorable settlement for my country, if I can do so without having to put the millions of my countrymen and countrywomen, and even children, through this ordeal of fire. It can be a matter of no joy and comfort to me to lead them again to a fight of that character, but, if a further ordeal of fire has to be our lot, I shall approach that with the greatest joy and with the greatest consolation that I was doing what I felt to be right, the country was doing what it felt to be right, and the country will have the additional satisfaction of knowing that it was not at least taking lives, it was giving lives; it was not making the British people directly suffer, it was suffering. Professor Gilbert Murray told me – I shall never forget that, I am paraphrasing his inimitable language – "Do you not consider for one moment that we Englishmen do not suffer when thousands of your countrymen suffer, that we are so heartless?" I do not think so. I do know that you will suffer; but I want you to suffer because I want to touch your hearts; and when your hearts have been touched then will come the psychological moment for negotiation....

Whilst there is a yet a little sand left in the glass, I want you to understand what this Congress stands for. My life is at your disposal. The lives of all the members of the Working Committee, the All-India Congress Committee, are at your disposal. But remember that you have at your disposal the lives of all these dumb millions. I do not want to sacrifice those lives if I can possibly help it. Therefore, please remember, that I will count no sacrifice too great if, by chance, I can pull through an honourable settlement. You will find me always having the greatest spirit of compromise if I can but fire you with the spirit that is working in the Congress, namely, that India must have real liberty. Call it by any name you like; a rose will smell as sweet by any other name, but it must be the rose of liberty that I want and note the artificial product. If your mind and the Congress mind, the mind of this conference and the mind of the British people, means the same thing by the same word, then you will find the amplest room for compromise, and you will find the Congress itself always in a compromising spirit. But so long as there is not that one mind, that one definition, not one implication for the same word that you and I we may be using, there is no compromise possible.....

... It is for friendship I crave. My business is not to throw overboard the slave-holder and tyrant. My philosophy forbids me to do so, and today the Congress has accepted that philosophy, not as a creed, as it is to me, but as a policy, because the Congress believes that is the right an the best thing for India, a nation of 350 millions, to do....

But what is that nation does? To summarily, or at all, dismiss Englishmen? No. its mission is today to convert Englishmen. I do not want to break the bond between England and India, but I do want to transform that bond, I want to transform that slavery into complete freedom for my country. Call it complete independence or whatever you like. I will not quarrel about that word, and even though my country men may dispute with me for having taken some other word, I shall be able to bear down that opposition so long as the content of the word that you may suggest to me bears the same meaning. Hence, I have times without number to urge upon your attention that the safeguards that have been suggested are completely unsatisfactory. They are not in the interests of India.

. . . I will not be baffled. I shall be here as long as I am required because I do want to revive civil disobedience. I want to turn the truce that was arrived at in Delhi into a permanent settlement. But for heaven's sake give me, a frail man 62 years gone a little bit of a chance. Find a little corner for him and the organization that he represents. You distrust that organization though you may seemingly trust me. Not for one moment differentiate me from the organization of which I am but a drop in the ocean. I am no greater than the organization to which I belong. I am infinitely smaller than that organization; and if you find me a place if you trust me I invite you to trust the Congress also. Your trust in me otherwise is a broken reed. I have to authority save what I derive from the Congress. If you will work the Congress for all it is worth, then you will say goodbye to terrorism, then you will not need terrorism. Today you have to fight the school of terrorists which is there with your disciplined and organised terrorism because you will be blind to the facts or the writing on the wall will you not see the writing that we do not want bread made of wheat, but we want the bread of liberty; and without that liberty there are thousands today who are sworn not to give themselves peace or to give the country peace.

I urge you then to read that writing on the wall. I ask you not to try patience of a people known to be proverbially patient. We speak of the mild Hindu, and the Musalman also who by contact good or evil with the Hindu has himself become mild. And that mention of the Musalman brings me to the baffling problem of minorities. Believe me, that problem exists here, and I request what I used to say in India – I have not forgotten those words – that without the problem of minorities being solved there is no Swaraj for India, there is no freedom for India. I know and I realize it; and yet I came here in the hope "perchance" that I might be able to pull through a solution here. But I do not despair of some day or other finding a real and living solution in connection with the minorities problems. I repeat what I have said elsewhere that so long as the wedge in the shape of foreign rule divides community from community and class from class, there will be no real living solution; there will be no living friendship between these communities.

It will be after all and at best a paper solution. But immediately you withdraw that wedge, the domestic ties, the domestic affections, the knowledge of common birth—do you suppose that all these will count for nothing?

Were Hindus and Musalmans and Sikhs always at war with onc another when there was no British rule, when there was no English face seen there? We have chapter and verse given to us by Hindus historians and by Musalman historians to say that we were living in comparative peace even then. And Hindus and Musalmans in the villages are not even today quarreling. In those days they were not known to quarrel at all. The late Maulana Muhammad Ali often used to tell me and he was himself a bit of an historian. He said ? "If God" – "Allah" as he called God-' gives me life. I propose to write the history of Musalman rule in India; and then I will show through documents that British people have preserved, that Aurangzeb was not so vile as he has been painted by the British historian that the Mogul rule was not so bad as it has been shown to us in British history and so on." And so have Hindu historian written. This quarrel is not old; this quarrel is coeval with this acute shame. I dare to say; it is coeval with the British advent, and immediately this relationship, the unfortunate, artificial, unnatural relationship between Great Britain and India is transformed into a natural relationship, when it becomes, if it does become, a voluntary partnership to be given up to be dissolved at the will of either party, when it becomes that, you will find that Hindus Musalmans, Sikhs, Europeans, Anglo Indians, Christians, Untouchables, will all live together as one man.

. . . Last of all my last is a pleasant task for me. This is perhaps the last time that I shall be sitting with you at negotiations. It is not that I want that. I want to sit at the same table with you in your closets and to negotiate and to plead with you and to go down on bended knees before in take the final leap and final plunge.

But whether I have the good fortune to continue to tender my co-operation or not does not depend upon me. It largely depends upon you. But it may not even depend upon you. It depends upon so many circumstances over which neither you nor we may have any control whatsoever. Then, let me perform this pleasant task of giving my thanks to all from their Majesties down to the poorest men in the East End where I have taken up any habitation.

In that settlement, which represents the poor people of the East London, I have become one of them. They have accepted me as a member, and as a favoured member of their family it will be one of the richest treasures that I shall carry with me. Here, too, I have found nothing but courtesy and nothing but a genuine affection from all with whom I have come in touch. I have come in touch with so many Englishmen. It has been a priceless privilege to me. They have listened to what must have often appeared to them to be unpleasant, although it was true. Although I have often been obliged to say these things to them they have never shown the slightest impatience or irritation. It is impossible for me to forget the things. No matter what befalls me, no matter what the fortunes may be of this Round Table Conference, one thing I shall certainly carry with me, that is, that from high to low I have found nothing but the utmost courtesy and the utmost affection. I consider that it was well worth my paying this visit to England in order to find this human affection.

It has enhanced, it has deepened by irrepressible faith in human nature that although Englishmen and Englishwomen have been fed upon lies that I see so often disfiguring your press, that although in Lancashire, the Lancashire people had perhaps some reason for becoming irritated against me, I found no irritation and no resentment even in the operatives. The operatives, men and women, hugged me. They treated me as one of their own. I shall never forget that.

I am carrying with me thousand upon thousands of English friendship I do not know them but I read that affection in their eyes as early in the morning I walk through your streets. All this hospitality, all this kindness will never be effaced from my memory, no matter what befalls my unhappy land. I thank you for your forbearance.

❖ ❖ ❖

IV

SIMON COMMISSION

GENERAL SURVEY AND CONCLUSION

362. We have now reached the end of our task. By the terms of our Warrant of Appointment, and by the provisions of the section on which it was based, we have been required to survey the working of the existing system of government in British India and to make recommendations for its amendment. In particular, we are directed to report "as to whether and to what extent it is desirable to establish the principle of responsible government or to extend, modify, or restrict the degree of responsible government' now existing. The previous parts of this volume give our detailed and considered answer to these questions. But we realize how difficult it is, in dealing with matters so various and complicated, to present to those who may not be experts on the subject of the Indian constitution, a clear picture of the main constitutional or to extend, modify, or restrict the degree of responsible government' now existing. The previous parts of this volume give our detailed and considered answer to these questions. But we realize how difficult it is, in dealing with matters so various and complicated, to present to those who may not be experts on the subjects of the Indian constitution, a clear picture of the main constitutional results which would be achieved if our suggestions were incorporated into the existing system. We propose, therefore, in this final chapter to point out the more important of the changes which we recommend. What follows must not be treated as a summary of this volume, for not only is it impossible in a brief survey to cover all its contents, but a bald statement of conclusions would tends to mislead if it were not accompanied by a consideration of the arguments which have led us to reach them we shall, therefore, add, at each point which we are going to mention, the necessary references to earlier portion of our Report.

The Scope of our Proposals

363. British India at present has a constitution, based for the most part on the Government of India Act, which includes (1) a Central

Executive – the Governor General in Council; and a Central legislature – the council of State and Legislative Assembly; and (2) nine Provincial Governments, each associated with a Provincial Council Council, and covering between them 97 percent of the whole area. The balance is represented by the North- West Frontier Province and other minor administrations. Out proposals touch every part of this constitution. We will venture to repeat words which we used in the first paragraph of our former volume, when we wrote that we were entering upon our task upon the basis and assumption that the goal defined by Mr. Montagu represents the accepted policy to be pursued, and that the only proposals worthy to be considered are proposals conceived in the spirit of the announcement of 20th August, 1917, and inspired with the honest purpose of giving to it its due effect." We have kept this principle steadily in mind throughout the whole of our deliberations, and our recommendations are based upon it.

Outline of Provincial Changes

364. In the provinces, the main consequences of adopting our proposals would be as follows.

The boundary now set up between departments of which Indian Ministers may take charge and departments from which they are excluded will be removed, and thus diarchy will terminate.

The conduct of provincial administration as a whole will rest with a provincial Cabinet the members of which will be chosen by the Governor. These Ministers, whether elected members of the legislature or not, will have joint responsibility for action and policy. The constitution of the provincial Cabinet will be elastic and, where and when the Governor considers it necessary, it will contain an official element.

The powers of the Governor for certain essential purposes, such as the protections of minorities and of the civil service, will be defined, and will be exercised within the limits and under the conditions we have described.

Full powers of intervention in the event of a breakdown will remain in the hands of the Governor, subject to the directions of the Governor-General.

The provincial Legislature will be based upon a widened franchise – the extension we propose would treble the electorate and would include the admission of a large number of women voters.

Certain important minorities will be adequately protected by the by the continuance of communal electorates unless and until agreement can be reached upon a better method.

The Depressed Classes will get representation by reservation of seats.

The legislatures will be enlarged, and the constituencies reduced to a more manageable size. The provincial Councils instead of being, as at present, purely legislative bodies, will acquire certain powers of recasting their own representative system, so that each province may advance to self-government on lines which are found to be best suited for its individual needs, subject always to securing that the vote of the majority shall not introduce constitutional changes which would prejudice minority rights.

The provinces will be provided with enlarged financial resources.

As for provincial areas, the question whether some redistribution is desirable will at once be taken up; such cases as those of Sind and the Oriya-speaking people will be the first to be considered.

Burma, which is admittedly not a natural part of British India, will be separated forthwith. Provision must be made without delay for framing its future constitutions.

The administered areas of the North-West Frontier Province will now receive an advance in constitutional status represented by the creation of a local legislature, with powers which we have described. Both it and Baluchistan will acquire the right to representation at the center.

The complicated and interlacing system of administration of the Backward Tracts will be revised, and such parts of these as remain excluded areas will come under the charge of the central administration.

Modification at the Centre

365. We now pass to the center.

The Legislative Assembly, which should be called the "Federal Assembly" will be reconstituted on the basis of the representation of the Provinces and other areas in British India according to population. Members representing Governors Provinces will be elected by the Provincial Councils by the method of proportional representation, which will ensure that members belonging to minority communities will be included in sufficient number in the Federal Assembly. Members will be returned from the North-West Frontier Province and other areas outside the Governor's Provinces by methods appropriate in each case. The official member of the Federal Assembly will consist of such members of the Governor General's Council as sit in the Lower House, together with twelve other nominated officials.

The council of State will continue with its existing functions as a body of elected and nominated members chosen in the same proportion as at present. Its members who must have high qualifications, will, so far as they are selected, be chosen by indirect election carried out by provincial Second Chambers if such bodies are constituted, or, failing this, by the Provincial Councils.

The existing legislative and financial powers of the two chambers of the Central Legislature will remain as at present, but the Federal Assembly will also have the special function of voting certain indirect taxes, collected by a central agency, the net proceeds of which will fall into a provincial Fund for the purpose of being distributed amongst the different units represents in the Federal Assembly.

The central Executive will continue to be the Governor General in Council, but the Governor-General will henceforth be the authority who will select and appoint his Executive Councillors. Existing qualifications will remain, but will be laid down in statutory rules made under the new Government of India Act, so that when occasion arises to modify these conditions hereafter this may be done without passing a new Act of Parliament. But any modification in the statutory rules made for this purpose would require to be laid before both Houses of Parliament and the approval of both Houses expressed by resolution.

It is proposed that among the members of the Governor General's Council should be one whose primary function it would be to lead the Federal Assembly. We have made other suggestions relating to the composition and character of the Governor-General's Council, and we propose that the Commander-in-chief should no longer be a member of it, or of the Central Legislature.

The Army

366. We have suggested for consideration a method by which if agreement could be reached, the obstacle which the composition and functions of the Army in India present to the more rapid development of responsible government might be removed through treating the

defence of India as a matter which would fall within the responsibilities of the Governor-General advised by the Commander in-chief, as representing the Imperial authorities instead of being part of the responsibilities of the Government of India in relation to the Central Legislature.

Civil Services, High Courts, India Office

367. As regard the Civil Service of India, the Security Service must continue to be recruited as All-India Service by the Secretary of State, and their existing structure must be maintained. These security services include the Indian Civil Service and the Indian police Service. It is a matter for consideration whether the Irrigation Service and the Forest Service should not be similarly recruited. The privilege of premature retirement will be extended.

The rates of Indianisation laid down by the Lee Commission for the Security Services will be maintained.

In addition to the existing Public Service Commission, we intend that there should be established by Statue similar bodies covering the provincial and subordinate services in all the provinces.

The High Courts will be centralized, and the expenses of the High Courts will become a central charge.

As regards the Indian office, the Governor-General in Council will remain in constitutional theory under the superintendence's, direction and control of he Secretary of State, and the extent to which this control is relaxed or falls into desuetude will depend upon future practice, and cannot be laid down in the Statue.

Apart from the Secretary of State's authority over the Governor General in Council, he will exercise no control over Provincial Government, save in so far as he does so in connection with the exercise of special powers vested in the Governor.

The functions and composition of the Council of India will be modified. Its size will be reduced, and the majority of its members should have the qualification of more recent India experience than is required at present. The council will exist primarily as an advisory body, but independent powers will continue for (1) the control of Service conditions, and (2) the control of non-votable Indian expenditure.

Indian States

368. Lastly for the purpose of promoting the closer association with British India of the Indian States in matters of common concern for India as a whole, we propose that the new lot should provide that it shall be lawful for the Crown to create a Council for Greater India, containing both representatives of the States and members representing British India. This council would have consultative and deliberative functions in regard to a scheduled list of "matters of common concern", together with a such other subjects of common concern as the Viceroy from time to time certifies as suitable for consideration by the council we refer to part VII of this volume for a more detailed account of the machinery and methods which we contemplate, and we put forward the proposals as designed to make a beginning in the process which may lead to the Federation of Greater India.

Conclusion

369. In writing this report we have made no allusion to the events of the last few months of India. In fact, the whole of our principal recommendations were arrived at and unanimously agreed upon before these events occurred. We have not altered a line of our Report on that account, for it is necessary to look beyond particular incidents and to take a longer view.

Our object throughout has been to bring to the notice of the British Parliament and the British people such information as we are able to supply about the general conditions of the problem which now awaits solution, together with our considered proposals. We hope, at the same time, that our Indian fellow-subjects, after doing us the courtesy of studying the Report as a whole (for isolated sentences may give to any readers a wrong impression), will find that what we have put forward has been written in a spirit of genuine sympathy.

No one of either ought to be so foolish as to deny the greatness of the contribution which British has made to Indian progress. It is not racial prejudice, nor imperialistic ambition, nor commercial interest, which makes us say so plainly. It is a tremendous achievement to have brought to the Indian sub-continent and to have applied to practice the conceptions of impartial justice, of the rule of law, of respect for equal civic rights without reference to class or creed, and of a disinterested and incorruptible civil service. These are essential elements in any state which is advancing towards well ordered self government. In his heart, even the bitterest critic of British administration in India knows that India has owed these things mainly to British. But, when all this is said, it still leaves out of account the condition essential to the peaceful advance of India, and Indian statesmanship has now a great part to play. Success can only be achieved by sustained goodwill and co-operation, both between the great religious communities of India which have so constantly been in conflict, and between India and Britain. For the Future of India depends on the collaboration of East and West, and each has much to learn from the other.

We have grown to understand something of the ideals which are inspiring the Indian national movement, and no man who has taken part in working the representatives institutions of British can fail to sympathise with the desire of others to secure for their own land of similar development. But a constitution is something more than a generalization; it has to present a constructive scheme. We submit our Report in the hope that it may furnish materials and suggest a plan by means of which Indian constitutional reconstruction may be peacefully and surely promoted.

All of which we submit for your Majesty's gracious consideration.

JOHN SIMON, *Chairman*
BURNHAM,
STRATHCONA
EDWARD CAGOGAN
VERNON HARTSHORN
G. R. LANE FOX
C.R. ATLEE.

S. F. STEWART,
Secretary
London, 27th May, 1930.

❖ ❖ ❖

V

STATEMENT MADE BY HIS MAJESTY'S GOVERNMENT ON JUNE 3, 1947

INTRODUCTION

1. On 20th February 1947, His Majesty's Government announced their intention of transferring power in British India to Indian hands by June 1948. His Majesty's Government had hoped that it would be possible for the major parties to co-operate in the working out of the Cabinet Mission plan of the 16th May 1946, and evolve for India a constitution acceptable to all concerned. This hope has not been fulfilled.

2. The majority of the representatives of the provinces of Madras, Bombay, the United Provinces, Bihar, Central Provinces and Berar, Assam, Orissa and the North-West Frontier Province, and the representative of Delhi, Ajmer-Merwora and Coorg have already made a progress in the task of evolving a new constitution On the other hand, the Muslim League party, including in it a majority of the representatives of Bengal, the Punjab and Sind, as also the representative of British Baluchistan, has decided not to participate in the Constituent Assembly.

3. It has always been the desire of His Majesty's Government that power should be transferred in accordance with the wishes of the Indian people themselves. This task would have been greatly facilitated if there had been agreement among the Indian political parties. In the absence of such agreement, the task of devising a method by which the wishes of the Indian people can be ascertained has devolved upon His Majesty's Government. After full consultation with political leaders in India, His Majesty's Government has decided to adopt for this purpose the plan set out below.

His Majesty's Government wishes to make it clear that they have no intention of attempting to frame any ultimate constitution for India; this is a matter for the Indians themselves. Nor is there anything in this plan to preclude negotiations between communities for a united India.

Issues to be Decided

4. It is not the intention of His Majesty's Government to interrupt the work of the existing Constituent Assembly. Now that provision is made for certain provinces specified below, his Majesty's Government trust that, as a consequence of this announcement, the Muslim League representatives of those provinces, a majority of whose representatives are already participating in it, will now take their due share in its labours. At the same time, it is clear that any constitution framed by this Assembly cannot apply to those parts of the country which are unwilling to accept it. His Majesty's Government are satisfied that the procedure outlined below embodies the best practical method of ascertaining the wishes of the people of such areas on the issue whether their constitution is to be framed :

a. in the existing Constituent Assembly; or

b. in a new and separate Constituent Assembly consisting of the representatives of those areas which decide not to participate in the existing constituent Assembly.

When this has been done, it will be possible to determine the authority or authorities to whom power should be transferred.

Bengal and the Punjab

5. The provincial Legislative Assemblies of Bengal and the Punjab (excluding the European members) will, therefore, each be asked to meet in two parts, one representing the Muslim majority districts and the other the rest of the province. For the purpose of determining the population of districts, the 1941 census figures will be taken as authorative. The Muslim majority districts in these two provinces are set out in the appendix to this announcement.

6. The members of the two parts of the each legislative assembly sitting separately will be empowered to vote whether or not the province should be partitioned. If a simple majority of either part decides in favour of partition, division will take place and arrangements will be made accordingly.

7. Before the question as to the partition is decided, it is desirable that the representatives of each part should know in advance which Constituent Assembly the province as a whole would join in the event of the two parts subsequently deciding to remain united. Therefore, if any member of either legislative assembly so demands there shall be

held a meeting of all members of the legislative assembly (other than Europeans) at which a decision will be taken on the issues as to which Constituent Assembly the province as a whole join, if it were decided by the two parts to remain united.

8. In the event of partition being decided upon, each part of the legislative assembly will, on behalf of the areas of the areas they represent, decide which of the alternatives in paragraph 4 above to adopt.

9. For the immediate purpose of deciding on the issue of partition, the members of the Legislative Assemblies of Bengal and the Punjab will sit in two parts according to Muslim majority districts (as laid down in the appendix)and non-Muslim majority districts. This is only a preliminary step of a purely temporary nature as it is evident that, a detailed investigation of boundary questions will be needed; and, as soon as a decision involving partition has been taken for either province, a Boundary Commission will be set up by the Governor General, the membership and terms of reference of which will be settled in consultation with those concerned. It will be instructed to democrate the boundaries of the two parts of the Punjab on the basis of ascertaining the contiguous majority areas of Muslim and non-Muslims. It will also be instructed to take into account other factors. Similar instructions will be given to the Bengal Boundary Commission. Until the report of a Boundary Commission has been put into effect, the provisional boundaries indicated in the appendix will be used.

Sind

10. The Legislative Assembly of Sind (excluding the European members) will, at a special meeting, also take its own decision on the alternatives in Paragraph 4 above.

North-West Frontier Province

11. The position of the Northwest Frontier Province is exceptional. Two of the three representatives of this province are already participating in the existing Constituent Assembly. But it is clear, in view of its geographical situation and other considerations, that if the whole or any part of the Punjab decides not to join the existing Constituent Assembly, it will be necessary to give the North-West Frontier Province an opportunity to reconsider its position. Accordingly, in such an event, a referendum will be made to the electors of the present Legislative Assembly in the North-West

Frontier Province to choose which of the alternatives mentioned in paragraph 4 above they wish to adopt. The referendum will be held under the aegis of the Governor-General and in consultation with the provincial government.

British Baluchistan

12. British Baluchistan has elected a member, but he has not taken his seat in the existing constituent Assembly. In view of its geographical situation, this province will also be given an opportunity to reconsider its position and to choose which of the alternatives in paragraph 4 above to adopt. His Excellency the Governor-General is examining how this can most appropriately be done.

Assam

13. Though Assam is predominantly a non-Muslim province, the district of Sylhet which is contiguous to Bengal is predominantly Muslim. There has been a demand that, in the event of the partition of Bengal, Sylhet should be amalgamated with the Muslim part of Bengal. Accordingly, it is decided that Bengal should be partitioned, a referendum will be held in Sylhet district under the aegis of the Governor-General and in consultation with the Assam Provincial Government to decide whether the district of Sylhet should continue to form part of the Assam province or should be amalgamated with the new province of Eastern Bengal, if that province agrees. If the referendum results in favour of amalgamation with Eastern Bengal, a Boundary Commission with terms of reference similar to those for the Punjab and Bengal will be set up to demarcate the Muslim majority areas of Sylhet district, and contiguous Muslim majority areas of adjoining districts, which will then be transferred to Eastern Bengal. The rest of the Assam Province will in any case continue to participate in the proceedings of the existing constituent Assembly.

Representation in Constituent Assembly

14. If it is decided that Bengal and the Punjab should be partitioned, it will be necessary to hold fresh elections to choose their representatives on the scale of one for every million of the population according to the principle contained in the Cabinet Mission plan of 16th May 1946. Similar elections will also have to be held for Sylhet in the event of it being decided that this district should form part of East

Bengal. The Number of representatives in which each area would be entitled is as follows:

Province	*General*	*Muslims*	*Sikhs*	*Total*
Sylhet District	1	2	..	3
West Bengal	15	4	..	19
East Bengal	12	29	..	41
West Punjab	3	12	2	17
East Punjab	6	4	2	12

15. In accordance with the mandates given to them, the representatives of the various areas will either join the existing constituent Assembly or form the new Constituent Assembly.

Administrative Matters

16. Negotiations will have to be initiated as soon as possible on the administrative consequence of any partition that may have been decided upon –

a. between the representatives of the respective successor authorities about all subjects now dealt with by the Central Government, including defence, finance and communications;
b. between different successor authorities and His Majesty's Government for treaties in regard to matters arising out of the transfer of power;
c. in the case of provinces that may be partitioned, as to the administration of all provincial subjects such as the division of assets and liabilities, the police and other services, the High Courts, provincial institutions, etc.

Tribes of North West Frontier

17. Agreements with the tribes of the North-West Frontier of India will have to be negotiated by the appropriate successor authority.

The States

18. His Majesty's Government wish to make it clear that the decisions announced above relate only to British India and that their

policy towards Indian State contained in the Cabinet Mission memorandum of 16th May 1946 remains unchanged.

Necessity for Speed

19. In order that the successor authorities may have time to prepare themselves to take over power, it is important that all the above processes should be completed as quickly as possible. To avoid delay, the different provinces or parts of province will proceed independently as far as practicable within the conditions of this plan. The existing Constituent Assembly and the new Constituent Assembly (if formed) will proceed to frame constitutions for their respective territories : they will of course be free to frame their own rules.

Immediate Transfer of Power

20. The major political parties have repeatedly emphasized their desire that there should be the earliest possible transfer of power in India. With this desire His Majesty's Government are in full sympathy, and they are willing to anticipate the date of June 1948, for the handing over of power, by the setting up of an independent Indian Government or government at an even earlier date. Accordingly, as the most expeditious and indeed the only practicable way of meeting this desire. His Majesty's Government propose to introduce legislation during the current session for the transfer of power this year on a Dominion Status basis to one or two successor authorities, according to the decisions taken as a two successor authorities, according to the decision taken as a result of this announcement. This will be without prejudice to the right of the Indian constituent Assemblies to decide in due course whether or not the part of India in respect of which they have authority will remain within the British Commonwealth.

Further Announcement by Governor-General

21. His Excellency the Governor-General will from time to time make such further announcement as may be necessary in regard to procedure or any other matters for carrying out the above arrangements.

VI

OBJECTIVES OF THE RESOLUTION

On 15th December, 1946 Jawaharlal Nehru moved an important resolution defining the Constituent Assembly's aims and objects in the following terms :

*1. This Constituent Assembly declares its firm and solemn resolve to proclaim India as an independent sovereign republic and to draw up for her future governance a constitution;

*2. wherein the territories that now compromise British India, the territories that now form the Indian states, and such other parts of India as are outside British India and the States, as well as such other territories as are willing to be constituted into the independent sovereign India, shall be a union of them all; and

*3. wherein the said territories, whether with their present boundaries or with such others as may be determined by the Constituent Assembly and thereafter according to the law of the constitution, shall possess and retain the status of autonomous units, together with residuary powers, and exercise all powers and functions of government and administration, save and except such powers and functions as are vested in or assigned to the union, or as are inherent or implied in the union or resulting there from; and

*4. wherein all powers and authority of the independent sovereign India, its constituent parts and organs of government, are derived from the people; and

*5. wherein shall be guaranteed and secured to all the people of India justice, social, economic and political; equality of status, of opportunity and before the law; freedom of thought, expression, belief, faith, worship, vocation, association and action, subject to law and public morality; and

*6. where adequate safeguard shall be provided for minorities, backward and tribal areas and depressed and other backward classes; and

*7. whereby shall be maintained the integrity of the territory of the republic and its sovereign rights on land, sea and air, according to justice and law of civilized nations; and

*8. this ancient land attains its rightful and honoured place in the world and makes its full and willing contribution to the promotion of world peace and the welfare of mankind."

INDEX

A

Act of 1919, 101, 111, 113, 114, 115, 152, 169, 174, 216, 217
Ahmed Khan Sir Syed, 70, 71, 79, 80, 81, 274
Andhra circular, 320
Andhra Jateeya Kalasala, 94
Andhra Mahasabha, 323
Annie Besant, 49, 102, 105, 274, 289, 291
Arya Samaj, 39, 41, 42, 43, 136, 140, 282, 328, 330
Aurobindo Ghosh, 91

B

Bahadur shah, 13
Bardoli, 160, 161, 163, 164, 185, 186, 188, 192, 234, 298, 300, 343
Bengal Famine, 247
Bhagat Singh, 178, 189, 190, 210, 211, 212
Bipin Chandra Pal, 4, 82, 91, 93, 154, 155, 283, 284
Birendra Kumar Ghose, 207
Bombay Association, 58

C

Cabinet Delegation, 259, 260
Chandrasekhar Azad, 209
Chauri Chaura, 163, 172
Civil Disobedience, 160, 180, 187, 193, 229, 295, 312, 318, 336
  in Andhra, 295
Communal Award, 196, 215, 216, 219, 220
Congress Ministries, 223, 226, 228
Cornwallis, 6
Council of National Education, 90

D

Dadabhai Naoroji, 54, 60, 72, 97, 284
Dandi March, 183
Dayananda Saraswati, 39, 41, 54, 274
Devendra Nath Tagore, 37, 38
Divide and Rule, 230, 274

E

East India Association, 60
European Defence Association, 61, 62

F

Freedom Movement in Andhra, 288

G

Gandhiji entry into politics, 291
  Calcutta session, 98, 154, 195, 284, 302
  experience in South Africa, 118, 121
  Gujrati Sabha, 126, 129
  Hindu Muslim Unity, 122, 126
  Irwin Pact, 188, 189, 316
  Rowlatt Satyagraha, 131, 135, 141, 143–44, 149, 159, 291, 293
  Satyagraha, 4, 118, 120, 121, 122, 123, 125, 126, 127, 128, 129, 130, 131, 132, 133, 134, 135, 136, 137, 138, 140, 141, 142, 143, 144, 145, 151, 153, 160, 161, 165, 183, 184, 193, 197, 198, 214, 215, 227, 231, 291,

298, 302, 308, 309, 312, 330, 332, 333, 336, 338, 339, 340, 341
Satyagrahas, 133, 134
Untouchability, 122
women, 89, 122, 158, 165, 184, 202, 272, 329
Ghadar Movement, 204
Gokhale, 59, 66, 96, 99, 103, 116, 125, 126
Government of India Act of 1935, 115, 214, 216, 221, 226, 316
Elections, 221
Government of India Act of 1919, 113, 152, 174, 216
Great Revolt, 7, 11, 17, 19, 21
Central provinces, 15, 213, 319
Failure, 21, 254, 256
Immediate cause, 11
Nature of, 22, 30, 68, 135, 241, 277, 314, 327
Pillars of, 19
Results, 17
Spreads to Kanpur, 13
Gujarati Sabha, 126, 129

H

Harisarvothama Rao, 92, 284, 287, 289, 290
Hindu Mahasabha, 170, 174, 177, 187, 217, 239, 330
Hume, 62, 63, 64, 65, 66, 67, 68, 71
Hunter Committee, 149, 153

I

Ilbert Bill, 61, 62, 63
Indian Association, 9, 19, 58, 60, 62, 66
Indian Independence Act, 270, 271, 324
Indian National Army, 204, 225, 249, 250, 251, 252, 257, 272
Indian National Congress, 32, 33, 50, 54, 57, 61, 62, 64, 65, 66, 72, 74, 76, 80, 118, 165, 189, 198, 212, 280, 281, 327, 331
Individual Civil Disobedience, 231, 318, 319
Interim Government, 261, 262, 263, 264, 265, 266, 268, 269

J

Jatin Mukherjee, 205
Jawaharlal Nehru, 117, 176, 178, 180, 221, 226, 229, 251, 262, 305, 311, 341, 362
Jhansi Lakshmi Bai, 16
Jinnah's demands, 173, 177
14 points, 217

K

Kaira Satyagraha, 131
Khilafat Movement, 151, 328
Kotappa Konda riot, 287
Kripalani, 127, 130

L

Lala Lajpat Rai, 82, 92, 116
Lord Wavell, 247, 248, 255, 258, 259, 265, 267, 323

M

Madras Native Association, 58, 59
Mahendra Pratab, 208
Mangal Pandey, 12
Maulana Azad, 162, 168, 219, 229, 232, 236, 256, 262
Michael O'Dwyer, 145, 149, 150, 161
Montagu, 105, 106, 107, 108, 109, 110, 143, 148, 149, 166, 171, 179, 290, 291, 349
Montagu-chelmsford Reform, 143, 166
Disillusionment, 166
Motilal Nehru, 117, 153, 154, 158, 162, 164, 167, 169, 170, 172, 176, 177, 293, 294, 300
Muslim League, 104, 108, 126, 165, 170, 172, 173, 175, 216, 220, 221, 222, 223, 225, 227, 228, 230, 231, 232, 237, 239, 248, 249, 254, 256, 258, 259, 261, 262, 263, 264, 265, 268, 270, 355, 356
Muslim Politics, 76, 217, 231
Indian Councils Act, 19, 72, 99
Separatist movement, 77, 79

N

Nana Saheb, 13, 14, 15, 22
Nationalism–Growth, 28
  A religious Creed, 85
  English Education, 28
  Meaning, 26
Nehru Committee, 177, 178, 217, 307
Non-cooperation, 83, 91
  Congress resolution, 229

Q

Queen Victoria's, 71, 73
  Proclamation, 71, 73
Quit India Movement, 4, 199, 210, 241, 253, 272, 318, 319, 331
  Course, 241
  In Andhra, 318
  Results, 243
  Revolution, 23, 71, 278

R

Raja Ram Mohan Roy, 53, 80, 274
Rajagopalachari, 117, 263, 272, 315, 336
Rajendra Prasad, 127, 130, 231, 263, 265, 269, 271
Ramadas Pantu, 300, 301
Ramakrishna Mission, 43, 45, 201, 282
Ramananda Tirtha, 330
Ramsay Macdonald, 179, 187, 191, 192, 196, 215, 220
Ranade, 38, 54, 59
Rippon, 61, 62, 63, 66
Rowlatt Satyagraha, 131, 134, 135, 141, 143, 144, 149, 159, 291, 293
  Outcome, 143, 291

S

Simla Conference, 256, 257, 259, 323
Simon Commission, 174, 175, 176, 178, 186, 191, 211, 214, 215, 302, 306, 307
  Visit to Andhra, 306
Social Reforms, 53
Surendra Nath Banerjee, 284
Surya Sen, 209, 210
Swarajya Party, 167, 168, 220, 300, 301
  In Andhra, 300

T

Tatya Tope, 15, 16, 22, 24
Tej Bahadur Sapru, 159
Theosophical Society, 48, 49, 63, 103, 282, 289
  Work of Blavatsky, 48, 49

V

Vallabhbhai Patel
Vandemataram Movement, 4, 88, 283, 284, 288
  Genesis, 88
  Goes underground, 94
  Outcome, 96
  Long term effects, 101
Venkatarangaiya M. 4,
Venkatarao Kala, 335
Village Community, 4
Vivekananda, 27, 38, 45, 46, 47, 49, 50, 123, 201, 274, 328
  As religious reformer, 48

W

Willingdon Lord, 196

❖ ❖ ❖